Critical Medical Anthropc

EMBODYING INEQUALITIES: PERSPECTIVES FROM MEDICAL
ANTHROPOLOGY

Series Editors
Sahra Gibbon, UCL Anthropology
Jennie Gamlin, UCL Institute for Global Health

This series charts diverse anthropological engagements with the changing dynamics of health and wellbeing in local and global contexts. It
includes ethnographic and theoretical works that explore the different
ways in which inequalities pervade our bodies. The series offers novel
contributions often neglected by classical and contemporary publications
that draw on public, applied, activist, cross-disciplinary and engaged
anthropological methods, as well as in-depth writings from the field. It
specifically seeks to showcase new and emerging health issues that are
the products of unequal global development.

Critical Medical Anthropology

Perspectives in and from Latin America

Edited by Jennie Gamlin, Sahra Gibbon, Paola M. Sesia and Lina Berrio

First published in 2020 by
UCL Press
University College London
Gower Street
London WC1E 6BT
Available to download free: www.uclpress.co.uk

ISBN: 978-1-78735-584-2 (Hbk.)
ISBN: 978-1-78735-583-5 (Pbk.)
ISBN: 978-1-78735-582-8 (PDF)
ISBN: 978-1-78735-585-9 (epub)
ISBN: 978-1-78735-586-6 (mobi)
DOI: https://doi.org/10.14324/111.9781787355828

Contents

List of figures

List of tables

List of contributors

Editors

Jennie Gamlin is a Wellcome Trust Senior Research Fellow based in the Institute for Global Health at UCL. Jennie has carried out extensive research in Mexico and the UK on reproductive and maternal health and has worked for the past 10 years with indigenous Wixárika communities. She is also co-director of the UCL Centre for Gender and Global Health and teaches and writes about the political economy of gender and health.

Sahra Gibbon is associate professor in the Medical Anthropology Department at UCL. She has carried out research in the UK, Cuba and Brazil examining developments in genomics, public health, activism, gender and identity. Her recent publications include (as co-editor) *The Routledge Handbook of Genomics, Health and Society* (2018) and she is editor, with Jennie Gamlin, of the UCL Press book series *Embodying Inequalities*.

Paola M. Sesia is a full-time researcher and professor at the Centre for Research and Advanced Studies in Social Anthropology (CIESAS) in the city of Oaxaca, Mexico. She is a medical anthropologist and public health specialist with a PhD in cultural anthropology from the University of Arizona, Tucson and a master's degree in public health from the University of California, Berkeley. Her current research interests focus on maternal, neo-natal and reproductive health, maternal mortality, obstetric violence, health policies and indigenous peoples in Mexico.

Lina Berrio is a researcher and professor at the Centre for Research and Advanced Studies in Social Anthropology (CIESAS) in the city of Oaxaca, Mexico. She holds a PhD in anthropological sciences from the UAM-Iztapalapa. Her research topics are sexual and reproductive health, gender, indigenous peoples, public health policies and feminist anthropology. She has coordinated several research projects on maternal health in indigenous areas and works in collaboration with organisations of indigenous women and non-governmental organisations. She is integrated into the National System of Researchers and coordinates the specialism in medical anthropology at CIESAS-Pacífico Sur.

Contributors

Waleska Aureliano is an associate professor at the State University of Rio de Janeiro in the Social Science Institute, Department of Anthropology. Her field of interest is the anthropology of health at the interface with gender, the family and kinship, religion and emotions. Since 2013 she has been conducting research among families living with rare inherited diseases in Brazil.

Kimberly C. Brouwer is a full-time researcher and professor at the University of California, San Diego.

Melania Calestani is a lecturer at Kingston and St George's (University of London) in the joint Faculty of Health, Social Care and Education. She is an anthropologist with post-doctoral experience in health services research and social sciences. She teaches research methods and public health on undergraduate and postgraduate courses in midwifery and on the MRes in clinical research. She has carried out fieldwork on social and cultural constructions of wellbeing and health in Andean Bolivia with indigenous communities. In the UK, she has conducted ethnographic research on processes of decision-making in the NHS, from the perspectives of both patients and healthcare professionals.

Eliana E. Diehl is a retired professor in the Department of Pharmaceutical Sciences and the graduate programme in pharmaceutical assistance, Federal University of Santa Catarina, and member of the national research institute Plural Brazil (Instituto Brasil Plural). With a doctorate in public health from the Oswaldo Cruz Foundation, Rio de Janeiro, her interdisciplinary investigations draw on collective/public health, anthropology and pharmaceutical sciences for the study of indigenous health, indigenous health policy and the quality of pharmaceutical services and assistance.

Carmen Fernández Casanueva is a full-time professor and researcher at the Centre for Research and Advanced Studies in Social Anthropology (CIESAS) in San Cristobal de las Casas, Chiapas, Mexico.

Claudia Fonseca is full professor in the Department of Postgraduate Studies in Social Anthropology at the Federal University of Rio Grande do Sul (Brazil) and in the doctoral programme in anthropology at the National University of San Martin (Argentina). Her research interests include kinship, gender studies, legal anthropology and the anthropology of science and technology. Since 2012 she has been conducting research in connection with former leper colonies in Brazil, looking at questions of medical care, social movements for reparation, stigma and deficiency. Simultaneously, she is working with lower-income urban families, examining the interaction between community/kin networks and public policies for the care of dependent members of the household.

Rebecca Irons is a PhD candidate in medical anthropology at UCL. Her doctoral research explores the implementation of the Peruvian national family planning programme with Quechua indigenous women in the Andes, and addresses questions of race, subjectivity and kinship. Rebecca holds an MRes from UCL, and an MA in development and social transformation from the University of Sussex. She undertook ethnographic fieldwork based on women's reproductive health in Peru for both master's degrees. Her broader research interests include reproductive and sexual health, biopolitics, indigeneity, maternity, inequality and Latin America.

Frida Jacobo Herrera is a professor and researcher in the Centre of Anthropological Studies (CEA) of the Faculty of Social and Political Science, UNAM (Mexico). She has a degree in social anthropology from UAM-Iztapalapa and a master's degree in anthropology with a specialisation in medical anthropology, as well as a doctoral degree from the Centre for Research and Advanced Studies in Social Anthropology (CIESAS). She is a member of the National Network of Researchers in Sociocultural Emotional Studies (RENISCE-Mexico) and coordinator of the interdisciplinary seminar 'Emotions on Both Sides: Researchers and Social Actors. Ethnographical Record of the Affective Dimension in Social Sciences'. She is a member of the National System of Researchers, CONACYT-Mexico.

Esther Jean Langdon is a researcher and coordinator of the national research institute Plural Brazil (Instituto Brasil Plural). She is a retired professor in the graduate programme in anthropology at the Federal University of Santa Catarina. She focuses on the field of anthropology of health with particular emphasis on indigenous health and public policy and has been published throughout the Americas and Europe.

Eduardo L. Menéndez is an emeritus professor at the Centre for Research and Advanced Studies in Social Anthropology (CIESAS) in Mexico City. He has published some 30 books, 102 scientific papers and 101 book chapters. His principal publications include *Cure and Control* (1978), *Power, Stratification and Health* (1981), *Death from Alcohol: Knowledge and Medical Ideology* (1990), *The Denied Part of Culture* (2002), *Fears, Risks and Insecurities* (2009), *Of Subjects, Knowledge and Structures* (2009), *Racisms are Eternal, but Racists are Not* (2018) and *Of Traditional, Popular and Scientific Medical Knowledge* (2018).

Sonia Morales Miranda is a full-time researcher in the HIV Unit, Universidad del Valle de Guatemala.

Laura Montesi is a researcher in the Cátedras Programme CONACyT (National Council of Science and Technology) at the Centre of Research and Advanced Studies in Social Anthropology (CIESAS) in the city of Oaxaca, Mexico. Her work focuses on the lived experiences and social representations of diabetes and other chronic conditions in Mexico. She has carried out field research in rural indigenous Mexico and, more recently, in urban health centres with mutual-aid groups for chronic patients. She has published in international social science journals on issues such as diabetes and gendered violence, syndemics of alcohol abuse and diabetes, and diabetes and healthy eating. She is involved in civil society organisations working on gender equality, environmental sustainability, food and energy sovereignty.

Rubén Muñoz Martínez is a full-time professor and researcher at the Centre for Research and Advanced Studies in Social Anthropology (CIESAS), in Mexico City. His area of expertise is medical anthropology, specialising in HIV, mental health, indigenous populations and migrants' healthcare, and intercultural health. He has carried out several research projects, mainly in Latin America. Muñoz was a post-doctoral fellow or guest researcher at the Facultad Latinoamericana de Ciencias Sociales (FLACSO) in Ecuador, the Universidad Nacional Autónoma de México (UNAM), Mexico, the Université Libre de Bruxelles (ULB), Belgium, the Global Public Health Division at the University of California, San Diego, USA and CIESAS, in the city of San Cristobal de las Casas, Chiapas, Mexico.

Olga Lidia Olivas Hernández is a professor and researcher in the Cátedras Programme CONACyT (National Council of Science and Technology) at the Department of Social Studies of El Colegio de la Frontera

Norte. She has a PhD in social sciences with emphasis in social anthropology from Ciesas Occidente and was a post-doctoral fellow at El Colegio de la Frontera Norte (2014–15) and at the University of California, San Diego (2016–17). Her research interests are focused on the US–Mexico border, migratory trajectories and the processes of health/illness/care. Her recent publications are: *¿Dejar las drogas con la ayuda de dios? Experiencias de internamiento en centros de rehabilitación fronterizos* (2018), and *Danzar la Frontera: Procesos socioculturales en la tradición de danza azteca en la frontera de las Californias* (2018).

David Orr is senior lecturer in social work in the School of Education & Social Work at the University of Sussex. He holds a PhD in social anthropology from UCL and his primary research interests lie in cultural aspects of mental health and of adult safeguarding. He has carried out ethnographic fieldwork in Peru and the UK, sits on the editorial board of the international journal *Anthropology in Action* (published by Berghahn) and is co-editor of the *Palgrave Handbook of Sociocultural Perspectives on Global Mental Health* (2017).

Rosa María Osorio Carranza is a medical anthropologist and has been a professor/researcher at the Centre for Research and Advanced Studies in Social Anthropology (CIESAS), Mexico City, since 1987. She studied physical anthropology (1984) and obtained an MA in social anthropology (1994) at the National School of Anthropology and History (ENAH, Mexico City); she has a master's degree in medical anthropology (1996) and PhD in social and cultural anthropology (1998) from the Universitat Rovira i Virgili (Tarragona, Spain). She has conducted research on chronicity, disability and ageing processes; maternal medical culture, medical pluralism and the self-care structure; and illness trajectories.

Preface
Critical medical anthropology in Latin America: Trends, contributions, possibilities

Eduardo L. Menéndez

In Mexico the trend for writing critical medical anthropology (CMA) emerged in the 1970s from a questioning of integrationist perspectives that had been dominant from 1940 to 1960 (notwithstanding the contributions of authors such as Gonzalo Aguirre Beltrán or Julio de la Fuente). Beyond their – sometimes radical – differences, these CMA works merge with contemporary critique and find common cause in seeking a solution to the exclusion, marginalisation and poverty of indigenous peoples, building on the contributions of Latin and Afro-American intellectuals including Guillermo Bonfil Batalla, Orlando Fals Borda and Frantz Fanon. Both in theoretical and ideological terms, this perspective is a critical continuation of proposals by authors such as Darcy Ribeiro and Pablo González Casanova in relation to US and European perspectives. This continuity persists, largely, through a focus on colonial/neocolonial situations and relationships, often framed by class structure, even when these studies are classified under other conceptual denominations (Menéndez 2002).

Regional Latin American CMA emerged through a shared concern for the high rates of avoidable deaths among indigenous people, and the accompanying dearth of solutions – either biomedical or material. While by no means excluding sociocultural factors, CMA locates political economy intrinsically within the process of health, disease, treatment and prevention (h/d/t-p). It is also an anthropology that draws on and utilises epidemiological data, while merging and interacting with trends in Latin American social medicine, particularly in the case of Brazilian anthropology.

Critiques, proposals and (whenever possible) intervention are an integral part of CMA. In a region like ours, characterised by poverty, stark socio-economic inequality and cultural and ethnic diversity, both 'hard' and soft scientists should not only try to create new low-cost drugs or prosthetics and incorporate traditional medicine but also offer descriptions, analysis, explications and proposals. This may involve improving healthcare services on all three levels of care, both in general and in relation to specific ethnic groups. Moreover, I think that CMA should not only be directed towards biomedically generated policies and activities in order to reduce maternal mortality, to take one example; it should also describe and analyse the role played by practising midwives, and traditional medicine in general, in the high rates of maternal and neo-natal mortality that occur when midwives attend the majority of deliveries. This is necessary in order to capture both the positive and negative aspects of all healing/healthcare that occurs in any real context. *All* forms and systems of healthcare need to be described and analysed in order to observe their structure, operation and degree of efficacy for addressing, preventing and resolving the healthcare issues of an ethnic community or nation. Similarly, we must identify the social meaning that these forms have for the population, which almost always go beyond the actual h/d/t-p processes themselves. This must be undertaken as part of an effort to contain, if not eliminate, our ideological preconceptions, which can end up distorting the very reality that we are studying. This is also the case when we study native communities' healthcare systems. We must observe the make-up of these systems and their efficacy in reducing mortality, and try to identify what sociocultural and ideological functions these systems serve for communities and for subjects. However, I stress that we must do so while trying to determine the efficacy that such systems have in actually reducing healthcare problems.

Currently, different Latin American trends of medical anthropology[1] (including CMA) study almost every process among very different social actors and sectors, with the goal of describing and understanding these processes and, to a lesser extent, influencing their outcomes. However, although the social actors examined here are not exclusively indigenous peoples, they continue to be central to Latin American studies. Latin American CMA has made significant contributions in very different fields and issues. It has propelled the use of qualitative methods and technologies in the study of h/d/t-p processes, gathering strategic information and explanations not otherwise obtained by statistical methods and approaches. Recognition of the benefits of qualitative techniques has led to their extensive use by biomedical researchers, a use that has frequently been questioned by anthropologists, mostly in terms of the need to apply these techniques to the medium- and long-term fieldwork being done by these researchers: we must assume that, in every sense, anthropological work is personalised work at every stage of a research project.

Medical anthropology evidences the connections that subjects and groups make between different forms of care that occur in specific contexts, and the processes of appropriation that all social sectors have of biomedical knowledge. Specifically, medical anthropology in Latin America has shown that traditional and alternative medicines are normalised aspects of treatment, and that all forms of care, not just biomedical care, are constantly changing. It has also demonstrated that society and culture, along with biomedical and traditional healers, can *create* the ailments that they subsequently treat and can sometimes cure or heal.

Medical anthropology increasingly studies the power dynamics of healers and patients and within other relationships when these revolve around inequalities such as gender. It has permanently underscored the importance of fieldwork, although theory-driven proposals are constantly and intermittently generated. It has continued, where possible, to put forward a holistic view of h/d/t-p processes that question the unilateral and exclusionary perspective of the biomedical model. In summary, it has tried to consider h/d/t-p processes in a way that is not only different from but also in opposition to biomedical forms of thinking, generating new types of explanations and interpretations, and potential modes for action.

One of CMA's most consistent contributions is that of documenting and attempting to understand popular knowledge of h/d/t-p processes through the study of subaltern social actors. All areas of medical anthropology have tried to describe the rationality that different social and ethnic groups use to explain and counteract the ailments that affect them, and to understand their supposed or real rejection of biomedicine. Medical anthropology has also attempted to evidence the cultural and technical rationality of so-called traditional medicines in order to underscore their explanatory and applicative abilities while seeking to rehabilitate not only traditional 'medical' knowledge, but also the culture of indigenous peoples themselves.

Anthropological studies have demonstrated that every social group, regardless of its level of formal education, creates and uses preventative criteria regarding some of the illnesses – both real and imagined – that subjects and groups believe to impact their health and wellbeing. The majority of preventative criteria that social groups use are sociocultural;[2] but for anthropologists, the crux lies not in considering these correct or incorrect, but rather in considering how social groups necessarily create and replicate preventative social practices and ideas within their group, questioning the medical gaze that treats populations and subjects, particularly the 'uneducated', as though they reject preventative care. The development of preventative measures for real or imaginary threats therefore becomes a structural process in the life of social groups.

For medical questions such as 'Why do patients with high blood pressure, diabetes or HIV/AIDS not comply with their prescribed "treatment" and/or change their "habits" or lifestyles?' – or, 'Why are different vaccines increasingly rejected?' – anthropologists try to understand the cultural, economic, political and ideological rationales behind practices and behaviour. They make reference to the larger context in which these behaviours occur and they seek a rationale, based at least in part on the premise that scientific evidence does not immediately change the behaviour of some social sectors. Furthermore, CMA has documented that some actors – including healthcare professionals – use scientific arguments and new medical technology in order to justify, for example, the social and professional rejection of vaccination.

Hence, I reiterate, sociocultural, economic and technical rationales should not be sought only in the habits or lifestyles of the population, but also in those of medical staff and within the healthcare/disease industries. Often anthropologists appear only interested in describing and understanding the sociocultural rationality of traditional healers, but not of doctors – as if we only think of sociocultural rationality as it pertains to the first group – a fact that has negative consequences for understanding how to deal with communication difficulties that may exist between a doctor and an indigenous patient; or in promoting changes in communities in order to foster self-detection of diseases such as Chagas, or to reduce the consumption of sugary beverages to prevent chronic and degenerative diseases.

Some specific changes have been difficult to achieve, while others have happened more quickly than expected. To understand why this happens we must analyse the often contradictory messages and practices with which we live (Bateson 1985; Ruesch and Bateson 1965) and understand both traditional knowledge and the latest digital practices on h/d/t-p processes, so that the actions of subjects and micro-groups can be guided accordingly (Menéndez 1998).

Intentionally or not, by analysing h/d/t-p processes, CMA describes the contexts of exclusion, degradation, racism and aggression, to which secondary social sectors in general, and some ethnic groups in particular, have been subjected. Medical anthropology has sought to expose these processes, identify possibilities for their reduction or elimination and boost mechanisms for empowerment through h/d/t-p processes. Indigenous peoples, and in recent years indigenous women in particular, have been the subjects of much of this research.

Latin American anthropologists have mostly tried to describe and understand alternative knowledge without considering it false or erroneous, independent of the efficacy that this knowledge may have and in stark contrast to biomedical knowledge and institutions. We have studied the knowledge that groups and communities have formed about their own ailments; nevertheless, these studies have, at least until the 1990s, dismissed the question of subjectivity. Under neoliberalism and together with cultural difference and ethnicity, paradoxically we also recover a focus on subjectivity. Thanks largely to theoretical tendencies emerging in the USA, the region began to develop an anthropology that considered questions such as addiction, suffering, experience and emotions. These analyses were essential in order to more fully explore subjectivity, to build on previous work and perspectives and so that we could take our understanding of cultural rationalities more deeply to the level of subject and group.[3]

One of CMA's principal contributions has been demonstrating that the majority of traditional illnesses are generated by social relationships, such that, for subjects, micro-groups and communities, the causes of physical, mental or psychosomatic illness may be the result of conflicts that occur within the family or among neighbours. We should be studying this issue in terms not only of traditional illnesses but also non-traditional ones, given that their causes and solutions can be mediated by the action of subjects and groups.

A review of the ethnographic bibliography on h/d/t-p processes shows that in the context of incidences of illness, the majority of interviewees made reference to conflictive relationships among subjects and micro-groups, transgressions of community norms, the role played by witchcraft and divine or magical schemes. Most of the people interviewed attributed their illnesses to daily hot or cold temperatures, to what happened with a neighbour, to not satisfying a craving, to not having money or milk to feed a newborn baby, to witnessing a sexual act at an inappropriate age, or to divine intervention or will. Ethnographic descriptions show not only that many of these illnesses generated by conflict or commonplace social problems (related to land-ownership, marriage agreements between families or other violence) but also that in the majority of these relationships a large role is played by envy in the context of poverty – a situation that that cultural, functional, structural and Marxist anthropologists have been describing and explaining since the 1940s. I consider that the relational aspect of these illnesses requires wider investigation, so that we might better explain economic-political issues and processes at both family and community levels and understand why some social rituals and murderous violence persist.

Some specific problems of CMA

As I have already noted, some principal anthropological contributions have been critiques of biomedicine and proposals for changing some of its elements. These critiques have been directed towards the theoretical, methodological, educational and interventionist aspects of the field, and especially biomedicine's negative treatment of indigenous peoples and, more recently, women of every social sector, including but not exclusively from these communities. Both directly and indirectly, the structure and function of biomedical institutions and knowledge have been described and analysed, weakly noting its positive aspects whilst homing in on its negative ones. Because biomedicine appears uninterested in obtaining information for understanding the rationality of subjects and groups undergoing care or in preventative procedures, the biomedical focus is often imposed through physical or symbolic violence.

Such critiques have generated different possibilities about the relationship between anthropology and biomedicine. One end of the spectrum argues that it is structurally impossible for biomedicine and the healthcare sector to take into account and apply specific cultural, political and subjective issues affecting the comprehension and solution of illness and ailments; the other end of the spectrum, although questioning certain aspects of medical knowledge and institutions, posits that there remains confidence in the possibility of change within biomedicine, and the potential for it to complement socio-anthropological proposals.[4] The first position suggests that a radical incompatibility exists between anthropological and biomedical perspectives, asserting that all professionals working within biomedical institutions – including anthropologists – will end up medicalising both their interventions and modes of thinking (Sarti 2010). Others hope that independent anthropological ways of thinking and acting can be maintained, even when working within biomedical institutions. Some authors even go further to propose a form of division of labour, by which the main focus of CMA is using its own perspectives to complement and fill in gaps in education, research or even interventions, overlooked by biomedicine.

Nevertheless, medicalisation remains among the most reported dangers by CMA. At least since the 1970s, US and European anthropologists and sociologists (Conrad and Schneider 1980; Conrad 1992) have been concerned about not only the medicalisation of behaviours, but also the increasing medicalisation of medical anthropology itself (Baer 1990; Morgan 1990; Singer 1989), as is also occurring in Latin America (Menéndez 2013). This is an extremely disquieting issue for Latin America, not only because it seems to be on the rise, but also because medicalisation reduces the potential for contributions from socio-anthropological perspectives, since the results generated through medicalisation are almost identical to those of biomedicine.

Even the most divergent among anthropological trends agree that biomedical perspectives tend to impose their ways of thinking and implementation. This becomes evident through, for example, how the healthcare sector manages family planning programmes, its negative (pre)conceptions about preventative care in certain groups, its simplistic notions about influencing the lifestyles of subjects and social groups, the way it tends to use qualitative techniques as fast-track research, and how it stigmatises self-medication – despite recognising the role played by 'self-care'.

For Latin American anthropologists, there is no doubt that h/d/t-p processes are an intrinsic part of the culture inhabited by different social groups, subjects and particularly, ethnic groups. These processes are part of the cultural identities of subjects and groups. It is possible that the majority of CMA specialists perceive the expansion of biomedicine, including its use by traditional healers, as a threat to the survival of traditional medicine itself, and to the cultural identity of the ethnic groups to whom it belongs. This growth is usually analysed through either of two basic positions. One focuses on the expansive character of biomedicine – and the social forces supporting it – invoking the increasing dominance of instrumental rationality or all-encompassing medical biopower that excludes the role of groups and subjects. The other, while recognising biomedical expansion, focuses its analysis on the persistence of traditional healing and its ability to remain relevant, relegating biomedical expansion and penetration to a secondary concern.

Rather than concentrating on the relationships of hegemony and subordination, power and resistance, each of these trends focuses on only one of these interrelated social forces or groups. Such power dynamics are created through different kinds of social transactions, which, although they reveal the expansion of biomedicine, include not only the persistence and redefinition of traditional medicines, but also the role that they play in questioning important aspects of biomedicine (Menéndez 2018). Hence, with exceptions, what we see in Latin America is the constant expansion of biomedicine in general, and as related to ethnic groups in particular. This demands an understanding of why biomedicine is produced and expands, but the analysis must not be Manichaean, referring exclusively, for example, to responses to interests of the chemical and pharmaceutical industry. Rather, an analysis must attempt to examine the roles of every important social actor related to biomedical expansion, including both the pharmaceutical industry and secondary social actors – not only ethnic groups, but also indigenous healers. We must explain why the ethnic groups that have most strongly propelled indigenous empowerment in political terms are those that least resist biomedical expansion. We must explain why pro-indigenous governments (like that of Evo Morales in Bolivia, which engages in indigenous identitarian discourse leading to the creation of an Intercultural Health sub-ministry within the Bolivian healthcare system) nevertheless devote resources almost entirely directed to promoting biomedicine, especially biomedical treatment, rather than traditional medicine. One explanation lies in the efficacy of conventional medicine compared with traditional medicine, for treating and reducing the illnesses that have been historically responsible for the highest mortality rates. I also attribute it to the mandate that governments receive from their citizens, including ethnic groups, for promoting the biomedical services sought by the population. But additionally, NGOs, and religious institutions from Catholic, Protestant and other denominations, have also played an influential role in criticising traditional medicine and promoting biomedical treatment.

Recognising biomedical expansion does not undermine the many critiques that can be made about biomedicine and the healthcare sector. But it must be emphatically noted that if we do not identify and analyse the positive functions that biomedicine fulfils for some social groups, the results of these studies will scarcely be relevant to the common, dominant processes and tendencies emerging in the coming years. Notwithstanding the existence of Latin American ethnic groups that have experienced low biomedical penetration, we need to assume that the majority will eventually experience this process, even so-called 'forest peoples' (Hill and Oliver 2011; Kelly 2011; Kroeger et al. 1991; Zent and Freire 2011). Additionally, in various regional contexts, subjects and ethnic groups not only prefer biomedicine for certain aliments, but also prefer private medicine to official public medicine.

Not only does CMA question biomedicine, but doubts also emerge about some of its objectives and results, in which medical anthropologists have played a (sometimes leading) role. In several countries in the region, special healthcare services for ethnic groups were created and intercultural healthcare policies formulated by regional governments, and supported by the Pan-American Health Organization. Although most of these healthcare services have been questioned on several grounds, intercultural healthcare policies have had little impact and, with the exception of a few cases, are considered failures and have been discontinued, as is the case of mixed (intercultural or multicultural) hospitals (see Menéndez 2016).

A set of critiques have been made regarding the healthcare subsystems for indigenous peoples that were created under neoliberalism, of which the most common and important are: insufficient financing and/or poor financial administration; bureaucratic and corrupt administration of services; bad patient care; a lack of coordination between biomedicine and indigenous medicine; a strong tendency to impose a biomedical model and exclude indigenous medicine; subordination, asymmetry and verticality between healthcare staff and the indigenous population (including its healers) and the homogenisation of inherently distinct ethnic groups (Cardoso 2015; Freire 2015; Kelly 2011; Langdon and Garnelo 2017; Puerta Silva 2004). Several of the intercultural tendencies that have developed since the 1980s proposed and anticipated a level of coordination between biomedicine and traditional medicine that has never played out, proving, for many anthropologists, the incompatibility of anthropology and biomedicine. Despite biomedicine's apathy towards, and even rejection of, the intercultural healthcare programmes promoted during the 1980s and 1990s, we must critically analyse them, since most were destined to failure. The influence of biomedical dominance (in opposing or ignoring these types of programmes) was not taken into account, nor were these ethnic groups' conditions (in economic, influence, and cultural terms) or urgent needs considered, a fact that also led to apathy towards these programmes, insofar as they lacked both resources and institutional management.

A second issue meriting reflection, and a cause of ongoing concern, is related to the capacity and quality of the agency that secondary social sectors have over h/d/t-p processes. Here I am not questioning the agency and capacity of 'managers' at the micro-group (such as family) level in addressing the illnesses suffered by the members of their group. My doubts relate to civil society's capacity for creating autonomous alternative organisations, such that they will not be co-opted or redirected by dominant social forces. I am also concerned as to whether civil society can foment resistance, empowerment or concrete action on h/d/t-p processes so that it can achieve (or at least 'impose' or generate consensus on) some of its ideas, requests and proposals. Thus, without denying the existence of resistance organisations and efforts (Berrio 2017; De Melo e Silva 2017), the things I see, particularly in Mexico, are troubling. H/d/t-p processes do not often appear to be central to ethnic movements, their leaders or scholars, beyond their rhetorical value. With few exceptions ethnic leaders or movements do not seem to really promote their own forms of healing as potential alternatives to biomedicine, nor do they consistently demand improved biomedical healthcare services. We do find that the population itself requests services such as healthcare centres, permanent physicians or even hospitals. Similar self-propelled efforts are also manifested in the work of small groups of activists on HIV/AIDS, and for women in particular the efforts focus almost exclusively on procedures and violence related to reproductive health. It is worth noting that these groups are composed of many kinds of professionals, including anthropologists.

On a related note, we must refine some issues. What constitutes resistance, not only in terms of social movements, but also for individuals, micro-groups and communities? Such a determination implies making interpretative decisions that can be difficult to establish, such as, for example: when is not going to the doctor the consequence of a lack of doctors or economic resources? And when is it actually the result of a negative attitude towards biomedicine? When does self-medication constitute a form of empowerment with regard to biomedicine? And when is it a social process of rational time management or economic saving for a subject or micro-group? (Dias-Scopel 2015; Ortega and Palma 2017).

Central to these and other questions is the power of establishing the capacity for agency in subjects and subordinate groups, so they can not only practise self-care or resistance but also negotiate and, especially, advance their own proposals for the improvement or modification of healthcare activities and policies operating within their territories. This should include real recognition at the governmental and healthcare-sector levels of their particular forms of care (Cardoso 2015). Fostering agency in terms of h/d/t-p processes is an issue that requires urgent analysis in every Latin American country, given that it is the capacity for collective agency that can – at least temporarily – maintain traditional forms of care that are effective in addressing illness, while continuing to serve as a principal means of asserting identity through curative ritual. Collective agency can also be a mechanism for the social control of biomedical policies, activities and directions, especially through different alternatives for self-care.

Notes

1. I consider that the denomination 'medical anthropology' is not the most appropriate; nevertheless, anthropology of healthcare, anthropology of medicine or ethnomedicine are even less appropriate because of their ideological connotations, incongruence or specificity. Hence we retain the name, despite criticism, for the simple reason that we most commonly use it.
2. Subjects and ethnic groups increasingly use preventative biomedical criteria, whether or not these have been culturally redefined.
3. While, between the 1930s and 1950s, a set of anthropological currents developed in the United States recovering the subject, or at least the person, in Latin America these tendencies were frequently questioned as psychologising, especially by authors who adhered not only to functionalism or structuralism but also to anti-colonialist and/or anti-classicist theories. It is interesting that the tendencies that in fact recovered the subject in this region did not usually make reference to, for example, a large number of biographies, autobiographies or life-stories that North American anthropologists and sociologists developed during this period. This is even the case when we leave aside, in the case of Mexico, the biography of Juan Chamula developed by Ricardo Pozas, and practically the entire oeuvre of Oscar Lewis about Mexico City.
4. A large part of the criticisms of biomedicine and the healthcare sector by CMA is not only correct, but also necessary; nevertheless, others are characterised by a unilateral perspective, such that they only acknowledge negative biomedical perspectives and actions and omit many of the contributions related to its efficacy. Even anthropologists denounce some medical deficiencies, including, for example, failing to recognise the symbolic efficacy of these professionals, when at least some of them know that both doctors and medications can have a placebo effect.

References

Baer, Hans A. 1990. 'The Possibilities and Dilemmas of Building Bridges between Critical Medical Anthropology and Clinical Anthropology: A Discussion', *Social Science and Medicine* 30 (9): 1011–13.

Bateson, Gregory. 1985. *Pasos hacia una ecología de la mente*. Buenos Aires: Carlos Lohlé.

Berrio, Lina. 2017. 'Una década de intervenciones gubernamentales y desde la sociedad civil en torno a la salud materna en Guerrero'. In *Salud y mortalidad materna en México: Balances y perspectivas desde la antropología y la interdisciplinariedad*, edited by Graciela Freyermuth Enciso, 168–200. Mexico City: Centro de Investigaciones y Estudios Superiores en Antropología Social.

Cardoso, Marina D. 2015. 'Políticas de saúde indígena no Brasil: Do modelo assistencial à representação política'. In *Saúde indígena: Políticas comparadas na América Latina*, edited by Esther Jean Langdon and Marina D. Cardoso, 83–106. Florianópolis: Editora da Universidade Federal de Santa Catarina.

Conrad, Peter. 1992. 'Medicalization and Social Control', *Annual Review of Sociology* 18: 209–32.

Conrad, Peter and Joseph W. Schneider. 1980. *Deviance and Medicalization: From Badness to Sickness*. St. Louis: Mosby.

De Melo e Silva, Núbia Maria. 2017. *"A conversa de hoje é que parir é no hospital": Implicações e desafios à saúde indígena*. Rio de Janeiro: Fundação Oswaldo Cruz.

Freire, Germán, ed. 2011. *Perspectivas en salud indígena: Cosmovisión, enfermedad y políticas públicas*. Quito: Ediciones Abya-Yala.

Freire, Germán. 2015. 'Políticas de salud indígena en Venezuela (con un comentario sobre la participación y el contexto)'. In *Saúde indígena: Políticas comparadas na América Latina*, edited by Esther Jean Langdon and Marina D. Cardoso, 61–82. Florianópolis: Editora da Universidade Federal de Santa Catarina.

Hill, Jonathan and Myla Oliver. 2011. 'Curanderos rituales, salud y medicina moderna entre los curripaco del Amazonas'. In *Perspectivas en salud indígena: Cosmovisión, enfermedad y políticas públicas*, edited by Germán Freire, 251–85. Quito: Ediciones Abya-Yala.

Kelly Luciani, José A. 2011. 'Equívocos sobre identidad y cultura: Un comentario sobre la formulación de políticas para los pueblos indígenas en Venezuela'. In *Perspectivas en salud indígena: Cosmovisión, enfermedad y políticas públicas*, edited by Germán Freire, 417–61. Quito: Ediciones Abya-Yala.

Kroeger, A., M. Mancheno, W. Ruiz and E. Estrella, eds. 1991. *Malaria y leishmaniasis cutanea en Ecuador: Un estudio interdisciplinario, aspectos históricos, epidemiológicos, antropológicos, entomológicos y métodos de control*. Quito: Museo Nacional de Medicina.

Langdon, Esther Jean and Marina D. Cardoso, eds. 2015. *Saúde indígena: Políticas comparadas na América Latina*. Florianópolis: Editora da Universidade Federal de Santa Catarina.

Langdon, Esther Jean and Luiza Garnelo. 2017. 'Articulación entre servicios de salud y "medicina indígena": Reflexiones antropológicas sobre política y realidad en Brasil', *Salud Colectiva* 13 (3): 457–70.

Menéndez, Eduardo L. 1998. 'Estilos de vida, riesgos y construcción social: Conceptos similares y significados diferentes', *Estudios Sociológicos* 16 (46): 37–67.

Menéndez, Eduardo L. 2002. *La parte negada de la cultura: Relativismo, diferencias y racismo*. Barcelona: Edicions Bellaterra.

Menéndez, Eduardo. 2013. 'Miradas antropológicas o miradas medicalizadas: Reflexiones sobre las diferencias entre ciencias médicas y antropología social'. In *Miradas concurrentes: La antropología en el diálogo interdisciplinario*, edited by Virginia García Acosta and Guillermo de la Peña, 225–52. Mexico City: Centro de Investigaciones y Estudios Superiores en Antropología Social.

Menéndez, Eduardo Luiz. 2016. 'Salud intercultural: Propuestas, acciones y fracasos', *Ciência e Saúde Coletiva* 21 (1): 109–18.

Menéndez, Eduardo L. 2018. *Poder, estratificación social y salud: Análisis de las condiciones sociales y económicas de la enfermedad en Yucatán*. Tarragona: Publicacions de la Universitat Rovira i Virgili.

Morgan, Lynn M. 1990. 'The Medicalization of Anthropology: A Critical Perspective on the Critical–Clinical Debate', *Social Science and Medicine* 30 (9): 945–50.

Ortega, Judith and Judzil Palma. 2017. 'Comunicación, género y autoatención: Acción social en prevención de cánceres'. In *Cánceres en mujeres mayas de Yucatán: Pobreza, género y comunicación social*, edited by Judith Ortega Canto and José Pérez Mutul, 199–244. Mérida: Universidad Autónoma de Yucatán.

Paiva Dias-Scopel, Raquel. 2015. *A cosmopolítica da gestação, do parto e do pós-parto: Práticas de autoatenção e processo de medicalização entre os índios Munduruku*. Brasília: Paralelo 15.

Puerta Silva, Claudia. 2004. 'Roles y estrategias de los gobiernos indígenas en el sistema de salud colombiano', *Revista Colombiana de Antropología* 40: 85–121.

Ruesch, Jurgen and Gregory Bateson. 1965. *Comunicación: La matriz social de la psiquiatría*. Buenos Aires: Paidós.

Sarti, Cynthia Andersen. 2010. 'Saude e sufrimiento'. In *Horizontes das ciências sociais no Brasil: Antropologia*, edited by Carlos Benedito Martins and Luiz Fernando Dias Duarte, 197–223. São Paulo: ANPOCS.

Singer, Merrill. 1989. 'The Limitations of Medical Ecology: The Concept of Adaptation in the Context of Social Stratification and Social Transformation', *Medical Anthropology* 10 (4): 223–34.

Zent, Stanford and Germán Freire. 2011. 'La economía política de la salud, enfermedad y la cura entre los piaroa'. In *Perspectivas en salud indígena: Cosmovisión, enfermedad y políticas públicas*, edited by Germán Freire, 327–83. Quito: Ediciones Abya-Yala.

Introduction

Paola M. Sesia, Jennie Gamlin, Sahra Gibbon and Lina Berrio

Latin American critical medical anthropology (LA-CMA) is a product of its context. Social histories of inequality, ethnocide, racism and internal and external colonialism, aggravated by a spate of dictatorships interspersed by foreign military interventions, civil war and rebellion, have marked Latin America and its academic production as deeply as its richly diverse cultural and ethnic landscape. When universities took on a central social role during the decades of economic development in the 1940s–60s, academic voices began generating critical commentary regarding the human fallout of economic, political and social processes. Anthropological and sociological works that documented similar and contrasting social patterns in Central America, Mexico, the southern cone and Andean regions contributed to critical debates drawing on Marxist and Gramscian thought, dependency theories and Soviet-era communism, while Catholic liberation theology and indigenous epistemologies added ideological and ideational perspectives to interpretations of history, development, culture and wellbeing.

As we outline in this volume, Latin American critical theory has been particularly influential at the intersection of medicine, epidemiology and anthropology, leading to the development of whole fields of study. These have been pivotal in the development of Latin American social sciences since the mid-twentieth century. Yet in the ethnocentric anglophone-dominated academic world, where literature produced in languages other than English is little known and rarely cited, acknowledged contributions to the field of LA-CMA are scarce.[1] Waitzkin et al. (2001: 315) suggest that this lack of impact 'reflects an erroneous assumption' that the 'intellectual and scientific productivity of the "third world" manifest a less rigorous and relevant approach to the important questions of our age'. Narotzky (2002) points out that hegemonic Anglo-American academia has systematically ignored anthropological production published in Spanish, including by those who work from similar political economy perspectives. Martínez Hernáez (2008), for his part, argues that there are multiple ironies to this obliteration. This includes Anglo-American anthropologies' and CMA's claim to ownership of political economy and neo-Marxist theoretical approaches that originated in Latin American critical thought (such as dependency or under-development theories) or in southern Europe (Gramsci's theory of hegemony), while they ignore social science production that builds upon these traditions in Portuguese, Spanish or Italian.[2] Other progressive theories such as collective health and social medicine have been marginalised and colonised,[3] while the epistemic hierarchy of scientific knowledge production and the hegemony of the anglophone academic systems of ranking and qualification remain unchallenged (Santos 2014).

For these reasons, research about this region by Latin American theorists rarely has global impact. Concerned with this dismissal and well aware of theoretical contributions from Latin America, the editors of this book organised a series of events, beginning with a workshop in Oaxaca, Mexico, at which anthropologists working in the UK, Mexico and Brazil were invited to present their research on theory and practice in CMA. The event generated great interest and enthusiasm, covering fields as diverse as chronic diseases, ethnographies of maternal health, rare genetic diseases, judicialisation and human rights, violence and mental health. As a result, we learned of the breadth of CMA's ongoing relevance to contexts across the globe as threats to social cohesion grow, as much among dementia patients in the UK as among Central American migrants.

Riding on the success of this event, a second meeting and a series of conference panels were organised in London, Lisbon and Florianópolis, Brazil, taking a deeper look at Latin American critical theory around health inequalities and drawing together critical anthropologists from Argentina, Brazil, Ecuador, Mexico, the UK and the USA. This book is a product of these collaborations. To the best of our knowledge it is the first to bring together Latin American ethnographic contexts and theories of CMA in the English language.

The editors sought to create a volume that included a significant number of authors whose work has rarely or never been published in English, with an implicit focus on both the ethnographic context and the generation or reinterpretation of Latin American critical theory. The book provides a showcase for cutting-edge ethnographically informed anthropological research focused on and informed by Latin American social and historical contexts, including original theoretical contributions. The collection includes work spanning four regions in Latin America (Mexico,

Brazil, Guatemala and Peru) as well as the trans-migratory contexts they connect and are defined by. It draws on research that is focused on diverse social practices and contexts pertaining to health, including reproduction, sex work, rare and chronic diseases and the use of pharmaceuticals. In doing so it addresses themes of central relevance to medical anthropology and global health, such as agency, identity, reproductive politics, indigenous health and human rights. Given the wealth of research being undertaken in Latin America and given its specific history of engagement with critical theory, there is an urgent need to provide wider access to this expertise for an English-speaking audience who can engage in dialogue with, and learn from, anthropological work being undertaken in the region.

Several of the chapters were co-authored by Latin American and European or North American scholars, providing a double perspective that adds value to this collaborative endeavour. The final product, we hope, explores the hugely valuable contribution that LA-CMA can play in understanding, explaining and potentially addressing some of the most pressing health concerns facing our globalised world today.

What is Latin American critical medical anthropology?

Theoretical developments in LA-CMA offer sharp critical interpretations of the causes and contexts of health, illness, suffering and wellbeing because this academic work is based on research, practice and experience that reflect a shared history. In contrast to the 'us and them' that characterises much 'northern' anthropology, in Latin America there is a tendency to reflect on ethnographic experiences from within the historical, social and political contexts of Latin America, defined by highly unequal structures of race/ethnicity, gender and social class. This has been referred to as a 'culture of social critique', reflecting on 'visible signs of extreme socio-political authoritarianism and inequality' and 'social unfairness in the global economy' (Breilh 2008: 745). Several of the authors in this volume make reference to the work of the Mexican anthropologist Guillermo Bonfil Batalla (1935–1991) as a pre-eminent figure in this field who called attention to the conditions of inequality and marginalisation experienced in the mid- to late twentieth century, especially among indigenous populations (Bonfil Batalla 2006 [1962]), and the need for policy and practice interventions to overcome these conditions.

Latin American medical anthropologists[4] and those of us who position ourselves within this sub-field tend in fact to be immersed in contexts of profound inequalities, which makes it almost inevitable that our professional commitment, definition of research interests and subscription to theoretical orientations will fall within the field of CMA; this often occurs even if we do not openly label ourselves as critical medical anthropologists. These research orientations often reside on an ethnographically grounded and theoretically oriented understanding of social inequalities, often combining research and involvement in transformative action. This link between research and action – the attempt to understand and act upon multiple social inequalities – is one of the prime contributions of LA-CMA, and constitutes an underlying idea for many authors in this edited collection.

In contrast, CMA as a discipline of its own originated in the late 1980s in Anglo-American academia to account for a Marxist and, at times, practice-oriented perspective (Singer and Baer 1995; Morgan 1987; Singer 1986, 1990; Singer et al. 1990). Anglophone CMA evolved as an alternative to what was considered mainstream medical anthropology. From its inception, CMA embraced the political economy of health, sickness, health-seeking and healthcare delivery. It brought a materialist, systemic and macro-social perspective to medical anthropology in order to study how biomedicine, the biomedical model of care and the medicalisation of everyday life have expanded in North America and Western Europe as well as in most of the rest of the world. It showed how epidemiological profiles, social vulnerability and health resources are unequally distributed in today's globalised and neoliberal world. It unravelled the corporate production of harm through the deregulated commoditisation of pharmaceuticals, food, cosmetics, guns, agriculture and medical implants (Singer and Baer 2009). Finally, it enquired into everyday micro-dynamics in health and illness to reveal underlying macro forces and deepening power asymmetries linked to monopoly capitalism and neoliberalism, persistent imperialist drives, colonial, neocolonial or post-colonial heritages, and even racist and ethnocentric nationalism and xenophobia.

In later years, Anglo-American CMA expanded to become more inclusive of post-structuralist cultural critiques of individuals' and collectives' experience of suffering, ill health and harm within contexts of structural or symbolic violence (Scheper-Hughes, 1992; Scheper-Hughes and Bourgois 2017); ideological and cultural processes behind the expansion of medicalisation, the role of the state and biopolitics; hegemonic social representations around entitlements, bodily regimes, health and welfare politics at the expense of the poor; and the production of knowledge and scientific discourse intertwined with dominant societal notions of gender, race and ethnicity.

Despite their different beginnings, in practice Latin American and anglophone CMA converge in many ways. Both have become theoretical and methodological orientations that are vigilant of structural determination and power relations around health, illness and healing, while their fields of inquiry include individual and collective responses (Seppilli and Otegui 2005). Both take a political economy approach within medical anthropology, generated through ethnographically grounded and theoretically oriented understandings of social inequalities and power asymmetries in health, sickness and healing combined with a keen interest in understanding and naming those problems in order to transform them (Farmer 1992, 1999, 2005; Freyermuth Enciso 2003; Freyermuth and Sesia 2006; Holmes 2013; Ponce et al. 2017; Singer and Baer 1995, 2009). CMA and LA-CMA have both demonstrated how epidemiological profiles, social vulnerability and health resources are unequally distributed in today's globalised and neoliberal world. Both scrutinise micro-relations and subjective experiences of pathologies and health-seeking, within larger systemic issues and contexts of power and inequalities (Betancourt Rodríguez and Pinilla Alfonso 2011; Farmer 1992; Mendoza González 2011; Scheper-Hughes 1992; Holmes 2013). Perhaps most emphatically, the Latin American version acknowledges its debt to Marxism and the Gramscian concept of hegemony that is widely used, particularly by Eduardo Menéndez – one of the most influential Latin American medical anthropologists working today (see Menéndez 1981, 1984, 1990; Módena 1990).

This positionality within CMA has been particularly well developed in Latin America, where anthropologists have critically examined intercultural perspectives on health and the relationship between 'traditional' and 'hegemonic' models. In so doing they have also explored and expanded on the classical anthropological notions of disease and illness, and wider efforts to study this as a process that is socially determined.

These orientations have led to the development of influential theoretical concepts such as structural violence (Farmer 1999 and 2005), which has been widely applied to regional realities by critical medical anthropologists within Latin America. Other conceptual categories, such as medical pluralism (Leslie 1980), were rediscovered and repurposed in LA-CMA in the context of the hegemony of biomedicine and its simultaneous asymmetrical coexistence with other medical models, including indigenous traditional medicine and domestic health-seeking or self-care. This sub-field is complemented by theoretical developments such as *salud intercultural* (intercultural health; see Campos Navarro 2016; Fernández Juárez 2004, 2006; Ramírez Hita 2009), *intermedicalidade* (intermedicality; see Greene 1998; Follér 2004; Langdon 2018), *la determinación social de la salud* (the social determination of health; see Breilh 2008, 2013), and *proceso salud/enfermedad/atención* (the health/illness/care process), *autoatención* (self-care) and *el modelo hegemónico bio-médico* (the hegemonic biomedical model; see Menéndez 1984; 1990). These conceptualisations of the relationship between different societies and medicine have enjoyed a broad dissemination within LA-CMA for their ability to explore and explain socio-medical realities that are widespread in the region. However, their theoretical applicability transcends Latin American borders, and yet they are almost unknown outside the region.

LA-CMA did not follow one specific route, but many. Although its embeddedness in a social context of inequality established CMA as a branch of social critique, within this broad field LA-CMA follows a variety of anthropological traditions linked to the development of different national schools in Argentina, Brazil, Colombia, Mexico and Peru – to name but a few. These national traditions developed throughout the twentieth century in conjunction with specific hegemonic projects of state formation in each country; they were also influenced by Anglo-American and French anthropological schools to varying degrees. In Mexico, the influence of North American anthropology was predominant, although medical anthropology developed from the 1950s very much building on the work of Gonzalo Aguirre Beltrán (1908–1996), whose theoretical orientation was inspired by structuralist Marxism and a historicist approach (1955; 1986). Brazilian anthropology, on the other hand, was more influenced by French ethnology; here too, a national anthropological tradition coalesced around the development of an anthropology of health whose distinctive ethos was linked to Brazil's specific historical and social processes (Langdon and Follér 2012). The idea of a Latin American anthropological tradition in CMA as a coherent and homogenous field is challenged by these diversities, including the existence of linguistic barriers between the Portuguese and Spanish languages that limit dialogue. In this sense, this book is also a wager on strengthening these regional dialogues.

Structure of the book

This book is structured across four thematic sections that bring new insight and understanding to how critical medical anthropology is being examined and addressed by those both living and working in Latin America.

The first section of the book focuses on intercultural and indigenous health in Latin America, rethinking critical approaches and current challenges. Intercultural health has often been defined in terms of the 'integration of western and traditional indigenous medicine' (PAHO 2002). For some time it has been an area of concern and engagement by a wide range of medical anthropologists working in Latin America, who have demonstrated the diversity of practices, hegemony and power involved in these relationships and the failure of intercultural health policies in a majority of regions (Campos Navarro et al. 2017; Menéndez 2012). The chapters in this section shed further light on these dynamics, demonstrating how efforts at developing 'intercultural' approaches must be critically and reflexively examined in relation to questions of power, interdisciplinarity and activism.

Esther Jean Langdon and Eliana Diehl reflect on how the emergence of the public health system in Brazil in the late 1980s, as a product of two decades of campaigning by the sanitary reform movement, also created opportunities for the involvement of indigenous participation in specific areas of Brazilian healthcare organisation and delivery. They show how this has shaped the 'anthropology of health' in Brazil as distinct from critical 'medical anthropology' in North America. Most importantly, they draw attention to the ambivalent involvement of indigenous communities and representatives, illustrating how, as the specific case of the Kaingang NGO highlights, external priorities force indigenous NGOs to work within a centralised and bureaucratic landscape that undermines efforts at intercultural healthcare. The authors also draw on Menéndez' work to demonstrate how Latin American CMA has not achieved the influence of North American anthropology, despite the incredible diversity of therapeutic processes analysed and examined.

Building on more than a decade of ethnographic work with Mexican indigenous communities, Jennie Gamlin and Lina Berrio's chapter gives an overview of critical medical anthropology with indigenous communities, focusing on what long-term ethnographic work and 'practivists' or intellectual activists have learned from the field and the theoretical contributions that these relationships have made to key theories within LA-CMA. Drawing on case studies from their own work on maternal health with Mexican indigenous communities, the authors point to the role of responsive indigeneity and indigenous anti-colonial resistance in the development of new theories. They propose that by its very nature intellectual activism generates theory that must be attributed as much to the indigenous critical view of their social context as to the work of intellectuals.

David Orr and Frida Herrera make use of comparative ethnographic research in Mexico and Peru to revisit classic anthropological terrain concerning how to understand and interpret a condition that is common across Latin America, *susto*, often defined as 'soul loss' or 'fright sickness'. They demonstrate the value of committing to an approach that aligns critical medical anthropology and its attention to structural inequalities with recent work in the anthropology of emotions, suggesting that the failure to do so has in part been due to a colonial legacy of seeing *susto* in terms of 'non-Western somatisation'. In doing so they not only highlight the variability and diversity of how *susto* is experienced in different regions of Latin America but also ask important questions concerning the need to better integrate structural inequalities, subjective accounts and phenomenological approaches to better understand what it means to 'live in conditions of fright'.

Drawing on a political economy framework, Rebecca Irons provides another important perspective on questions of intercultural health and health pluralism as 'self-care', focusing on the use of 'post-coital' pills in Lima, Peru. Drawing on rich ethnographic data, she shows how in a context of limited resources and options for low-income women in Lima, the meanings of these pharmaceuticals are multiple, deeply dependent on both flexible interpretations of religious beliefs and local understandings of the temporalities that configure conception and foetal development. It is this situation, however, that ultimately both reflects and reproduces inequalities, given how structures of reproductive governance in Peru fail to address and account for these differences in developing appropriate interventions for low-income and indigenous women.

Globalisation and contemporary challenges of border spaces and biologised difference

In the second section of the book we turn to examine how globalisation, whilst a contested and diverse phenomenon that is neither homogeneous nor unidirectional (Lowenhaupt Tsing 2005), nevertheless creates new contexts and challenges for examining how structural inequalities are entangled with and help to create 'border spaces' as well as biologised boundaries of difference. The first comes sharply into focus in the discussion of two chapters which examine how Central American migrants' lives and experiences in the US–Mexico border region are shaped at a nexus in which structural inequalities, vulnerabilities and discrimination inform life trajectories and opportunities. In the discussion by Olga Hernández we see how drug consumption among specific migrant communities in the US (mostly Mexican men, in this case) is pursued and made meaningful as a form of 'self-care', even as this is shaped by injustice, inequality and violence. By foregrounding individual experiences and daily physical and emotional struggles that contribute to the precarity of migrants' lives, we witness the diverse embodied contexts and consequences of drug use as a 'care' strategy in efforts to overcome the challenges of social, economic and political inclusion in the new environments that these Mexican migrants now live in. Similarly focused on the border spaces of the US–Mexican region, Rubén Muñoz Martínez and his co-authors focus on the specific vulnerability that Central American male migrants experience in relation to drug use, sex work and HIV exposure. Adopting a 'social mapping' approach, this chapter importantly highlights how particular public/private spaces in urban border cities in Mexico create and facilitate the structural vulnerability of these migrants in specific ways, as they navigate highly precarious 'border spaces' of the Mexico–Guatemala frontier.

If diverse aspects of biological, cultural and social globalisation shape how the fluid border spaces of migration are lived, they can also entail the remaking of other, more entrenched boundaries and categories of difference. In their chapter Melania Calestani and Laura Montesi examine how the globalising discourse of genomics (Gibbon et al. 2018), and the recent enormous investment in genomic research aimed at elucidating how genetic difference relates to categories of race and ethnicity (Wade et al. 2014; Saldaña-Tejeda and Wade 2018), are central to understanding and intervening in health disparities. Providing an important comparative perspective, they examine how discourses about population difference and genetic aetiologies, as this concerns type 2 diabetes in Mexico and chronic kidney disease in the UK, undermine a necessary wider focus on how health inequities are embedded in broader social histories, neoliberal ideologies and 'infrastructures for racialization' (Lee 2005). Drawing on Breilh's concept of 'critical epidemiology' (2008) and also pointing to an emerging field of epigenetic research and recent social science work on the 'somatisation' of race, they urgently underline the need for an approach that includes the biological as always situated within wider social and material ecologies in addressing and intervening on health disparities.

Political economy and judicalisation

A political economy perspective has been a central tenet of the critical medical anthropology approach, which is attentive to how historical and political forces and social institutions shape the distribution of economic resources in diverse healthcare arenas. Whilst such a perspective continues to be of vital importance to many of the contributors in this edited collection, a number of them are also attentive to the changing parameters within which these dynamics function in specific Latin American contexts, and the uneven consequences this has for action and agency with regard to how rights and choices relating to health are sought and secured. In the final section of the book we explore these questions through the lens of three contributions. The first, by Rosa María Osorio, directly examines the uneven benefits and burdens that are brought about by the incorporation of new forms of privatised primary healthcare services within pharmacies in Mexico – a phenomenon that has expanded rapidly in the last 10 years, particularly in urban areas. Whilst these novel public/private alignments in the provision of healthcare in Mexico reflect the 'niche' expansion of the pharmaceutical industry, multiplying both its markets and consumers, we also see that this is not sufficient to understand the complex dynamics at stake in these developments. These include greater and easier access to professional medical care for a wider range of often poorly served publics even as this community, rather than the state, absorbs the cost of this expanded but not closely regulated form of healthcare provision. Yet as this chapter outlines, these clinics 'annexed' to pharmacies constitute an easy and relatively swift way of expanding healthcare that is nevertheless gradually displacing efforts to redress deteriorating public health services.

A similar sense of complexity and also ambivalence is evident in the two chapters that constitute the final section of the edited collection, reflecting in complementary and contrasting ways on the expanded space of judicialisation in Latin America for pursuing human rights and accessing healthcare services and biomedical resources. In the penultimate paper of the book Paola Sesia examines how novel forms of 'counter-hegemonic' activism have emerged in the context of maternal care in Mexico in response to persistent racial discrimination against indigenous women. Drawing on one particular high-profile case, Sesia shows how these have become mobilised through media visibility and an articulation of what is described as 'obstetric violence'. Accompanied by judicial actions, these processes appear to offer a mode of public redress, compensation and potential transformation of the healthcare system.

Yet it is clear that whilst judicialisation can be successful in the field of human rights and maternal care in Mexico, it is not a panacea. The ongoing gap between the immediate success achieved in one high-profile case and wider efforts to shape healthcare institutions and infrastructures illuminates how judicialisation is only ever at best a partial and temporary solution.

The final chapter in the collection turns to another arena in which questions of activism, political economy and the expanding realm of judicialisation have become complexly entwined in the context of rare genetic disease in Brazil. Waleska Aureliano and Sahra Gibbon examine how an exponential increase in efforts to secure healthcare services and resources in Brazil by entering into judicial actions in relation to a wide range of disease conditions, including HIV/AIDS medications and cancer, have also become significantly evident in the context of rare genetic diseases – conditions that are thought to affect between 13 and 15 million people in Brazil. Drawing on ethnographic research and analysis of media and public discourse, they examine how a discourse about the 'right to life' is diversely mobilised by implicated communities that include government, civil society and the pharmaceutical industry in disputes that oscillate between the budgetary limits of the state and the commercial interests of the market. They powerfully show how in a context where the commodification of health weakens the public health system, rare-disease patients and their families are placed in situations of profound uncertainty and instability, with little choice but to judicialise.

Concluding remarks

The process of editing this collection has provided a valuable opportunity to reflect upon the wider relevance of LA-CMA beyond this region, to Europe and North America, as well as further afield within the Global South. When we initially conceived of this project several years ago, the socio-political context of Latin America appeared to stand out as a global example of how neoliberalism, unabated and unchallenged, in a context of extreme inequality and built upon fragile states with segmented populations, had created complex scenarios of violence, apparently unsolvable social frictions often based on racial and ethnic divisions and varying responses from within civil society, academia and the political economy itself. Within Latin America, Brazil and Mexico are two powerful recent examples of how people and political systems are responding on the Right and Left, each hoping that an institutional effort can solve their national crises.

Three chapters in particular allude to this in different ways: Paola Sesia gives a human face to human rights activism around obstetric violence; Jennie Gamlin and Lina Berrio talk about how indigenous women are subtly seeking ways to influence unequal gender relations through maternal health; and Sahra Gibbon and Waleska Aureliano describe activist processes around access to medications. These are examples of responses to the human fallout of a political economy that has not sought to ensure health and wellbeing or social justice for the population as a whole. They are examples of structural violence where the means and knowledge required for greater wellbeing exist, but resources are unequally distributed to the detriment of certain groups within society. As we conclude the editing of this book, it becomes evident that what once appeared to be confined to the socio-historical context of Latin America and the Global South – regions and nations that to varying degrees and for different time frames have been, or continue to be, subject to colonial rule – is in fact a pattern that is diversely repeated the world over. Populist governments, racially motivated massacres, climate denial, the post-truth society, social media corporations usurping democracy, whole political systems falling apart under the weight of divided populations – all these are signs of the dysfunctional, even dystopian state of globalisation. This context leaves no doubt about the relevance of LA-CMA to the health of the world population, now and in the coming turbulent times.

While we can clearly vouch for the global relevance of LA-CMA, any attempt at an overview of this broad and diverse field will face the impossibility of including each and every one of the many themes and populations that it comprises. The large number of works on the health of indigenous peoples included in the book demonstrates their importance in Latin American anthropological production, including medical anthropology. Urban populations are also amply represented, from Central American and Mexican migrants in Mexico and the United States to migrants of multiple nationalities in the UK and middle-class sectors in Brazil and Mexico. However, we have been unable to include work on the health of Afro-descendant populations, despite their numerical importance in the region and the conditions of vulnerability that most of them face. In 2015 the Economic Commission for Latin America estimated the total number of people of African descent in Latin America to be 130 million people, equivalent to more than 20 per cent of the total Latin American population. The majority are located in Brazil with 97 million, followed by Cuba, Colombia, Mexico, Ecuador and Venezuela

(Del Popolo and Rangel 2017: 51). We are also indebted to rich regional productions, particularly from Brazil and more recently research carried out in Colombia and Ecuador, on the characteristics and health conditions of Afro-descendant populations, even more so considering that we are writing during the Decade of People of African Descent (2015–24). Promoting a greater circulation of anthropological works in this field should undoubtedly be considered a priority for further research on CMA. We also recognise regional specialisations, in particular the considerable body of theoretical work produced in Argentina, which has been relevant and influential in its own national context as well as to research at a theoretical-methodological level throughout the region, and is host to landmark journals within this field including the influential *Salud Colectiva*. In conclusion, by drawing attention to some of the thematic and theoretical gaps in this current volume, as well as the absence of work from the Andean area and southern cone of Latin America, we hope to stimulate further research in the region, and more importantly to highlight the rich opportunities for ongoing engagement with and development of critical medical anthropology in and from Latin America.

Notes

1. This exclusion encompasses medical anthropological production from Italy and Spain, besides Latin America. At the same time, there has been significantly a high degree of cross-fertilisation between LA-CMA (especially from Argentina and Mexico) and CMA from southern Europe (Seppilli and Otegui 2005: 8).
2. Martínez Hernáez (2008: 153) ventures that this exclusion is the result of two concomitant phenomena: intellectual domination (others would label it 'intellectual colonialism') and the commodification of knowledge production in English-speaking academia. Intellectual domination is argued to occur because anglophone academia suffers from a peculiar form of ethnocentrism that consciously or unconsciously excludes all production in languages other than English as invalid, irrelevant or non-existent. The commodification of knowledge refers to a relentless process of theoretical innovation that is constantly and mostly produced in the English language to be consumed in the global academic market – a phenomenon from which even CMA cannot escape.
3. Breilh (2008), a leading critical epidemiologist from Ecuador, highlights that when European social and health scientists developed the social determinants of health model for WHO in 2005–8, they disregarded pioneering social medicine and collective health literature produced since the 1970s by Latin American critical thinkers. He argues that this omission cannot be explained simply by linguistic barriers. It may be due instead to an epistemic and political disinclination to include a critical approach that deeply questions power relations in an increasingly unequal market society. Social medicine integrates capitalist accumulation and exploitation, gender domination, racism and ethnic discrimination into its theoretical analysis of historically structured health profiles and lifestyles among individuals as well as collectives.
4. In this category we include the many 'adopted' anthropologists and committed academics from Europe and North America who have dedicated much of their life's work to the development of Latin American anthropology and/or working in Latin American academia.

References

Aguirre Beltrán, Gonzalo. 1955. *Programas de salud en la situación intercultural*. Mexico City: Instituto Indigenista Interamericano.

Aguirre Beltrán, Gonzalo. 1986. *Antropología médica*. Mexico City: Centro de Investigaciones y Estudios Superiores en Antropología Social.

Betancourt Rodríguez, Carlos Fabian and María Yaneth Pinilla Alfonso. 2011. 'Apreciaciones sobre el contexto sociocultural del VIH-Sida en las comunidades indígenas en Colombia', *Desacatos* 35: 75–86.

Bonfil Batalla, Guillermo. 2006. *Diagnóstico sobre el hambre en Sudzal, Yucatán: Un ensayo de antropología aplicada*. Mexico City: Centro de Investigaciones y Estudios Superiores en Antropología Social.

Breilh, Jaime. 2008. 'Una perspectiva emancipadora de la investigación y acción, basada en la determinación social de la salud'. Paper presented at the Latin American Workshop on Social Health Determinants, Latin American Social Medicine Association (ALAMES), Mexico City, 30 September–2 October 2008.

Breilh, Jaime. 2013. 'La determinación social de la salud como herramienta de transformación hacia una nueva salud pública (salud colectiva)', *Revista Facultad Nacional Salud Pública* 31 (Supplement 1): 13–27.

Campos Navarro, Roberto, ed. 2016. *Antropología médica e interculturalidad*. Mexico City: McGraw-Hill.

Campos Navarro, Roberto, Edith Yesenia Peña Sánchez and Alfredo Paulo Maya. 2017. 'Aproximación crítica a las políticas públicas en salud indígena, medicina tradicional e interculturalidad en México (1990–2016)', *Salud Colectiva* 13 (3): 443–55.

Del Popolo, Fabiana and Marta Rangel. 2017. *Situación de las personas afrodescendientes en América Latina y desafíos de políticas para la garantía de sus derechos*. Centro Latinoamericano y caribeño de demografía (CELADE)-División de Población de la Comisión Económica para América latina (CEPAL). Accessed 31 October 2019. https://repositorio.cepal.org/handle/11362/42654.

Farmer, Paul. 1992. *AIDS and Accusation: Haiti and the Geography of Blame*. Berkeley: University of California Press.

Farmer, Paul. 1999. *Infections and Inequalities: The Modern Plagues*. Berkeley: University of California Press.

Farmer, Paul. 2005. *Pathologies of Power: Health, Human Rights, and the New War on the Poor*. Berkeley: University of California Press.

Fernández Juárez, Gerardo, ed. 2004. *Salud e interculturalidad en América Latina: Perspectivas antropológicas*. Quito: Ediciones Abya-Yala.

Fernández Juárez, Gerardo, ed. 2006. *Salud e interculturalidad en América Latina: Antropología de la salud y crítica intercultural*. Quito: Ediciones Abya-Yala.

Follér, Maj-Lis. 2004. 'Intermedicalidade: A zona de contato criada por povos indígenas e profissionais de saúde'. In *Saúde dos povos indígenas: Reflexões sobre antropologia participativa*, edited by Esther Jean Langdon and Luiza Garnelo, 103–16. Rio de Janeiro: Contra Capa/Associação Brasileira de Antropologia.

Freyermuth, Graciela and Paola Sesia. 2006. 'Del curanderismo a la influenza aviaria: Viejas y nuevas perspectivas de la antropología médica', *Desacatos* 20: 9–28.

Freyermuth Enciso, Graciela. 2003. *Las mujeres de humo: Morir en Chenalhó: Género, etnia y generación, factores constitutivos del riesgo durante la maternidad*. Mexico City: Centro de Investigaciones y Estudios Superiores en Antropología Social.

Gibbon, Sahra, Susie Kilshaw and Margaret Sleeboom-Faulkner. 2018. 'Genomics and Genetic Medicine: Pathways to Global Health?', *Anthropology and Medicine* 25 (1): 1–10.

Gramsci, Antonio. 1971. *Selections from the Prison Notebooks of Antonio Gramsci*, edited and translated by Quintin Hoare and Geoffrey Nowell Smith. New York: International Publishers.

Greene, Shane. 1998. 'The Shaman's Needle: Development, Shamanic Agency, and Intermedicality in Aguaruna Lands, Peru', *American Ethnologist* 25 (4): 634–58.

Holmes, Seth M. 2013. *Fresh Fruit, Broken Bodies: Migrant Farmworkers in the United States*. Berkeley: University of California Press.

Langdon, Esther Jean. 2018. 'Salud indígena en Brasil: Pluralismo médico y autoatención', *Desacatos* 58: 8–15.

Langdon, Esther Jean and Maj-Lis Follér. 2012. 'Anthropology of Health in Brazil: A Border Discourse', *Medical Anthropology* 31 (1): 4–28.

Lee, Sandra Soo-Jin. 2005. 'Racializing Drug Design: Implications of Pharmacogenomics for Health Disparities', *American Journal of Public Health* 95 (12): 2133–38.

Leslie, Charles. 1980. 'Medical Pluralism in World Perspective', *Social Science and Medicine – Part B: Medical Anthropology* 14 (4): 191–95.

Lowenhaupt Tsing, Anna. 2005. *Friction: An Ethnography of Global Connection*. Princeton: Princeton University Press.

Martínez Hernáez, Ángel. 2008. *Antropología médica: Teorías sobre la cultura, el poder y la enfermedad*. Barcelona: Anthropos.

Mendoza González, Zuanilda. 2011. *De lo biomédico a lo popular: El proceso salud-enfermedad-atención en San Juan Copala, Oaxaca*. Mexico City: Universidad Nacional Autónoma de México.

Menéndez, Eduardo L. 1981. *Poder, estratificación y salud: Análisis de las condiciones sociales y económicas de la enfermedad en Yucatán*. Mexico City: Centro de Investigaciones y Estudios Superiores en Antropología Social.

Menéndez, Eduardo L. 1984. *Hacia una práctica médica alternativa: Hegemonía y autoatención (gestión) en salud*. Mexico City: Centro de Investigaciones y Estudios Superiores en Antropología Social.

Menéndez, Eduardo L. 1990. *Antropología médica: Orientaciones, desigualdades y transacciones*. Mexico City: Centro de Investigaciones y Estudios Superiores en Antropología Social.

Menéndez, Eduardo L. 2009. *De sujetos, saberes y estructuras: Introducción al enfoque relacional en el estudio de la salud colectiva*. Buenos Aires: Lugar Editorial.

Menéndez, Eduardo L. 2012. 'Metodología cualitativa: Varios problemas y reiteradas omisiones', *Index de Enfermería* 21 (1/2): 62–68.

Menéndez, Eduardo L. 2016. 'Cuestiones metodológicas sobre antropología e interculturalidad'. In *Antropología médica e interculturalidad*, edited by Roberto Campos Navarro, 1–12. Mexico City: McGraw-Hill.

Módena, María Eugenia. 1990. *Madres, médicos y curanderos: Diferencia cultural e identidad ideológica*. Mexico City: Centro de Investigaciones y Estudios Superiores en Antropología Social.

Morgan, Lynn M. 1987. 'Dependency Theory in the Political Economy of Health: An Anthropological Critique', *Medical Anthropology Quarterly* 1 (2): 131–54.

Narotzky, Susana. 2002. 'The Political Economy of Political Economy in Spanish Anthropology'. In *Culture, Economy, Power: Anthropology as Critique, Anthropology as Praxis*, edited by Winnie Lem and Belinda Leach, 33–46. Albany: State University of New York Press.

PAHO (Pan American Health Organization). 2002. *Health in the Americas*. Washington, DC: Pan American Health Organization.

Pineda, Roberto. 2012. 'El Congreso Indigenista de Pátzcuaro, 1940, una nueva apertura en la política indigenista de las Américas', *Baukara: Bitácoras de antropología e historia de la antropología en América Latina* 2: 10–28.

Ponce, Patricia, Rubén Muñoz and Matías Stival. 2017. 'Pueblos indígenas, VIH y políticas públicas en Latinoamérica: Una exploración en el panorama actual de la prevalencia epidemiológica, la prevención, la atención y el seguimiento oportuno', *Salud Colectiva* 13 (3): 537–54.

Ramírez Hita, Susana. 2009. 'Políticas de salud basadas en el concepto de interculturalidad: Los centros de salud intercultural en el altiplano boliviano', *Avá: Revista de Antropología* 14: 1–28.

Saldaña-Tejeda, Abril and Peter Wade. 2018. 'Obesity, Race and the Indigenous Origins of Health Risks among Mexican Mestizos', *Ethnic and Racial Studies* 41 (15): 2731–49.

Santos, Boaventura de Sousa. 2014. *Epistemologies of the South: Justice against Epistemicide*. Boulder, CO: Paradigm Publishers.

Scheper-Hughes, Nancy. 1992. *Death without Weeping: The Violence of Everyday Life in Brazil*. Berkeley: University of California Press.

Scheper-Hughes, Nancy and Philippe Bourgois, eds. 2017. *Violence in War and Peace: An Anthology*. Malden, MA: Blackwell Publishing.

Seppilli, Tullio and Rosario Otegui. 2005. 'Antropología médica crítica: Presentación', *Revista de Antropología Social* 14: 7–13.

Singer, Merrill. 1986. 'Developing a Critical Perspective in Medical Anthropology', *Medical Anthropology Quarterly* 17 (5): 128–29.

Singer, Merrill. 1990. 'Reinventing Medical Anthropology: Toward a Critical Realignment', *Social Science and Medicine* 30 (2): 179–87.

Singer, Merrill and Hans Baer. 1995. *Critical Medical Anthropology*. Amityville, NY: Baywood Publishing Company.

Singer, Merrill and Hans Baer, eds. 2009. *Killer Commodities: Public Health and the Corporate Production of Harm*. Lanham, MD: AltaMira Press.

Singer, Merrill, Hans A. Baer and Ellen Lazarus. 1990. 'Critical Medical Anthropology in Question', *Social Science and Medicine* 30 (2): V–VIII.

Wade, Peter, Vivette García Deister, Michael Kent, María Fernanda Olarte Sierra and Adriana Díaz del Castillo Hernández. 2014. 'Nation and the Absent Presence of Race in Latin American Genomics', *Current Anthropology* 55 (5): 497–522.

Waitzkin, Howard, Celia Iriart, Alfredo Estrada and Silvia Lamadrid. 2001. 'Social Medicine in Latin America: Productivity and Dangers Facing the Major National Groups', *The Lancet* 358 (9278): 315–23.

Part I
Intercultural health: Critical approaches and current challenges

1
Anthropological engagement and interdisciplinary research: The critical approach to indigenous health in Brazil

Esther Jean Langdon and Eliana E. Diehl

In 1986, the First National Conference for the Protection of Indian Health was held in Brazil to discuss indigenous health policy in the face of the proposed health reform. The reform was part of the return to democracy after two decades of dictatorship in Brazil and also part of the larger social medicine movement in Latin America. This movement was guided by a positive notion of integral health, challenging the statistical epidemiological model of public health and valuing the social sciences as key for revealing the cultural and political dimensions of sanitary conditions and practices (Waitzkin et al. 2001). Brazil's reform, known as collective health (*saúde coletiva*), promoted the establishment of the Unified Health System (Sistema Único de Saúde/SUS) based on the municipalisation of primary care in order to guarantee the universal right to health and to promote citizen participation. The First National Conference was concerned with the provision of health services for Brazil's native peoples in the face of the proposed municipal control and global discussions of indigenous rights and interculturality, defined as articulation and mutual respect in different sociocultural settings (Coelho and Shankland 2011). Attended by indigenous leaders, health professionals, representatives of non-governmental organisations (NGOs) and anthropologists, the conference marked the beginning of a long struggle that led to the founding of the Indigenous Health

Subsystem in 1999 and the definition of a National Policy of Healthcare for Indigenous Peoples (Brasil. Fundação Nacional de Saúde 2002). The inclusion of academic researchers in the First National Conference also marked the beginning of a network of anthropologists and health professionals united in an effort to contribute to indigenous health policy and the provision of primary care within a democratic and multicultural perspective.

The objective of this chapter is to explore the principles and modes of engagement that represent the 'critical' perspective in Latin America as it has developed in Brazil. For this purpose, it traces the formation and consolidation of the Indigenous Health Workgroup of the Brazilian Association of Collective Health (Associação Brasileira de Saúde Coletiva/ABRASCO) that grew out of the Latin American health reform movement and the First National Conference for the Protection of Indian Health. This network of researchers, composed of anthropologists and health professionals, has worked to develop critical approaches adequate for the specific characteristics and concerns of the region. It is concerned with research and analytical models adequate for analysing public policy and services that recognise the diversity of cultures and health practices. Critical engagement is a central characteristic of this network, as its members articulate research activities with participation in public forums designed to formulate and evaluate the implementation of health policy. In order to examine this articulation between research and policy, we focus on one group in the network, the Nucleus for the Study of Indigenous Knowledge and Health (NESSI). Associated with the Graduate Programme in Social Anthropology of the Federal University of Santa Catarina, it includes members from the Health Sciences Centre and is an example of a critically engaged research group. Its research is primarily guided by ethnographic qualitative research methods, and focuses on the communities' perspectives and health practices.

The critical position of the larger interdisciplinary network, as well as that of NESSI, has received little recognition from Brazilian or international anthropologists. As is the case with most Latin American research efforts to develop concepts adequate for understanding the region's specificity and plurality of therapeutic practices, the network remains peripheral to theoretical debates[1] of global medical anthropology (Langdon and Follér 2012). Moreover, reviews of the development of the field of anthropology of health in Brazil have either ignored studies of indigenous populations or have characterised them as limited to ethnomedicine (Diniz 1997; Carrara 1994; Leibing 2007; Sarti 2010). They fail to recognise that these studies share interests in the transformation of health practices and public policy that are characteristic of the field as a whole. This chapter argues that studies in indigenous health contribute to discussions of a Latin American critical approach through examination of the network's history and strategic investigations related to health policy for indigenous peoples. The analysis of NESSI's activities demonstrates that engagement is expressed through the articulation of research with policy development and evaluation, participation in governmental health forums and the training of health workers. We also examine the group's contribution to the construction of concepts capable of capturing a Latin American 'critical' perspective.

A Latin American critical approach

As Seppilli and Otegui (2005) indicate in their introduction to a special number of the *Revista de Antropología Social* dedicated to health research, the 'Latin' approach does not identify with the label of 'critical medical anthropology' as developed by anthropologies of the Global North. Decades before its emergence in the 1990s, the Mexican anthropologist Guillermo Bonfil Batalla (1966) expressed Latin America's critical approach, pointing out that economic and political structural factors are responsible for poor health conditions and not cultural practices as implied by North American applied anthropology. Regional historical and political processes define the problems examined by South American anthropologies of health. These include long-standing consciousness of the colonial situation, the impact of late development of capitalism and modernisation and, in the case of Brazil, the sanitary reform movement of the 1970s and 1980s that promoted integral health as a universal right and responsibility of the state. It is important to recognise that biomedical hegemony in Latin America has not eradicated other practices. The region is characterised by a diversity of different therapeutic systems that are autonomous and continue to play an important role in health (Menéndez 2003), a situation different from the Global North, where medical pluralism is more limited (Cueto and Palmer 2015). The autonomous articulation between these practices in the search for health by indigenous people, Afro-descendants and other marginalised groups throughout all of Latin America must be perceived as political as well as therapeutic.

The critical stance of anthropology of health in Brazil entails a rejection of medical anthropology as a label, because of perceptions that it subordinates anthropological knowledge through reproducing medical science's biological and psychological empiricism for the understanding of suffering and emotion (Sarti 2010: 205).[2] Research among indigenous populations examines the impact of discriminatory practices and economic development on health conditions (Coimbra Jr et al. 2002; Welch et al. 2013), diversity of knowledge systems and political relations between medical professionals and the populations they serve (Teixeira and Dias da Silva 2013). In collaboration with other Latin Americans, Brazilians seek to develop concepts adequate for understanding the effects of the expansion of biomedical hegemony and asymmetrical power relations. Since its beginning, the research network has sought to construct, together with the populations studied, a more adequate health policy and the provision of services that recognise the multiplicity of practices, the autonomy of the target populations and their active role in articulating the diverse therapeutic traditions, including those of biomedicine.

Indigenous health policy in Brazil and forms of engagement

Prior to the First National Conference in 1986, there were few services and no clear health policy for indigenous peoples. Itinerant health teams of the National Indian Foundation (Fundação Nacional do Índio/ FUNAI) and NGOs circulated irregularly (Langdon 2010), and access to public health institutions was limited. The Conference examined the precarious health situation, the importance of traditional practices and indigenous demands for a separate system based on ethnic difference (CEBES 1988). Four sectors of Brazilian society were represented in the political debate: governmental agencies, NGOs, research institutions and indigenous peoples. Researchers included anthropologists and those from medical professions. The considerable number of indigenous representatives was evidence of their growing movement and their role in the constitutional reform process. The Conference's concluding resolutions called for the establishment of a specific subsystem linked directly to the Ministry of Health, the construction of a model of intercultural health (later called 'differentiated care' – *atenção diferenciada*) and the inclusion of indigenous communities in the planning, organisation, execution and evaluation of health services. The participation of anthropologists in health teams was recommended. In 1988, the National Constitutional Assembly instituted the SUS, establishing municipal control of health services, citizen participation and humanised services. However, there was no provision regarding health services for indigenous peoples.

The 1988 Federal Constitution was followed by a decade of political advocacy and negotiation for the construction of an indigenous health policy that would satisfy the principles outlined in the First National Conference (universal access, respect for cultural practices and social oversight). The creation of health districts, independent of the municipalities, was proposed as the organisational basis; primary care would be organised according to districts administered by the federal government with the creation of citizen health councils at the local and district levels guaranteeing democratic participation (Mendes 1995).[3] The Coordination of Indian Health (Coordenação da Saúde do Índio/COSAI) was created in 1991 as a division of the National Health Foundation (Fundação Nacional de Saúde/FUNASA) and was responsible for the administration of health services for indigenous peoples. COSAI was not granted adequate financial or human resources to establish effective health services. Moreover, its creation did not satisfy the demand for a separate system organised according to indigenous health districts linked directly to the Ministry of Health.

Along with COSAI, the Intersectoral Commission of Indigenous Health (CISI), composed of representatives from indigenous, governmental and non-governmental organisations, was established as a technical advisor to the National Health Council for the purposes of *controle social* at the national level (Teixeira et al. 2013). *Controle social*, best translated as social oversight (Cornwall and Shankland 2008), refers to the participation of civil society 'in the management of public policies in order to control them to meet the demands and interests of the collective group' (Correia 2000: 11). During the 1990s, CISI advocated for the approval of the Indigenous Health Subsystem based on health districts.

The National Programme for the Control of Sexually Transmitted Diseases and AIDS (Monteiro and Villela 2009) was the most heavily funded health programme during the 1990s. The division dedicated to the indigenous population and directed by an anthropologist/physician sponsored a number of regional conferences for addressing the issues of alcohol abuse and STDs, including AIDS (Ministério da Saúde 1997). Indigenous presence was an important component of all events in the effort to create a democratic process of participation and deliberation. Subsequently, projects for education on STDs were conducted throughout Brazil, funded by the Ministry of Health and coordinated by university researchers and NGOs working with indigenous peoples.

Indigenous health services suffered throughout the decade from inadequate funding, poorly defined institutional responsibilities and conflicts between federal and municipal governmental agencies, nongovernmental organisations and universities.[4] Due to lack of resources and its organisational structure, COSAI failed to counter the deplorable epidemiological situation of Brazil's indigenous peoples or to improve access to health services. The health district model with its local and district health councils was not implemented until the approval of the Indigenous Health Subsystem in 1999 and creation of 34 Special Indigenous Health Districts (Distrito Sanitaria Especial Indígena/DSEI) (Garnelo 2012). Significant financial resources were injected into the Subsystem,[5] finally enabling the expansion of primary healthcare for all indigenous territories. As a Subsystem of the SUS, problems requiring more specialised care are to be resolved by municipal and regional services.

Throughout the process leading to the approval of the Subsystem, anthropologists interacted with advocates of indigenous health in the various conferences and other events organised by governmental and NGO institutions and an interdisciplinary network began to form. In an encounter examining the relation between traditional and Western medicine held in 1988 (Buchillet 1991), researchers engaged in the advocacy of indigenous health agreed to form a network for strategic research in order to contribute to the construction of public policy and intercultural services. Recognising the paucity of epidemiological and sociocultural data on the health of Brazil's indigenous groups, they hoped to create a database that contemplated the extreme diversity characteristic of the country's native populations.

Although this group was never formally constituted, the network grew throughout the 1990s and was consolidated in 2001 as the Indigenous Health Workgroup (https://www.abrasco.org.br/site/gtsaudeindigena/) associated with the collective health association ABRASCO. It is composed of professors and investigators from the diverse fields of collective health, social sciences, epidemiology and administration and planning, and its academic and political agenda includes workshops, courses and sessions in academic and governmental conferences. Governmental represent- atives participate in its workshops for policy discussions. Its members are representatives in different councils and commissions, such as CISI[6] and others of the Ministry of Health, and also involved in research and graduate teaching. The Ministry of Health and Pan-American Health Organisation have appointed members of the Workgroup to committees establishing research priorities and evaluation (Garnelo et al. 2003). In 2008–10, the Workgroup directed the First National Investigation of Health and Nutrition of Indigenous Peoples (Coimbra Jr. et al. 2013).

The Workgroup, with its 14 official members, is the nucleus of a larger network that extends throughout Brazil and Latin American, including Argentina, Venezuela, Colombia and Mexico. Many members are trained in anthropological and biomedical or biological sciences. Anthropologists are found in both medical institutions and in anthropol- ogy departments in universities throughout the country. It is important to stress the interdisciplinary nature of this group, in which a number of non-anthropologists employ qualitative methods along with quantitative approaches characteristic of the medical sciences.

In sum, the larger network represented by ABRASCO's Indigenous Health Workgroup is inter-institutional, interdisciplinary, international and political. Their critical stance is evidenced by political and interdis- ciplinary research questions that focus on relations of power and health services in intercultural settings. They are engaged researchers whose activities have constructed a strong interface between research and polit- ical advocacy as they interact with governmental agencies and indige- nous leaders and communities to construct adequate policy and services that guarantee universal access, articulation with native practices and citizen participation.

Strategic research as critical engagement: The Nucleus for the Study of Indigenous Knowledge and Health

We examine here, as an example of strategic research that has accompa- nied policy formation and implementation of the Subsystem, the activ- ities of the Nucleus for the Study of Indigenous Knowledge and Health (NESSI). Officially formalised in 1994 by researchers in anthropology and health sciences of the Federal University of Santa Catarina, the group has maintained its interdisciplinary character since its inception. All members are committed to the value of long-term ethnographic field-work in order to understand global and national health issues at the local level and to research that contributes to public policy. Its members are part of ABRASCO's Workgroup as well as the health research network of the National Institute of Science and Technology: Brazil Plural.[7]

Given its interdisciplinary nature, NESSI strives to create dia-logue with the health field as well as with the indigenous communi-ties studied via the ethnographic method. It has collaborated over the years with other participants in the ABRASCO Workgroup in research, publications, workshops and special courses for health professionals. Since 2009, the group has intensified its collaborations with other Latin American countries, particularly with Mexico and Colombia (Langdon and Cardoso 2015). NESSI participates in methodological and theoret-ical discussions concerned with the development of concepts adequate for understanding the medical pluralism characteristic of Latin America. Its researchers reaffirm the value of the ethnographic method for exam-ining micro-political relations and indigenous agency and autonomy as manifested in interactions between medical professionals and the popu-lations they serve.

The objectives of NESSI's research reflect what can be characterised as the Brazilian critical approach in anthropology. In the 1990s, its mem-bers participated in public forums working to establish the Indigenous Health Subsystem and investigated autonomous therapeutic practices and the health/illness/care process among indigenous groups in Santa Catarina and elsewhere in Brazil. Once the Subsystem was approved, its research assumed a more political focus, examining the principles of the National Policy of Healthcare for Indigenous Peoples.

> [Implementation of healthcare] requires the adoption of a *comple-mentary and differentiated* model of organisation of services – aimed at the protection, promotion and recuperation of health – that guar-antees indigenous peoples the exercise of citizenship in health […] *a network of services* […] making possible the application of the principles and directives of decentralisation, universality, equity, *community participation* and *social control*. In order for these prin-ciples to be implemented, it is necessary that healthcare be deliv-ered in a *differentiated form, taking into consideration the cultural, epidemiological and operational specificities of these peoples*. Thus, it is necessary to develop and make use of appropriate technologies

through the adjustment of conventional Western ways of service organisation. (Brasil. Fundação Nacional de Saúde 2002: 6; emphasis added)

In Brazil, the term 'differentiated' is used for both educational and health policy rather than the more widespread term of 'interculturality'. With respect to indigenous health it refers to a special network of primary care services that adapts to and articulates with indigenous knowledge and practices and includes citizen participation in all phases of planning, execution and evaluation of health actions and services. NESSI's members investigate and evaluate the implementation of differentiated care, seeking to develop concepts that permit understanding of pluralities of knowledge and practices and the political nature of primary care intervention (Langdon 2004).

Certain concepts developed by Eduardo Menéndez (1992; 2003), such as that of 'self-care practices' (*prácticas de autoatención*),[8] have furnished an analytical orientation for much of NESSI's research. Menéndez is concerned with a relational approach that recognises medical pluralisms and the agency of social actors in the search for prevention and resolution of health problems. It shifts attention from medical professionals and traditional healers by recognising the autonomy of social groups as central actors in health dramas (Menéndez 2016). It also frees analysis from the binary dichotomies of traditional/modern, science/magic, natural/supernatural and personal/impersonal that have plagued anthropological discussions of 'primitive' medicine since its origins and convey an image of ethnomedicine as primitive and static.

The concept of self-care practices, in its ample sense, is related to social practices necessary to assure the *biosocial* reproduction (emphasis by the authors) of the subjects and groups at the local level, in particular the domestic group. These include not only care and prevention of sickness, but also notions of corporality; alimentary and hygienic norms; social organisation; rituals; subsistence practices; environmental resources; and all other activities that maintain the wellbeing of the group. It includes the socialities and ontologies of daily life that go beyond the biomedical domain of health and illness and are concerned with social and cultural reproduction as well as the biological. Taken at a more restricted level, the concept refers principally to knowledge, scientific or not, sickness representations and healing practices and care. Much of the 'qualitative' research conducted by biomedical researchers recognises only this more restricted level, ignoring larger social and cultural processes that are central to integral health (Menéndez 2012).

'Intermedicality' (Greene 1998), another concept useful for NESSI's interests, highlights the political, economic and ideological aspects involved in interactions between medical professionals and indigenous groups and in native praxis that incorporates and appropriates biomedical substances and practices. This concept was amplified by Follér (2004) in order to analyse asymmetry in relations as well as hybridity of practices between the medical team of Médecins Sans Frontières and the Shipibo-Conibo. Follér indicates that intermedicality points to the expansion of biomedical services among indigenous people as a contact zone in which social reality is constituted by negotiations between politically active subjects, recognising that all the actors exhibit social agency.

Finally, studies that investigate the new opportunities for indigenous participation in the Subsystem have adopted the concept of 'border space' in order to analyse the autonomy of action and decision-making in new participatory contexts created by national policy (Diehl and Langdon 2015). Border space is understood as a communicational relational field that attempts to 'account simultaneously for the nature of what is constructed in this contact zone, as well as for the fluidity and constitutional character of the relationships that develop between different social agents in contact' (Boccara 2007: 60). The new spaces of action and participation, also called 'practices of borderization' (Briones and Del Cairo 2015), are based upon democratic assumptions that differ from indigenous modes of social and political organisation (Garnelo and Sampaio 2003; Shankland 2014).

Ethnographic research in Santa Catarina

We take as an example of NESSI's research its investigations into the implications of differentiated care among the Kaingáng of Santa Catarina. Research has concentrated primarily on Xapecó, an indigenous territory with 3,935 inhabitants (IBGE 2010). Xapecó is located on the highland plateau in the interior of the state, surrounded by farmers of German or Italian descent and with a history of ethnic intolerance, prejudice and violence in one of the most prosperous regions of the country. After decades of intensive contact, the Kaingáng are no longer visually distinctive. The majority speak Portuguese and not all are fluent in their native language, which belongs to the Jê language family. The lack of diacritical signs for ethnic distinctiveness often leads health professionals to claim that the Kaingáng have lost their 'culture' and thus do not need differentiated healthcare as stipulated by national health policy.

NESSI's first investigations in Xapecó identified the existence of a variety of health practices, drawing from traditional knowledge and contemporary religious practices as well as articulation with available biomedical services. Although few governmental medical services existed in the 1990s, the Kaingáng were accustomed to acquiring pharmaceutical products to treat their ailments (Diehl 2001), and their therapeutic itineraries also articulated with healing/religious practices of their *caboclo*[9] neighbours. Popular Catholicism and evangelical cults were, and continue to be, important sources of Kaingáng autonomous therapeutic practices (Almeida 1998, 2004; Ghiggi Junior 2015; Haverroth 1998, 2004; Oliveira 1997a, 2000). An example of the dynamics of intermedicality is the 'Church of Health', founded by a Kaingáng traditional leader, a former *kujã* (a type of shamanic healer) and a young *cabocla* woman of mixed descent. For several years, these three articulated practices originating in shamanism, messianic popular Catholicism, spiritualistic surgeries and industrialised medicines have been used in the treatment of indigenous and non-indigenous patients (Oliveira 1997b).

After the implementation of the Subsystem in 1999 and increased access to primary services, research has concentrated on articulation between self-care practices and biomedical services. Other studies have focused on specific health conditions that are the object of governmental intervention, such as free distribution of medicines (Diehl 2016); alcohol abuse (Ghiggi Junior and Langdon 2014); maternal and infant health (Aires-Oliveira 2012) and alimentary practices (Hanna de Almeida Oliveira 2008, 2009). Portela García (2010) examined self-care practices in Kaingáng patients diagnosed with diabetes and high blood pressure. Her ethnographic descriptions of the national programme implemented to educate and medicate these patients and interactions between health team members and patients reveal professional–patient communication to be asymmetrical, linear and unidirectional, ignoring the comments and perceptions of the indigenous patients. Interactions between professionals and patients are shown to be a clear example of communicative hegemony (Briggs 2005), a concept associated with processes of the hegemonic medical model (Menéndez and Di Pardo 1996).

NESSI's research, guided by the concepts of self-care practices and intermedicality, has directed attention to corporal, social and cosmological dynamics involved in biosocial reproduction in its more ample sense, demonstrating that health must be understood within a larger perspective recognising plurality, the dynamics of knowledge systems and processes related to the body, forms of sociality, cosmology and ontology. Research has also demonstrated that, despite the expansion of biomedical primary care and the specific programmes stimulated by the global health agenda (maternal and infant care; diabetes; STDs such as AIDS; alcohol abuse; malnutrition), biomedicine is not supplanting indigenous forms of knowledge and practices as collective groups continue to be the central actors who articulate with biomedical services.

By focusing on indigenous perspectives and actions at the level of micro-groups, the studies contribute specifically to the evaluation of intervention and interaction between medical teams and indigenous peoples. They are strategic and critical studies, in the sense that they provide ethnographic descriptions examining local perspectives and the political nature of interactions between indigenous patients and professionals in health services. Research among the Kaingáng has demonstrated that healthcare professionals working among indigenous groups do not receive a clear definition or training for the delivery of 'differentiated care'. Health workers and the Kaingáng have different understandings of the term's implications for health services. Moreover, most professionals fail to recognise the autonomous nature of the self-care practices of Kaingáng patients and, in general, continue to operate according to the biomedical model organisational logic that results in asymmetrical relations. Contrary to the National Policy of Healthcare for Indigenous Peoples, organisation and primary care services offered in indigenous territories in Santa Catarina do not adapt to the local contexts, practices and knowledge.

A second strand of research carried out by NESSI's members reflects a more explicit political focus on the Indigenous Health Subsystem's guarantee of 'citizen participation in all phases of planning, execution and evaluation of health actions' (Brasil. Fundação Nacional de Saúde 2002: 6). NESSI's investigators have analysed the potential of participation and governance in three border spaces of interaction instituted by the Subsystem: the indigenous health agents (Agentes Indígenas de Saúde/ AIS) (Langdon et al. 2006, 2014; Diehl et al. 2012), Kaingáng representation on health councils (Langdon and Diehl 2007); and administration of health services by a Kaingáng NGO contracted as an outsourced provider of primary care in Xapecó (Diehl and Langdon 2015). These studies have sought to analyse Kaingáng agency and citizenship in the border spaces of intercultural interaction created by the state since the end of the twentieth century (Diehl and Langdon 2018).

The Indigenous Health Agent (AIS)

The role of the AIS was implemented in order to develop forms of mediation between medical traditions, to increase indigenous participation in health services and to contribute to the quality of services. As a member of the multi-professional health team, the AIS should belong to the community and participate in primary care activities and health promotion and prevention. More importantly, the role is understood as the link between traditional and biomedical knowledge as well as between the community and health team. The AIS's role is conceived as central to the practice of differentiated care, one that articulates with indigenous practices (Brasil. Fundação Nacional de Saúde 2002: 15–16).

Ethnographic research conducted with Kaingáng AIS indicates a number of limitations of the role as idealised by the National Policy of Healthcare for Indigenous Peoples (Langdon et al. 2006; Diehl et al. 2012). The AIS reported distant relationships with the rest of the health team members and complained of the number of written reports they were required to complete. Few received any prior training or on-the-job supervision. Basic first-aid activities, such as measuring temperatures or blood pressure, were duties assigned to other health team members, thus reducing their role primarily to that of courier between the health post and community households. They also felt constrained to recommend traditional practices to the patients. Examination of manuals developed for AIS training revealed a strong biomedical bias, with no information preparing them for articulation with indigenous health practices (Brasil. Fundação Nacional de Saúde 2005).

The AIS is the lowest member of a hierarchical team organised according to medical specialisms and responsibilities. Relations with other members of the health team are asymmetrical, and their activities are bureaucratised in various ways that curb their autonomy. Although expected by the team to operate independently of community demands, as community workers they are enmeshed in local expectations and networks of obligations and demands that influence their daily rounds, distribution of medications and other activities. Although Brazilian health policy envisions the role of the AIS as central to the mediation between the health team and the community and between the different forms of knowledge and practices, NESSI's studies have shown that in practice there have been no advances or innovations in the bureaucratic or biomedical logic that organises primary healthcare.

The research also found that the Kaingáng highly appreciate the opportunities the AIS position offers and also that the AIS are commonly chosen for new political roles created by the state.[10] They are frequently selected as representatives for both local and district health councils designed to guarantee democratic participation. The emergence of the AIS as an important political actor in the border spaces of health councils and conferences is not due to their knowledge of traditional medicine, but a reflection of their position in the traditional power structure and privileged access to biomedical knowledge and services as a member of the health team.

Health council representation

The local and district health councils create a border space for indigenous participation and governance in the decision-making process related to planning, evaluation and financial control of health programmes in their communities. Local councils consist of only community members and membership on district health councils follows the logic of parity: representation is divided between local council representatives, members of professional teams, and health providers and administrators.

As university representatives, both authors have accompanied district council meetings of the Special Indigenous Health District Inland South (DSEI Interior Sul) meetings from 2002 to 2006 (Langdon and Diehl 2007; Diehl and Langdon 2018). We observed that district health councils have not always provided a forum for full democratic participation and identified a number of problems that have subsequently been noted by other researchers (Shankland and Athias 2007; Teixeira 2010; Teixeira et al. 2013; Toledo et al. 2013). Democratic representation as idealised by the *controle social* process is not well understood. Indigenous representatives who are also employees of the service provider or of the government (such as the AIS) expressed a conflict of interest between voicing the demands of their communities and facing possible disapproval or repression by the institutions that employed them. In a debate about parity at one meeting, for example, one indigenous representative asked: 'Who do I represent? I work for FUNAI and I am Indian' (Langdon and Diehl 2007).

The role of councillor and concepts of democratic representation, selection and responsibilities are not well understood. This is aggravated by inadequate preparation. Training programmes for councillors, as called for by national policy, have not been a priority and few have been offered over the years. We observed indigenous councillors voicing individual complaints and demands rather than attempting to influence the formulation, management and evaluation of health programmes and policies (Langdon and Diehl 2007; Diehl et al. 2012).[11] Lack of preparation is compounded by high turnover. While rotation of representatives is part of the democratic exercise, in the case of indigenous health councillors it has contributed to continuing problems of understanding the workings of the bureaucratic-administrative culture and health policy.

One problem we observed with respect to district councils, also reported for other districts (Shankland and Athias 2007; Toledo et al. 2013), has been irregularity of meetings due to organisational, financial and other difficulties. As observed in encounters between health professional supervisors and AIS, district council meetings, as an interactional space, favour the bureaucratic-administrative dimension at the expense of the political. Questions discussed were primarily operational, punctuated by individualised accusations and demands. Administrative concerns occupied a central role, providing little space for the negotiation of divergent interests or development of full participation and social control processes expected of these councils.

Kaingáng NGO as health service provider

With the creation of health districts, primary care services have been provided through contracts established with NGOs or municipalities. In Amazonia, several indigenous NGOs were contracted between 1996 and 2004, but due to a series of problems, this policy was reversed and municipalities were increasingly favoured for outsourced service management (Garnelo 2012: 47).

During the period of the demise of Amazonian indigenous organisations due to accusations of mismanagement and corruption, a Kaingáng NGO was created in 2003 and contracted to manage primary care services for the Xapecó indigenous territory. In contrast to the 250 Amazonian indigenous organisations created in the 1990s for defence of territory and political activism (Albert 2000), it was founded as a private non-profit entity specifically to substitute the municipality as primary care provider for the Kaingáng. In an interview in 2007, its president affirmed that FUNASA had encouraged the creation of the NGO with the expectation that it would become a model of indigenous management and that its indigenous founders were seeking 'power and autonomy to begin to assume our own direction' (Diehl and Langdon 2015: 227). However, NESSI's research found that this opportunity to assume health service management contradicted both the principles of differentiated attention and the motivations of the indigenous NGO.

During the 58 months of its activity as health provider between 2003 and 2008, the NGO received approximately US$1.1 million (Diehl and

Langdon 2015: 226). Although it hoped for greater autonomy in order to diversify its activities beyond those of health services, FUNASA's central administration restricted the application of resources to pre-defined actions. The NGO's capacity to execute local organisation of services was weakened because of inconsistent support and centralised management of administrative-bureaucratic flow in the District Coordination Office of the FUNASA, located some 500 kilometres away in Florianópolis. Constant changes of district coordination and the failure to transfer financial resources to the NGO as scheduled disrupted health services. In turn, the community blamed the NGO for the disruptions caused by the consequences of the delays.

Governmental administrative control affected the NGO's relationship with the health team, causing it to become task-oriented in order to fulfil bureaucratic demands. Use of resources as stipulated in the agreement between FUNASA and the NGO did not match the community's needs. The lack of a formalised local coordinator in the health clinics, discontinuity in work conditions (interruptions in transportation, telephone, medications or other supplies) and high turnover of health professionals jeopardised the activities and produced indignation among the team and community members. Inter-institutional and interpersonal conflicts plagued the provision of health services until the contract was terminated in 2008. In 2011 contracts with indigenous NGOs as outsourced providers in Brazil ceased totally.

The role of indigenous NGOs as health providers was seen as an opportunity for participation in the governance of health services and a strategy to support indigenous forms of organisation, creating a space for the expression and strengthening of identity as well as for empowerment (Shankland and Athias 2007). However, the responsibility of managing primary care shifted the role of indigenous organisations from that of political activism to that of professional management (Albert 2000), converting them into possible reproducers of the dominant system or weakening their activism (Shankland 2010). As is evident from the Kaingáng experience, the priorities, planning and execution of health assistance became defined by external sources and limited indigenous prominence and autonomy.

Final considerations

As Teixeira and Dias da Silva (2013) demonstrate, anthropological research on indigenous health has witnessed an extraordinary increase since 2000. The political process instituted by the establishment of the Indigenous Health Subsystem combined with increased financing for global health problems, such as sexuality, maternal and infant health, ageing, nutrition, endemic diseases, substance abuse and suicide, have stimulated the recent consolidation of indigenous health research in Brazil. As outlined in the introduction to this chapter, research on indigenous health has its origins in the collective health movement, the return to democracy and the rise of the interdisciplinary and international network engaged in health reform in Latin America. The collective health movement is critical of functional and biological paradigms and has looked to the social sciences to help understand the interaction between the biological and psychosocial and the sociocultural, historical and political dimensions of the health/illness/care process. The interdisciplinary network of indigenous health research has its origins in the struggle for the establishment of the Subsystem that began with the First National Conference for the Protection of Indian Health, and researchers have been protagonists in the construction and evaluation of national policy. Their research efforts were consolidated in 2000 with the formation of ABRASCO's Indigenous Health Workgroup.

The critical engagement of the members of this network is exhibited by its commitment to the production of knowledge in order to contribute to health policy and services, to the elimination of inequalities in social inclusion and health and to the construction of citizenship. The focus is upon local and national problems with research designed to impact upon services, policy, the formation of human resources and political participation. Researchers are active, along with indigenous peoples, in extension courses, conferences and forums of social participation. Ethnographic research seeks to highlight local health knowledge and practices as well as local perceptions of health problems. The network's members collaborate for the development of concepts that account for the plurality, dynamics and autonomous articulation of health practices that are relatively independent of the expectations of individual responsibility implied in health professionals' evaluations of 'self-care'.

The Latin American critical approach, as exhibited by the research network and that of NESSI examined here, affirms that ethnographic qualitative fieldwork is fundamental not only for the understanding of local processes but also for establishing dialogue that involves listening, respecting and creating symmetrical relations (Biehl 2016). Pluralism of knowledge refers to recognition of the diversity of knowledge systems, ontologies and practices present in the groups studied and invokes a more ample conception of health and qualitative research than that which is implied within the domain of biomedicine or by rapid assessment methods (Menéndez 2012). Brazilian anthropologists reject what is perceived as the instrumentalisation of anthropological methods in applied research that is directed by the concerns and presuppositions of biomedicine. Research in indigenous health highlights other systems of knowledge and praxis in the face of the increased expansion of medical services by the Indigenous Health Subsystem. It aims to study not only the diversity of medical traditions, but also the political dynamics of how indigenous people articulate their knowledge and practices with those of biomedical services (Langdon 2016).

Another characteristic of the Latin American critical approach is its analysis of the new roles created by the state (Briones and Del Cairo 2015). In the case of Brazil, the National Policy of Healthcare for Indigenous Peoples has created new spaces of interaction on the local, regional and national levels through its concept of differentiated attention that calls for indigenous participation and governance in the planning, evaluation and financial control of health programmes in their communities. The investigations carried out by members of NESSI have investigated to what extent indigenous actors have been able to exercise their rights and make autonomous decisions in the different intercultural spaces created by the state. Specifically, NESSI's ethnographic research focuses on indigenous participation on local and regional levels through the examination of indigenous health agents, district health representatives and outsourced providers of primary care.

The findings point to a general tendency towards centralisation on the part of the state that institutionalises participation and limits responsibilities and autonomy (Langdon and Garnelo 2017). The role of AIS as mediators between different systems of knowledge and socio-political organisations is undermined by bureaucratic tasks and biomedical logic that reduces their autonomy in decisions and action. The democratic process of participation and social oversight envisioned for indigenous councillors on health councils is also contradictory, being characterised by a lack of understanding of democratic representation, the high turnover of councillors with little preparation and bureaucratic priorities in meeting agendas and interaction.

Finally, with respect to indigenous NGOs' role as outsourced service managers, the potential for autonomy and agency is limited by the contradictions observed in this border space of negotiation with the state. Problems originating from the centralised model determined provider responsibilities and actions, ignoring community needs and practices. The Kaingáng NGO was caught between the demands of its employer and the indigenous community. It was blamed for service disruptions caused by the delays in resources, problems with the medical team and accessibility of medications. The indigenous NGO was forced to follow plans, goals, deadlines and budgets that were shaped by priorities defined in spaces external to the local groups.

Notes

1. See Pereira (2015) as an example of a review of the field international health that ignores Latin America's contribution to conceptual development.
2. Brazilian anthropology has traditionally opposed an applied, instrumental role of anthropology. The first studies related to health focused on the impact of expanding capitalism on alimentary practices among peasant and proletarian groups (Woortman 1978; Langdon and Follér 2012).
3. During the 1990s, only the Yanomami Health District was created.
4. The Escola Paulista de Medicina and Fundação Oswaldo Cruz were pioneers in health intervention and training for work with indigenous communities (Baruzzi and Junqueira 2005; Confalonieri and Verani 1993). In 1982 the first interdisciplinary group with anthropologists and biomedical researchers, the Centro de Estudos e Pesquisas em Antropologia Médica (CEPAM), was founded in the School of Health Sciences at the University of Brasília. It was organised by the anthropologist Martin Ibáñez-Novion, but most members were from the biological and medical sciences, among them Carlos Coimbra Jr, who was instrumental in creating the ABRASCO work group.
5. US$96 million in 1999/2000, increasing gradually to the value of approximately US$426 million in 2013 (Diehl and Langdon 2015: 226).
6. Both ABRASCO and the Brazilian Association of Anthropology have representation on the CISI.
7. Brazil Plural (IBP) was founded in 2009 as an inter-institutional research programme in support of anthropological investigations that inform public policy formulation and implementation and contribute to the political struggles of the communities studied (Langdon and Cardoso 2015; Langdon and Grisotti 2016; Montardo and Rufino 2017).
8. We emphasise *practices* in his concept to distinguish from biomedicine's 'self-care', which expects the patient's individual responsibility to comply with biomedical values and instructions. Menéndez emphasises the autonomy of the patient's group in the dynamics of articulation of therapeutic resources.
9. We are using *caboclo* here to refer to traditional peoples of mixed ethnic heritage.
10. This is true of research on AIS in other parts of Brazil. For a full comparative review of research on AIS in Brazil see Langdon et al. (2014).
11. See Shankland (2014) for a more recent discussion of the differences between representation and mediation based on interviews with three indigenous district council presidents.

References

Aires-Oliveira, Ewerton. 2012. 'Saberes, espaços e recursos em saúde: Práticas de autoatenção frente aos adoecimentos em crianças Kaingáng da Terra Indígena Xapecó, Santa Catarina'. Master's thesis in Collective Health, Universidade Federal de Santa Catarina.

Albert, Bruce. 2000. 'Associações indígenas e desenvolvimento sustentável na Amazônia Brasileira'. In *Povos Indígenas no Brasil, 1996–2000*, edited by Carlos Alberto Ricardo, 197–203. São Paulo: Instituto Socioambiental.

Almeida, Ledson Kurtz de. 2004. 'Religiões cristãs entre os povos indígenas: O exemplo Kaingang', *Inclusividade* (Centro de Estudos Anglicanos-Porto Alegre) 7: 97–110.

Almeida, Ledson Kurtz de. 1998. 'Dinâmica religiosa entre os Kaingang do Posto Indígena de Xapecó-SC'. Master's thesis in Anthropology, Universidade Federal de Santa Catarina.

Baruzzi, Roberto G. and Carmen Junqueira, eds. 2005. *Parque Indígena do Xingu: Saúde, cultura e história*. São Paulo: Universidade Federal de São Paulo.

Biehl, João. 2016. 'Theorizing Global Health', *Medicine Anthropology Theory* 3 (2): 127–42.

Boccara, Guillaume. 2007. 'Poder colonial e etnicidade no Chile: Territorialização e reestruturação entre os Mapuche da época colonial', *Tempo* 12 (23): 56–72.

Bonfil Batalla, Guillermo. 1966. 'Conservative Thought in Applied Anthropology: A Critique', *Human Organization* 25 (2): 89–92.

Brasil. Fundação Nacional de Saúde. 2002. *Política Nacional de Atenção à Saúde dos Povos Indígenas*, 2nd edn. Brasília: Ministério da Saúde/Fundação Nacional de Saúde.

Brasil. Fundação Nacional de Saúde. 2005. *Formação Inicial para Agentes Indígenas de Saúde: módulo introdutório*. Brasília: Fundação Nacional de Saúde.

Briggs, Charles L. 2005. 'Perspectivas críticas de salud y hegemonía comunicativa: Aperturas progresistas, enlaces letales', *Revista de Antropología Social* 14: 101–24.

Briones, Claudia and Carlos del Cairo. 2015. 'Prácticas de fronterización, pluralización y diferencia', *Universitas Humanística* 80: 13–52.

Buchillet, Dominique, ed. 1991. *Medicinas tradicionais e medicina ocidental na Amazônia*. Belém: Edições CEJUP.

Carrara, Sergio. 1994. 'Entre cientistas e bruxos: Dilemas e perspectivas da análise antropológica da doença'. In *Saúde e doença: Um olhar antropológico*, edited by Paulo César Alves and Maria Cecília de Souza Minayo, 33–45. Rio de Janeiro: Fiocruz.

CEBES (Centro Brasileiro de Estudos de Saúde). 1988. 'A Saúde do Índio', *Saúde em Debate*, special issue.

Coelho, Vera and Alex Shankland. 2011. 'Making the Right to Health a Reality for Brazil's Indigenous Peoples: Innovation, Decentralization and Equity', *MEDICC Review* 13 (3): 50–53.

Coimbra Jr, Carlos E.A., Nancy M. Flowers, Francisco M. Salzano and Ricardo V. Santos. 2002. *The Xavánte in Transition: Health, Ecology, and Bioanthropology in Central Brazil*. Ann Arbor: University of Michigan Press.

Coimbra Jr, Carlos E.A., Ricardo Ventura Santos, James R. Welch, Andrey Moreira Cardoso, Mirian Carvalho de Souza, Luiza Garnelo, Elias Rassi, Maj-Lis Follér and Bernardo L. Horta. 2013. 'The First National Survey of Indigenous People's Health and Nutrition in Brazil: Rationale, Methodology, and Overview of Results', *BMC Public Health* 13, Article 52: 1–19. Accessed 13 September 2019. https://doi.org/10.1186/1471-2458-13-52.

Confalonieri, Ulisses E.C. and Cibele B.L. Verani. 1993. 'Agentes indígenas de saúde'. In *Saúde de populações indígenas: Uma introdução para profissionais de saúde*, edited by Ulisses E.C. Confalonieri, 45–51. Rio de Janeiro: Escola Nacional de Saúde Pública.

Cornwall, Andrea and Alex Shankland. 2008. 'Engaging Citizens: Lessons from Building Brazil's National Health System', *Social Science and Medicine* 66 (10): 2173–84.

Correia, Maria Valéria Costa. 2000. *Que controle social? Os conselhos de saúde como instrumento*. Rio de Janeiro: Editora Fiocruz.

Cueto, Marcos and Steven Palmer. 2015. *Medicine and Public Health in Latin America: A History*. New York: Cambridge University Press.

Diehl, Eliana Elisabeth. 2001. 'Entendimentos, práticas e contextos sociopolíticos do uso de medicamentos entre os Kaingáng (Terra Indígena Xapecó, Santa Catarina, Brasil)'. Doctoral thesis in Public Health, Escola Nacional de Saúde Pública Sérgio Arouca, Fundação Oswaldo Cruz.

Diehl, Eliana E. 2016. 'Estudos sobre medicamentos em uma perspectiva interdisciplinar'. In *Políticas públicas: Reflexões antropológicas*, edited by Esther Jean Langdon and Márcia Grisotti, 83–104. Florianópolis: Editora da Universidade Federal de Santa Catarina.

Diehl, Eliana E. and Esther Jean Langdon. 2015. 'Transformações na atenção à saúde indígena: Tensões e negociações em um contexto indígena brasileiro', *Universitas Humanística* 80: 213–36.

Diehl, Eliana Elisabeth and Esther Jean Langdon. 2018. 'Indigenous Participation in Primary Care Services in Brazil: Autonomy or Bureaucratization?', *Regions and Cohesion* 8 (1): 54–76.

Diehl, Eliana Elisabeth, Esther Jean Langdon and Raquel Paiva Dias-Scopel. 2012. 'Contribuição dos agentes indígenas de saúde na atenção diferenciada à saúde dos povos indígenas brasileiros', *Cadernos de Saúde Pública* 28 (5): 819–31.

Diniz, Débora. 1997. 'O Que é isso Que Chamamos Antropologia da Saúde no Brasil?', *Revista Brasiliense de Pós-Graduação em Ciências Sociais* 1 (1): 213–34.

Follér, Maj-Lis. 2004. 'Intermedicalidade: A zona de contato criada por povos indígenas e profissionais de saúde'. In *Saúde dos povos indígenas: Reflexões sobre antropologia participativa*, edited by Esther Jean Langdon and Luiza Garnelo, 103–16. Rio de Janeiro: Contra Capa/Associação Brasileira de Antropologia.

Garnelo, Luiza. 2012. 'Política de saúde indígena no Brasil: Notas sobre as tendências atuais do processo de implantação do subsistema de atenção à saúde'. In *Saúde indígena: Uma introdução ao tema*, edited by Luiza Garnelo and Ana Lúcia Pontes, 18–58. Brasília: SECADI/UNESCO.

Garnelo, Luiza, Guilherme Macedo and Luiz Carlos Brandão. 2003. *Os povos indígenas e a construção das políticas de saúde no Brasil*. Brasília: Organização Pan-Americana da Saúde.

Garnelo, Luiza and Sully Sampaio. 2003. 'Bases sócio-culturais do controle social em saúde indígena: Problemas e questões na Região Norte do Brasil', *Cadernos de Saúde Pública* 19 (1): 311–17.

Ghiggi Junior, Ari. 2015. 'Uma abordagem relacional da atenção à saúde a partir da Terra Indígena Xapecó'. Doctoral thesis in Anthropology, Universidade Federal de Santa Catarina.

Ghiggi Junior, Ari and Esther Jean Langdon. 2014. 'Reflections on Intervention Strategies with Respect to the Process of Alcoholization and Self-Care Practices among Kaingang Indigenous People in Santa Catarina State, Brazil', *Cadernos de Saúde Pública* 30 (6): 1250–58.

Greene, Shane. 1998. 'The Shaman's Needle: Development, Shamanic Agency, and Intermedicality in Aguaruna Lands, Peru', *American Ethnologist* 25 (4): 634–58.

Hanna de Almeida Oliveira, Philippe. 2008. 'Aspectos da vida diária Kaingang: Papéis de gênero na aquisição, distribuição e preparo dos alimentos'. Accessed 31 October 2019. http://www.fazendogenero.ufsc.br/8/sts/ST6/Philippe_Hanna_de_Almeida_Oliveira_06.pdf.

Hanna de Almeida Oliveira, Philippe. 2009. 'Comida forte e comida fraca: Alimentação e fabricação dos corpos entre os Kaingáng da Terra Indígena Xapecó (Santa Catarina, Brasil)'. Master's thesis in Anthropology, Universidade Federal de Santa Catarina.

Haverroth, Moacir. 1998. 'Kaingang: Relação entre classificação das plantas e organização social', *Revista de Divulgação Cultural* 20 (64): 32–47.

Haverroth, Moacir. 2004. 'Análise da etnotaxonomia kaingáng das formas de vida vegetais'. In *Novas contribuições aos estudos interdisciplinares dos Kaingang*, edited by Kimiye Tommasino, Lúcio Tadeu Mota and Francisco Silva Noelli, 83–144. Londrina: Editora da Universidade Estadual de Londrina.

IBGE (Instituto Brasileiro de Geografia e Estatística). 2010. 'Tabela 3.1 – Pessoas residentes em terras indígenas, por condição de indígena, segundo as Unidades da Federação e as terras indígenas – Brasil – 2010'. Accessed 15 May 2013. ftp://ftp.ibge.gov.br/Censos/Censo_Demografico_2010/Caracteristicas_Gerais_dos_Indigenas/pdf/tab_3_01.pdf.

Langdon, Esther Jean. 2004. 'Uma avaliação crítica da atenção diferenciada e a colaboração entre antropologia e profissionais de saúde'. In *Saúde dos povos indígenas: Reflexões sobre antropologia participativa*, edited by Esther Jean Langdon and Luiza Garnelo, 33–51. Rio de Janeiro: Contra Capa/Associação Brasileira de Antropologia.

Langdon, Esther Jean. 2010. 'The Notion of Inclusion in Brazilian Indian Health Policy: Services and Cultural Practices', *Anales Nueva Época* 13: 153–81.

Langdon, Esther Jean. 2016. 'Os diálogos da antropologia com a saúde: contribuições para as políticas públicas em saúde indígena'. In *Políticas públicas: Reflexões antropológicas*, edited by Esther Jean Langdon and Márcia Grisotti, 17–42. Florianópolis: Editora da Universidade Federal de Santa Catarina.

Langdon, Esther Jean and Marina D. Cardoso. 2015. 'Introdução'. In *Saúde indígena: Políticas comparadas na América Latina*, edited by Esther Jean Langdon and Marina D. Cardoso, 11–30. Florianópolis: Editora da Universidade Federal de Santa Catarina.

Langdon, Esther Jean and Eliana E. Diehl. 2007. 'Participação e autonomia nos espaços interculturais de saúde indígena: Reflexões a partir do sul do Brasil', *Saúde e Sociedade* 16 (2): 19–36.

Langdon, Esther Jean, Eliana Elisabeth Diehl, Flávio Braune Wiik and Raquel Paiva Dias-Scopel. 2006. 'A participação dos agentes indígenas de saúde nos serviços de atenção à saúde: A experiência em Santa Catarina, Brasil', *Cadernos de Saúde Pública* 22 (12): 2637–46.

Langdon, Esther Jean, Eliana E. Diehl and Raquel Paiva Dias-Scopel. 2014. 'O papel e a formação dos agentes indígenas de saúde na atenção diferenciada à saúde aos povos indígenas brasileiros'. In *Saúde indígena em perspectiva: Explorando suas matrizes históricas e ideológicas*, edited by Carla Costa Teixeira and Luiza Garnelo, 213–40. Rio de Janeiro: Editora Fiocruz.

Langdon, Esther Jean and Maj-Lis Follér. 2012. 'Anthropology of Health in Brazil: A Border Discourse', *Medical Anthropology* 31 (1): 4–28.

Langdon, Esther Jean and Luiza Garnelo. 2017. 'Articulación entre servicios de salud y "medicina indígena": Reflexiones antropológicas sobre política y realidad en Brasil', *Salud Colectiva* 13 (3): 457–70.

Langdon, Esther Jean and Márcia Grisotti, eds. 2016. *Políticas públicas: Reflexões antropológicas.* Florianópolis: Editora da Universidade Federal de Santa Catarina.

Leibing, Annette. 2007. 'Much More than Medical Anthropology: The Healthy Body and Brazilian Identity'. In *Medical Anthropology: Regional Perspectives and Shared Concerns*, edited by Francine Saillant and Serge Genest, 58–70. Oxford: Blackwell.

Mendes, Eugenio V. 1995. *Distrito sanitário: O processo social de mudança das práticas sanitárias do Sistema Único de Saúde.* Rio de Janeiro: HUCITEC/ABRASCO.

Menéndez Eduardo. 1992. 'Modelo hegemónico, modelo alternativo subordinado, modelo de autoatención: Caracteres estructurales'. In *La antropología médica en México*, edited by Roberto Campos, 97–114. Mexico City: Universidad Autónoma Metropolitana.

Menéndez, Eduardo L. 2003. 'Modelos de atención de los padecimientos: De exclusiones teóricas y articulaciones prácticas', *Ciência e Saúde Coletiva* 8 (1): 185–207.

Menéndez, Eduardo L. 2012. 'Metodología cualitativa: Varios problemas y reiteradas omisiones', *Index de Enfermería* 21 (1/2): 62–68.

Menéndez, Eduardo Luiz. 2016. 'Salud intercultural: Propuestas, acciones y fracasos', *Ciência e Saúde Coletiva* 21 (1): 109–18.

Menéndez, Eduardo L. and Renée B. Di Pardo. 1996. *De algunos alcoholismos y algunos saberes: Atención primaria y proceso de alcoholización.* Mexico City: Centro de Investigaciones y Estudios Superiores en Antropología Social.

Ministério de Saúde. 1997. *Anais da 1a Oficina Macrorregional de Estratégia, Prevenção e Controle das DST/Aids para as Populações Indígenas das regiões Sul e Sudeste, e do Mato Grosso do Sul.* Londrina: Coordenação Nacional de DST/AIDS/Programa Municipal para DST/AIDS.

Montardo, Deise Lucy O. and Márcia Regina C.F. Rufino, eds. 2017. *Saberes e ciência plural: Diálogos e interculturalidade em antropologia.* Florianópolis: Editora da Universidade Federal de Santa Catarina.

Monteiro, Ana Lucia and Wilza Vieira Villela. 2009. 'A criação do Programa Nacional de DST e Aids como marco para a inclusão da idéia de direitos cidadãos na agenda governamental brasileira', *Revista Psicologia Política* 9 (17): 25–45.

Oliveira, Maria Conceição de. 1997a. 'Percepção corpórea e a questão da dieta em momentos de liminaridade: O exemplo Kaingáng'. In *Anais da 1a Oficina Macrorregional de Estratégia, Prevenção e Controle das DST/Aids para as Populações Indígenas das regiões Sul e Sudeste, e do Mato Grosso do Sul*, 69–78. Londrina: Coordenação Nacional de DST/AIDS/Programa Municipal para DST/AIDS.

Oliveira, Maria Conceição de. 1997b. *Os especialistas Kaingáng e os seres da natureza: Curadores da Aldeia Xapecó – Oeste de Santa Catarina.* Florianópolis: Fundação Catarinense de Cultura.

Oliveira, Maria Conceição de. 2000. 'Dinâmica do sistema cultural de saúde Kaingang – Aldeia Xapecó Santa Catarina'. In *Uri e Wãxi: Estudos interdisciplinares dos Kaingang*, edited by Lúcio Tadeu Mota, Francisco Silva Noelli and Kimiye Tommasino, 327–77. Londrina: Editora da Universidade Estadual de Londrina.

Pereira, Pedro. 2015. 'Antropologia da saúde: Um lugar para as abordagens antropológicas à doença e à saúde', *Revista de Antropología Experimental* 15 (3): 23–46.

Portela García, Sandra Carolina. 2010. 'Diabetes e hipertensão arterial entre os indígenas Kaingang da Aldeia Sede, Terra Indígena Xapecó (SC): Práticas de autoatención em um contexto de intermedicalidade'. Master's thesis in Anthropology, Universidade Federal de Santa Catarina.

Sarti, Cynthia Andersen. 2010. 'Saúde e sofrimento'. In *Horizontes das ciências sociais no Brasil: Antropologia*, edited by Carlos Benedito Martins and Luiz Fernando Dias Duarte, 197–223. São Paulo: ANPOCS.

Seppilli, Tullio and Rosario Otegui. 2005. 'Antropología médica crítica: Presentación', *Revista de Antropología Social* 14: 7–13.

Shankland, Alex. 2010. 'The Indigenous Peoples' Movement, "Forest Citizenship" and Struggles over Health Services in Acre, Brazil'. In *Mobilizing for Democracy: Citizen Action and the Politics of Public Participation*, edited by Vera Schattan P. Coelho and Bettina von Lieres, 99–119. London: Zed Books.

Shankland, Alex. 2014. 'Mediation as Diplomacy: Dynamics of Governance and Representation in Brazilian Indigenous Societies'. In *Mediated Citizenship: The Informal Politics of Speaking for*

Citizens in the Global South, edited by Bettina von Lieres and Laurence Piper, 183–202. Basingstoke: Palgrave Macmillan.

Shankland, Alex and Renato Athias. 2007. 'Decentralisation and Difference: Indigenous Peoples and Health System Reform in the Brazilian Amazon', *IDS Bulletin* 38 (1): 77–88.

Teixeira, Carla Costa. 2010. 'Autonomia em saúde indígena: Sobre o que estamos falando?', *Anuário Antropológico* 2009/1: 99–128.

Teixeira, Carla Costa and Cristina Dias da Silva. 2013. 'Antropologia e saúde indígena: Mapeando marcos de reflexão e interfaces de ação', *Anuário Antropológico* 2012/1: 35–57.

Teixeira, Carla Costa, Diego da Hora Simas and Nilton Miguel Aguilar de Costa. 2013. 'Controle social na saúde indígena: Limites e possibilidades da democracia direta'. *Tempus: Actas de Saúde Coletiva* 7 (4): 97–115.

Toledo, Maria Elvira, Maria Ferreira Bittencourt, Alexander Shankland and Hélio Barbin. 2013. 'O olhar das representações indígenas sobre a sua saúde e a interface com o subsistema de saúde indigena', *Tempus: Actas de Saúde Coletiva* 7 (4): 117–30.

Waitzkin, Howard, Celia Iriart, Alfredo Estrada and Silvia Lamadrid. 2001. 'Social Medicine in Latin America: Productivity and Dangers Facing the Major National Groups', *The Lancet* 358 (9278): 315–23.

Welch, James R., Ricardo Ventura Santos, Nancy M. Flowers and Carlos E.A. Coimbra. 2013. *Na primeira margem do rio: Território e ecologia do povo Xavante de Wedezé*. Rio de Janeiro: Museu do Índio-FUNAI.

Woortmann, Klaas. 1978. *Hábitos e ideologias alimentares em grupos sociais de baixa renda: Relatório final* (Série Antropologia 20). Brasília: Fundação Universidade de Brasília.

2

Critical anthropologies of maternal health: Theorising from the field with Mexican indigenous communities

Jennie Gamlin and Lina Berrio

Latin America's relationship with its colonial past and indigenous people has been catalytic of the development of critical paradigms in social science (Menéndez 2012, 2018; Langdon and Diehl, this volume). Indigenous historical and sociocultural systems and communities, although ethnically extremely diverse, have become important spaces through which medical anthropologists understand and explore illness experience and causality (Segato in García Pérez 2017; Flores 1991). Most notably, the presence throughout Latin America of diverse indigenous medical systems has informed anthropological theory, adding new perspectives to interpretations of wellbeing, and alternative subjectivities from which to theorise. Close engagement with indigenous communities through collaborative work has taught us about the structure of these health systems, about the social determination of health and illness and how activism around specific structural injustices, such as class, ethnicity and gender, can create access points for addressing important health concerns. The theoretical insights we wish to highlight in this chapter point to the generation of critical theory about medicine and healthcare that is emergent from indigenous lifeworlds.

Mexico's 10 million indigenous people continue to lag behind the national population in all health indicators. Social security coverage in health is minimal at a national level: 49.9 per cent of the population rely on Seguro Popular, a health protection scheme for the uninsured, while in indigenous municipalities this rises to 91.1 per cent (CDI 2015). These health inequalities, the consequence of a historical pattern of disenfranchisement, are maintained in the present day by poorquality education and healthcare, the imposition of biomedical notions of wellbeing, the undermining of indigenous authoritative knowledge and weakening traditional medical systems that were integral to communities' cultural and social survival (Fajardo Santana 2007; PNUD 2010). Ethnographic work has established the social structure and role of indigenous traditional medical systems and the vision of health as essentially holistic, spiritual and environmental, as opposed to individual and biomedical (Zolla et al. 1992; Menéndez 1984, 1994). This has led, on the one hand, to work on biomedicine as a hegemonic medical system (Menéndez 1992), and on the other to a critique of the manner and methods through which healthcare is provided, including the biomedicalisation of birth and the conditionality and bureaucratisation of access to care (Campos 1992a, 1992b; Ortega Canto 2010; Smith-Oka 2009). These anthropologies often take the form of activist or engaged research processes (Juárez et al. 2017).

The purpose of this chapter is to draw out the contributions that collaborative and long-term ethnography with indigenous communities have made to critical theory within medical anthropology, proposing that such theory would not have been possible had it not been for indigenous agency around health and anthropological research. We argue that these critical theorisations about biomedicine and healthcare provision, welfare and development that are *learned* from indigenous communities are essentially underpinned by differing forms of activism: i) activism in the form of resistance to medical care that challenges and questions the biomedical model, ii) demands for social justice and better-quality healthcare and welfare, and iii) activism in the form of resilience of traditional forms of care in spite of decades of colonialism. To illustrate and explore this argument we outline three important theoretical ideas within critical medical anthropology (CMA) that have emerged through research with and about Latin American indigenous communities. We then draw on examples of collaborative projects around maternal health with indigenous communities, focusing specifically on the relationship between agency, activism and research to propose a new paradigm for activism and social justice within CMA.

Latin American CMA: Theorising from indigenous communities

Coloniality/colonialism and inequality

Indigeneity is defined relationally and politically in terms of a group's status and identity within a nation state (Merlan 2007). Critically, this definition hinges on indigenous people belonging to groups with historical continuity to original inhabitants of invaded territory (Stephens et al. 2006). The concepts of colonialism and indigeneity are inextricably linked by meaning, with indigenous identity being given to original inhabitants of a nation before colonialism or invasion, who continue to live with varying degrees of continuity to their past as a group that is ruled by a settler population. Laws, knowledge production, education and medical systems that are put into place at a national level are defined by the settler population – a category that includes Latin America's Spanish- and Portuguese-speaking white and mestizo groups.[1] The concept of coloniality, which defines colonialism as an ongoing process as opposed to an event (Lugones 2008; Mignolo 2008), refers to the continued imposition of social and cultural structures that are mostly of Western and European origin. With few exceptions, Latin America has been ruled by and for white and mestizo groups since independence, leaving indigenous populations essentially under continuing colonial rule. In this paper we use this concept to discuss the role of biomedicine in indigenous people's lives, as an imposed form of medical care of a different cultural origin. As we describe in the following pages, the manner in which the structure of biomedicine has come to dictate social practices is colonial in nature, in that indigenous people are subjected to its biopolitical practices and processes, while indigenous medical systems are devalued. We refer to this dynamic as the coloniality of biomedicine.

Anthropological work documenting this dynamic began to emerge in the mid-twentieth century, through the visibilisation of health inequalities (Menéndez 2012). Influential works followed, such as those of Bonfil Batalla (1966), which conceptualised high levels of indigenous morbidity and mortality as racial and class discrimination, forming a critical turning point. In *Del indigenismo de la revolución a la antropología crítica*, Bonfil Batalla (1983) critiques the post-revolutionary discourse of *indigenismo* that promoted assimilation and integration, arguing instead for a revision of anthropological discourse about cultural diversity. 'The indian cannot remain marginalised', he argued, but neither should they become obliterated through integration. Using this politicised reconceptualisation of indigenous social reality as a springboard, Bonfil Batalla proposed an anthropology that sought to understand cultural diversity and developed conceptual tools for explaining social problems on a much greater scale. The indigenous context became fertile ground for developing Latin American CMA – or critical theory of the anthropology of health. By reflecting on diversity, a broader understanding was brought to the meaning and praxis of medical systems.

Indigenous therapeutic systems and medical pluralism

Reflections on the hegemony of biomedicine constitute a critical interpretation of the role of biomedicine in and of itself, and as the dominant method and nosology of wellbeing. Among the theories that have emerged are the conceptualisation of biomedicine as the hegemonic model, the biomedicalisation of healthcare and illness, and a redefinition of the various forms of home treatment that fall under the banner of *autoatención* or self-care (see for example Menéndez 1994; Aguirre Beltrán 1992; Langdon 2016; Langdon and Garnelo 2017). From a critical standpoint within the anthropology of health, we conceptualise 'biomedicine' as referring to a positivist and Western nosology and system of healthcare delivery that uses scientific methods to ascertain causality and develop curative procedures. It is the principal medical doctrine used in modern and capitalist societies, covering prevention, diagnosis and treatment, although local biomedical cultures differ both in relation to political economy – in some countries private healthcare systems are dominant while in others the state provides most or all healthcare – and local patterns of illness, treatment and care. Although biomedicine emerged within modern and European cultures, it has become universalised, most recently through the structures and institutions of Global Health, as the solution to saving lives and increasing life expectancy. In relation to this, biopolitics refers to the strategies and mechanisms through which human lives are managed by authorities or governments; critically, the biopolitics of global health agencies in settler colonial or European nations is driven by the doctrine of biomedicine and the prevailing political economy.

Menéndez studied illness and treatment behaviour over many decades and through public health practice to define the existence of parallel models. Crucially, understanding and conceptualising the non-biomedical – indigenous – health system visibilised the structure and role of therapeutic systems as a whole (Menéndez 1992, 1994). It is a social fact that every society has developed representations and practices to understand and treat illnesses (Menéndez 1994; Pérez Tamayo

1991; Finkler 1992). The strategies or medical system that social groups develop follow a similar pattern in all societies: an institutionally recognised group of healers becomes established and authorised to deal with specific threats to health and uphold an authority over treatment, dictating what is the best way to deal with illness. This authority provides a hegemony over behaviour, embedding social and ideological control within medical systems (Menéndez 1994; Finkler 1992). This (medical) structure defines a determined set of behaviours as deviant, with corresponding stigma and negative connotations attached to unhealthy behaviour. Social institutions become responsible for delivering or ensuring adherence to the 'correct' set of norms and practices, leading to a degree of social control through medical and healthcare delivery. Those institutionally recognised as healers hold a position in the social hierarchy that authorises them to dictate the strategies for action or techniques for treating illness. For example, it is well established that Wixárika *mara'akate* (healers) occupy an important social and or religious role and though their leadership treat the collective as well as the individual (Fajardo Santana 2007; Neurath 2002), while Mayan midwives provide social, emotional and ritual guidance to women (Cosminsky 2012; Ortega Canto 2010). A further idea that emerged in response to understandings of Latin American indigenous health systems is that the coloniality of knowledge defines science as the basis of academic praxis, ensuring biomedicine is established as the 'hegemonic' model that deals with recognised diseases, while traditional and alternative medicine have become subaltern (Santos 2014; Connell 2015). The parallel use of more than one of these different models is viewed as medical pluralism. While the degree of syncretism varies considerably, the continued hegemony of biomedicine and the cultural and wellbeing implications of this are foremost (Menéndez 2003).

From indigenous models of health, to a critique of biomedicine: The individual versus the collective

The hegemonic/traditional dichotomy also represents two separate understandings of the concept of wellbeing: on the one hand a biomedical understanding of individual and behaviour-related health, and on the other a concept of wellbeing that is embedded in communities, spiritualities and social and environmental dynamics within any given community (see for example Valeggia and Snodgrass 2015; Paradies 2016). While traditional medicine is practised in indigenous communities, *public* (as opposed to biomedical) health within Latin America has been concep-tualised as a social science, and both 'collective health' and 'social med-icine' approaches have become important conceptual and applied tools. Although the political and theoretical construction of social medicine and collective health has its origins in Marxism, the collective perspec-tive of health that is present in indigenous health systems is an extension of their own worldview and how this applied. Both indigenous and non-indigenous concepts coincide in emphasising the collective dimension in contrast to the individual view of biomedicine, forming the basis of Latin American critical theories of about health. CMA has embraced these con-cepts, although their origins are not specifically anthropological; hence by moving between a critical theory about health and medical anthro-pology we aim to blur the disciplinary boundaries, understandings and application of theories about health. While the practice of indigenous therapeutic medicine has remained this, largely confined to indigenous and culturally close communities, the ideological conception of health as a social phenomenon rather than individual and biological is cen-tral to the fields of social medicine and collective health. The nosology and practices of social and collective approaches to health speak to the social *determination* of illness (Spiegel, Breilh and Yassi 2015), featur-ing interventions that focus on the collective as a subject (Laurell 1982). This understanding of health is now widely influential in anglophone CMA (Farmer et al. 2006; Castro and Singer 2004), both academically and increasingly in practice within the fields of global and public health (UNFPA 2019).

In defining health and illness as a social and historical process within human groups, the social determinants position argues that the modern, scientific conception of health is not false, but partial, and there-fore treatment options – such as hospital care – that focus only on bio-logical processes are not treating the social causes (Laurell 1982). Like indigenous health systems, social medicine and collective health (SM/CH) focus on the broad context within which illness occurs (Waitzkin et al. 2001) and although it would be tenuous to argue that these theories have developed from indigenous medical systems, as models of illness and care they share the conceptualisation of illness as social and histori-cal, and the ideology that biomedicine is only a partial therapy, treating symptoms but not underlying causes (Fajardo Santana 2007). Essentially both indigenous health systems and social medicine work with an epis-teme of health as other than, or far more than, individual or biological unwellness. While we cannot assume a direct relationship – that SM/CH were learned through understanding indigenous health systems – we wish to make the point that indigenous nosologies and health systems are relevant far beyond their own social reality.

Activist knowledge: Learning from the field

The relationship between anthropologists and health policy has been varied – with both close and distant alliances forged (Castro and Singer 2004). An important sector of applied anthropology grew out of a 'pursuit of social justice' (Lamphere 2018), which seeks to solve contemporary public health problems, while bringing forward the voices of unrepresented people. In her discussion of transnational feminism, Conway (2017) argues that a post-colonial and post-structuralist theoretical reconsideration of activist practice, one that goes beyond the applied concept, is needed. In this section, taking as an example research and activism around maternal mortality, we argue that collaborations between academic and non-academic researchers are co-producing anti-colonial critical anthropological theory and social policy in relation to health and wellbeing, and that in so doing, they are producing a post-critical knowledge.

Context: Research and activism around indigenous maternal health

The combination of feminist foci, indigenous justice, human rights abuse and long-standing anthropological interest has made the causes and contexts of indigenous maternal mortality an area of medical anthropology where critical research, activism and indigeneity collide. The reality of inequality in Mexican indigenous communities is acted out in interpersonal relationships, experienced in clinical settings and reinforced by welfare services such as the *Prospera* programme that makes financial support conditional, subject to adherence to a centrally defined set of healthcare practices. Unequal structures of gender, race and class, compounded by health system weaknesses, have led to high rates of preventable maternal morbidity and mortality with maternal mortality rates (MMR) in the poorest southern states of Chiapas, Guerrero and Oaxaca between 58.3 and 45.9 per 100,000, compared to 36.7 at a national level and increasing to 78.1 in indigenous municipalities (Freyermuth 2019). For Mexico's indigenous women the experience of maternal care has been marked in many cases by ineffective or late interventions, and problems with human resources and infrastructure. The structural deficiencies that are evident in this pattern of care are compounded by deep gender inequalities that are acted out in interpersonal and family relationships, experienced in clinical settings and reinforced by wider development and educational services (Sesia 2017; Freyermuth Enciso 2003, 2017; Berrio 2017a).

The theoretical positions described above are highly relevant to maternal and reproductive health, as this field of health reproduces colonial relations of subordination within Mexican society, in particular unequal structures of race, gender and social class. Fundamental and hugely symbolic events, such as birth, have been gradually displaced from the community and home to the hospital as a means of achieving specific targets for reducing maternal mortality. Targets for reducing maternal mortality have been linked to the millennium development goals, also forming an important catalyst for the politicisation of maternal mortality in Mexico. By linking the right to life and health with social and gender inequality, pregnancy and birth moved beyond the health sector to become a battleground of feminist organisations, while the medicalisation of birth became a priority in order to achieve internationally set targets (see *The Lancet* 2016). In a region where conservative values dominate the political landscape, maternal health became an uncontroversial tool for advancing in the controversial field of sexual and reproductive health and rights. Maternal mortality reduction became a vehicle for advancing women's and indigenous people's rights, while also addressing the more complicated concerns of gender inequality and reproductive rights. It is this context we draw on, to discuss how researchers and indigenous partners mobilised around shared concerns for social justice through collaborative research projects.[2]

Through the following two case studies we explore the birth experiences of two indigenous women and report on the responses of researcher–activist collaborations around maternal and gender equality concerns that emerged in each context. The first is the case of Sukulima, a young indigenous Wixárika woman experiencing her first birth. Sukulima's pregnancy was documented as part of a collaborative community project that followed 64 pregnancies over a period of 24 months in the state of Jalisco. The second case focuses on Juana, a Na Saavi woman whose baby died in the womb, leading to conflicts around gender and healthcare provision. This case is linked to CAMI (*Casa de la Mujer Indigena* – Indigenous Women's House), a community project for women's health in Guerrero state. For each case we describe the associated knowledge co-production that emerged as a result of the researcher–activist collaboration and go on to discuss how collaborations such as these have contributed to the field.

Sukulima's pregnancy: Three versions

The following section is an extract from a field diary.

I (Gamlin) first met Sukulima in 2011 when she, her sister and her cousin were companions on the five-hour walk down to a valley community for a fiesta. At only 13, Sukulima was by far the strongest walker and ran most of the way, arriving well ahead. I heard that she had had a baby a few years later when I returned to their community. In fact, by then, all three young sisters were mothers. Sukulima had been studying at secondary school in a small town outside their community. I had known her in-laws for some years, and it was they who told me the first version of the baby's birth.

Her father-in-law, Juan, recounted how Sukulima had gone into labour early, at seven months' gestation. She was living with her husband Raul and his parents and at only 14 was afraid to give birth at home. As she reached the final stage of labour Raul put her in his father's truck and drove her the 200 metres down a bumpy hill to the clinic. According to Juan's version of events, Raul ran into the clinic asking for help and was told that because Sukulima had not been for any ante-natal checks and was not registered with the *Seguro Popular*, the health system for the uninsured, she could not be attended in the clinic. The doctor refused to let her in and she gave birth in the truck outside the clinic. Her baby was tiny, born still inside the amniotic sac. She was then taken by ambulance down to the municipal town, and from there to the nearest city where her baby spent the next two months in an incubator.

This version was confirmed in later conversations with her cousins, Liliana and Chabela, who picked up on Juan's comment about the *Seguro Popular*. Liliana spoke to me about how government services seemed selective and always politically motivated. She described how the new 'Campaign Against Hunger' reduced them to hungry people: 'We are not all just dying of hunger', she told me. Since these welfare programmes are enforced by staff in the health clinic, they use this authority to reprimand patients for not seeking ante-natal care and failing to follow hygiene and nutritional advice.

Chabela then talked about Sukulima, and how she had been beaten harshly by Juan, one day arriving at their house with a split lip and blood down her chin. Chabela had taken her to the clinic but she had refused to make an official complaint as the potential repercussions might mean she had to leave the community. Liliana had told her how she had no reason to put up with this – she had rights – but gradually over the next few months Sukulima saw them less and less, having returned to her husband's home and withdrawn from the family.

On another occasion Sukulima arrived at their house with her little boy, having been beaten. She had argued with Raul and he had beaten her and told her to leave, throwing her belongings out of the house. Sukulima's sister and her husband were sent to collect the belongings while Chabela took her to the clinic, but they were sent away by Juan, who shouted to his son that he should sort things out with Sukulima, bring her back and treat her better. These episodes continued for many years.

That afternoon I visited Sukulima and asked her about her birth. Her mother-in-law was with us in their kitchen as Sukulima made tortillas and we chatted. Sukulima's version of her birth was that she had been feeling unwell the day before. At about midnight she felt pains, but thought it couldn't be the baby as she was only seven months' pregnant. At 6.30 a.m. Raul put her in the truck and drove her to the clinic. He knocked on the door and shouted but no-one let them in, so they returned home. At 8.40, in a lot of pain, Rosa said they should go to see the *mara'akame* (shaman). This they did; the *mara'akame* confirmed that she was just about to give birth, and should go straight to the clinic. By then Sukulima could barely move and was unable to sit due to the position of the baby, but Raul helped her into the truck and drove to the clinic. The baby came so quickly that she wasn't able to make it inside the clinic and there, in the front seat of the truck, outside the clinic, she gave birth. The baby was born still in its amniotic sac. It was tiny. She signalled to me with her hands how small the baby was. The doctor came straight out and attended her there in the truck, cutting the cord and helping her and the baby into the clinic. There was no-one to drive the ambulance so Raul drove her and the baby straight down to the municipal town and from there she went on to the city hospital. I asked if the doctor had explained why she might have gone into labour at seven months and she repeated that she had been really ill and felt awful the day before – she thought that must have been it. I asked why she hadn't been to the ante-natal clinic. She just said she had felt fine, that was all.

As we walked away Chabela and I discussed Sukulima's story. I commented that I had thought she had been denied access to the clinic but in fact it seemed not to be the case. There Chabela interjected, 'But the day before Raul had beaten her. She had come to us in tears, but then went back home, feeling sick and ill. She had been ill all day because she had been beaten.' When I asked what Sukulima's father had thought of all this, she responded that he had been indifferent, suggesting that they were young and would sort their problems out. 'Everyone knows that Raul beats Sukulima, but no-one dares to get involved', she told me.

Knowledge co-production

The research project from which this case study was drawn sought to understand the social and structural determinants of maternal mortality and identify community-based responses, by working with the semi-autonomous indigenous community structure and ethnomedical practices. One of the authors of this chapter (Gamlin) was research coordinator for this project. The community of San Pedro mobilised directly around the issue of access to healthcare firstly by organising a team of women to document experiences of maternal healthcare and secondly with direct action. As part of an academic-led study of the structural determinants of maternal morbidity and mortality,[3] eight women from across the governorship formed a maternal health group – giving themselves the name 'Wimari' in reference to an important female deity – to gather data on pregnancies and births. Sixty-four sets of interviews were conducted with women while pregnant and after the birth of their babies. The results of this study have been published elsewhere (Gamlin and Osrin 2018; Gamlin and Holmes 2018).

The structural and social factors identified included a stratified gender system, whereby women were largely responsible for childcare and men largely for decision-making regarding care-seeking and financial resources. Control of this system is often enforced through violence and the lack of access to healthcare is exacerbated by inadequate transport and communications, aggravated by scarce financial resources at both family and community level, generalised poverty, a fear of authorities leading to avoidance of care-seeking and an inadequate system of referral and ante-natal support. These social and collective issues were discussed with the maternal health group Wimari.

Trained by an experienced indigenous reproductive health leader from a different ethnic group, Wimari brought the issue of maternal health to community meetings and discussed options for a sustainable and community-managed approach to improving maternal health that would not require state maintenance or input and could be sustained at a community level. A first stage in this was the installation of radio communication throughout the 16 'agencies' that make up their politically bounded governorship, so that isolated hamlets are able to make contact with clinics, and from there hospitals. A second stage would be focusing on seeking institutional and community support for training midwives. There was recognition that openly focusing on gender inequality would be complicated and potentially unacceptable within the community in the immediate future.

Key to the project's success was working closely with the indigenous community structure, at once facilitator and generator of collective health. The Wimari project rapidly gained the support of community authorities and women began to acquire the courage to speak at community meetings about both the project and ongoing concerns over health provision. Prompted by the antagonistic decisions of a medical doctor who complicated access to care in one of the governorship's two health clinics, a direct action was organised. This began with a series of letters to seven different ministries within the state-level government, including health, social welfare, indigenous affairs and education. The letters were followed by a sit-in protest at which they demanded major improvements to health service provision and fulfilment of previous promises on resources. Following this, a team of community authorities, including one of the Wimari group members, made a trip to the state capital to directly confront state-level ministers.

These different actions generated three new types of knowledge: knowledge on the social/structural determinants of health and in particular the role of gender; knowledge about local actions and activisms at community and political levels; and knowledge about indigenous agency and how this operates within the context of inequality.

Between community and health services: Juana's case

At the start of the millennium San Luis Acatlán was one of the municipalities with repeatedly high rates of maternal death. It is also one of the municipalities of Guerrero with the largest number of indigenous midwives, with a history of health promoters that in 2010 led to the foundation of Casa de la Mujer Indígena (CAMI; Indigenous Women's House), coordinated and attended by a group of 20 indigenous Meph'a and Na Saavi midwives and health promoters. The CAMI was originally built with municipal funds, but some of the resources for its operation come from the National Commission for the Development of Indigenous Peoples (known in Mexico as the Comisión de Desarrollo Indígena or CDI). The CAMI is a community project that operates as a link between communities and health services. Women in labour are attended by midwives and accompanied by their relatives. *Sobadas* (massages) and the follow-up care of women during their pregnancy are carried out by the CAMI midwives. Workshops and health promotion activities are carried out in communities by a network of promoters. Pregnant women from distant indigenous communities can travel in advance of their baby's due date and stay at the CAMI until labour begins. Patients can be transferred to the primary care hospital nearby in case of an emergency. For several years the CAMI has been supported by academics and civil society organisations, who have helped build a series of policy demands that have been raised with local health authorities. The author (Berrio) has accompanied this organisational process since its inception, originally as an activist within a non-governmental organisation that worked to strengthen indigenous midwives' and promoters' capacity in reproductive health, and subsequently as an academic accompanying the CAMI as it carried out research and evaluation of intercultural health services and tracking maternal health policy with regards to midwifery.

Case study

In June 2016 I accompanied Apolonia, the CAMI coordinator, to visit Juana, a young woman whose baby had died in the womb a few weeks before. She needed medical assistance in the regional hospital, more than three hours away from home. Apolonia warned me that Juana's relatives had become very angry with her, and she wanted to explain to them why she had made the decision to take Juana to the hospital. After knocking and asking permission, we entered the small house where Juana and her partner lived with her in-laws and other members of the family. They received us with kindness but distance, and asked us to go Juana's room, where she was lying on her bed looking very pale.

The whole conversation took place in Tuun Saavi. Juana spoke little, answering the questions Apolonia asked about how she felt. Most of the responses were given by her husband, a man of around 25 years of age. He talked a lot, and through his body language indicated that something serious and delicate was being discussed between the couple, Apolonia and the in-laws, who also entered the small room. Everyone spoke quickly and loudly and they scolded Apolonia, who in turn spoke to them. Now and then one of them – usually the husband – would turn to me and summarise in Spanish what they were discussing. 'She did wrong', they said, 'the midwife did wrong to take her to the hospital without me'. 'We told her that she should wait for her husband to arrive, that he could not get her to San Luis', the in-laws replied. 'But the baby was already dead inside her belly for more than a day, [she] was at risk of an infection, she had to go to the hospital to have it [the baby] removed, and that was what the midwife did', replied Apolonia. After about an hour it seemed the issue had been resolved satisfactorily. Although the family was angry because Juana had been taken to the hospital without her husband's authorisation, they recognised that the baby had already died.

After leaving, Apolonia explained the case in full. The woman had come to her attention a couple of weeks before: one of the indigenous professional midwifery students made a routine check of all pregnant women in the community and identified this woman whose baby had not had foetal movements in the past 24 hours. The midwife explained to Juana – in her own language because both are Na Saavi women – that it was likely that the baby had died and she would need to go to the health centre about 20 minutes away. She also explained this to the in-laws, who proposed waiting for her husband to return from the field. The midwife explained the seriousness of the matter and the importance of acting quickly, so they finally agreed to go to the health centre.

There were no doctors at the health centre (they had all left for the day), so the midwife communicated with the hospital, an hour and a half away, asking for guidance on what to do and was told to take the patient there immediately. They were seen upon arrival but told that Juana could not be treated there and they would have to go to the nearest city, a further hour and a half away. By that time her husband had arrived. As Juana did not want to leave, they called Apolonia to explain and convince her in their language. They also called the police. Finally they agreed to go to the city hospital. It was another three days before, after a long and complicated induction, the baby was delivered. By this time Juana and her husband were so angry they decided to file a complaint against the midwife.

Knowledge co-production

Demands for a higher quality of care and for the intercultural adaptation of services were documented in a joint evaluation made between the CAMI and a civil society organisation accompanying the process. More than 100 interviews were carried out with service users asking about the types of attention they received and what they would like to receive. Workshops with health promoters and midwives about wider experiences of intercultural maternal health policy in Latin America were also documented. In May 2018, these demands led to an agreement between the primary care clinic, the health jurisdiction and the CAMI. Among these were the following commitments:

The hospital would commit to:

- Eliminate pressure on women to use contraceptives, especially intrauterine devices, immediately post partum.
- Eliminate scolding and mistreatment by health personnel.
- Allow women to choose their birth position and decide what to do with the placenta.
- Allow a CAMI member to accompany women to the hospital (the admission of anyone into the labour and delivery ward – including family members – is currently prohibited).
- Regional health authorities would arrange for interpreters within hospitals to accompany indigenous pregnant women.
- Several of these agreements have already been put into place; others have been more difficult, but this type of written and signed agreement is part of ongoing dialogue between the communities and the health sector, in which anthropologists have been present in Mexico and in Latin America.

Discussion: Theorising from the field

Dual medical systems and the coloniality of care

Both of the case studies described above evidence the tension between indigenous and Western biomedical healthcare systems. In their search for a safe birth environment Sukulima and Juana alternate between seeking biomedical care and traditional care, using both medical systems without conflict; in both cases a traditional healthcare provider recommends their patient seek clinical care. Both cases also demonstrate the existence of gatekeepers to biomedical care, potentially bringing into question the automatic right to treatment. Sukulima was reluctant to visit the clinic and her father-in-law rumoured that the doctors would not help her because she did not have Seguro Popular, an insurance plan for those who do not have access to the social security system. Juana was taken to hospital, but must await a doctor before being channelled onto the next level of care.

Langdon and Diehl's work (this volume) recounts the process through which interdisciplinary collaborations between anthropologists, indigenous organisations and health workers evidenced the political role of autonomous (traditional) therapeutic systems as resistance to the hegemonic form of medical provision. This itself became a form of resisting ongoing internal colonialism beyond the provision of medical care per se. In the case of Sukulima, this resistance may be a resistance to the control implicit in the conditionality of care that is attached to welfare programmes such as Prospera – a programme which in various forms has been providing welfare to indigenous populations for over two decades (Suárez and Herrera 2013). The biopolitics of motherhood from birth through to the conditionality of welfare has been documented, with institutions defining how indigenous bodies should be treated – in particular when it comes to reproductive health (Smith-Oka 2012; Gamlin 2013). Langdon and Diehl describe how maintaining indigenous care and wellbeing practices gives communities a role in the governance of their own health, and explain that engaging indigenous health NGOs in this process served the dual purpose of addressing the coloniality of healthcare provision and increasing indigenous agency in their ability to determine their own health outcomes (Langdon and Diehl, this volume). This point is emphasised more widely in research by indigenous academic/activists such as Tuhiwai Smith (1999) and Morgensen (2014).

Concerns about conditionality and resistance are central to decolonising indigenous research and healthcare globally and connect widely with anti-colonial indigenous researchers whose methodological focus and ideological position define both health and research as colonial institutions (Morgensen 2014; Tuhiawi Smith 1999; Connell 2015). Although it is recognised that biomedicine has been a principal contributor to improved indigenous health, methods of delivery and differentiated medical ontologies create barriers to care-seeking (Morgensen 2011; Stephens et al. 2006), while the coloniality of institutional care and welfare programmes removes communities' control over their own wellbeing (Gamlin 2013; Smith-Oka 2009). The cases of Sukulima and Juana evidence this dynamic through the critical relationship between members of the community, the clinic and welfare programmes in general. They suggest a distrust towards health services and the institutions aligned to them, with recognition of the paternalistic relationship between institutions and community indicated by the discussions about the Seguro Popular and the welfare programme 'campaign against hunger', the call to the police and demands brought against care in the case of Juana. This critical standpoint is a form of resistance that reflects recognition on the part of indigenous research participants of the ongoing coloniality of healthcare provision. The simultaneous rejection on the part of Sukulima, who chose not to seek ante-natal care, and the critical position of her father-in law and cousins suggests an antagonism towards institutional care and programmes that is also shared by Juana and her family, pointing to a politicised awareness of indigenous people's own lives that is illuminated through ethnographic engagement.

Articulating gender rights through maternal health

Research on maternal health developed from the perspective of CMA not only aims to visibilise the issue, but also to bring into the discussion the depth of gender inequalities entwined within this field. A strong link with feminism and the feminist movement in Mexico has helped articulate discussion around the sexual and reproductive rights of women and strengthen the demands of the movement for greater gender equity. Many indigenous women's movements have mobilised around maternal health, demanding improvements to state health provision (Juárez Ramírez et al. 2017) as well as discussion spaces within communities to rethink how gender is ordered. In both Sukulima and Juana's cases, social interactions that take for granted the hierarchical gender structure which endorses their husbands' authority over their bodies, or the attention they should receive, are a given. We argue that discourse around the prevention of maternal mortality has opened up spaces of reflection on women's rights in communities, including questioning naturalised inequalities and the role of intimate partner violence.

Activism around maternal health has been an important concern of medical anthropologists, often engaging from a feminist perspective on gender equality as a structural determinant of health with a clear understanding of how gender dynamics contribute to maternal health outcomes (Ortega Canto 2010). Participatory research has evidenced a circular dynamic between gender equality and maternal health: research addressing the former also brings improvements to the latter, while programmes that aim to improve maternal health outcomes generally lead to greater gender equality. The intersection between indigeneity and gender is a central concern of women's NGOs in Mexico and maternal health has become an uncontroversial concern through which to work with indigenous women without specifically seeking to up-end a delicate gender imbalance. Historical research beyond Mexico has demonstrated the important role of midwifery as a community asset for women more generally and struggles for women's rights and equality (Mies 1989; Stone 2016; Davis-Floyd and Cheyney 2009). The narratives of Juana and Sukulima's births reveal the role of gender inequality in decision-making, intimate partnerships and the wider family and community. In the case of Sukulima, her cousin Chabela points to gender violence as a causal factor in Sukulima's early labour. This may or may not have been the case, but Chabela offers an articulation of the role of gender inequality in birth outcomes, and uses her dual position as both research participant and activist/collaborator to talk about gender inequality within the context of health. As an activist she brings forward the problem of gender violence at a community level, pointing also to the impossibility of *directly* challenging gender inequality within the existing community structures.

For Juana, the midwife uses her authority as a healthcare provider to subvert the convention of waiting for the husband before making a decision about care. Apolonia then explains to the in-laws and husband why these decisions were made, putting Juana's wellbeing before an established gender norm. This case also demonstrates the important role that traditional midwives play within communities as advocates for women and for maternal health. In Sukulima's community, where there is no tradition of midwifery (Gamlin and Hawkes 2015), women have no advocates within the community and there are no authorities who will stand up for women. Apolonia has the double advantage of belonging to the same ethnic group – Na Saavi – and commanding authority through her knowledge of midwifery; from this position she is able to defend a decision to override the husband and in-laws' authority. Sukulima has no recourse to a midwife, and Chabela points to the impossibility of addressing gender violence, yet the research assistant makes a point of utilising her research participation to emphasise the role of gender inequality, possibly looking for someone sympathetic to this concern. The project itself led to Wimari developing and proposing political actions that included directly confronting policy makers (direct actions) regarding the provision of healthcare, while within the community the process of participation became transformative as women were appointed to political positions. In both cases, though in quite different ways, maternal health has provided an opportunity for challenging gender inequality without directly confronting hierarchies.

The CAMI further indirectly engages with gender equality by bringing indigenous women to the policy table in relation to the issue of maternal health. This occurs within a health policy context that seeks increasing medicalisation of childbirth and de-traditionalisation of the birthing process (Freyermuth Enciso 2018). In line with WHO guidelines (WHO 2015) for the non-promotion of traditional midwives as birth attendants, Mexican health policy does not encourage their practice. Although CAMI is thus clearly positioned within the health sector as a subaltern form of provision, it offers a location specifically for indigenous women to work directly alongside academics and activists to develop policy recommendations. This particular situation as a subaltern form of health provision has provided an opportunity to challenge the coloniality of biomedicine by creating a space through which indigenous women can engage together around their shared concerns.

This cyclical process, wherein maternal health and gender both generate and harness agency, brings into question the theoretical basis for the dichotomisation of structure and agency. In the previous section we described how the non-utilisation of health services is in itself an act of resistance; in this case we see an interaction with the process of research itself, as the knowledge generated with and by indigenous participants about health brings into question the importance of structure to gender forms and practices.

Post-critical medical anthropology: Adding agency to critique

The concept of structural violence articulates linkages between global structures – starting with neoliberal political economy and encompassing ongoing processes such as colonialism and institutionalised social hierarchies of gender and race – and avoidable harm to populations, referring to 'social structures that put people in harm's way' (Farmer et al. 2006). Ethnographies of maternal health in Mexico in the works of Freyermuth Enciso (2017; 2018), Sesia (2017) and Berrio (2017a; 2017b) provide rich examples of these links between inequalities and health. However, this now universalised concept *does not* provide a useful platform for exploring and proposing how we can address this harm, and crucially, by tracking harm back to structures of the global political economy, dichotomises structure and agency.

Structural violence theories have also failed to capture the *collective* nature of health, focusing instead on the biomedical and individual approach. As a structure of this medical nosology, global health institutions dictate a superstructure that is the best and healthiest way to live our lives as individuals within the confines of globalisation and capitalism (Morgensen 2011, 2014). The WHO's push for universal healthcare (WHO 2018) is the preferred strategy for improving global health worldwide as a one-size-fits-all policy. We propose the concept of *post-critical medical anthropology* to look more broadly at the coloniality of health and how collectives, such as indigenous communities, do not fit neatly into the policy dictates of healthcare provision. On the one hand the coloniality of care structures, as described above, means that communities have little control over the methods and conditions of healthcare provision, and on the other, the individual focus reduces health interventions to addressing causal factors. The proposed concept attempts to join a structural violence perspective with an anti-colonial positionality that draws on participant agency to indicate ways forward. By shifting our attention from causes to processes (such as coloniality, racism and relational gender dynamics) we also capture what Spiegel, Breilh and Yassi (2015) refer to as the 'emancipatory forces', the actions and agency of collective groups around health. Analyses of these processes would benefit greatly from a transformational perspective that not only asks about structural determinants, but also explores how populations can respond, and what forms of parallel non-biomedical approaches are beneficial. This also implies de-emphasising the biomedical outcomes over and above the processes of delivery and conditions of care. Importantly, it speaks to wrestling with the biopolitics of global health and rejection of a dysfunctional system. Post-critical medical anthropology implies going beyond political economy critiques such as structural violence to incorporate pushback and resistance and describe how this reshapes institutions. Critical theory must shift beyond the written format and while CMA clearly positions itself as an important voice demonstrating politically and economically how existing systems are harmful, we need to theorise around the role of agency rather than vulnerability from our ethnographies of health and wellbeing.

Proponents of the community participation paradigm, Nelson and Prilleltensky (2010) argue that if research is truly collaborative it can also be transformative. It is insufficient to engage participants in research, unless the process itself leads to greater social justice. This only happens when research participants themselves are agents of knowledge production (Tuhiwai Smith 1999). Anthropology accepts the role of participants as agents of their own change and transformation; what we wish to emphasise here is their agency in the production of critical knowledge and theory. As Biehl and Moran-Thomas (2009) highlight in their work on subjectivities and social ills, there is a tendency for certain anthropologists to 'depict people as subjects of structural violence', as if this were a 'critical end point' of a linear form of political and economic violence' (Biehl and Moran-Thomas 2009: 275). Here we attempt to depict them in relation to violent social structures but also as agents of change in this process.

In these case studies we have emphasised how indigenous women and families are responding to structural inequalities and what their role in the process and delivery of healthcare is. Gender inequality is a very real determinant of health, but it does not reduce women to victims of an unequal structure. They are actively involved in reshaping the process of healthcare in the ways that we have described above: returning to traditional healthcare providers that are culturally and socially safer and do not require access permission from a gatekeeper; resisting certain forms of treatment and in some cases refusing care; and seeking indirect means of advocating for their rights. Here we propose that post-critical anthropology is needed to document the role of agency and resistance while specifically pointing to ongoing relationships of domination and control and critiquing the coloniality of care and unequal social structures. We argue that this must be conceptualised as co-production of critical knowledge that is the result of agency and resistance: a post-critical anthropology.

Conclusions: The co-production of anti-colonial knowledge

These case studies demonstrate some of the outstanding theoretical contributions of indigenous communities to CMA, specifically exploring the anti-colonial perspective that sets Latin American critical theory apart from its northern counterparts, and emphasising the role of indigenous agency in collaborative research to define this as a process of knowledge co-production. Drawing on examples of collaborations around maternal and infant health, we have demonstrated the multidisciplinary processes through which public health, long-term ethnography, medical anthropology and community organisations intersect to improve maternal health, from an anti-colonial positionality.

In their ethnography of maternal mortality, Freyermuth Enciso and Argüello Avendaño (2010) demonstrate how the intersection of gender and racial inequality leading to maternal mortality is a form of structural violence, essentially state-sanctioned neglect that had become 'naturalised' through substandard care and poor registration. These positions evidence work such as that of Wolfe, who argues that the state neglect of indigenous communities is part of the 'logic of elimination' (Wolfe 1999): neglecting to care for health, and in particular the maternal health of indigenous women, would lead to their eventual ethnic assimilation or elimination. We have proposed that indigenous communities have resisted this 'logic of elimination' through both activism and anti-colonial critique, resistance and demands. Yet this critical theory, emerging from the voices and experiences of indigenous Latin Americans, for whom colonialism has not ended, remains obscured by the language of anthropologists. Speaking to this epistemic bias, Santos (2014: 7) notes how although he has 'been deeply involved in the struggles of the indigenous people of

Latin America, I am unable to determine to what extent my thoughts are part of a collective without a name, and without clear outlines'. Calling himself an 'intellectual-activist', the author acknowledges the impossibility of collective authorship that recognises the intellectual contributions of indigenous peoples. Indigenous agency in research has been and continues to be important in the co-production of a critical anti-colonial position in medical anthropology, although indigenous knowledge has only very rarely been considered as theoretical work. As De Sousa Santos (2014) notes, it has been a long-standing premise that since indigenous people cannot speak for themselves, we must speak for them.

With the concept of a post-critical medical anthropology, we suggest the need to move beyond straightforward critical paradigms. This position resonates with branches of anthropology such as activist and public anthropology (see for example Choudry 2015; Davis and Craven 2016; Hedican 2016), while taking as a starting point the conceptualisation of health as a collective and social phenomenon. The shared history of many Latin American indigenous groups is also one of activism (Quijano 2000), through their 'dynamic agency' (Langdon and Garnelo 2017), yet its contribution to social theory has long been overlooked.

We argue that the developments that have emerged from extended collaborations have come to constitute a form of *knowledge co-production*, linking activism, academic research and indigenous participation in their own health and wellbeing to a decolonial and critical standpoint (Leyva et al. 2015; Mora 2011; Leyva and Speed 2008).

It is our position that academic activism around indigenous health both feeds and is fed by its context, essentially contributing to critical theoretical concepts and constructs that speak as widely to biomedicine as they do to indigeneity, and embrace rather than reject activism as a generator of theory. Because of the common definition of theory as a form of academic production that is the preserve of the Global North and must adhere to rigorous academic formulae (Connell 2015), knowledge that challenges this status quo has been excluded. A very significant portion of feminist and critical theory has been generated through activist knowledge, although this knowledge has been relegated within the global hierarchies of theoretical production (Connell 2015; Conway 2017). In spite of the devaluation of knowledge arising from activism, this has been a method of southern academic production – particularly in Latin America – that is closely attuned to people's lives, and enables the depth of understanding that comes with long-term ethnographic work that is enriched by the insider perspective and is reciprocal, embedding social justice in the methods of research.

Breilh, Menéndez, Langdon and Diehl all point to the role of collaboration with activists in the development of their critical research (Spiegel, Breilh and Yassi 2015; Langdon and Diehl, this volume; Menéndez 2009). It has also been the case that public health and medical programmes have worked closely alongside anthropologists to develop culturally appropriate programmes, with the work of Aguirre Beltrán (1992), Fajardo Santana (2007) and Paredes Solís et al. (2018) standing out for their practice-based ethnographies of health within indigenous communities. These lessons from the field have opened up new theoretical terrains to examine the nature and structure of healthcare systems and, importantly, the coloniality of biomedical structures of care. A post-critical medical anthropology would open new fields of critical inquiry and draw on activism to embed within theory solutions to the contemporary challenges of globalisation.

Notes

1. Mestizo, in its original usage, essentially defined an inter-racial category that was neither white nor indigenous (Fisher and O'Hara 2009: 4). In present-day usage mestizos are the dominant group and the term defines cultural as opposed to racial differentiation. In Mexico vital registration systems only use indigenous and non-indigenous categories, with no racial subdivisions within either group.
2. Such projects were not confined to work with indigenous people, and concepts such as obstetric violence – see Sesia in this volume – were also a product of social justice work around reproductive health within medical anthropology.
3. This was a Wellcome Trust-funded project, 'Structural vulnerability and maternal health among Mexican indigenous populations'.

References

Aguirre Beltrán, Gonzalo. 1992. *Medicina y magia: El proceso de la aculturación en la estructura colonial*. Mexico City: Fondo de Cultura Económica.

Berrio Palomo, Lina. 2017a. 'Una década de intervenciones gubernamentales y desde la sociedad civil en torno a la salud materna en Guerrero'. In *Salud y mortalidad materna en México: Balances y perspectivas desde la antropología y la interdisciplinariedad*, edited by Graciela Freyermuth Enciso, 168–201. Mexico City: Centro de Investigaciones y Estudios Superiores en Antropología Social.

Berrio Palomo, Lina Rosa. 2017b. 'Redes familiares y el lugar de los varones en el cuidado de la salud materna entre mujeres indígenas mexicanas', *Salud Colectiva* 13 (3): 471–87.

Biehl, João and Amy Moran-Thomas. 2009. 'Symptom: Subjectivities, Social Ills, Technologies', *Annual Review of Anthropology* 38: 267–88.

Bonfil Batalla, Guillermo. 1966. 'Conservative Thought in Applied Anthropology: A Critique', *Human Organization* 25 (2): 89–92.

Bonfil Batalla, Guillermo. 1983. 'Del indigenismo de la revolución a la antropología crítica'. In *La quiebra política de la antropología social en México*, edited by Andrés Medina and Carlos García Mora, 209–42. Mexico City: Universidad Nacional Autónoma de México.

Breilh, Jaime. 2008. 'Latin American Critical ("Social") Epidemiology: New Settings for an Old Dream', *International Journal of Epidemiology* 37 (4): 745–50.

Briggs, Charles L. 2005. 'Perspectivas críticas de salud y hegemonía comunicativa: Apuerturas progresistas, enlaces letales', *Revista de Antropología Social* 14: 101–24.

Campos, Roberto, ed. 1992a. *La antropología médica en México, Tomo 1*. Mexico City: Universidad Autónoma Metropolitana.

Campos, Roberto, ed. 1992b. *La antropología médica en México, Tomo 2*. Mexico City: Universidad Autónoma Metropolitana.

Castro, Arachu and Merrill Singer, eds. 2004. *Unhealthy Health Policy: A Critical Anthropological Examination*. Walnut Creek, CA: AltaMira Press.

CDI (Comisión Nacional para el Desarrollo de los Pueblos Indígenas). 2015. *Indicadores socioeconómicos de los pueblos indígenas de México, 2015*. Mexico City: Comisión Nacional para el Desarrollo de los Pueblos Indígenas. Accessed 23 September 2019. https://www.gob.mx/cms/uploads/attachment/file/239921/01-presentacion-indicadores-socioeconomicos-2015.pdf.

Choudry, Aziz. 2015. *Learning Activism: The Intellectual Life of Contemporary Social Movements*. Toronto: University of Toronto Press.

Colombara, Danny V., Bernardo Hernández, Alexandra Schaefer, Nicholas Zyznieuski, Miranda F. Bryant, Sima S. Desai, Marielle C. Gagnier, Casey K. Johanns, Claire R. McNellan, Erin B. Palmisano, Diego Ríos-Zertuche, Paola Zúñiga-Brenes, Emma Iriarte and Ali H. Mokdad. 2016. 'Institutional Delivery and Satisfaction among Indigenous and Poor Women In Guatemala, Mexico, and Panama', *PLoS ONE* 11 (4), Article e0154388: 1–17. Accessed 18 September 2019. https://doi.org/10.1371/journal.pone.0154388.

Connell, Raewyn. 2015. 'Meeting at the Edge of Fear: Theory on a World Scale', *Feminist Theory* 16 (1): 49–66.

Conway, Janet M. 2017. 'Troubling Transnational Feminism(s): Theorising Activist Praxis', *Feminist Theory* 18 (2): 205–27.

Cosminsky, Sheila. 2012. 'Birth and Blame: Guatemalan Midwives and Reproductive Risk'. In *Risk, Reproduction, and Narratives of Experience*, edited by Lauren Fordyce and Amínata Maraesa, 81–101. Nashville: Vanderbilt University Press.

Davis, Dána-Ain and Christa Craven. 2016. *Feminist Ethnography: Thinking through Methodologies, Challenges, and Possibilities*. Lanham, MD: Rowman and Littlefield.

Davis-Floyd, Robbie and Melissa Cheyney. 2009. 'Birth and the Big Bad Wolf: An Evolutionary Perspective'. In *Childbirth across Cultures: Ideas and Practices of Pregnancy, Childbirth and the Postpartum*, edited by Helaine Selin and Pamela K. Stone, 1–22. Dordrecht: Springer.

De Moura Pontes, Ana Lúcia. 2012. 'Entrevista: Eduardo Luis Menéndez Spina', *Trabalho, Educação e Saúde* 10 (2): 335–45.

Fajardo Santana, Horacia. 2007. *Comer y dar de comer a los dioses: Terapéuticas en encuentro, conocimiento, proyectos y nutrición en la Sierra Huichola*. Lagos de Moreno: Universidad de Guadalajara.

Farmer, Paul E., Bruce Nizeye, Sara Stulac and Salmaan Keshavjee. 2006. 'Structural Violence and Clinical Medicine', *PLoS Medicine* 3 (10), Article e449: 1686–91.

Finkler, K. 1992. 'El cuidado de la salud: Un problema de relaciones de poder'. In *La antropología médica en México*, edited by Roberto Campos, 202–24. Mexico City: Universidad Autónoma Metropolitana.

Fisher, Andrew B and O'Hara, Matthew. 2009. *Imperial Subjects. Race and Identity in Colonial Latin America*. Durham, NC: Duke University Press.

Flores, Javier. 1991. 'Voz de los antiguos: Medicina indígena y conocimiento universal', *México Indígena* 18: 21–22.

Freyermuth Enciso, Graciela. 2003. *Las mujeres de humo: Morir en Chenalhó: Género, etnia y generación, factores constitutivos del riesgo durante la maternidad*. Mexico City: Centro de Investigaciones y Estudios Superiores en Antropología Social.

Freyermuth Enciso, Graciela, ed. 2017. *Salud y mortalidad materna en México: Balances y perspectivas desde la antropología y la interdisciplinariedad*. Mexico City: Centro de Investigaciones y Estudios Superiores en Antropología Social.

Freyermuth Enciso, Graciela, ed. 2018. *Los caminos para parir en México en el siglo XXI: Experiencias de investigación, vinculación, formación y comunicación*. Mexico City: Centro de Investigaciones y Estudios Superiores en Antropología Social.

Freyermuth, Graciela. 2019. Calculation of maternal mortality rates based on data for 2017 from SINAC (Subsistema de Información sobre Nacimientos) and INEGI (Instituto Nacional de Estadística y Geografía), Mexico. Unpublished.

Freyermuth Enciso, Graciela and Hilda E. Argüello Avendaño. 2010. 'La muerte prematura de mujeres en Los Altos de Chiapas: Un análisis desde la violencia', *Revista Pueblos y Fronteras Digital* 6 (10): 181–216.

Gamlin, Jennie B. 2013. 'Shame as a Barrier to Health Seeking among Indigenous Huichol Migrant Labourers: An Interpretative Approach of the "Violence Continuum" and "Authoritative Knowledge"', *Social Science and Medicine* 97: 75–81.

Gamlin, Jennie B. and Sarah J. Hawkes. 2015. 'Pregnancy and Birth in an Indigenous Huichol Community: From Structural Violence to Structural Policy Responses', *Culture, Health and Sexuality* 17 (1): 78–91.

Gamlin, Jennie and Seth Holmes. 2018. 'Preventable Perinatal Deaths in Indigenous Wixárika Communities: An Ethnographic Study of Pregnancy, Childbirth and Structural Violence', *BMC Pregnancy and Childbirth* 18, Article 243, 1–10. Accessed 18 September 2019. https://doi.org/10.1186/s12884-018-1870-6.

Gamlin, Jennie and David Osrin. 2018. 'Preventable Infant Deaths, Lone Births and Lack of Registration in Mexican Indigenous Communities: Health Care Services and the Afterlife of Colonialism', *Ethnicity and Health*: 1–15. Accessed 18 September 2019. https://doi.org/10.1080/1 3557858.2018.1481496.

García Pérez, Guillermo. 2017. 'Contrapedogías de la crueldad', *La Tempestad*, 120. Accessed 20 September 2019. https://www.latempestad.mx/rita-segato/.

Hedican, Edward J. 2016. *Public Anthropology: Engaging Social Issues in the Modern World*. Toronto: University of Toronto Press.

Juárez Ramírez, Clara, Felipe José Hevia de la Jara, Ana Eugenia López Ricoy and Laura Georgina Freyermuth Joffre, eds. 2017. *Entre el activismo y la intervención: El trabajo de organizaciones de la sociedad civil y su incidencia para la salud de las mujeres indígenas en México*. Mexico City: Alternativas y Capacidades.

Lamphere, Louise. 2018. 'The Transformation of Ethnography: From Malinowski's Tent to the Practice of Collaborative/Activist Anthropology', *Human Organization* 77 (1): 64–76.

Langdon, Esther Jean. 2016. *Políticas públicas: Reflexões antropológicas*. Florianópolis: Editora da Universidade Federal de Santa Catarina.

Langdon, Esther Jean and Luiza Garnelo. 2017. 'Articulación entre servicios de salud y "medicina indígena": Reflexiones antropológicas sobre política y realidad en Brasil', *Salud Colectiva* 13 (3): 457–70.

Laurell, Asa Cristina. 1982. 'La salud-enfermedad como proceso social', *Cuadernos Médico Sociales* 19: 1–11.

Laurell, Asa Cristina. 1989. 'Social Analysis of Collective Health in Latin America', *Social Science and Medicine* 28 (11): 1183–91.

Leyva, Xochitl, Araceli Burguete and Shannon Speed, eds. 2008. *Gobernar (en) la diversidad: Experiencias indígenas desde América Latina: Hacia la investigación de co-labor*. Mexico City: Centro de Investigaciones y Estudios Superiores en Antropología Social.

Leyva Solano, Xochitl, Camila Pascal, Axel Köhler, Hermenegildo Olguín Reza and María del Refugio Velasco Contreras, eds. 2015. *Prácticas otras de conocimiento(s): Entre crisis, entre guerras*. Mexico City: Cooperativa Editorial Retos.

Lugones, María. 2008. 'Colonialidad y género: Hacia un feminismo descolonial'. In *Género y descolonialidad*, edited by Walter Mignolo, 13–54. Bueno Aires: Ediciones del Signo.

Menéndez, Eduardo L. 1984. 'Estructura y relaciones de clase y la función de los modelos médicos: Apuntes para una antropologia medica critica', *Nueva Antropología* 6 (23): 71–102.

Menéndez, Eduardo. 1992. 'Modelo hegemónico, modelo alternativo subordinado, modelo de auto atención: Caracteres estructurales'. In *La antropología médica en México*, edited by Roberto Campos, 1: 97–114. Mexico City: Instituto Mora, Universidad Autónoma Metropolitana.

Menéndez, Eduardo. 1994. 'La enfermedad y la curación: ¿Qué es medicina tradicional?', *Alteridades* 4 (7): 71–83.

Menéndez, Eduardo L. 2003. 'Modelos de atención de los padecimientos: De exclusiones teóricas y articulaciones prácticas', *Ciência e Saúde Coletiva* 8 (1): 185–207.

Menéndez, Eduardo L. 2009. *De sujetos, saberes y estructuras: Introducción al enfoque relacional en el estudio de la salud colectiva*. Buenos Aires: Lugar Editorial.

Menéndez, Eduardo L. 2012. 'Sustancias consideradas adictivas: Prohibición, reducción de daños y reducción de riesgos', *Salud Colectiva* 8 (1): 9–24.

Menéndez, Eduardo Luiz. 2016. 'Intercultural Health: Proposals, Actions and Failures', *Ciência e Saúde Coletiva* 21 (1): 109–18.

Menéndez, Eduardo L. 2018. 'Antropología médica en América Latina 1990–2015: Una revisión estrictamente provisional', *Salud Colectiva* 14 (3): 461–81.

Merlan, Francesca. 2007. 'Indigeneity as Relational Identity: The Construction of Australian Land Rights'. In *Indigenous Experience Today*, edited by Marisol de la Cadena and Orin Starn, 125–49. Oxford: Berg.

Mies, Maria. 1989. *Patriarchy and Accumulation on a World Scale: Women in the International Division of Labour*. London: Zed Books.

Mignolo, Walter. 2008. 'Introducción: ¿Cuáles son los temas de género y (des)colonialidad?'. In *Género y descolonialidad*, edited by Walter Mignolo, 7–12. Bueno Aires: Ediciones del Signo.

Mora Bayo, Mariana. 2011. 'Producción de conocimientos en el terreno de la autonomía: La investigación como tema de debate político'. In *Luchas "muy otras": Zapatismo y autonomía en las comunidades indígenas de Chiapas*, edited by Bruno Baronnet, Mariana Mora Bayo and Richard Stahler-Sholk, 79–110. Mexico City: Universidad Autónoma Metropolitana.

Morgensen, Scott Lauria. 2011. 'The Biopolitics of Settler Colonialism: Right Here, Right Now', *Settler Colonial Studies* 1 (1): 52–76.

Morgensen, Scott Lauria. 2014. 'Indigenous Transnationalism and the AIDS Pandemic: Challenging Settler Colonialism within Global Health Governance'. In *Theorizing Native Studies*, edited by Audra Simpson and Andrea Smith, 188–206. Durham, NC: Duke University Press.

Nelson, Geoffrey and Isaac Prilleltensky, eds. 2010. *Community Psychology: In Pursuit of Liberation and Well-Being*. 2nd ed. Basingstoke: Palgrave Macmillan.

Neurath, Johannes. 2002. *Las fiestas de la casa grande: Procesos rituales, cosmovisión y estructura social en una comunidad huichola*. Mexico City: Instituto Nacional de Antropología e Historia.

Ortega Canto, Judith Elena. 2010. *Género, generaciones y transacciones: Reproducción y sexualidad en Mayas de Yucatán*. Zamora: Colegio de Michoacán.

Osmo, Alan and Lilia Blima Schraiber. 2015. 'The Field of Collective Health: Definitions and Debates on Its Constitution', *Saúde e Sociedade* 24 (Supplement 1): 201–14.

Paradies, Yin. 2016. 'Colonisation, Racism and Indigenous Health', *Journal of Population Research* 33 (1): 83–96.

Paredes Solís, Sergio, Abraham de Jesús Gracía, Geovani Valtierra Gil, David Gasga Salinas and José Legorreta Soberanis. 2018. 'Percepción de los cambios producidos por la enseñanza de parteras tradicionales experimentadas de Xochistlahuaca, Guerrero'. In *Los caminos para parir en México en el siglo XXI: Experiencias de investigación, vinculación, formación y comunicación*, edited by Graciela Freyermuth Enciso, 194–203. Mexico City: Centro de Investigaciones y Estudios Superiores en Antropología Social.

Pérez Tamayo, Ruy. 1991. 'La medicina alopática y las otras medicinas', *México Indígena* 18: 202–51.

PNUD (Programa de las Naciones Unidas para el Desarrollo). 2010. *Informe sobre el desarrollo humano de los pueblos indígenas en México: El reto de la desigualdad de oportunidades*. Mexico City: Programa de las Naciones Unidas para el Desarrollo. Accessed 23 September 2019. http://hdr.undp.org/sites/default/files/mexico_nhdr_2010.pdf.

Quijano, Aníbal. 2000. 'Coloniality of Power and Eurocentrism in Latin America', *International Sociology* 15 (2): 215–32.

Santos, Boaventura de Sousa. 2014. *Epistemologies of the South: Justice against Epistemicide*. Boulder, CO: Paradigm Publishers.

Sesia, Paola. 2017. 'Quince años de investigaciones en la prevencion y la reduccion de la muerte materna en Oaxaca: Perspectivas y aportes cualicuuantitativos desde la antropología y la salud pública'. In *Salud y mortalidad materna en México: Balances y perspectivas desde la antropología y la interdisciplinariedad*, edited by Graciela Freyermuth Enciso, 168–201. Mexico City: Centro de Investigaciones y Estudios Superiores en Antropología Social.

Smith-Oka, Vania. 2009. 'Unintended Consequences: Exploring the Tensions between Development Programs and Indigenous Women in Mexico in the Context of Reproductive Health', *Social Science and Medicine* 68 (11): 2069–77.

Smith-Oka, Vania. 2012. 'Bodies of Risk: Constructing Motherhood in a Mexican Public Hospital', *Social Science and Medicine* 75 (12): 2275–82.

Spiegel, Jerry M. and Jaime Breilh. 2017. 'Advancing Health Equity in Healthy Cities: Framing Matters', *Journal of Public Health Policy* 38 (2): 234–39.

Spiegel, Jerry M., Jaime Breilh and Annalee Yassi. 2015. 'Why Language Matters: Insights and Challenges in Applying a Social Determination of Health Approach in a North–South Collaborative Research Program', *Globalization and Health* 11, Article 9: 1–17. Accessed 20 September 2019. https://doi.org/10.1186/s12992-015-0091-2.

Stephens, Carolyn, John Porter, Clive Nettleton and Ruth Willis. 2006. 'Disappearing, Displaced, and Undervalued: A Call to Action for Indigenous Health Worldwide', *The Lancet* 367 (9527): 219–28.

Stone, Pamela K. 2016. 'Biocultural Perspectives on Maternal Mortality and Obstetrical Death from the Past to the Present', *American Journal of Physical Anthropology* 159 (Supplement 61): 150–71.

Suárez, Julia and Carmen Herrera. 2013. *Atención de la salud y de la salud reproductiva de las mujeres indígenas en México*. Mexico City: Abogadas y abogados por la Justicia y los derechos humanos.

The Lancet. 2016. *Maternal Health 2016*. Series of six papers published in vol. 388. Accessed 1 November 2019. https://www.thelancet.com/series/maternal-health–2016.

Tuhiwai Smith, Linda. 1999. *Decolonizing Methodologies: Research and Indigenous People*. London: Zed Books.

UNFPA (United Nations Population Fund). 2012. 'The Social Determinants of Maternal Death and Disability'. Accessed 20 September 2019. https://www.unfpa.org/resources/social-determinants-maternal-death-and-disability.

Valeggia, Claudia R. and J. Josh Snodgrass. 2015. 'Health of Indigenous Peoples', *Annual Review of Anthropology* 44: 117–35.

Vega, Rosalynn Adeline. 2017. 'Commodifying Indigeneity: How the Humanization of Birth Reinforces Racialized Inequality in Mexico', *Medical Anthropology Quarterly* 31 (4): 499–518.

Vickery, Joan, Shannon Faulkhead, Karen Adams and Angela Clarke. 2007. 'Indigenous Insights into Oral History, Social Determinants and Decolonisation'. In *Beyond Bandaids: Exploring the Underlying Social Determinants of Aboriginal Health*, edited by Ian Anderson, Fran Baum and Michael Bentley, 19–36. Casuarina, NT: Cooperative Research Centre for Aboriginal Health.

Waitzkin, Howard, Celia Iriart, Alfredo Estrada and Silvia Lamadrid. 2001. 'Social Medicine in Latin America: Productivity and Dangers Facing the Major National Groups', *The Lancet* 358 (9278): 315–23.

WHO (World Health Organization). 2015. 'WHO Recommendation on Partnership with Traditional Birth Attendants (TBAs)', World Health Organization, 31 May. Accessed 20 September 2019. https://extranet.who.int/rhl/topics/improving-health-system-performance/who-recommendation-partnership-traditional-birth-attendants-tbas.

WHO (World Health Organization). 2018. 'Universal Health Coverage: Launch of Pilot Programmes in Kenya', World Health Organization, 13 December. Accessed 20 September 2019. https://www.who.int/universal_health_coverage/en/.

Wolfe, Patrick. 1999. *Settler Colonialism and the Transformation of Anthropology: The Politics and Poetics of an Ethnographic Event*. London: Cassell.

Zolla, Carlos, S. del Bosque, V. Mellado, A. Tascón and C. Maqueo. 1992. 'Medicina tradicional y enfermedad'. In *La antropología médica en México*, edited by Roberto Campos, 2: 71–104. Mexico City: Instituto Mora, Universidad Autónoma Metropolitana.

3

Susto, the anthropology of fear and critical medical anthropology in Mexico and Peru

Frida Jacobo Herrera and David Orr

Susto, usually glossed as 'fright sickness' or 'soul loss,' has been much studied from a variety of theoretical perspectives in Mexico, Mesoamerica and the Andean region. It occurs when a person experiences a fright, causing their soul to start out of the body. The soul's absence leads to a range of symptoms, which may appear immediately or gradually over time. These commonly include, but are not limited to, tiredness, disturbed sleep, loss of appetite, diarrhoea, bodily aches, sadness and weakness. *Susto* is strongly associated with infants, whose souls are not yet securely attached and who startle easily, but adults are also affected by it, often severely. The volume of research carried out into *susto* attests to its prevalence and importance in the lives of indigenous, and often non-indigenous, populations in Latin America. This goes well beyond strictly anthropological interest, with *susto* included as one of nine 'cultural concepts of distress' within an appendix to the American Psychiatric Association's *Diagnostic and Statistical Manual of Mental Disorders, 5th Edition*, or DSM-5 (APA 2013).

Susto is only one of a range of illnesses associated with experiences of intense emotion that are found across most of Latin America (Cartwright 2007; Tapias 2015).[1] These reflect how health and emotions are envisaged as inextricably linked in prevailing concepts of the person. Accounting adequately for the emotional dimensions of experience presents a potential challenge for critical medical anthropology. One criticism often heard is that critical medical anthropology's relentless focus on socio-economic forces risks reducing individual lives to ciphers that do little more than play out familiar narratives of oppression, leaving no space for agency or local interpretations (the cultural syndromes) of illness. The ethical imperative to call attention to structural violence can sometimes lead to the assumption that the experience of – and by implication, solution to – suffering is the same everywhere (Robbins 2013); this view is particularly contested in the field of illnesses with emotional, mental and/or spiritual components (Calabrese 2008; Kirmayer 2012), such as *susto*, where cultural influences on the conceptualisation of the person are closely implicated. As a blanket characterisation of critical medical anthropology this is undeniably a caricature, for many works within the school succeed in combining incisive structural analysis with careful accounts of cultural frameworks of meaning and individual agency. Yet despite these worthy exceptions, there are many examples of scholarly treatments of *susto* that seek *either* to unmask the structural violence lying behind it *or* to take seriously local understandings of the condition. Negotiating this dichotomy is a perennial challenge for critical medical anthropology (Hannig 2017: 5–7).

Maria Tapias' (2015) exploration of *arrebato* (the transfer of a mother's unexpressed feelings of rage to her child through breast milk) in Punata, Bolivia, offers an instructive example of how structural analysis and thick description (Fassin 2012: 245) of emotion illnesses can be reconciled. Following lines of argument that have been well established in critical medical anthropology, she shows how diagnoses such as *arrebato* may serve to cast blame on individual women for their illnesses and those of their children, by attributing them to their inability to control their emotions and thereby contain the negative effects they have on health. Rage is seen as unfeminine and, above all unmaternal, and succumbing to it therefore represents a failure of role and of responsibility. *Arrebato* thus acts to direct responsibility towards individual failings and away from the structural (and in many cases, literal) violence with which these women live and which causes the anger they may feel but are discouraged from expressing. From a schematically critical perspective, therefore, local interpretations of emotion illnesses such as *arrebato* might seem straightforwardly oppressive, and the priority becomes to expose and discredit them. Yet Tapias' fine-grained description of lived experience also shows that 'illness talk' is too multifaceted to stop at this point; diagnoses may be doubted and contested, particularly where illnesses are ongoing or complex to resolve, as is often the case with emotion illnesses, but equally their implications may be questioned. Women are sometimes able to marshal arguments that their anger, and therefore illness, is a justified response to abusive partners or economic exploitation, and even thereby to attract support. *Arrebato* may therefore act to draw attention to, and allow individual women to contest, gendered inequalities, rather than inevitably obscuring them as a more schematic critical reading might suggest. By taking seriously the complexity of situated interpretation rather than rushing to critique and unmask cultural syndromes, Tapias produces a far more meaningful analysis. Emotions are produced within a social context, shaped along lines of culture, gender and society, and interpret interpersonal and social realities through their effects on health. Far from being tangential, a focus on emotions alongside a critical medical anthropology perspective is therefore central to a holistic understanding of health and wellbeing in these contexts.

We have therefore turned to the anthropology of emotions to provide new perspectives on *susto*. We first review the literature on *susto*, showing the different ways in which the condition has been explained, often in terms of something else fundamental – be that biomedical health conditions, psychology or 'society' – lying beneath it. Limited attention has been paid to the 'fear' or 'fright' that is central to the diagnosis, causal attributions and treatments. It is difficult to generalise about the precise relationship between fear and *susto*, because both may vary according to context: like other emotions, fear reflects individual experience, but from the perspective of the anthropology of emotions it is also a lens through which to view societies and cultures. The fears people develop and are exposed to are partly shaped by the gendered, ethnic- or class-based positions they occupy in the social structure, while the cultural environment establishes norms and defines the meaning of behaviours and emotional expression. The notion of 'emotional communities' (Rosenwein 2002) expresses how distinctive forms of social life produce distinctive emotional repertoires and triggers. Ethnographic data relating to cases of *susto*, drawn from fieldwork experiences in Cuetzalan, Mexico (Jacobo Herrera 2016), and Paucartambo, Peru (Orr 2012), are then used to demonstrate how the focus on fear offers critical insight into the vulnerabilities experienced by particular groups within society.

Susto and affect

Susto is widespread across Latin America, though its symptoms may vary widely within and between regions (Carey 1993; Greenway 1998; O'Nell and Selby 1968: 96; Trotter 1982; Valdivia Ponce 1975: 80–6). Many scholars have attempted to 'translate' *susto* into terms recognised by biomedical or 'Western' psychological knowledge categories. Critical biocultural anthropologists noted the structural conditions of deprivation in which the most affected populations lived and suggested that the 'real' causes of *susto* could be found in physical causation pathways, e.g. hypoglycaemia (Bolton 1981) or internal parasites (Signorini 1982). From a psychological perspective, *susto* has been linked to loss/ grief reaction (Houghton and Boersma 1988), post-traumatic syndrome (Bourbonnais-Spear et al. 2007), or stress and depression (Weller et al. 2008); these studies highlight the importance of the emotional dimension, but apply an analytical grid deriving from Euro-American clinical practice rather than sociocultural engagement with the affective worlds of the populations concerned. Meanwhile, literature that focused on social roles and the stresses they produced saw the diagnosis of *susto* as primarily a way of reinforcing internal community norms rather than an ethnomedical response to distinctive illness or distress (Aramoni 1990; Greenway 1998; O'Nell and Selby 1968; O'Nell 1975; Rubel et al. 1984).

Critical medical anthropologists built on the role-stress analysis to ask who gets *susto*. O'Nell and Selby (1968) argued that *susto*'s greater frequency among females than males reflected the more restrictive gender roles that women experienced in Zapotec communities. Crandon (1983) suggested that in the Bolivian highland town of Kachin, ethnic status determined a diagnosis of *susto*. This was the negotiated product both of strategic identity claims by sufferers and their families, allowing them more readily to mobilise resources and support from the social grouping to which they purported to belong, and of ascription by others. *Susto* was seen as an 'Indian' disease, but was commonly experienced by mestizos who, because of the distinct downward social trajectory they were undergoing at the time, had become more liable to this diagnosis. Mysyk (1998), in a critical review of the *susto* literature, built on this analysis to argue that *susto* was primarily an 'illness of the poor' – not just those identified as indigenous, but labourers and peasants who are downwardly mobile or entrenched in poverty. Re-examining earlier evidence that suggested no clear link between *susto* and socio-economic status (SES), her reading argued that the prevalence of and susceptibility to *susto*, like many illnesses, is determined by class and therefore indexes the inequalities in opportunities for health and wellbeing produced by contemporary societies in which it is found. The role played by SES is debated, with others finding no significant differences in occurrence by income or educational level within the communities they studied (Weller et al. 2008). Yet for all these advances in knowledge, there has been limited focus on the phenomenology of the triggering fear, what it was like to be *asustado* ('frightened'), and how the fears that contribute to *susto* are culturally and socially shaped within communities. Perhaps because of the urge to 'explain' *susto* in biomedically recognisable terms or through social-role stress, or perhaps because of an assumption that the 'fright' owes more to physiological startle reflex than to culturally elaborated fears subject to interpretive analysis, relatively few studies have engaged with the anthropology of emotions and its implications for how fear is experienced. Among the exceptions, Green's ethnographic study of fear amidst political violence in Guatemala is particularly evocative. Killings, disappearances, witnessed violence and constant threat made fear so palpable and ubiquitous that Green was driven to reassess anthropological approaches to *susto*, asking:

> might we take them at their word, that they are *asustado* (frightened) and that *el espíritu se fue* (the spirit/soul has left the body)? I suggest that this is an accurate, literal description of what has happened to them.
>
> (Green 1994: 248)

Tapias' (2015) exploration of folk illnesses among women in Punata, Bolivia, similarly charts how social conditions produce emotional responses that become embodied in illness. Focusing on the role of anger rather than fear, she traces the connections between local understandings of emotions and the 'social suffering' resulting from the frustrations of a neoliberal economy, gender inequalities and the indirect effects of the US-led 'war on drugs'. Both ethnographies point to the need to leaven analyses of structural inequalities or social-role norms with carefully observed attention to the lived emotions that, for those who find themselves suffering from *susto*, are at its heart.

There is a long tradition of such anthropological engagement with the emotions to draw from, dating back to the 1970s when the discipline 'became interested in understanding emotional life not only as a private matter but as a relational and cultural phenomenon' (Calderón 2012: 15). Key authors advanced the view that culture concerns not only what we think but also what we feel (Geertz 1973; Rosaldo 1984; Lutz and White 1986), or, as Geertz put it, 'Not only ideas but emotions too are cultural artefacts' (1973: 81), and therefore amenable to anthropological study. From an early focus on disembodied emotion concepts, the anthropology of emotions has moved towards an approach centred on 'thinking-feeling' as it arose in specific episodes that could be contextualised within individual and group experience (Wikan 1987). The close enmeshment of culture in the formation of emotion and subjectivity, and consequent need for caution in translation of emotion discourse across societies, is today widely accepted within the discipline (Beatty 2013). While it is challenging to measure emotions or analyse them confidently, they are relevant to the social sciences as an essential part of social being.

Nevertheless, anthropology has engaged much less with the emotion of fear than it has with love, anger or shame. Curiously, historians have been more active in studying fear and the ways it has changed (Bourke 2005). Historians of emotions have traced how key shifts in societal fears, such as natural phenomena, divine punishments, wars, illnesses and various 'others', have been influenced by the social, cultural and historical context of the time, and hence how 'fear' may be universal but its content and import vary significantly (Bourke 2005; Delumeau 1989, 2002; Gonzalbo 2008; Gonzalbo, Staples and Torres 2009) between emotional communities. Christine Tappolet makes this point in considering how different cultures may identify or foreground differently nuanced variations on the common theme of fear, such as the subtle distinctions drawn in English between 'anxiety, anguish, apprehension, worry, phobia, fright, terror, panic' or the distinctive notion of *megatu* among the Ifaluk, an emotion akin to fear but which has a positive valence (Tappolet 2010: 328); she goes on to claim that the objects that form the basis of fears may also give rise to substantive variations in the nature of fear in a specific historic-cultural context.

A useful framing for the study of emotions in anthropology is the influential concept of 'emotional communities' (Rosenwein 2002, 2010). Conceived as 'largely the same as social communities', these allow researchers to

> uncover systems of feeling, to establish what these communities (and the individuals within them) define and assess as valuable or harmful to them (for it is about such things that people express emotions); the emotions that they value, devalue, or ignore; the nature of the affective bonds between people that they recognize; and the modes of emotional expression that they expect, encourage, tolerate and deplore.
>
> (Rosenwein 2010: 10)

This definition shows the value of the 'emotional communities' notion, not only in identifying the common concerns of a group but also in following the faultlines revealed within those groups by how differently positioned individuals manifest specific emotions and the responses they receive. Like illnesses, emotions are not uniformly distributed, and expectations of appropriate emotions vary distinctively between genders, age groups and other identity markers; they are therefore significant for the critical study of inequalities within those groups. To varying extents, individuals participate in, and move in and out of, these diverse emotional communities within their daily lives (Rosenwein 2002: 842). They shape episodes of fright or fear such as might give rise to *susto*.

These experiences encompass social/historical, individual biographical and physiological dimensions (Beatty 2013), and arise in relation to a physical and societal environment, which may include structural violence, poverty, discrimination and other factors that differentially impact on the fears of individuals. The following ethnographic examples from Cuetzalan and Paucartambo are drawn from two differing but complementary fieldwork experiences: the former relied primarily on interviews and observations alongside healers and focused on their accounts of *susto*, the latter on community-based fieldwork that engaged with healers, sufferers and their families in the communities to explore help-seeking, accounts of illness and care. The accounts are partial and we do not focus here on first-hand experiential reports of what it is like to have *susto*. Intended to afford insights into the imbrications between structure and *susto*, rather than aspiring to present accounts representative of 'whole communities', together they show that attention to *susto* and to fear can tell us much not only about the sociocultural production of these emotional experiences, but also about how communities may link conditions such as *susto* to 'social suffering' – and in particular gendered experiences of abuse and oppression – more often than is sometimes recognised.

Susto in Cuetzalan, Puebla, Mexico

The municipality of Cuetzalan is located in the Sierra Norte de Puebla region. Of its approximately 47,000 inhabitants, 29,261 are registered as speaking an indigenous language, most commonly Nahua (CONAPO 2006). Most are small peasant-farmers. The principal driver of Cuetzalan's economy is now tourism, boosted by the governmental *Pueblo Mágico* (Magical Towns) programme which promotes festivals, local crafts and archaeological and ecotourism sites. The town of Cuetzalan (population 5,957) has a hospital run by the *Secretaría de Salud* and other private and social security-funded clinics. Nahua medicine can be found in several settings: a 'Traditional Medicine' department within the hospital;[2] *Talkampa*, a hotel run by a group of *curanderos* who offer traditional treatments;[3] and advertisements displayed at the municipal offices for traditional healers and bonesetters.

The ethnographic data described below were gathered over 10 months of fieldwork studying emotion-related illnesses in 2010–11 and 2012. I (Jacobo Herrera) carried out ethnographic interviews and observations with six *curanderos*, who use Nahua knowledge and healing techniques.

In Cuetzalan, *susto*, or *nemoujtil* (in Nahuatl), is thought to result either from natural causes or from intentional malevolence by other people. For the Nahua, human beings possess an animating aspect, or soul, known as *tonalli*. This is the individual's vital force, the source of the energy necessary to realise one's daily labours. It regularly leaves the body during sleep and travels to unknown places, but may also leave following a strong emotional shock or fright. This is *susto*, and in such cases the person usually consults a *curandero* to undergo a healing process that brings the body back into balance and allows recovery from what fear has caused.

The historians Echevarría García and López Hérnandez (2013) discuss the history of *susto* in their work on fear in seventeenth-century Nahua culture. Considering the fears inspired by natural phenomena as well as those caused by immoral behaviours that violated social conventions, they explore how gender, age and status differences determined who was permitted to feel and express fear, and who was not. For example, men were expected to show a warrior's attitude, characterised by bravery in the face of the enemy. Women, associated more with the 'safe' places of the domestic hearth, were not,[4] save for those giving birth, midwives and the older women who took care of the bodies of women who had died in childbirth. In confronting the dangers of childbirth they took on a warrior's role (Echeverría and López 2013: 153). This historical work shows how fears – and by implication cases of *susto* – are linked to attitudes and values that designate distinctive expectations by gender and by age. The emotions were located according to the Nahua conceptualisation of the body, with the heart and liver the organs that allowed the person to respond to situations of danger that might trigger *susto* (Echeverría and López 2013: 153; López Austin 1980). Individual traits of bravery, cowardice or fearfulness were determined by the day on which the person was born, and therefore not generally subject to autonomous self-cultivation.

Today the Nahua of Sierra Norte de Puebla have two principal explanations for *susto* cases: one linked to the four elements, water, fire, wind and earth, and the entities associated with them; and one involving human beings and their peer relationships, occurring due to another person's hostility or envy. The latter type is perhaps more complex and requires the *curandero* to identify the incorrect behaviour that occasioned ill feeling. In both types emotions are an important factor permeating the condition.

I now present some examples of these different types of *susto*, narrated from the perspectives of two *curanderas*. These specialists offer their services in different settings, but both illustrate very well the cultural conceptions of this affliction. Maribel is a *curandera* who works in her home and in the traditional medicine department of the hospital. She speaks Spanish only with difficulty and so sometimes requires an interpreter with non-Nahua-speaking clients. The second *curandera*, Linda, works in the health division of the *Casa de la Mujer Indígena* (CAMI; House of the Indigenous Woman), a civil association established in 2003 to support women who have experienced domestic violence. CAMI responds to considerable need, with Nahua women triply disadvantaged by gender, class and ethnicity. Inheritance norms have traditionally marginalised women from smallholding ownership; patriarchal attitudes ran through both customary and state legal systems until recent legal reforms; and gender norms have long stigmatised victims of sexual violence (Martínez-Corona 2012; Terven Salinas 2017). The centre integrates different therapeutic traditions – Nahua (through Linda), allopathic and psychological – in a holistic approach to restoring patients' confidence, emotional health and physical wellbeing. Linda herself speaks Spanish as her first language; she understands but does not consult in Nahua. These two contexts show different facets of healing in Cuetzalan and identify variations in how the *curanderas* talked about *susto*. Linda's experience of working in the women's service changed her conception of the ways in which it is possible to become ill with *susto*, and she now considers the factors of violence and the difficult lives of indigenous women.

Summer is the rainy season in Cuetzalan, marked by torrential storms with considerable thunder and lightning. *Curanderos* frequently mentioned this natural phenomenon, as in this season they attend people who have *susto* occasioned by lightning. During my time with her, Maribel attended two such patients. One was a girl who was at home when 'lightning struck, frightened her and burnt the television'.[5] The other was a young man who was clearing the brush with a machete when a storm began. The metal machete attracted the lightning, which struck the man. He was unconscious until he was found and taken to hospital, where he was treated both by doctors and by Maribel.

For Maribel, *susto* caused by lightning is difficult to treat because it implicates multiple elements: water, air and earth. The 'spirit' of the frightened person leaves with the lightning (which is at once water and air) but the earth is also involved (as the place where the lightning strikes). It is therefore necessary to entreat all these elements. The healing procedure takes place in different stages.[6] First, a *limpia* (cleansing) is done in order to diagnose and determine what *llamadas espirituales* (soul callings)[7] will be needed. Once these have been done, Maribel travels in her dreams to the place where the soul is and there negotiates with the entities that inhabit it. These entities retain the person's soul, causing the *susto* sickness. The *curandero*'s role is to make offerings and entreat these entities, but also to take food – beans, tortilla and chilli – to the place where the person was frightened.

Linda, meanwhile, indicated that *susto* can be occasioned by a strong shock, by a feeling of fear or insecurity. Among the symptoms she recognises are headaches and lack of appetite. To cure it, she applies the following techniques: *paladeada*;[8] *limpia* with herbs and egg; *llamada*. The *llamada* is done at night and Linda warns her patients not to worry if they have nightmares. After carrying out a first *limpia* for diagnosis, that night she looks in her dreams for the place where the soul can be found, whether in earth, water, fire or air. In these dreams she also finds out whether or not she will be able to treat the person successfully. For Linda, women and children have the greatest propensity to suffer from *susto*. She explained that this is because women are commonly victims of abusive treatment and that this also affects their children, who are harmed by the domestic environment. Linda regularly receives women who take refuge at the CAMI because of domestic abuse, all of whom she treats for *susto*, and acknowledges that her work there has given her a different perspective on the unequal gender relations within her indigenous culture. She has integrated the perspectives she encountered on domestic violence in the training she received at the CAMI, and lists sessions on self-care, relaxation workshops and working to help develop women's self-esteem alongside the more traditional practices of preparing medicinal infusions, *limpias* and *llamadas* that are her core activities. Her efforts to recover the absent *tonalli* are an integral part of working to break down deeply ingrained fears springing from the frequent histories of abuse by fathers and partners with which her clientele present to the centre (Mejía Flores and Palacios Luna 2011).

These two accounts, in which the *curanderas* explained causes and treatments, show the relationship between daily practices and the risks of suffering *susto*. They further identify links with domestic and gender-based violence. In all cases, cultural perceptions of fear are present within the discussion of the four elements and the entities that inhabit them, and the daily mistreatments experienced by women. This points the way to an analysis of fear and its relationship with *susto*. Fear is an individual experience and in that sense subjective, but the explanation of suffering can be found through an emotional community that affords a socially mediated way of understanding it. Among the Nahua, it is related to relationships between humans and nature or with other humans, and with situations that escape the control of the person, violence being a key example. These dangers reflect the sociocultural norms of the populations concerned. Conflict between family members or neighbours, violence and related experiences generate life conditions that lead individuals to experience fear in their daily lives.

Susto in Paucartambo, Cusco, Peru

Paucartambo is a rural province of the Peruvian department of Cusco. The province's population was 45,877 in the 2007 national census (18.6 per cent urban, 82.4 per cent rural). In the highlands, men and younger women are bilingual between Spanish and the indigenous Quechua language, but many rural-dwelling older women speak Spanish tentatively or not at all. Until the 1969 agrarian reform, much of the land belonged to locally powerful mestizo *hacendados*, who allowed peasant families to farm it in return for produce and services. The reforms went some way to breaking up this dominance and today the local economy is characterised by agricultural smallholdings. Income is also generated through migration to Cusco city or the jungle for work. However, the province continues to be considered poor by national standards, with implications for the health of the population; at the time of fieldwork infant mortality was 104 per 1,000 against a national average of 58, and child malnutrition was 66 per cent against a national average of 11 per cent (Municipalidad Provincial de Paucartambo 2006: 65). There is a health centre in the town of Paucartambo and a number of *postas* (health posts) elsewhere in the area, but the scattered population, difficult terrain, limited resources and professional reluctance to serve extended periods in rural areas mean that accessing adequate medical care can be difficult. Vernacular healers, commonly known as *yachaqs* ('those who know') or *brujos* ('witches'), are a frequently consulted alternative. *Yachaq* practices draw primarily on Catholic and indigenous animist cosmologies, and on the use of herbal and animal *materia medica* to achieve healing; there is individual variation in how different *yachaqs* position themselves between these interwoven bodies of knowledge as they seek to differentiate their healing practices from others (Orr 2012), but dramatic divergence from these frameworks is very rare in Paucartambo. Many Paucartambinos consult both *yachaqs* and biomedical services, but the two systems do not work together.

The Jesuit chronicler Father Bernabé Cobo reported something resembling *susto* in his *Historia del Nuevo Mundo* (cited in Valdivia Ponce 1975: 82). Valdivia Ponce (1975: 82) notes other colonial sources who wrote of the effect of fright caused by thunder and lightning, and that it required healing. Moving forward in time to the early twentieth century, Valdizán and Maldonado's study of popular medicine found *susto* to be widespread and, from a perspective imbued with biomedical positivism, described it as 'a capricious grouping of different misfortunes of diverse nature' (1922: 61). With regard to the intervening period, historians (Rosas Lauro 2005) have explored in some detail the large-scale fears that periodically swept Peru (political instability, piracy), but little information has been gathered about everyday frights or how they might have provoked cases of *susto*. In the present day, Quechua-speaking Peruvians talk of the *manchay tiempo*, or 'time of fear', to refer to the vicious conflict of the 1980s and 1990s between the Maoist group *Sendero Luminoso* (Shining Path) and the Peruvian army. Paucartambo was spared the intensity of violence that developed elsewhere in the country, though some guerrillas were killed there in the mid-1980s (Mucha 2017: 56). Consequently, fear was not threaded through the social fabric in the same way as in Ayacucho and other regions (Theidon 2001). Though violence is implicated in cases of *susto*, as will be shown, it is not the violence of societal conflict that is found elsewhere in the country.

I (Orr) spent 12 months doing fieldwork (2007–8) in the town and villages of Paucartambo, returning briefly in 2010 and 2014. Focusing on madness and severe emotional distress, I observed and conversed extensively with sufferers, their families, clinic staff and *yachaqs*. In many of the cases identified, *susto* was proposed as a possible cause, though causation was rarely definitive and often contested. *Susto*, in Paucartambo as throughout Latin America, is associated primarily with children, but can affect adults. Several things can produce the fright that gives rise to *susto*, ranging from the traumatic (near-death experiences) to the apparently trivial (tripping, unexpectedly glimpsing an animal). The fright leads to the escape of the *animo*, an invisible animating essence akin to air or the breath, which provides the person with the energy to move and work.[9] There is not a fully elaborated typology of four elements such as Jacobo Herrera describes among the Nahua, although it is well known that *susto* is significantly harder or impossible to cure if the *animo* falls into water. Another complicating factor occurs when the *animo* is captured by spiritual entities that inhabit and animate the natural environment. Very mild cases of *susto*, often those involving infants, can sometimes be resolved by family members calling the *animo*; more serious cases require intercession by a *yachaq*.

Though a prototypical account of *susto* is recognised (lethargy, disturbed sleep/appetite, diarrhoea, one sunken eye – cf. Fernández Juárez 2004), *susto* has no single, definitive and universally shared set of symptoms in Paucartambo (Greenway 1998). Many *yachaqs* do not diagnose based on symptoms, but rather on reading the coca leaves or through spirit or dream revelations; symptomatology therefore holds only secondary importance. Treatment usually consists of one or more soul-calling ceremonies that bring the *animo* home to its body from the place where it is lost; if the *animo* has been captured by the earth or another spiritual entity, the *yachaq* must make a sacrificial offering to persuade this creature to relinquish it.

Beyond the view that babies are more likely to suffer from *susto* because their *animos* have not yet developed a strong bond with their bodies, there is no overall agreement in Paucartambo as to who is most susceptible. Some argue that the elderly are particularly prone because they are tired and worn out, but others take the view that younger adults are more active, travel more and are therefore more likely to experience frights. While most think that women are more likely to get *susto* because they are weaker or more emotional, or their souls are less firmly anchored to their bodies, others suggest that women are less likely to suffer *susto* because they spend more time at home and hence run less risk of being frightened. Certainly the mountainsides and paths outside the villages are typical locations for *susto* to occur. Equally, transit accidents on the area's narrow, precipitous roads and in poorly maintained and sometimes carelessly driven transportation were a regular concern (Orr 2016) and commonly mentioned by informants as liable to trigger the onset of *susto*; their suddenness and the threat they pose to life and limb make these incidents emblematic of 'sustogenic' incidents.

It may seem from this that *susto* is the result of mere happenstance and can tell us little about the structural conditions of Paucartambinos' lives or their fears as an emotional community, but closer examination of discourse around the condition reveals that this is not the case. Illness, including mental and spiritual illness, is often closely linked to hunger, reflecting both contemporary biomedical messages about malnutrition and earlier beliefs about the significance of food (Orr 2013). Inadequate nourishment is commonly implicated in rendering individuals vulnerable, by reducing their resistance to conditions such as *susto* if they experience a fright. Many people in Paucartambo, who lived through the severe economic crisis of the late 1980s and early 1990s, and continue to live with the high rates of child malnutrition reported above, drew connections between these conditions and vulnerability to *susto*. As one mother of a young woman who had experienced lengthy psychosis in her twenties speculated:

> When I was pregnant with this girl I had nothing. Maybe that could be it, couldn't it, for having been badly nourished my daughter is like this. Then from the *sustos* she had complications.

One respected *yachaq* explained some of the differences in course and severity of *susto* along similar lines:

> Due sometimes to weakness perhaps, they're weak, not well. Maybe something like vitamins is lacking.

In these instances, people speculate that poverty, structural exclusion and the resulting economic and nutritional deprivation, while not in themselves causes of fright or *susto*, can weaken the resilience a person may show when confronted with natural or man-made triggering shocks. Just as the *animo* becomes less attached to the body with age, as the person approaches death, so living in these conditions makes the *animo*'s tie to the body more tenuous, less firm in the face of challenges.

The overlaps between *susto* and other areas of one's life are particularly evident in the case of Hilario, who was in his early twenties in 2007–8. He would regularly disappear for days to wander the hills or sleep in the streets, ate from rubbish bins, shook wildly at times and was often barely able to engage in everyday social interactions. Everyone, family and neighbours alike, concurred that Hilario suffered from *susto*. His parents recounted how they had sought help from several *yachaqs*, at considerable expense but without benefit. His stepmother Asunta told me about one of the soul-calling ceremonies, and how the *yachaq* had asked her to provide guinea pigs (commonly reared for food in the Andes) for an offering, and several hens for payment. 'We said we'd spend whatever it took for him to get better,' she said, but all attempts failed. She reported that visits to the evangelical Maranata church and the regional psychiatric hospital similarly had no long-term benefits.

Asunta told two different stories about how Hilario had been 'frightened'. According to the first, which she told me when I first got to know the family, it had happened while she and his father were away. He had gone to the stream where he used to fish, and there had been frightened by '[a]n evil spirit maybe, you see. It grabbed his soul, sure. Satan, Satan, they say. It lives inside [the water], the siren they say.'

The siren is a spirit commonly said to inhabit mountain rivers and streams. Asunta had converted to the Maranata Evangelical Church a few years before, which may account for why she so readily equated the siren with Satan. Asunta recounted the second story some weeks later, after I had got to know her better, and it was variations of this narrative that circulated among her neighbours. In this version, both Hilario and Asunta had been fleeing their home after nightfall because Hilario's father was in a drunken, violent rage. Both Asunta and the father himself acknowledged that this had occurred regularly; indeed, it formed part of their common narrative about their religious conversion, and Asunta had told me the first time we met about the beatings he had given her. As they ran, Hilario had seen a red cockerel rearing up in the moonlight, flapping its wings, which had then disappeared. Since then, he had been struck almost dumb, and could no longer engage in normal social behaviour.

In cases such as this, where healing was unsuccessful at the first attempt and further *yachaqs* were therefore consulted, it is quite usual for there to be multiple stories about how the *susto* occurred. The two stories originated with different *yachaqs*. In theory at least, it is important for the *yachaq* to identify where the fright occurred, so that he or she can direct the intercession to the appropriate place in order to recover the *animo*; hence a first failure may be followed by another *yachaq* identifying that the *animo* was really lost elsewhere and that another ceremony is needed, directed at that second location. Over time, therefore, consultations may explore a range of experiences of fear. In Hilario's case, both stories centre on unexpected encounters outside the areas most frequented by human beings. The first highlights primarily the risks of solitary activity outside the home or village, and the dangers posed by nature spirits like the siren. However, the second raises other issues in accounting for how meeting an everyday, seemingly innocuous domestic fowl could lead to such a severe case of *susto*. Certainly it was not surprising for someone to be startled by such a sudden apparition, even if the animal had been entirely natural; that the bird was up and about during the night rendered the encounter uncanny, conjuring demonic associations. However, it is also of note that this story was never told without being contextualised against the background of the domestic violence. Inter-partner violence is common in many households, so that narratives of conversion to evangelical Protestantism more often highlight it as the key driver of change than not. Religious switching is the only resort left for

Quechua-speaking women whose concerns have until recently not been taken seriously by state institutions or the established Catholic church. As with the examples of malnutrition and poverty, in this instance *susto* became a way to highlight factors around the incident of fright itself, in this case abuse and alcohol consumption.

Discussion

This chapter has framed the study of *susto* against the background of the emotion of fear, something that has been done surprisingly rarely in the literature. Deep contextualisation of how fear is experienced in these emotional communities must await further fieldwork, but these initial indications hint at the ways this experience is shaped in varying ways by different emotional communities. As the anthropology of the emotions has shown, the fears of these communities respond to the specific threats that are relevant to them under particular socio-historical circumstances (violence, vulnerability to natural disasters), but also in ways shaped by internal divisions such as gender, socio-economic situation and age (not to mention, as the case of Asunta shows, religious loyalties). Conceptions of the body, the *tonalli* or *animo* which is central to its health and the interactions between humans and the spiritual powers that surround them are all central to why and how fear manifests through the absence of the 'soul' and the resulting physical and mental suffering. The two ethnographies presented focus on, respectively, healers and families in the community, but recurring themes come through, not only in aspects of the conceptualisation and healing of *susto*, but notably in how gender-based violence and its effects on women and young people are frequently implicated in the development of *susto* cases. The emphasis found in Paucartambo on poverty more generally (that is, other than as a constraint on the options of women subject to abuse) as a contributing factor in a number of cases of *susto* was not evident in the Cuetzalan ethnography; whether this reflects genuine differences in discourse or structural conditions between the two sites, or simply the different dimensions prioritised in the narratives of healers (Cuetzalan) and community members (Paucartambo) remains to be seen.

This chapter offers a preliminary example of how the affective dimension of fear may be introduced into critical medical anthropology studies of *susto*, which we hope will be developed in future fieldwork. An extensive academic literature has arisen seeking to explain what 'really' lies behind *susto*, as researchers find themselves confounded by its range and scope. Ironically, given the long-standing scholarly propensity for the stereotype that 'Westerners' emotionalise while others somatise (Beatty 2013: 418), this has led many scholars to focus on physiological or sociological explanations and factor out of their analyses the core issue identified by the people experiencing *susto*: fear. A rich toolkit of approaches can be found in the anthropology of emotions to support the further development of this analysis, from the semantic networks of emotion terms and emotion narratives, to embodied emotion and even dream analysis (Beatty 2013, 2014; Mattingly 2010; Nations 2013). An attentive focus by critical medical anthropologists on the sets of fears informing *susto* reveals how community members reflect not only on the proximate causes such as a lightning strike, but also on factors that contribute more subtly: ongoing situations of domestic violence or a pervasive sense of poverty and marginalisation.

Across settings, females, children and the elderly are commonly perceived as more vulnerable to *susto*. This vulnerability reflects dominant perceptions of bodily/spiritual development and resistance, as shown in accounts emphasising the weak bonds between the person and their *tonalli/animo* during infancy and old age, or the construction of women as particularly prone to emotionality, sometimes attributed to suggestions that they have more 'souls' than males (Fernández Juárez 2004).[10] Yet as the significance of gender oppression in the two ethnographies highlights, such vulnerability to *susto* also corresponds – while not being entirely reducible to – the patterns of disadvantage discerned and shaped by society, with these groups being consistently excluded from positions of power and influence. In one sense, two orders of explanation for *susto* can be identified. From the emic point of view, the situation that led directly to the condition may be highlighted, e.g. lightning, a shock, violence. In external analysis, these trigger factors are often 'translated' into suffering linked to structural conditions of unequal social relations or access to resources, which manifest in poverty, malnutrition, discrimination or physical conditions such as hypoglycaemia or infection with parasites. As our review showed, analysis has often stopped at this point. Yet ethnographic engagement with the full details of how people live through and think about *susto* blurs the boundaries between these two orders; *susto* discourse in action, far from exclusively identifying immediate triggers, also brings out the wider conditions that contribute to fear and vulnerability. Fears are constructed in socially specific ways and may encompass several concerns, both immediate and broader. Due attention to such emotions and their cultural situatedness – without rushing to interpret them prematurely in other terms, be they physiological, psychological or sociological – can be valuable in sensitising critical medical anthropologists to the multidimensional forms of exclusion and vulnerability that populations experience, and to what they themselves have to say about them. The factors implicated in *susto* causation, and the fears that give rise to it, shift and change alongside social trends, as they respond to growing recognition of the effects of gender-based violence or malnutrition, just as they have been characterised by continuities and disruptions through the historical periods traced in this chapter. Both meaning and structural vulnerability are inextricably intertwined in making sense of such challenges; socio-economic structures are key factors in the shaping of emotional communities (Dureau 2012), but equally emotions cannot be considered as extraneous to how individuals and communities deal with the effects of such structures. Both narratives and their underlying emotional formations on the one hand, and critical perspectives on the production and distribution of ill health on the other, are central to understanding *susto* and related conditions.

Notes

1. Others include syndromes related to anger (*coraje, colerina, bilis*), anxiety (*nervios*), desire (*antojos*) or sadness (*llaki, pena*).
2. Cuetzalan's integrated hospital has seen collaboration between biomedical and traditional knowledge since 1958.
3. Among these can be found *temazcales* (steam baths), *limpias* (passing herbs and/or an egg over the body of the sick person in order to draw out the cause of the illness), massages and their own traditional medications.
4. Joyce (2000) notes that the perceptions of Fray Bernardino de Sahagún, García and Hérnandez's main source, and his informants, reflected their own male perspective, so these reports of how fears were gendered should not be accepted uncritically.
5. Houses in this area are typically built with cement, but the kitchens are constructed traditionally with palm roofs and earthen floors, making them more liable to lightning strikes.
6. The precise number of *limpias* and *llamadas* depends on the duration and cause of the *susto*.
7. These *llamadas* are a ritual performed by the *curandero* to call the missing soul. They normally take place at night and are directed to the element where the soul was trapped. This may involve singing to water, or beating the earth with a wooden stick while saying the name of the person.
8. The *paladeada* involves introducing the index finger into the patient's mouth to try to reach the uvula. If the uvula is twisted it indicates *susto* and the *curandero* must return it to its regular position.
9. See Boyer 2006, La Riva González 2005 and Fernández Juárez 2004 for further details.
10. See López Sánchez 2013 for an analysis of how Mexican biomedicine constructed women's bodily constitution as inherently emotional. There are intriguing resonances with the ethnomedicinal frameworks we have explored here.

References

APA (American Psychiatric Association). 2013. *Diagnostic and Statistical Manual of Mental Disorders: DSM-5*. 5th ed. Washington, DC: American Psychiatric Association.

Aramoni, María Elena. 1990. *Talokan tata, talokan nana: Nuestras raíces: Hierofanías y testimonios de un mundo indígena*. Mexico City: Consejo Nacional para la Cultura y las Artes.

Beatty, Andrew. 2013. 'Current Emotion Research in Anthropology: Reporting the Field', *Emotion Review* 5 (4): 414–22.

Beatty, Andrew. 2014. 'Anthropology and Emotion', *Journal of the Royal Anthropological Institute* 20 (3): 545–63.

Bolton, Ralph. 1981. 'Susto, Hostility, and Hypoglycemia', *Ethnology* 20 (4): 261–76.

Bourbonnais-Spear, Natalie, Rosalie Awad, Zul Merali, Pedro Maquin, Victor Cal and John Thor Arnason. 2007 'Ethnopharmacological Investigation of Plants Used to Treat Susto, a Folk Illness', *Journal of Ethnopharmacology* 109 (3): 380–87.

Bourke, Joanna. 2005. *Fear: A Cultural History*. London: Virago.

Boyer, Isabela Neila. 2006. 'El samay, el "susto" y el concepto de la persona en Ayacucho, Peru'. In *Salud e interculturalidad en America Latina: antropologia de la salud y critica intercultural*, edited by Gerardo Fernández Juárez, 187–215. Quito: Abya-Yala.

Calabrese, Joseph D. 2008. 'Clinical Paradigm Clashes: Ethnocentric and Political Barriers to Native American Efforts at Self-Healing', *Ethos* 36 (3): 334–53.

Calderón Rivera, Edith. 2012. *La afectividad en antropología: Una estructura ausente*. Mexico City: Centro de Investigaciones y Estudios Superiores en Antropología Social (CIESAS)/Universidad Autónoma Metropolitana Iztapalapa.

Carey, James W. 1993. 'Distribution of Culture-Bound Illnesses in the Southern Peruvian Andes', *Medical Anthropology Quarterly* 7 (3): 281–300.

Cartwright, Elizabeth. 2007. 'Bodily Remembering: Memory, Place, and Understanding Latino Folk Illnesses among the Amuzgos Indians of Oaxaca, Mexico', *Culture, Medicine and Psychiatry* 31 (4): 527–45.

CONAPO (Consejo Nacional de Población). 2006. *Proyecciones de la población de México 2005–2050*. Mexico City: Consejo Nacional de Población. Accessed 18 September 2019. http://alianzacivica.org.mx/guia_transparencia/Files/pdf/desarrollo/14_PROYECCIONESDELAPOBLACION-DEMEXICO/14_PROYECCIONESDELAPOBLACIONDEMEXICO.pdf.

Crandon, Libbet. 1983. 'Why Susto', *Ethnology* 22 (2): 153–67.

Delumeau, Jean. 1989. *El miedo en Occidente (siglos XIV–XVIII): Una ciudad sitiada*. Madrid: Taurus.

Delumeau, Jean. 2002. 'Miedos de ayer y de hoy'. In *El miedo: Reflexiones sobre su dimensión social y cultural*, by Jean Delumeau, María Teresa Uribe de Hincapié, Jorge Giraldo Ramírez, Pilar Riaño Alcalá, Alejandro Grimson, Norbert Lechner, Silvia Álvarez Curbelo, Soledad Niño Murcia, Jorge Echavarría Carvajal, Luz Amparo Sánchez Medina, Marta Inés Villa Martínez and Ana María Jaramillo Arbeláez, 9–21. Medellín: Corporación Región.

Dureau, Christine. 2012. 'Translating Love', *Ethos* 40 (2): 142–63.

Echevarría García, Jaime and Miriam López Hérnandez. 2013. 'La expresión corporal del miedo entre los antiguos nahuas', *Anales de Antropología* 47 (1): 143–66.

Fassin, Didier. 2012. *Humanitarian Reason: A Moral History of the Present*. Berkeley: University of California Press.

Fernández Juárez, Gerardo. 2004. 'Ajayu, animu, kuraji: El "susto" y el concepto de persona en el Altiplano aymara'. In *Gracias a Dios y a los achachilas: Ensayos de sociología de la religión en los Andes*, edited by Alison Spedding Pallet, 185–217. La Paz: Instituto Técnico Ecuménico Andino de Teología.

Geertz, Clifford. 1973. *The Interpretation of Cultures: Selected Essays*. New York: Basic Books.

Gonzalbo Aizpuru, Pilar. 2008. 'El nacimiento del miedo, 1692: Indios y españoles en la Ciudad de México', *Revista de Indias* 68 (244): 9–34.

Gonzalbo Aizpuru, Pilar, Anne Staples and Valentina Torres Septién, eds. 2009. *Una historia de los usos del miedo*. Mexico City: Colegio de México.

Green, Linda. 1994. 'Fear as a Way of Life', *Cultural Anthropology* 9 (2): 227–56.

Greenway, Christine. 1998. 'Hungry Earth and Vengeful Stars: Soul Loss and Identity in the Peruvian Andes', *Social Science and Medicine* 47 (8): 993–1004.

Hannig, Anita. 2017. *Beyond Surgery: Injury, Healing, and Religion at an Ethiopian Hospital*. Chicago: University of Chicago Press.

Houghton, Azula A. and Frederic J. Boersma. 1988. 'The Loss–Grief Connection in Susto', *Ethnology* 27 (2): 145–54.

Jacobo Herrera, Frida. 2016. 'Miradas antropológicas y sociológicas de las emociones: El análisis de la envidia en el pueblo nahua de Cuetzalan, Puebla'. In *Emociones, afectos y sociología: Diálogos desde la investigación social y la interdisciplina*, edited by Marina Ariza, 373–95. Mexico City: Universidad Nacional Autónoma de México.

Joyce, Rosemary A. 2000. *Gender and Power in Prehispanic Mesoamerica*. Austin: University of Texas Press.

Kirmayer, Laurence J. 2012. 'Cultural Competence and Evidence-Based Practice in Mental Health: Epistemic Communities and the Politics of Pluralism', *Social Science and Medicine* 75 (2): 249–56.

La Riva González, Palmira. 2005. 'Las representaciones del animu en los Andes del sur peruano', *Revista Andina* 41: 63–88.

López Austin, Alfredo. 1980. *Cuerpo humano e ideología: Las concepciones de los antiguos nahuas*. Mexico City: Universidad Nacional Autónoma de México.

López Sánchez, Oliva. 2013. 'La pertinencia de una historia de la construcción emocional del cuerpo femenino en México entre 1850–1910: Abordaje desde el construccionismo social', *Revista Latinoamericana de Estudios sobre Cuerpos, Emociones y Sociedad* 5 (12): 51–64.

Lutz, Catherine and Geoffrey M. White. 1986. 'The Anthropology of Emotions', *Annual Review of Anthropology* 15: 405–36.

Martínez-Corona, Beatriz. 2012. 'Género, participación social, percepción ambiental y remediación ante desastres naturales en una localidad indígena, Cuetzalan, Puebla', *Ra Ximhai: Revista de Sociedad, Cultura y Desarrollo Sustentable* 8 (1): 113–26.

Mattingly, Cheryl. 2010. *The Paradox of Hope: Journeys through a Clinical Borderland*. Berkeley: University of California Press.

Mejía Flores, Susana and Adriana Palacios Luna. 2011. *Voces diversas frente a la violencia: Sistematización de la experiencia de atención a mujeres indígenas en situación de violencia de género en Cuetzalan, Puebla*. Mexico: CADEM/INDESOL/SEDESOL.

Mucha, Witold. 2017. *Why Do Some Civil Wars Not Happen? Peru and Bolivia Compared*. Opladen: Budrich UniPress.

Municipalidad Provincial de Paucartambo. 2006. *Plan de desarrollo: Provincia de Paucartambo 2006–2010*. Paucartambo: Municipalidad Provincial de Paucartambo.

Mysyk, Avis. 1998. 'Susto: An Illness of the Poor', *Dialectical Anthropology* 23 (2): 187–202.

Nations, Marilyn. 2013. 'Dead-Baby Dreams, Transfiguration and Recovery from Infant Death Trauma in Northeast Brazil', *Transcultural Psychiatry* 50 (5): 662–82.

O'Nell, Carl W. 1975. 'An Investigation of Reported "Fright" as a Factor in the Etiology of Susto, "Magical Fright"', *Ethos* 3 (1): 41–63.

O'Nell, Carl W. and Henry A. Selby. 1968. 'Sex Differences in the Incidence of Susto in Two Zapotec Pueblos: An Analysis of the Relationships between Sex Role Expectations and a Folk Illness', *Ethnology* 7 (1): 95–105.

Orr, David M.R. 2012. 'Patterns of Persistence amidst Medical Pluralism: Pathways toward Cure in the Southern Peruvian Andes', *Medical Anthropology* 31 (6): 514–30.

Orr, David M.R. 2013. '"Now He Walks and Walks, as if He Didn't Have a Home Where He Could Eat": Food, Healing, and Hunger in Quechua Narratives of Madness', *Culture, Medicine, and Psychiatry* 37 (4): 694–710.

Orr, David M.R. 2016. 'Regulating Mobility in the Peruvian Andes: Road Safety, Social Hierarchies and Governmentality in Cusco's Rural Provinces', *Ethnos* 81 (2): 238–61.

Robbins, Joel. 2013. 'Beyond the Suffering Subject: Toward an Anthropology of the Good', *Journal of the Royal Anthropological Institute* 19 (3): 447–62.

Rosaldo, Michelle Z. 1984. 'Toward an Anthropology of Self and Feeling'. In *Culture Theory: Essays on Mind, Self, and Emotion*, edited by Richard A. Shweder and Robert A. LeVine, 137–57. Cambridge: Cambridge University Press.

Rosas Lauro, Claudia, ed. 2005. *El miedo en el Perú: Siglos XVI al XX*. Lima: Pontificia Universidad Católica del Perú.

Rosenwein, Barbara H. 2002. 'Worrying about Emotions in History', *American Historical Review* 107 (3): 821–45.

Rosenwein, Barbara H. 2010. 'Problems and Methods in the History of Emotions', *Passions in Context: Journal of the History and Philosophy of the Emotions* 1: 1–32.

Rubel, Arthur J., Carl W. O'Nell and Rolando Collado-Ardón. 1984. *Susto: A Folk Illness*. Berkeley: University of California Press.

Signorini, Italo. 1982. 'Patterns of Fright: Multiple Concepts of Susto in a Nahua-Ladino Community of the Sierra de Puebla (Mexico)', *Ethnology* 21 (4): 313–23.

Tapias, Maria. 2015. *Embodied Protests: Emotions and Women's Health in Bolivia*. Urbana: University of Illinois Press.

Tappolet, Christine. 2010. 'Emotion, Motivation, and Action: The Case of Fear'. In *The Oxford Handbook of Philosophy of Emotion*, edited by Peter Goldie, 325–45. Oxford: Oxford University Press.

Terven Salinas, Adriana. 2017. 'Domestic Violence and Access to Justice: The Political Dilemma of the Cuetzalan Indigenous Women's Home (CAMI)'. In *Demanding Justice and Security: Indigenous Women and Legal Pluralities in Latin America*, edited by Rachel Sieder, 51–71. New Brunswick, NJ: Rutgers University Press.

Theidon, Kimberly. 2001. 'Terror's Talk: Fieldwork and War', *Dialectical Anthropology* 26 (1): 19–35.

Trotter, Robert T. 1982. 'Susto: The Context of Community Morbidity Patterns', *Ethnology* 21 (3): 215–26.

Valdivia Ponce, Oscar. 1975. *Hampicamayoc: Medicina folklórica y su substrato aborigen en el Perú*. Lima: Universidad Nacional Mayor de San Marcos.

Valdizán, Hermilio and Angel Maldonado. 1922. *La medicina popular peruana*. Lima: Torres Aguirre.

Weller, Susan C., Roberta D. Baer, Javier Garcia de Alba Garcia and Ana L. Salcedo Rocha. 2008. 'Susto and Nervios: Expressions for Stress and Depression', *Culture, Medicine, and Psychiatry* 32 (3): 406–20.

Wikan, Unni. 1987. 'Public Grace and Private Fears: Gaiety, Offense, and Sorcery in Northern Bali', *Ethos* 15 (4): 337–65.

4

Post-coital pharmaceuticals and abortion ambiguity: Avoiding unwanted pregnancy using emergency contraception and misoprostol in Lima, Peru

Rebecca Irons

> With this pill [misoprostol] you cannot abort. Abortion is the job that a doctor does, introducing things so that he can take 'it' out, it's very different. – Female Nurse

> It's not an abortion [ECP]. Scientifically it's not a human being, it's nothing more than a cell, like so many other cells that are born and die ... for me there's no conflict. – Female Art Student

Manufacturers may intend for pharmaceuticals to function the same way everywhere, on bodies perceived to be universally biologically identical, but they are not, in fact, unproblematically transported across cultures: potential markets are socially, culturally and subjectively diverse (Petryna and Kleinman 2006). As Van der Geest et al. suggest, 'the cultural efficacy of pharmaceuticals lies in their capacity to carry meanings' (1996: 169), and furthermore, pharmaceuticals can directly affect corporeal subjectivities and experience because of the intimate nature of their application (Van der Geest et al. 1996: 171). It has been argued that 'wrong use' of a global product without considering local contexts could result in the pharmaceutical being meaningless (Van der Geest et al. 1996: 156), but this implies that there is alternatively a 'right' use and does not consider the potential multiplicity of such medical objects, as Mol (2002) suggests.

Pharmaceuticals act within a complex web of relationships beyond that between manufacturers and consumers. Importantly, they frequently concern the state. Governmental pens are often poised over pharmaceutical policy documents, deciding whether a pill will be available legally or not (as is the case with the post-coital pharmaceuticals discussed in this chapter). This is so whether they are dispersed directly by governments (such as in ministries of health and state-run hospitals) or acquired from the market by private citizens and organisations (Van der Geest et al. 1996).

Peru's relationship to pharmaceuticals, and particularly those used within a family planning framework, has a long history involving multiple actors beyond the state. For example, Necochea López (2014) describes how the Catholic church has long held influence over the state, dictating which (reproductive) pharmaceuticals have reached the market. Although the state is now secular, the church and other actors (such as NGOs) continue to influence pharmaceutical availability and acceptability, particularly with regard to post-coital pills, which are contested terrain (Chávez and Coe 2007). Pharmaceuticals in Peru make sense within such a context of ongoing liberal and conservative push and pull, with women users at the centre of this tug of war.

Pharmaceutical involvement with a political economy of health invites a critical medical anthropology (CMA) framework of analysis (Singer et al. 1990). CMA critically examines how the structural relationship between class, wealth and power affects people's health (Joralemon 2010), or the relationship between 'health and wealth'. It has been suggested that in questions of maternal health and motherhood (or the avoidance of motherhood, in the case of this chapter), CMA is a particularly well-situated framework with which to examine the power dynamics at play in the lives and bodies of women (Newnham et al. 2016), and this may apply particularly to Latin America, given the pluralities and diverse nature of medical systems that coexist there (Menéndez 2016). Furthermore, the contention that 'Western biomedicine' should be analysed as another cultural system interacting with a rich and varied network of alternatives allows the interrogation of pharmaceuticals and their supposedly 'given' nature, in addition to the structural considerations of health incorporated in the CMA framework. Gamlin (2013) argues that CMA 'takes political and historical issues as a starting point with the aim of taking a step back from the medical interpretation ... to look at underlying causal factors' (2013: 35). This chapter will do so in relation to the question of post-coital pills in Peru, approaching a contested subject (abortion) that entails illegalities. The discussion here will support an alternative (political) approach to post-coital pharmaceuticals, which are both legal and illegal at present in Peru, that will contribute towards debate on a topic that is mired in a restrictive political and historical context at present. Furthermore, as this approach questions the wider social and political structures at work in medicine, it is of great relevance and use when querying the use of medicines in a low-income context.

However, it is not just the application of pharmaceuticals that may differ in varying sociocultural contexts, but also the bodies of the users. Lock and Nguyen's discussion of 'local biologies', the concept that physical bodies in different cultures may be biologically different due to their sociocultural and environmental situation, resulting from a 'biosocial differentiation in action over time' (2010: 314), further complicates matters. Lock and Kaufert (2001) give an example of how these local biologies are understood to work through their study on menopause across different contexts, when they found that women in Japan, Canada and the United States, despite going through the 'same' biological process, had distinctly different risk levels for associated disease. Thus, local biologies 'reflect the very different social and physical conditions of women's lives from one society to another' (2001: 494). This concept introduces the question of whether, on an anatomical level, pharmaceuticals may work differently in different bodies.

How to make sense of this? Mol (2002) offers the theoretical framework of 'multiple realities'. When one object, in this case a pill, is 'enacted' in different ways by different actors, that object ceases to be singular and becomes multiple. Mol writes that if the realities enacted through an object 'do not run parallel they may be objects in their own right. Different objects' (2002: 67). This underscores the fluid realities of pharmaceuticals, and highlights the fact that the *same* pill can be understood literally and metaphorically as *different* depending on the context into which it is inserted. Moving beyond an analysis of varied 'local', 'indigenised' understandings of pharmaceuticals (Van der Geest et al. 1996: 170), then, Mol suggests that these objects may in fact become different 'things' depending on how they are used and perceived. With 'local biologies' also in mind and incorporating an understanding of biomedicine as a cultural system in itself, the notion that a specific pill is the same 'thing' everywhere is further unravelled. However, this is not to say that all 'realities' are considered acceptable, particularly when we speak of post-coital pharmaceuticals and the debate about the beginning of life among informants in Lima. When one reality dominates another, this can be seen as a form of 'reproductive governance' (Morgan and Roberts 2012), where the bodies of citizens are controlled by institutions, the state and civil society.

Post-coital pharmaceuticals

This chapter addresses two pharmaceuticals that can be taken after unprotected intercourse, the emergency contraception pill (ECP) and misoprostol (an 'abortion pill'), which are available (legally and illegally, respectively) to women in Lima who wish to avoid unwanted pregnancy. Hereafter they shall be termed post-coital pharmaceuticals. Abortion is currently illegal in Peru, except therapeutically, and can be difficult to obtain at any rate, especially considering that medical practitioners in Peru have a 'limitless' ability to refuse on grounds of conscientious objection (Casas 2009). Despite this illegality, an estimated 350,000+ abortions are practised yearly, often clandestinely and dangerously (Ferrando 2006). These pharmaceuticals are critically important for women who do not wish to carry a pregnancy to term, nor to take the risk of an 'underground' abortion; thus this topic informs the political economy of reproductive health in Peru as an urgent issue of concern.

From a theoretical perspective, the pills are particularly complex because they have the potential ability to intervene in 'life' (depending on when one perceives 'life' to begin). This complication has resulted in strong and continuous condemnation from the Catholic (and increasingly Evangelical) church in Peru, which argues that life begins at the moment when a sperm fertilises an egg, and is thus opposed even to the ECP (Chávez and Coe 2007).

The ongoing abortion debate focuses on the rights of the foetus versus those of the mother, and on the question of whose rights are prioritised. Feminist groups advocate that a woman should be considered as an end in herself, and not as a vehicle for the development of an unborn entity. The woman becomes invisible in such patriarchal societies, it has been argued (Lamas 2003), and her rights should be privileged. Peruvian feminist organisations such as Manuela Ramos and Flora Tristán also advocate for the rights of a woman to decide over her body. In the work of these feminist groups, the termination of unwanted pregnancy is named as an 'abortion', as evidenced by the report commissioned and published by Flora Tristán, 'Clandestine *abortion* in Peru' (Ferrando 2006; emphasis added). Some organisations in Peru have gone so far as to actively reject the 'ethnomedical' menstrual regulation (*atraso menstrual*, discussed below) and to advocate for a direct discussion of 'abortion' named as such. For example, a public seminar was held at a Lima university in September 2018 to promote just this, entitled *Se llama aborto no atraso menstrual* ('It's called an abortion, not menstrual regulation').[1] However, these perspectives already assume that all parties accept and understand that an 'abortion' is at play in the debate. But what if the ingestion of post-coital pills was not perceived as an 'abortion' (understood as the termination of a life) at all?

Indeed, scientifically the ECP is not considered abortifacient, as from this perspective pregnancy occurs after implantation of the fertilised egg (three days after intercourse) (Trussell 2012). Both scientific and religious viewpoints would consider misoprostol to be abortifacient in all cases. Therefore, as biomedical technologies have advanced and the medical 'gaze' has penetrated even further into the anatomy of women's intimate and enclosed bodies (Foucault 2003), the question of when 'life' begins inside the uterus has been 'objectively' discussed. The first at-home pregnancy test, invented in 1968 (Wide 2005) gave further weight to an objective proof of pregnancy, and biomedicine has rushed to fill in certain gaps of knowledge, thereby supplementing personal experience with 'expert' certainty. Marta Lamas further suggests that the visual impact of the foetus – photographs of which were widely publicised in 1965 – has become a political tool used to impede women seeking interruptions as 'life' can be envisaged (2003: 154).

However, a leading theme in these perceptions is the *concept of time*. Any pill can only abort if there is a living entity to abort in the first place. Yet the time it takes after intercourse for 'life' to exist can vary wildly in perceptions; immediately, after three days, two weeks, three months. It depends on whose reality is being questioned. Therefore, paradoxically the 'same' pill can be abortion for one person and something else for another; they are 'multiple' (Mol 2002). These discrepancies should not only encourage the probing of pharmaceutical 'given-ness', but also have consequences for the way that women use and perceive the pharmaceuticals available to them. In a context where options are already limited for post-coital pregnancy avoidance, and the abortions available to women come with risks of complications and death, exploration of these pills in context is timely and crucial, with CMA offering an appropriate framework within which to interrogate the social and political forces at work in low-income Lima women's freedom of choice and subjectivities in this matter.

This chapter will discuss how – contrary to the 'biomedical' understandings of the ECP and misoprostol as contraceptive and abortifacient respectively – it was found that understandings and use of post-coital pills are closely related to local concepts of time in foetal development, which expressed much more ambiguity than is allowed for in the biomedical model. A woman's perception of the abortifacient nature of different pharmaceuticals was influenced by her understandings about the start of 'life' after unprotected intercourse.

The 'life' time frames ran from: three days after intercourse, the time required for the egg to implant and 'medical' pregnancy to be identified; two weeks, when a positive result could be indicated on pregnancy tests; three months, which follows a pan-Andean understanding of the developing 'entity' as blood clots without independent life from the mother before this time (Platt 2002; Hammer 2001; Morgan 1997).

Because of these understandings, paradoxically, even a pill widely indicated as abortifacient in medical discourse (misoprostol) could instead be considered as more of a contraceptive if taken within an identified time frame of non-foetal 'life', as there is no perceived 'life' to remove through (induced) abortion, thereby suggesting 'multiple realities' (Mol 2002).

Methodology

This chapter is based on three months of ethnographic research in a suburb of Lima, Villa Cristo (pseudonym). All interviews and observations took place in Villa Cristo. This is one of the poorer regions that make up the Lima conos,[2] with an estimated 75 per cent of residents living in conditions of extreme to moderate poverty (Matos Mar 2004: 135). Whilst 'safer', doctor-led medical abortions are available (illegally) in Lima, they come with a high price tag. Wealthier acquaintances reported paying around S/1,500–2,000 (US$400–600) for vacuum-aspiration abortions in high-end clinics, for example. The average monthly income in Villa Cristo is around $200 (Matos Mar 2004), which makes such methods financially unavailable for poorer women. This structural inequality therefore creates a higher necessity for cheaper alternatives such as pills, whilst also fostering an environment for clandestine practices to flourish, such as those advertised as *atraso menstrual* on public spaces in poorer neighbourhoods (discussed below).

Due to the high rates of poverty in Lima, to study women's experiences Rousseau suggests that it is necessary to go to the shanty towns (2009: 97). Furthermore, Boesten observes that 'it is often assumed that Lima is an entirely different cultural and socio-political space than the Andean highlands, but this is certainly not true' (2010: 14), suggesting that the issues raised within this sample may resonate with other regions of the country also. That said, González-López (2004) introduces the concept of 'regional patriarchies', showing that the regional socio-political and economic context in which people live can further affect inequalities from a gendered perspective. Whilst she distinguishes between urban and rural patriarchies, the structural dimensions found in the *conos* may be economically and socially more comparable to those in the rural Andes than wealthier urban centres (particularly as the population of the *conos* is composed largely of internal migrants). From this perspective, women who live in the poorer urban regions may face greater inequality and lack of ability to act upon their own bodies than those living in more affluent areas, suggesting a greater need to research within this group.

Semi-structured interviews were undertaken with 13 women, two semi-structured interviews with male informants who had accompanied their partners during abortions, one semi-structured interview with a health psychologist working with young women who had a variety of experiences concerning the subject matter, one focus group with four participants, three questionnaires with pharmacists in the area, and numerous informal conversations and interviews that structure the wider context of this research. Participant observation was also undertaken as the researcher lived for three months in this community, being able to observe and experience the daily context in which perspectives and practices towards post-coital pills are formed. All personal and place names have been changed to protect participant confidentiality.

Conception and concepts of time

Ever since a dedicated ECP was made available in 1996 (Wynn 2012: 6), it has been embroiled in controversy about its potentially abortifacient properties. A lack of scientific certainty about the mechanism of action, and the fact that it is taken post-coitally, has left the door open for a variety of interpretations about what it does exactly (Trussell 2012). Scientifically, ECP is not considered abortifacient, but for the Church it is seen to be (Trussell 2012: 28–9). These varying opinions hinge on the different concepts of time and foetal development. In Peru, the ECP has been legally available in pharmacies since 2001, but until August 2016, under the presidency of Pedro Pablo Kuczynksi, it was not offered alongside other contraceptive methods in national family planning clinics, nor were they permitted to educate about it (Chávez and Coe 2007). The lack of 'official' discourse on this pill, coupled with the Church's anti-ECP promotional materials, may have led to confusion about how it works exactly, a similar situation to that which has been observed in Mexico (Schiavon and Westley 2012). However, among women in Lima a key factor in perceptions about the mechanism of action was the time in which they considered that 'life' was developing after unprotected intercourse had occurred. Necochea López suggests that the concept of 'abortion' is dependent on whether a woman perceives herself to be 'pregnant' or not (2014: 52). Following from this, taking the ECP (or misoprostol for that matter, as will later be discussed) within a time frame of 'non-pregnancy', as one sees it, cannot be necessarily considered abortion. But what is this time frame in Lima? Responses differed depending on the measurement used by individual women, suggesting that this pill exists in 'multiple realities' in this context (Mol 2002).

The central Catholic Christian religious discourse in Peru insists that 'life' begins at the moment of conception, when the sperm meets the egg,[3] meaning that any intervention is considered an abortion. Whilst this may be considered the dominant religious view throughout the continent, individual women who self-identified as Catholic (or Evangelical Christian) did not necessarily follow this, instead relying on what they considered to be 'scientific knowledge'. For example, one informant who had taken ECP once and had been raised with a Catholic education stated that:

I understand that the church has a very radical discourse on this … scientifically this is not a living human, it's a cell, nothing more, like so many cells that are born and die, I don't have a conflict with this … I believe more in science than religion, even though I had a religious upbringing.

Another informant, the daughter of an Evangelical pastor, said that although her church taught that the ECP was abortion and was 'bad', personally she was not against this method, nor did she see it as such:

As a Christian, I don't accept all the ideas of the church … I don't believe that it's abortion, I think it's the same as a condom.

Similarly, during an interview concerning the ECP a health psychologist who also worked as a guidance counsellor in an Evangelical Christian church articulated that in her role as a professional psychologist, the ECP was one thing, but in the Church, it was another. She said it must depend on how it works in the body and could not conclude on the matter herself, because of the differing information she had received about it.

These conversations suggest that religious teachings are not necessarily seen as a barrier to use even by women who self-identify as Catholic/Christian, and this is not specific to Peru. In Mexico, Hirsch (2008) found that women would frequently employ 'culturally creative' strategies when using contraception and seeking permission to do so, such as travelling to priests with more 'favourable' viewpoints, in order to use the methods of their choice. Among informants in Lima, they were similarly discarding the dominant religious doctrine in favour of using ECP where they felt it was necessary, for example by selecting different discourses (e.g. psychology versus the church), to better suit their wishes/needs. Additionally, this suggests that informants may be practising what Anzaldúa termed a 'folk Catholicism' (1987: 27) – a syncretism between local belief systems and Catholic teachings. However, it should be kept in mind that the (Catholic) Church itself is not always consistent, promoting 'double standards of sexual morality' in Mexico, for example (González-López 2013), and inconsistencies of support (regarding hormonal contraception, for example) in Peru (Necochea López 2014).

This pluralist nature of decision-making is not uncommon in Peruvian society, which is often analysed as pluri-medical and pluri-ethnic (Koss-Chioino et al. 2003; De la Cadena 2000; Tartakoff 2016) in which people will simultaneously use medicine from a variety of practices. Medical pluralism is common across the continent, although the approach to health from an intercultural perspective should not be romanticised. As Menéndez (2016) suggests, the issue of racism, for example, is often omitted when examining medical pluralism, and this factor plays a central role in access to, and use of, different health systems.

Regardless of religious belief, most informants were aware that there was a window of time after intercourse during which one could take the pill and not become pregnant, although these understandings ranged from 24 to 72 hours. Questionnaires distributed to three local pharmacists also showed how women are often confused about the window of time when the ECP will be effective. This confusion may be down to it being commonly referred to as the 'morning-after-pill', leaving some women to wrongly believe it only has effectiveness for one day after unprotected sex.[4] Even amongst those who recognised the 72-hour window, there was some discrepancy in ideas as to why this was so.

During a focus group discussion with four participants on the ECP's mechanism of action, three of them insisted that it created a 'barrier' to stop the sperm reaching the ovum, so fertilisation of the egg could not take place. This barrier lasted an estimated 2–5 days, and therefore the question of 'abortion' was not central for them, as no union of sperm and egg was ever perceived to be created.

More varied time frames were also suggested, ranging from two weeks to three months, with these beliefs based on different forms of 'evidence'. One way of telling if there was 'life' or not was the pregnancy test. Speaking about whether she considered the ECP to be abortifacient or not, one informant responded:

> I believe that it's not abortion as there still isn't conception, fifteen days have to pass, then you can do a pregnancy test, just two weeks after then there's conception.

Another suggested:

> I believe it's a contraceptive method, because abortion implies more than fourteen days, when this fusion arrives to its 'house' to develop, it starts to form from fourteen days, it sticks then.

From these perspectives, life only develops after two weeks (when a pregnancy test shows as positive), and therefore taking any pill up until this point cannot be considered abortion, as there is not yet life to remove. The reference to the at-home pregnancy test is also of note. In using a 'scientific' test as 'proof' of pregnancy and therefore identifiable 'life', it brings into question the reliance of biomedical knowledge to define one's embodied experience. Before this 'biomedical evidence' could suggest a scientifically objective pregnancy, these women concluded that the pregnancy was somehow more ambiguous and not 'formed life' yet. Only once the two-week point had passed, the point when one could 'scientifically' indicate pregnancy (in their perceptions), could they accept that they were definitely pregnant. This indicates that some women may be using the Western scientific-biomedical narrative with which to understand their bodies, and thus their subjectivity (Good 1994). The question of subjectivity and biomedicine has been previously raised in Latin America, and although is not within the scope of this chapter to examine it fully, it is worth noting that biomedical technologies are frequently accused of altering subjectivity and impacting lives in both positive and negative ways (Berry 2010; Roberts 2012). That said, the two-week pregnancy test was not the only notable perception of 'time' and ECP. As well as the two-week mark, other informants suggested a three-month time frame before identifiable human life could be perceived. For example, one woman, a Catholic nurse, said that:

> we all know that until three months we are all still blood clots, we aren't a foetus, there's nothing formed, until three months there's no foetus.

Another participant, an office worker, also commented:

> From three months it's considered like a 'person', in quotations. It wouldn't be considered an abortion before, it's forming, but it's not a person.

The three-month time frame for identifiable life is common across the Andes. In the southern Bolivian Andes for example, it has been observed how women consider a 'pregnancy' to be clotted blood (from the perception of retained menstrual blood in the uterus) until three months has passed (Hammer 2001; Platt 2002). In the Ecuadorian Andes, Morgan (1997) describes how the 'tissue-matter' inside the uterus is not considered to be independent from the mother, and therefore not a 'person' until a few months have passed. Paradoxically, this time frame may have had Catholic influence, even if the contemporary Church insists that life begins at the moment of fertilisation of the egg. A century ago Catholic discourse suggested that ensoulment did not take place until after 40 to 80 days (male/female) (Necochea López 2014: 53). Therefore any 'entity' inside the uterus until this point did not have a soul and could not be considered as a 'person' in the eyes of God.

The ambiguities surrounding perceptions of time and uterus contents in this context may contribute to understandings about the origins of disparate views as to how post-coital pills work in the body and what can be considered an abortion, in the Peruvian context. The way that women think about and understand the mechanism of action of ECP affects the way they will *enact* that object – as a method of abortion, as a method of menstrual regulation, as just another hormonal contraception, thus suggesting that the ECP has 'multiple realities'. It could be argued that if this object can invariably be an abortion for one, but a contraceptive pill for another, then in fact it becomes multiple, different objects. This leads to a discussion of another other 'object' that runs parallel to this post-coital pill.

Menstrual regulation and the expulsion of blood

Concepts of time and conception only form one part of the discussion. Women who take the ECP may experience some form of bleeding and/ or discharge when they take the ECP (although not all women do), even if they do not consider that foetal 'personhood' is present until three months. For example, one woman noted of her experience with the pill that it made her 'expel blood', and another had a similar experience (although she identified this as an abortion, whereas the first did not). How do they make sense of this, for those who do not interpret it as an abortion?

Further, how do other women interpret the uterus' 'contents' if it is not perceived as 'life', and how do they account for the expulsion of blood that can accompany the ingestion of ECP (and misoprostol)? Hormonal contraception, including the ECP, has uses beyond pregnancy prevention. For example, a female art student studying at a public university, who supported a two-week 'pregnancy-test' time frame following a medical-scientific discourse, suggested that 'scientifically this is not a living human, it's a cell, nothing more, like so many cells that are born and die, I don't have a conflict with this'.

She recognised the development of living cells, even if they were not perceived as 'human' (yet) and recognised that there were cells that could be expelled. However, there are other explanations also. These pills can also be used to regulate and/or stop menstruation for purported health and lifestyle benefits, beyond pregnancy concerns alone (Sanabria 2016). Regulation of menses is an important health concept in parts of Peru, as retained menstrual blood can be interpreted as a sign of internal imbalance and illness (Bastien 1985; Hammer 2001). This finds expression through the ethno- and (increasingly) biomedical term *retraso menstrual* (menstrual regulation). This condition is identified by irregular or late menses, which is not always considered to be due to pregnancy (although there is room for ambiguity). Retained or delayed menses (*retraso menstrual*) are interpreted as a blockage of menstrual blood that forms a hard ball, much like a 'pregnancy', although it is not a given that a foetus would develop from this clotting. Unblocking this, through traditional methods such as herbal teas, or increasingly through biomedical methods such as hormonal contraceptive pills, is considered to be good for one's health (Hammer 2001).

To illustrate in the words of a 25-year-old office worker from the *conos* who had been prescribed the ECP by her gynaecologist for irregular menstruation (as per her medical complaint):

> I used the ECP once because I had irregular menses and it was the gynaecologist herself who gave me the pill, she said it was necessary that I took it to make it come [my menstruation], to regulate myself, my month.

On discussing this further, it seemed that the gynaecologist may have mistaken her complaint of delayed or irregular menstruation (*retraso*) as a pregnancy scare and provided the ECP as an attempt at prevention. However, the informant herself did not consider it this way and had taken the ECP as she believed she could regulate her menses using the hormone.

Another informant, a 23-year-old *cono* rights activist, was also given hormonal contraception by her doctor when she complained of a delayed menses. Although she believed she had a hormonal imbalance and was not pregnant, when she went to the pharmacy they demanded the prescription as they apparently could not sell her the medicine without one, as it was considered abortifacient.

For more traditional methods, it is possible to obtain various plant-based medicines, commonly considered as abortifacient (*sangre de drago, japananchak, ruda*), from the weekly local market, by complaining of a *retraso*. For example, I was informed by an herbalist who sold me various plants, 'these will make you bleed', but without further explanation as to what blood (regular menses or abortifacient) that might be.

Such examples highlight the ambiguity within this concept. Without medical testing, delayed menses could be considered as an irregularity in the cycle, as *retraso* or as a potential pregnancy, depending on whether one believes oneself to be pregnant.

Thus, aside from clinical and at-home pregnancy tests that can provide an 'objective' answer, how do women differentiate a definitive pregnancy from an accumulation of 'matter' destined to end in a *retraso* treatment or a clot of blood in the body?

Pregnancy, and the process of becoming a parent, is not only a physical state, but a mental and emotional process also. It has been much discussed how the Cartesian dualism of this mind–body split can be found in Western contexts, where the physical development of a foetus can be separated from the psychological perception of that process (Goldberg 2002; Davis and Walker 2010). This is not the case for everyone in Peru. Through the various interviews regarding conception and contraception, the concept of will and development of a foetus was raised by several women.

For example, when a 31-year-old saleswoman and mother of two was talking about the moment of conception, she suggested: 'I believe that life begins in the form that you take it, if you want to have a child you become excited, but there are other people who it doesn't sit well with, and then it isn't [a life].'

For her, if two women had unprotected intercourse with their respective partners, but one desired to have a child and the other did not, their personal will is what could affect the reality of 'life' that could develop inside them. Another woman viewed this discrepancy in more concrete terms: 'You know what you're looking for, some [women] go to parties, they take antibiotics, it's not the same, they're not "pregnant" because one looks after one's pregnancy.'

Thus, if one perceives oneself to be pregnant, and has the will to be so, she will be more likely to care for her body and carry that pregnancy to term. If a woman does not want to be pregnant, her behaviour may reflect her choice and the pregnancy will not have the chance to develop. Hammer (2001) found a similar perspective among her Quechua informants, who she says may perform extra-strenuous physical tasks if they do not wish to be pregnant after unprotected sex (2001: 247). Whilst this could be seen as women's strategies to 'unconsciously' miscarry in order to prevent an unwanted pregnancy, that may be an oversimplification. Pregnancy may not be something that one's body 'does' by itself but something that begins in the emotions and will of the woman herself. Such an analysis further contributes to understanding menstrual regulation and *retraso* treatment, even in the case where a woman could be potentially pregnant (i.e. she recognises the consequences of unprotected intercourse). If she had not desired to become pregnant, she may see this delay as a health problem and deal with it accordingly. If she had wanted to be with child, then she may instead seek medical confirmation and take care *not* to miscarry. Further, if one sees ECP as preventative, then this may also translate into a lived reality as it being a contraceptive, rather than an abortive method, as the user is not considering or planning a pregnancy consciously. On the other hand, if one considers ECP to be abortive, and takes it anyway, then it could ontologically become abortive for that person's experience, due to their conception of life being formed from their unprotected intercourse. This supports the existence of 'multiple realities' as it is the process of using and understanding the ECP that creates the reality of a 'pregnancy' or not.

Misoprostol and abortion ambiguity

ECP is not the only post-coital pill available to women in Peru, as there also exists an 'abortion pill' on the market (though it is not available for that purpose). As a pharmaceutical, misoprostol has been legally available on prescription in Peru to treat gastric ulcers since 1985, though use of this pill explicitly for abortion was not reported until the year 2000 (Ferrando 2006). If one considers that more invasive methods of abortion have been used in Peru for nearly 200 years (Necochea López 2014), the concept of aborting with a pill can be seen as relatively new in Peru's history. Lamas calls it 'the pill of the 21st century', highlighting its recent place in the timeline of pregnancy avoidance (2003: 140). Indeed, the most common forms of abortion in Peru continue to include the introduction of substances, medicines and tools into the vagina to extract the contents of the uterus (Ferrando 2006). Whilst a lack of access to misoprostol may be a factor in relative under-use compared to other abortion methods, the perceptions about what is an abortion, and whether a pill has the power to abort or not, must also be taken into consideration.

It is of interest to note that the recommended maximum number of weeks during which a woman can successfully abort with a pill is twelve (WHO 2012). Beyond this point there is the risk of incomplete abortion and infection, and so it is medically unadvisable. This time frame is noteworthy considering perceptions of foetal development in the Peruvian context. If taking the ECP was not considered abortifacient up to the three-month (or two-week) mark for some (regardless of whether the ECP would work until that point), depending on perceptions of whether there is discernible life or not, then how is taking misoprostol within these time frames also perceived?

One informant who suggested that there were only blood clots up to three months, and therefore the ECP could be taken until this point, was asked whether taking misoprostol also within this time frame would constitute abortion. She responded: 'Extracting blood, it's not abortion, a pill that can produce haemorrhage, it's not abortion. Abortion is the labour that a doctor does introducing things so that they can take "it" out, it's very different.'

From this perspective, *anything* taken before the cut-off point of three months was not abortion, and furthermore, the ability of a pill to abort at all was questioned.

Women who had suggested that two weeks was the point at which life begins were also asked about this. An informant who correctly identified the window of time for taking ECP as three days later suggested that no real life was identifiable until after two weeks. She was asked if, following from this reasoning, taking misoprostol at ten days after intercourse (still within the two-week limit) would be abortion or not. She answered: 'I don't think that it would be abortion in this case, there's no life, there are two cells that have joined, but they don't have the medium to develop themselves.'

Thus, depending on when a person perceives 'life' to begin after intercourse affects their perceptions not only of ECP as abortifacient, but also of misoprostol as abortifacient. If misoprostol is not abortifacient in some realities, what is it?

The answers given by informants included: 'really strong hormones', '[a] really strong dose of female hormones'; and 'I imagine that if the ECP is strong hormones, then this pill is even stronger'. Some women therefore consider misoprostol to be a stronger 'version' of ECP, yet essentially composed of the same kinds of hormones. This suggests that the local reality of misoprostol is not necessarily as a pill distinct from the ECP, even if medically speaking they are completely different things. Here, misoprostol can be seen as on a hormonal continuum, along with other contraceptive pills such as the combined oral contraceptive and ECP, as part of this 'family' of pharmaceuticals. As the ECP is understood as an incremented dose 'up' from the combined oral contraceptive, so is misoprostol seen as a higher dose of these same hormones. As such, it inhabits an ambiguous grey area: not quite contraceptive as it is taken post-coitally, but not quite abortifacient as it is not perceived as powerful enough to abort beyond the time-concept framings. Of course, this depends on the individual perspective and the way that a person uses it. Sanabria, studying hormonal contraceptives in Brazil, suggests that if 'the pregnancy is not interpreted as having generated a "person"' (2016: 92), then any intervention to clear the uterus of its contents cannot be interpreted as definitive abortion.

Then again, some women do use misoprostol to abort (see for example the feminist literature released by CLIM 2014 and Drovetta 2015). This again points not to a singular object that produces abortion, but to a pill that can be perceived to perform multiple, very different tasks (the fact that misoprostol is intended for treatment of stomach ulcers would further complicate the multiple realities of this pill, although it was not a focus of discussion in this study).

A pill's ability to abort

Whilst some informants recognised misoprostol as potentially abortifacient, it was not considered to be effective at always doing the job on its own. For example, one man living in the *conos* spoke about his and his partner's experience with a misoprostol abortion. She was around three months pregnant when she took eight pills, four under the tongue and four inserted into her vagina. Whilst they had believed the pills were effective at first, she was later admitted to the hospital to have her uterus 'cleaned', as he termed it, because they did not perceive the pills to be completely successful at aborting. In this case, one could observe that this woman took the pills incorrectly (twelve pills are recommended, and either orally or vaginally but not both) and that she was at the maximum limit of the recommended time, and therefore the pills might not have functioned as they should. However, he mentioned no difficulties specifically, and the decision to visit the hospital was based on a perception about misoprostol's functionality, rather than an actual medical complication. If so, why would they not trust the pill on its own?

It is perhaps more enlightening to investigate cases where people actively *rejected* misoprostol, and their reasons for doing so. I discussed a clinical abortion with a male informant who had accompanied his partner to a *cono* 'clinic' when she was around one month pregnant. He knew about misoprostol, but they had decided not to use this method. When I asked why, he replied that these pills 'don't work' as they are not 'strong enough' to abort. He believed that a growing life 'stuck into the uterus' (referencing notions of the Andean 'aggressive foetus' that resists expulsion – Platt 2002), and that 'a mother's body' was incapable of expelling this entity on its own but needed an external force to enter the uterus and extract it. As far as he saw it, a mere pill would not have succeeded in aborting as the perceived will of the mother's uterus to protect the developing entity was stronger than anything that could be developed in a laboratory. His perception reflects the concept of *marianismo*, one could argue. First developed by Stevens (1973), *marianismo* is proposed as the female alternative to *machismo* (male dominance), with the 'ideal' woman emulating the Virgin Mary and motherhood being her most important and defining role. According to notions of *marianismo*, a woman's central role is to care for and nurture her children, to the exclusion of other pursuits. Motherhood is considered to be the most important social role that women have, and they are expected to act out this role with the same dedication as Mary is perceived to have done. As Anzaldúa states: 'Educated or not, the onus is still on woman to be a wife/mother: only the nun can escape motherhood. Women are made to feel total failures if they don't marry and have children' (1987: 17).

Another female informant made a comment that also reflects this idea: 'a mother is incapable of hurting her baby'. As misoprostol causes the uterus to contract and expel the entity 'from within', it relies on the 'mothering' body to reject the 'child' – which was viewed as an impossibility by some. According to the concept of *marianismo*, the female body is 'designed' to protect a baby, and certainly not to cause it any harm. Therefore, a pill that would cause the woman's body to 'aggressively' force out her 'baby' was perhaps not seen as a realistic possibility for some, resulting in the questioning of misoprostol as an abortion option. Because of this, misoprostol was not perceived to function completely, and a further external force was needed in the above-mentioned cases. If a woman's body was not perceived as able to abort by itself, then someone else needed to come along and pull the baby out. This may go some way towards explaining the prevalence of provider-led abortions over home abortions, and leaves room for ambiguity with misoprostol.

Alternative solutions to post-coital pills

In the neighbourhood of Villa Cristo, on every single lamp-post, one can find an advertisement for *atraso menstrual* along with a telephone number (figure 4.1). These can be found throughout the poorer *conos*, but are nowhere to be seen in the wealthier districts of Lima. Whilst the concept of an *atraso menstrual* (menstrual regulation/*retraso*) itself can be seen as an ethno- (and increasingly bio-) medical illness, as previously discussed, when presented in the standardised, identifiable format that is found on signposts, it refers to clandestine abortion services, according to informants. But why are these advertisements found only in the *conos* and not wealthier districts? Two informants both suggested that women in poorer areas might be getting pregnant more frequently, and therefore need more abortions. The idea that poorer women are more fertile is common in Peru (Boesten 2010). It can be a troubling perception, as it has led to past population-control programmes in this demographic, such as the forced sterilisations under President Fujimori's anti-natalist national family planning programme in the 1990s (Rousseau 2009).

However, it is not true that only women in poorer areas of Lima are aborting (Ferrando 2006). What is true is that they have different available options. One could argue that in poorer areas abortion is simply more visible through public advertisements, as opposed to in private clinics. In the absence of state intervention, Matos Mar (2004) suggests that the informal economy has taken precedence in the Lima *conos*. In areas such as Villa Cristo, he states that 'there's the sensation of living abandoned by a good government' (2004: 143) and that because of this people effectively self-govern: the community collectively constructs and responds to unwritten rules of behaviour. The widespread advertisements, which everyone living in the area can identify as relating to clandestine

Figure 4.1 *Atraso menstrual* advertisement (posters are misspelt).
Photo by the author.

abortion, are not necessarily *legal*. However, because the state is percep-
tibly absent from Villa Cristo due to a lack of effective police surveillance
or patrolling, such a practice becomes *legitimate*, as something that the
people need and want, and the market provides (Matos Mar 2004).
Goldstein (2004) further suggests that when a government's presence is
not felt, people may resort to self-governance out of both necessity and
resistance. Using this theory, he explains how illegal practices, in this
case the lynching of thieves in the Bolivian Andes, become acceptable
and commonplace. Whilst these adverts do not explicitly mention abortion, they are a code that everyone living in the area understands. In a
similar fashion, one may recognise that shoes tied onto telephone cables
indicate the house of a drug seller, or 'massage' advertisements indicate
prostitution. However, these cultural codes are illegible to outsiders, and
therefore indicate an informal economy outside the purview of the state
and managed by the market in these neglected districts. Women living in
wealthier districts do not access abortions in this way, because they have

the financial freedom to access private clinics where surgical abortions can be performed safely. They may even be able to fly to the United States for an abortion, one informant suggested, an option that is both financially and practically unobtainable for poorer women due to travel costs and visa restrictions.

Whilst the informal economy may provide a solution for poorer women that the state does not, this in no way suggests that it is safe or viable. Clandestine abortions, such as those accessed through these advertisements, are a leading cause of global maternal mortality (Faúndes and Shah 2015).

A Lima psychologist who works with women who have aborted clandestinely commented:

> It's in bad conditions, they have gone to hotels, the 'doctor' arrives with a dirty shirt with remains of blood, it's terrible, it's true that it's like a horror film. They have left them bleeding and left, it's almost always a man, and almost always with an ugly look, they do it really quickly.

Another informant, who had accompanied a friend, asserted:

> Oh my god it's like a horror movie, I'd compare it to that movie *Hostel*,[5] something like that, but less healthy! Because that was for rich people to torture others [in *Hostel*]. For sure they have killed people, it's very gory, very bloody.

Methods of choice in these scenarios may include medication, aspiration, forceps or other tools inserted into the vagina. Because of the lack of regulation and lack of qualification of practitioners, women frequently perish as a result of clandestine abortions in Peru, from compilations and infections (Ferrando 2006), and therefore the risk inherent in the narratives of these women may not be far from the reality.

Yet for women living in Lima's poorer districts, there may not be many other options. As one male informant who had accompanied his partner to four abortions under such circumstances mused: 'You all in Europe, when you have an abortion you just fill in a form. For us? These advertisements you seen on the posts, that's our form.'

With a lack of state promotion and the illegality of abortion (and therefore lack of regulated and professional abortion services), clandestine and dangerous abortions offered on the informal market become a prime option for Villa Cristo women.

Conclusion

Whereas scientific opinion views only misoprostol as abortifacient, widespread religious belief in Peru suggests that both the ECP and misoprostol can abort 'life'. Whilst it previously appeared as though the country was undergoing a process of change towards the ECP, with President Kuczynksi introducing the pill on the national health service in August 2016, his decision to officially pardon ex-president Fujimori (notorious for corruption and a policy of enforced sterilisations in the 1990s) and release him from prison in December 2017 led to wide criticism, and Kuczynksi's credibility (and policies) were thrown into question.[6] This was followed by the successful Peruvian tour of Pope Francis in January 2018, reasserting sectors of the country as 'Catholic' once more and nudging the pendulum of 'context' back in the other direction (Lamas 2000).

However, drawing on the experiences and opinions of low-income women in Lima, this chapter has argued that the key factor in determining whether a pill can 'abort' or not is that of *time*, on which people hold opinions that differ from those dominant in health and religious discourses, among others. This suggests that women's interpretations of this process may be different from those presented by the mainstream institutions that control policy and public opinion, leading to unforeseen uses and understandings amongst women. It supports the argument that biomedicine is one of many cultural systems of understanding in health, and should not remain unchallenged, and as Menéndez (2016) has argued, this is especially relevant in Latin America where multiple medical systems coexist. Furthermore, in arguing that the post-coital pills should be understood within the theoretical framework of 'multiple realities' and a context of structural vulnerability, it has been shown how conflicting realities can potentially further deepen the marginality and poor health of women in vulnerable positions. As Mol observes, if incompatible objects (in this case, opposing discourses on pregnancy termination) do not meet, 'they are in position to confront each other' (2002: 118), but when it comes to the practicalities of competing realities, 'one of them wins. The other is discarded' (2002: 66). In the present context, it may be the dominant reality concerning 'abortion', that of the church for example, that wins out, at the sacrifice of the women's reality. This is particularly true for those women who live in structural poverty, such as the people of Villa Cristo and similar areas, where agency is limited through the conditions of structural violence. This is concerning not only for the health of women who may face death due to clandestine practices used because of their structural marginality, but also for their democratic freedoms; 'reproductive rights are intrinsically democratic rights: they stem from freedom, particularly sexual freedom' (Lamas and Bissell 2000: 21). It could be said that the lack of these freedoms is a form of 'reproductive governance' (Morgan and Roberts 2012), as women are restricted in their capacity to access the healthcare that they deem appropriate according to their understandings of their own bodies. Finally, if one considers Lock and Nguyen's (2010) theory of 'local biologies', where physical bodies may actually differ according to locale, this governance can be seen as attempting to homogenise bodies where the biological 'realities' may differ.

One further implication of this is that even non-governmental interventions intended to promote safe(r) abortion with pills may be unsuccessful for some women, if they do not accept that misoprostol is wholly abortifacient in the first place. The widely available do-it-yourself abortion manuals, such as those released by feminist groups in Peru and the southern cone (figure 4.2; CLIM 2014; Drovetta 2015; LFDI 2010; LFDI 2012) advocate at-home abortion with misoprostol as a less dangerous alternative to attending clandestine and invasive 'underground' abortions. However, these manuals may also need to attend to (mis)understandings about misoprostol and its ability to abort if they aim to speak to the widest possible range of Latin American women. Furthermore, they should be made more readily available among poorer women living in structurally vulnerable conditions (by a distribution of printed copies for those who cannot access the internet, for example). That said, Lamas (2009) suggests that feminist groups are key to pressurising Latin American governments into open debate about abortion and should be worked with in order to incite changes in the realities of women in the continent.

This is not to suggest that competing 'realities' cannot be reconciled, as suggested by the work of Campos-Navarro (2010) and Duarte-Gómez et al. (2004) on intercultural health models that successfully address indigenous concerns within biomedical hospitals in Mexico. However, while the dominant reality triumphs, low-income women may continue to have certain understandings of their bodies mistranslated into policy and be at risk from clandestine abortions or other complications. Returning to the political economy of health mentioned in the introduction, this chapter contributes to a deeper understanding of the local conditions in Lima that influence the reproductive health of the population with regard to the wider political and economic context.

Furthermore, the framework of CMA can begin to address these structural inequalities, and discussions such as this one can further

Línea Aborto Chile:
El Manual

¿Cómo las mujeres pueden
hacerse un aborto con pastillas?

· Lesbianas y Feministas por el Derecho a la Información ·

Figure 4.2   Latin American abortion manuals: (left to right) Collective for Free Information for Women (CLIM, Peru, 2014); Lesbians and Feminists for the Decriminalisation of Abortion (LFDA, Argentina, 2012); Lesbians and Feminists for the Right to Information (LFDI, Chile, 2010). Source: Peru: http://abortoinfosegura.com, Chile: http://infoabortochile.org, Argentina: http://www.rednosotrasenelmundo.org.

develop understanding of them; however, further change at the policy level, which takes women's views into account, is needed to secure reproductive health for women in Lima.

Notes

1. 28 September 2018, Pontifica Universidad Católica de Peru, Faculty of Letters, Citizenship and Politics. Organisation Serena Morena.
2. The poor northern neighbourhoods of Lima (the 'cones' of the city).
3. The dominant view is that this may happen at the moment of intercourse, even if this is not scientifically accurate as there can be some delay.
4. Among informants the ECP was frequently known as the *pastilla del día siguiente*, whereas medical professionals may use the term 'AOE' (*anticoncepción oral de emergencia*).
5. A 2005 horror film, in which wealthy individuals pay to torture hostages to death in a dirty warehouse.
6. Kuczynksi was later replaced by Martín Vizcarra (March 2018) after a corruption scandal.

References

Anzaldúa, Gloria. 1987. *Borderlands/La Frontera: The New Mestiza*. San Francisco: Aunt Lute Books.

Bastien, Joseph W. 1985. 'Qollahuaya-Andean Body Concepts: A Topographical-Hydraulic Model of Physiology', *American Anthropologist* 87 (3): 595–611.

Berry, Nicole S. 2010. *Unsafe Motherhood: Mayan Maternal Mortality and Subjectivity in Post-War Guatemala*. New York: Berghahn Books.

Boesten, Jelke. 2010. *Intersecting Inequalities: Women and Social Policy in Peru, 1990–2000*. University Park: Pennsylvania State University Press.

Campos-Navarro, Roberto. 2010. 'La enseñanza de la antropología médica y la salud intercultural en México: Del indigenismo culturalista del siglo XX a la interculturalidad en salud del siglo XXI', *Revista Peruana de Medicina Experimental y Salud Pública* 27 (1): 114–22.

Casas, Lidia. 2009. 'Invoking Conscientious Objection in Reproductive Health Care: Evolving Issues in Peru, Mexico and Chile', *Reproductive Health Matters* 17 (34): 78–87.

Chávez, Susana and Anna-Britt Coe. 2007. 'Emergency Contraception in Peru: Shifting Government and Donor Policies and Influences', *Reproductive Health Matters* 15 (29): 139–48.

CLIM (Colectiva por la Libre Información para las Mujeres). 2014. *"Hablemos de aborto y Misoprostol": Información segura y experiencias sobre su uso*. Lima: Colectiva por la Libre Información para las Mujeres.

Davis, Deborah L. and Kim Walker. 2010. 'Re-Discovering the Material Body in Midwifery through an Exploration of Theories of Embodiment', *Midwifery* 26 (4): 457–62.

De la Cadena, Marisol. 2000. *Indigenous Mestizos: The Politics of Race and Culture in Cuzco, Peru, 1919–1991*. Durham, NC: Duke University Press.

Drovetta, Raquel Irene. 2015. 'Safe Abortion Information Hotlines: An Effective Strategy for Increasing Women's Access to Safe Abortions in Latin America', *Reproductive Health Matters* 23 (45): 47–57.

Duarte-Gómez, María Beatriz, Viviane Brachet-Márquez, Roberto Campos-Navarro and Gustavo Nigenda. 2004. 'Políticas nacionales de salud y decisiones locales en México: El caso del Hospital Mixto de Cuetzalan, Puebla', *Salud Pública de México* 46 (5): 388–98.

Faúndes, Anibal and Iqbal H. Shah. 2015. 'Evidence Supporting Broader Access to Safe Legal Abortion', *International Journal of Gynecology and Obstetrics* 131 (Supplement 1): S56–S59.

Ferrando, Delicia. 2006. *El aborto clandestino en el Perú*. Lima: Centro de la Mujer Peruana Flora Tristán.

Foucault, Michel. 2003. *The Birth of the Clinic: An Archaeology of Medical Perception*, translated by A.M. Sheridan. London: Routledge.

Gamlin, Jennifer Bridget. 2013. 'Pesticides and Maternal Child Health, Experience and the Construction of Knowledge among the Huichol'. PhD thesis, University College London.

Goldberg, Lisa. 2002. 'Rethinking the Birthing Body: Cartesian Dualism and Perinatal Nursing', *Journal of Advanced Nursing* 37 (5): 446–51.

Goldstein, Daniel M. 2004. *The Spectacular City: Violence and Performance in Urban Bolivia*. Durham, NC: Duke University Press.

González-López, Gloria. 2004. 'Fathering Latina Sexualities: Mexican Men and the Virginity of Their Daughters', *Journal of Marriage and Family* 66 (5): 1118–30.

González-López, Gloria. 2013. 'Incest Revisited: A Mexican Catholic Priest and His Daughter', *Sexualities* 16 (3/4): 401–22.

Good, Byron J. 1994. *Medicine, Rationality, and Experience: An Anthropological Perspective*. Cambridge: Cambridge University Press.

Hammer, Patricia J. 2001. 'Bloodmakers Made of Blood: Quechua Ethnophysiology of Menstruation'. In *Regulating Menstruation: Beliefs, Practices, Interpretations*, edited by Etienne van de Walle and Elisha P. Renne, 241–53. Chicago: University of Chicago Press.

Hirsch, Jennifer S. 2008. 'Catholics Using Contraceptives: Religion, Family Planning, and Interpretive Agency in Rural Mexico', *Studies in Family Planning* 39 (2): 93–104.

Joralemon, Donald. 2010. *Exploring Medical Anthropology*. 3rd ed. Upper Saddle River, NJ : Prentice Hall.

Koss-Chioino, Joan D., Thomas Leatherman and Christine Greenway, eds. 2003. *Medical Pluralism in the Andes*. London: Routledge.

Lamas, Marta. 2003. 'Aborto, derecho y religión en el siglo XXI', *Debate Feminista* 27: 139–64.

Lamas, Marta. 2009. 'La despenalización del aborto en México', *Nueva Sociedad* 220: 154–72.

Lamas, Marta and Sharon Bissell. 2000. 'Abortion and Politics in Mexico: "Context is All"', *Reproductive Health Matters* 8 (16): 10–23.

LFDI (Lesbianas y Feministas por el Derecho a la Información). 2010. *Todo lo que querés saber sobre cómo hacerse un aborto con pastillas*. Buenos Aires: Editorial El Colectivo.

LFDI (Lesbianas y Feministas por el Derecho a la Información). 2012. *Línea Aborto Chile: El manual: ¿Cómo las mujeres pueden hacerse un aborto con pastillas?* Santiago: Lesbianas y Feministas por el Derecho a la Información.

Lock, Margaret and Patricia Kaufert. 2001. 'Menopause, Local Biologies, and Cultures of Aging', *American Journal of Human Biology* 13 (4): 494–504.

Lock, Margaret and Vinh-Kim Nguyen. 2010. *An Anthropology of Biomedicine*. Chichester: Wiley-Blackwell.

Matos Mar, José. 2004. *Desborde popular y crisis del Estado*. Lima: Fondo Editorial del Congreso del Perú.

Menéndez, Eduardo Luiz. 2016. 'Intercultural Health: Proposals, Actions and Failures', *Ciência e Saúde Coletiva* 21 (1): 109–18.

Mol, Annemarie. 2002. *The Body Multiple: Ontology in Medical Practice*. Durham, NC: Duke University Press.

Morgan, Lynn M. 1997. 'Imagining the Unborn in the Ecuadorian Andes', *Feminist Studies* 23 (2): 322–50.

Morgan, Lynn M. and Elizabeth F.S. Roberts. 2012. 'Reproductive Governance in Latin America', *Anthropology and Medicine* 19 (2): 241–54.

Necochea López, Raúl. 2014. *A History of Family Planning in Twentieth-Century Peru*. Chapel Hill: University of North Carolina Press.

Newnham, Elizabeth C., Jan I. Pincombe and Lois V. McKellar. 2016. 'Critical Medical Anthropology in Midwifery Research: A Framework for Ethnographic Analysis', *Global Qualitative Nursing Research* 3: 1–6.

Petryna, Adriana and Arthur Kleinman. 2006. 'The Pharmaceutical Nexus'. In *Global Pharmaceuticals: Ethics, Markets, Practices*, edited by Adriana Petryna, Andrew Lakoff and Arthur Kleinman, 1–32. Durham, NC: Duke University Press.

Platt, Tristan. 2002. 'El feto agresivo: Parto, formación de la persona y mito-historia en los Andes', *Estudios Atacameños* 22: 127–55.

Roberts, Elizabeth F.S. 2012. *God's Laboratory: Assisted Reproduction in the Andes*. Berkeley: University of California Press.

Rousseau, Stéphanie. 2009. *Women's Citizenship in Peru: The Paradoxes of Neopopulism in Latin America*. New York: Palgrave Macmillan.

Sanabria, Emilia. 2016. *Plastic Bodies: Sex Hormones and Menstrual Suppression in Brazil*. Durham, NC: Duke University Press.

Schiavon, Raffaela and Elizabeth Westley. 2012. 'Mexico: Expanding Access through Partnerships and Persistence'. In *Emergency Contraception: The Story of a Global Reproductive Health Technology*, edited by Angel M. Foster and L.L. Wynn, 91–106. New York: Palgrave Macmillan.

Singer, Merrill and Hans Baer. 1995. *Critical Medical Anthropology*. Amityville, NY: Baywood Publishing Company.

Singer, Merrill, Hans A. Baer and Ellen Lazarus. 1990. 'Critical Medical Anthropology in Question', *Social Science and Medicine* 30 (2): V–VIII.

Stevens, Evelyn P. 1973. 'Machismo and Marianismo', *Society* 10 (6): 57–63.

Tartakoff, Laura Ymayo. 2016. 'Ethnic Identity and Gender in Pluralist Perú', *Society* 53 (1): 67–75.

Trussell, James. 2012. 'Emergency Contraception: Hopes and Realities'. In *Emergency Contraception: The Story of a Global Reproductive Health Technology*, edited by Angel M. Foster and L.L. Wynn, 19–35. New York: Palgrave Macmillan.

Van der Geest, Sjaak, Susan Reynolds Whyte and Anita Hardon. 1996. 'The Anthropology of Pharmaceuticals: A Biographical Approach', *Annual Review of Anthropology* 25: 153–78.

WHO (World Health Organization). 2012. *Safe Abortion: Technical and Policy Guidance for Health Systems*. 2nd ed. Geneva: World Health Organization.

Wide, Leif. 2005. 'Inventions Leading to the Development of the Diagnostic Test Kit Industry: From the Modern Pregnancy Test to the Sandwich Assays', *Upsala Journal of Medical Sciences* 110 (3): 193–216.

Wynn, L.L. 2012. 'United States: Activism, Sexual Archetypes, and the Politicization of Science'. In *Emergency Contraception: The Story of a Global Reproductive Health Technology*, edited by Angel M. Foster and L.L. Wynn, 39–55. New York: Palgrave Macmillan.

Part II

Globalisation and contemporary challenges of border spaces and biologised difference

5

Migrant trajectories and health experiences: Processes of health/ illness/care for drug use among migrants in the Mexico–United States border region

Olga Lidia Olivas Hernández

This chapter discusses the subjective experience related to drug use from the perspective of Mexican migrant men in the US–Mexico border region. Some studies have argued that migrants increase drug use after leaving their places of origin; the purpose of this study is to examine the overlap between their migration trajectory and drug use practices and meanings, analysing how the migration experience and its social, economic and political conditions affects migrants' mental health.

Migration experience impacts daily life at interpersonal and structural levels. Leaving their places of origin and distancing themselves from family while lacking social networks may emotionally affect some migrants; the lack of language abilities acts as a barrier not only culturally but also economically; not having documents for a legal stay in a country criminalises people and makes them subject to deportations and detentions. Others are simply exploited by a capitalist system seeking cheap labour but offering precarious labour conditions. In general, being a migrant (undocumented or returned) can place a person at the margins of society.

California (CA) has the highest percentage of Mexican immigrants in the United States: they make up 69 per cent of the state's unauthorised immigrant population, and numbered more than 1.5 million in 2016 – the highest total of any state (González-Barrera and Krogstad

2019) – while Baja California (BC), specifically Tijuana, receives the most returned migrants (whether forced or voluntary) in Mexico. In 2018, BC registered 54,625 repatriations from January to October, and around 56 per cent (30,475) of these were repatriated at the receiving point El Chaparral in Tijuana (Secretaría de Gobernación 2018).

Both states (CA and BC) rank among the highest in their respective countries for prevalence of drug use. According to the National Survey of Addictions (Encuesta Nacional de Adicciones), drug use is increasing in the north-western region of Mexico, particularly BC (INPRFM 2012). In CA, specifically Los Angeles County, there has been an increase in methamphetamine use (Brecht 2014). San Diego shows a significant increase in heroin use and a growth in heroin overdose death rates since 2013 as well as an increase in methamphetamine use from 2015 to 2017 (Wagner 2014; Meth Strike Force 2018).

Even though it is possible to identify social conditions in the Western US–Mexico border region that affect the development of health problems related to drug use, in this work I focus on the analysis of the processes of health/illness/care (h/i/c) for drug use through studying people's life trajectories and focusing on their migratory experience. According to Menéndez (1994), the process of h/i/c constitutes a universal that operates differentially in each society and is diversely experienced among different groups. From Menéndez' perspective, health conditions – and the societal response to those conditions – generate representations, produce practices and structure specific knowledge of the appropriate ways to understand, treat and whenever possible cure what is socially defined as illness (Menéndez 1994: 71).

Focusing on migrants' experience to explore the process of h/i/c for drug use allows me to distinguish the different meanings that consumption practices have for Mexican migrants. At the same time, analysing their migratory trajectories makes it possible to identify their understandings, practices and forms of care related to drug use and how these may change throughout their lives in the US–Mexico border zone.

This chapter begins by discussing the theoretical perspectives approached in this study, mainly from psychological/medical and critical medical anthropology, followed by a summary of research studies conducted in Mexico relating to drug use and focused on social perceptions, policies and treatments. The third section describes methodological procedures, giving an account of the different settings where the study was conducted in the US–Mexico border region.

The chapter then analyses the overlap between migratory and drug use trajectories, discussing how the experience of migration from Mexico to the United States has affected drug use practices and meanings. From a qualitative perspective, some experiences analysed demonstrate an increase and diversification of drug use in the border region in comparison to their homeland, suggesting that in the first stages of their trajectory, drugs use is experienced as a resource to deal with the challenges faced in this context as undocumented migrants. The following section analyses how drug use became a health problem in the later stages of their trajectory, leading them to deportation, homelessness and seeking treatment at the margins of the healthcare system.

Finally, the chapter concludes by synthesising how migratory and drugs use trajectories overlap in the experience of undocumented and returned migrants in the border region. It highlights the processes of marginalisation that exacerbate their health condition as well as their active role in creating therapeutic communities for their peers.

Theoretical perspective

The critical medical anthropology (CMA) perspective has made significant contributions to scholarly understanding of the social dimensions of health/illness/care processes. These contributions include analysing 1) the social construction of health and illness in relation to the world economic system; 2) health policies and the distribution of health resources; 3) the state's role in health fields; 4) contemporary understandings of medical pluralism; 5) the development of a critique of biomedical ideology; and 6) individual health behaviour as well as illness experience in the context of wider structures, processes and relations (Singer 1989). This chapter uses a life trajectories approach centred on the process of migration to analyse how the subjective experience of drug use is affected by the social, political, economic and cultural conditions experienced by migrants in the United States–Mexico border region.

Singer (1989) emphasises the importance of CMA prioritising the micro level of social analysis, specifically individual experience and behaviour, to discuss the conflict and struggles that happen at the macro social level, both inside and outside of healthcare systems. In accordance with this perspective, Scheper-Hughes and Lock (1986) emphasise the necessity of studying the subjective experience of illness and healing processes. In this case study, I examine the relationships people establish with others along their migratory trajectory, within different social contexts (e.g. the family, at work or among religious groups), as well as at institutions providing treatment for drug use. These relationships influence the lived experience of understanding, interpreting and reacting to drug use. According to Kleinman and Fitz-Henry (2007), this is an intersubjective process involving practices, negotiations and disputes. Therefore, by examining lived experience, I seek to understand collective realities as well as individual transformations and translations of those realities. Through engaging with migrants' life stories, it is possible to identify periods where their experiences of drug use are not understood as illness but rather as helping address the difficulties they face in daily life. Eventually, turning points in the lives of migrants (such as becoming homeless and starting to experience auditory hallucinations) affect the meaning of the experience as an illness and lead them to seek treatment.

Analysing the subjective experience of illness also requires consideration of gender and ethnicity, as they can affect the lived realities of health conditions (Jenkins and Schumacher 1999; Jenkins and Cofresi 1998; Jenkins 1997; Lerín 2004; Ramírez Navarro 2010). We can identify differences between men and women regarding drug use and its treatment processes. For example, in Baja California, 75 per cent of rehabilitation centres for drug abuse do not accept women, and the ones that do provide treatment for this group reinforce their gender role as mothers and caregivers since they incentivise internment by offering legal support to get back parental authority (Galaviz 2015). Thus, treatments for women are focused on the recovery of their social function as caregivers, giving special meaning to their role as homemaker, mother, and wife; while for men, the role of caregiver is oriented to their peers, especially to those who are part of their therapeutic community (Galaviz 2015). Women are less prone to following up rehabilitation treatments due to the social demand of taking care of their home rather than being in a process of internment. It is therefore important to point out that the participants in this study are Mexican men since it was more feasible to contact this population on both sides of the border.

The participants of this study have different migratory experiences that have brought them, from various places, to the US–Mexico border region. As part of their migration experience in the United States, this population often lacks housing, language skills, income and a social support network. Thus they often face specific difficulties related to being an undocumented immigrant, and disparities accessing health services (Holmes 2006). Following Holmes (2013), structural, everyday and symbolic forms of violence experienced by migrants, especially in relation to their ethnic origin and their migratory status as undocumented, make them more vulnerable to racism and unjust legal structures operating against them as conjugated forms of oppression, which often affect their health conditions. In some cases, undocumented migrants are blamed for their own health problems. The different forms of inequality and violence they are subjected to (in labour, health and justice systems) are not considered to affect their health condition, especially when talking about drugs use/abuse, since it has been criminalised rather than truly understood as a health problem. For example, under the Secure Communities Program,[1] drug offences (in many cases, possession) have been one of the causes for deportation.

Therefore, the understanding of migrants' health problems is also affected by the marginalisation and discrimination they are subjected to, in addition to the stigmatisation that exists towards drug use/abuse. Undocumented migrants have limitations accessing healthcare, and when it comes to drug use problems, the possibility of accessing a treatment is even more difficult: in some cases they are criminalised and blamed for their problem rather than perceived as needing help.

Active drug users face a different set of difficulties related to the social construction of addiction. Possession of illegal drugs sometimes implies that the person engages in illegal behaviours beyond drug use. For this reason, possession of or appearing to be under the influence of illegal drugs contributes to the stigma, marginalisation, criminalisation and social segregation of people who use drugs. The notion that drug use is an illness is sustained by the medical-psychological-psychiatric perspective embedded in the *Diagnostic and Statistical Manual of Mental Disorders* (*DSM*) as 'Substance-Related and Addictive Disorders', which is based upon a pathological set of behaviours related to the use of a substance (alcohol, caffeine, cannabis, hallucinogens, inhalants, opioids, sedatives, stimulants or tobacco): impaired control, social impairment, risky use and pharmacological criteria (APA 2013).

The association of this health condition with impaired control resulting from drug use has resulted in the development of specialised, temporary residential treatment. The therapeutic models of these treatment centres range from biomedical and psychological to religious and mutual aid. Depending on where the centre is within the US–Mexico border region, patients may enter in-patient treatment voluntarily or involuntarily; however, later on in the treatment process they may move to out-patient care. Each of these therapeutic models represents a different institutionalised form of care based on a specific understanding of the problem to be treated, which leads to particular intervention strategies to support and guide the process of quitting drug use.

In order to discuss participants' experience through a critical lens rather than as having a psychological disorder, I use the notion of 'extraordinary conditions' proposed by Jenkins (2015). According to the author, instead of labelling someone as marginal or abnormal, the extraordinary can be recognised as vital and integral. Therefore, an analysis from the first-person perspective seeks to criticise the notion of mental health problems in categorical versus continuous terms, in order to consider the indeterminate thresholds between the ordinary and the extraordinary, the routine and the extreme, the healthy and the pathological (Jenkins 2015). Jenkins argues the critical need for engagement with individuals' experience, understanding their problems in terms of daily life struggles and not simply as symptoms defining illnesses.

Following Jenkins, I discuss extraordinary conditions as situations experienced at the limits of precariousness where, in some cases, drug use is involved. For example, the economic pressures experienced by some participants in the study led them to use drugs to do overtime at work. This situation is understood to be the result of a condition of precariousness, a struggle and an extraordinary condition experienced by undocumented migrants who have informal and low-paid jobs, while also having the responsibility of being home providers. Turning to drug use in this specific case can be discussed as a consequence of the structural violence exerted over them by the US immigration system.

The term structural violence is understood as a 'way of describing social arrangements that put individuals and populations in harm's way … the arrangements are structural because they are embedded in the political and economic organization of our social world; they are violent because they cause injury to people' (Farmer et al. 2006: 1686).

The processes of criminalisation that undocumented migrants experience by being considered 'illegal immigrants' by the political-economic system in the United States exacerbates their conditions of precariousness by restricting access to formal jobs, healthcare services, housing and other social and material resources. According to Armenta (2017), the immigration enforcement system has become increasingly punitive, and restrictive immigration policies are the primary mechanism through which people of Mexican descent are excluded and racialised in the United States, subordinating their status in the racial hierarchy, with consequences for their social, cultural, political and economic situation.

Even though some undocumented immigrants manage to get a job and find a place to live, their social rights are undermined due to their situation as undocumented; their labour and housing conditions may increase their fear of deportation, leading to other social and, in many cases, health problems related to poverty, marginalisation and discrimination. The jobs they acquire are often temporary, unskilled, low-paid, and do not provide healthcare or other work benefits. Some of the participants in this study reported that they have had jobs where they did not receive a salary, but instead were compensated with a place to live or with drugs (alcohol and marijuana). In some cases, they work extended hours or have two different jobs to earn enough money to cover their basic needs in the US as well as send some money to their families in Mexico. Using drugs may become a way to relieve the pressures of daily life. Such precarious conditions show how structural violence is embodied in the experience of people living in poverty or marginalised by social inequality (Farmer 2004).

The situation Mexican migrants face in the process of aiming to live in the United States affects their health. Thus it is relevant to discuss the way migration affects the h/i/c processes for drug use. Through this analysis, I argue it is possible to identify the hegemonic ways of understanding and caring for drug use. There are different forms of care configured by social structures and health institutions at the macro level, as well as the strategies that people living in socially and economically precarious conditions use to deal with problems related to drug use at the micro level. Menéndez (2003) suggests that it is possible to identify forms of care that individuals and groups use to address their illnesses beyond the biomedical, traditional or alternative perspectives used by health specialists, in what he describes as self-care. Therefore, analysing the h/i/c processes for drug use through life trajectories allows us to discuss the different interpretations of drug use as an illness, a habit, a vice and a self-care strategy to face the difficulties experienced under conditions of precariousness, among others. Likewise, it sheds light on the institutional forms of care sought by the participants.

Analysis of the life trajectory centred on the forms of understanding and caring for problems related to drug use allows us to identify how different healthcare and self-care practices intervene to reduce, solve or exacerbate health problems.

Self-care practices synthesise the activities developed by social groups regarding the h/i/c process (Menéndez 2003), that is, the different strategies they use to deal with and care for their health condition. In some cases, self-care practices are related to institutional healthcare practices, due to migrants' past experiences of specific forms of treatment, or to other drug users' self-care practices. When participants discussed their drug use prior to their migration, they did not consider it as problematic; it was not until they found themselves in certain critical situations in the United States as undocumented migrants or returned migrants in Mexico that they felt their drug use became problematic and sought out care for it. In this sense, it is relevant to analyse the way in which their condition as migrants in the border region has impacted their intersubjective experience related to drug use, not only associated with consumption but also the forms of care they turn to.

Social perspectives on drug use practices, meanings and treatments in Mexico

Researchers have investigated a variety of problems related to drug use from both an anthropological and a sociological perspective. Some of these studies have analysed how different therapeutic models of treatment shape both conceptions of illness and the recovery or healing process. Although this paper is not focused on analysing a particular treatment model, it is relevant to review the studies that investigate the impact of cultural conceptions of the problem understood as drug abuse in Mexico, since it helps to understand personal, social, cultural, economic and political situations faced by people dealing with drug use problems in the border region between Mexico and the US.

Some scholars have studied residential self-help groups, in which people live together with the aim of mutually guiding each other's recovery process. This is one of the main forms of help for drug abuse problems in Mexico; it is modelled on Alcoholics Anonymous (AA), or the Twelve Steps.[2] Since the early 1980s, Menéndez (1983, 2003, 2009) has analysed alcohol use and the role of AA therapeutic communities in Mexico. He discusses the relevance of religious aspects in the processes of h/i/c for drug use, highlighting the role these therapeutic communities have in the development of support networks for different stigmatised populations, from those labelled as 'drug addicts' to migrant populations. Menéndez (2009) also analyses the way AA as a therapeutic model understands the illness and recovery process through social and cultural aspects related to the alcoholic identity, which differs vastly from the biomedical perspective of drug abuse as brain disease. Módena (2009) specifically studies the group dynamics within AA therapeutic communities; she pays special attention to the processes of identity, power relations and differences in the meanings of treatment among groups in the process of recovery. Similarly, Palacios Ramírez (2009) discusses the self-transformations during the recovery process among an AA community. On the other hand, Rosovsky (2009) gives a historical account of AA in Mexico, analysing the fragmentations of this treatment model over the last century.

Self-help treatments have been the most extensively used and affordable source of help for people dealing with drug use problems. Living the process of recovery in a community setting is meaningful for the experience of quitting drugs and building new social and cultural contexts where this can be sustained. Thus, these models of treatment are relationally based, which is fundamental especially when the people going through this process are marginalised or stigmatised, not only due to drug use in itself but because of their cultural, economic, ethnic and political condition, such as being an undocumented migrant or returned migrant of Mexican descent in the border region.

Another kind of therapeutic community that has been analysed in northern Mexico, specifically in Tijuana, is religiously oriented: Evangelical-Pentecostal rehabilitation centres. García Hernández (2014) has studied the dynamic narrative identities of people undergoing religious conversion through analysing their testimonies of recovery, which are stories about personal transformation showing how a person reached sobriety with God's help. González Tamayo (2016) and Velázquez Fernández (2016) have analysed the process of recovery in relation to gender, while Kozelka (2015) has studied the way the social environment of rehabilitation centres contributes to certain cultural conceptions of the illness 'drug addiction' and the people who have it. Other scholars have analysed the processes of subjectivation through the paradigm of embodiment (Olivas Hernandez and Odgers Ortiz 2015) and the hope for the recovery during in-patient treatment in these religiously oriented centres (Galaviz and Odgers Ortiz 2014).

Both modalities of treatment, based on the Twelve Steps (AA) and religiously oriented, can be understood as self-help approaches offering alternative ways of understanding and treating drug users and drug use problems. In some cases, these therapeutic communities permit upward social mobility due to the role as guides or leaders that some people develop in the task of supporting others in their processes; this can positively benefit their own process of recovery.

Finally, some studies have discussed the problems associated with the social marginalisation of drug users. For example, París Pombo (2013) analyses the way the enforcement of legal policies against drug trafficking actually affects the human rights of drug users in Tijuana. She argues that poverty has increased drug users' vulnerability since the criminalisation of poverty has been added to the 'war on drugs'. In a similar sense, Cajas Castro (2013) analyses how drug prohibition in Mexico as a result of the 'war on drugs' has had a paradoxical effect of stimulating the use of illegal substances, highlighting the failure of prohibition policies. Thus, analysing drug use is not limited to the understanding of it as a health problem, but involves conceptions of it as a condition affected by social, cultural, economic and political issues embedded in the use of drugs.

Muñoz, Morales, Fernandez and Brower (in this book) analyse the conditions of vulnerability under which Central American migrants live in the southern border of Mexico and the inequalities they face in a system that marginalises them. These forms of economic, social and political inequalities place migrant people at risk in relation not only to their health (drug use, STI, interpersonal violence) but also to the spaces and networks they become linked to, undermining their social security as a result of the structural and interpersonal violence they are subject to as sex workers, migrants and drug users.

Thus, analysing migration in relation to drug use in the border regions shows the structural violence exerted towards those who, in the process of seeking life improvement through migration, are placed at the margins of nation states, and their health, social and political condition is worsened in these contexts. The aforementioned studies address different aspects and levels of analysis concerning the experience of drug use in contemporary Mexican society. Using migrants' experiences as starting point, this chapter aims to articulate, from a CMA perspective, the interactions between the migratory condition and the subjective experience of drug use (practices, meanings and forms of care) in the border region between Mexico and the United States.

Methodological approach

This research is based on a qualitative longitudinal study that explores different participants' life stages related to the overlapping aspects of the migration experience, drug use and its forms of care, from leaving their places of origin until their settlement in the border region. This approach considers different variables (social, personal, cultural, economic and political, among others) as intertwined over a period of time, qualitatively paying attention to the subjective dimension of those variables from participants' experience. The study systematically analyses migrants' trajectories, from leaving their place of origin to settling in the border region between Mexico and the United States, and engaging with a form of treatment for drug use in California or Baja California.

The trajectory, as a theoretical and methodological tool, contributes to the systematisation of multi-spatiality during the migration experience (Rivera Sánchez 2012). It also aids understanding of changes, continuities and breakdowns in social, cultural, political, economic and personal aspects of individuals' life experiences. Specifically, the migratory trajectory approach permits the selection of an analytical period in the biography, allowing the order, systematisation and interpretation of drug use during a specific time interval, in this case migration between Mexico and the United States. Thus, this study discusses the relationship between personal situations and the context in which these experiences occur.

The study included 24 men between the ages of 25 and 65. Most of them reported methamphetamine, heroin or alcohol as the principal drug used. The majority of them were born in Mexico City and Tijuana, while a minority were from Nayarit, Jalisco, Michoacán and Durango. A few of those born in Tijuana emigrated to the United States with their parents or a relative during their childhood. However, the majority emigrated alone between the ages of 15 to 25, escaping from problematic situations in their places of origin, mainly drug use and violence, as well as economic and familial problems.

During the study, participants were recruited from three institutions providing low-cost self-help group services for drug use in the border region, which is the principal form of care in the Mexican side of the border (Galaviz and Odgers Ortiz 2014). Most of the people were of Mexican descent and treatment was provided in Spanish. Importantly, the people providing treatment have often had or are concurrently experiencing treatment as well. These self-help organisations outlined below were selected because they are more accessible for people with social and economic conditions of precariousness.

The first organisation is a religious rehabilitation centre located in Los Angeles that provides voluntary residential treatment for drug use. The religious approach to drug use rehabilitation understands the problem as spiritual and has the idea of God as saviour (Olivas Hernandez and Odgers Ortiz 2015). The second, located in San Diego, is a 24-hour AA group, which provides both out-patient and residential (in-patient) treatment. Even though it is an AA group, the users of this service have used drugs beyond alcohol, such as methamphetamine, alcohol, heroin and psychotropic pills, among others. The study participants attend out-patient self-help group sessions based on the Twelve Steps model. Finally, the third organisation located in Tijuana, is a rehabilitation centre also based on the Twelve Steps model, providing voluntary and involuntary residential treatment. The participants interviewed at this centre are returned migrants deported from the US.

During 2016, I conducted semi-structured interviews with 24 participants receiving treatment in each one of these organisations. In the interviews, I explored changes in their patterns of drug use and other familial, economic, emotional and social events that they had experienced after leaving their places of origin until their current involvement in the treatment. I specifically focused interviews on changes in drug use, their notions of health and illness, as well as the forms of care used to diminish their drug use, as most of the time they did not turn to specialised treatments. I also conducted observations of daily activities in the centres.

The migratory process and drug use

Some quantitative studies that have focused on the experience of migration between Mexico and the United States in relation to drug use have argued that people migrating from Mexico increase drug use once they are in the United States, while among returned migrants drug use diminishes once they are back in Mexico (Caetano and Medina Mora 1988; Sánchez-Huesca et al. 2006; Sanchez-Huesca and Arellanez-Hernández 2011). However, the quantity of consumption in Mexico continues to be high compared with their drug use practices before leaving their home country.

Other studies have focused on Mexican immigrants settled in the US. For example, one study argued that labour discrimination and exclusion are associated with alcohol abuse and dependence. In this case, social support did not act as a source of help among the people living with high to moderate rates of labour frustration and feeling unsatisfied (Finch et al., cited in Alvarez et al. 2007). Other research has shown that Latin American people living in the US have unequal access to treatments for drug use (SAMHSA, cited in Alvarez et al. 2007). Even if the possibility of accessing healthcare exists, they wait long periods of time to receive care, which they ultimately find unsatisfactory (Wells et al. cited in Alvarez et al. 2007). Finally, some studies discuss treatments' characteristics, emphasising that culturally specific out-patient and residential treatments could have better results for drug use among Latin American people settled in the US (Cervantes et al.; Hohman and Gait; Waters et al. – all cited in Alvarez et al. 2007).

Although the condition of Mexican immigrants in the US or returned migrants in Mexico is different due to their migratory status, they share some difficulties related to the process of mobility (voluntary or forced) between Mexico and the US. As stated before, the majority of participants in this study migrated from Mexico to the US when they were 15 to 25 years old; most of them were using marijuana or alcohol at the time. Even though some of them had a relative or friend living in the US, they did not contact them, or if they did, the relationship was temporary.

Some of the reasons to migrate from Mexico to the US were related to family problems (mainly with parents), substance consumption, situations of violence in their places of origin and economic difficulties. In most of the cases analysed, moving to a new context was framed as an attempt to modify and improve their social, cultural and economic condition, in comparison to their lifestyle in their places of origin.

Nevertheless, undocumented migrants in the US face conditions of precariousness in terms of their labour, economic and social needs, which are reinforced by their experience of social isolation. In the border region, migrants deal with adversities that affect the possibility of gaining social and material resources to integrate themselves in their new context, ultimately impacting their mental, emotional and physical health.

Participants' migratory experiences were often characterised by a change in their drug use patterns. During the mobility from their places of origin and their first weeks in the border region, there was a decrease in drug use. However, once they became employed and established relationships with other users, their drug use increased. Additionally, most of them demonstrated a diversification of the type of drugs used, such as using methamphetamine, crack, psychotropic pills, cocaine or heroin for the first time. Valentin, for example, was born in Durango, México and emigrated to the US alone after ending a relationship, when he was 23 years old. He used to consume alcohol in Mexico, but in the US, crack was the main substance of consumption.

> When I arrived [in the US], I was looking at everything differently. For example, it was easy for me to get into drug addiction here, because if you were on the street with a beer or a cigarette [marijuana], you just needed to hide it when the police were passing by, they were not aware of it … that made it easier for me (to use drugs) because being alone here is how I became addicted to marijuana. I was using meth, pills, PCP, crack, and I didn't know about all that until I arrived in this country.[3]

For most participants, their increased drug use was affected by their life circumstances in the border region, related to their working conditions, social isolation and living at the margins with other people in the same condition as undocumented migrants. Even though the kind of jobs they acquired have precarious conditions and low pay, most of them report an increased income, allowing them to have more access to drugs. They also find more social tolerance of drug use in the US, particularly among those sharing an apartment with other migrant men or in jobs where drugs were used to improve performance over long work shifts, like one of the participants describes.

Ricardo was born in Mexico State and migrated to the border region at 21 due to problems of gang violence in his neighbourhood. Even though the main drugs he used before starting rehabilitation were alcohol and cocaine, he describes the shifts from one drug to another and his experience with marijuana during his first employment in agriculture, where most undocumented migrants work in the US.

> We arrived at a place called Oceanside, there were tomato fields and, well, I didn't know anyone, I had to stay working in the field. There I met more friends and that's when I got back into marijuana. While working in the field and picking tomatoes, they told me: 'Look, with this [smoking marijuana] you are going to work more quickly', and I said: 'Well, let's see.' Then I started using marijuana and stopped drinking alcohol. That is how my life has been [switching from one drug to another]. I started smoking marijuana [in Mexico] but I didn't like it, then I used inhalant drugs [volatile solvents] for a long time, later for a while I drank alcohol and I quit when I was working in the tomato field. I started with marijuana when I came here [to the US] because it was easier to get drugs here. I was working and having more money ... I was smoking around ten cigarettes in a day.[4]

Ricardo did not have social networks when he first arrived in the US and he relied on other migrants to help him to settle in Los Angeles, California. The neighbourhood where he arrived was poor, with gang and drug use problems. Even though he met other undocumented migrant men in the US with whom he shared an apartment, he felt alone. Problematic emotional experiences on arriving at their migratory destination affected the increase and diversification of drug use among participants in this study, especially when settling into segregated neighbourhoods where drug trafficking is common. The feelings of loneliness and sadness experienced as a consequence of being away from their social networks in Mexico often caused an increase in drug use. In addition to the lack of affective bonds in the US, work stress, economic difficulties and marital problems influenced their emotional experience. For these men, drug use became a strategy to face the emotional challenges of living in these situations. As such, drug use could be understood as a form of 'self-care' in Menéndez's sense, to deal with the emotional pain, as another participant argues.

Dario was contacted in a rehabilitation centre in Mexico after being deported. It was his first experience of treatment. He was born in Tijuana and emigrated with an aunt to the US at the age of three months after his mother passed away. At the age of eight, he started to have problems with his aunt and left home. Later on, he started using drugs and was incarcerated many times, but not in rehabilitation centres, demonstrating how drug abuse is often criminalised but not understood as a health problem. Dario describes the experience of being away from his family as the reason for beginning and continuing his drug use:

> When I started using more drugs, it was because I was falling into a kind of depression; I started missing my brothers, my aunt and my cousins. At the beginning with the marijuana, you are always laughing, but as it gets inside of you, you are more focused on your thoughts, and you will be there just thinking about the problem. Later I tried mushrooms and I would hallucinate ... then the LSD, and later the pills. The pills (Rohypnol) started helping me more ... in the way that they blocked my thoughts ... I just started to think a little bit about my family and I would take three or four pills and that's how I was living.[5]

Even though many participants increased their drug use after the migratory experience, it was not perceived as problematic, because they felt capable of regulating their use by themselves. This notion was also associated with the benefits they were experiencing from drug use; it became a resource to deal with different situations in their lives. Moreover, some participants noticed that using drugs helped them to deal with their emotions. They registered an improvement in their social skills as they became self-confident and were able to work for longer periods under the influence of drugs, improving their income. They were also, however, spending more money on drugs, which later became a difficulty for some.

This situation gives an account of the levels of labour exploitation that some undocumented migrants face in the US. Since they have low-paid and irregular jobs and are always at risk of being deported, some of them try to make the highest profit from their time in the US, sometimes at the cost of their health and safety. Even though they experienced challenges due to drug use, most of them developed strategies to diminish those effects, reducing the quantity and frequency of use. One of the strategies was to change their place of residence in the US, as some started to have illegal trans-border mobility between Mexico and the US (mainly those who were born in Tijuana), especially during the 1990s, before the militarisation of the border (Heyman and Campbell 2012). The mobility allowed them to move away from the drug users' networks, although sometimes only temporarily.

Another strategy was to manage their money differently, spending more on their family, homes and personal belongings and less on drugs. Entering into romantic relationships and having a child were other strategies related to more responsibility or being aware of it. Another strategy was to diminish the adverse effects of drug use. For example, when they felt a lack of control over their drug use, they replaced one drug with another, or diminished the use of one drug while increasing another. These adjustments in drug use patterns can also be understood as forms of self-care. These strategies were undertaken to avoid being in a critical condition, as one participant describes.

Martín was born in Mexico City and migrated to the US when he was 20 due to family economic problems. He used to work seasonally in the US and go back with his family (parents and brothers) to Mexico. But when the militarisation of the border was enforced after 9/11, he stayed in the US and never went back to Mexico. The jobs he got were in small markets, with precarious labour conditions, such as low payment and no access to healthcare, but with minimal supervision, allowing him to drink alcohol at work. He began consuming alcohol at the age of 15 and explains why he replaced alcohol with methamphetamine while working.

> Here [in the US] I had the chance to drink at my job, there was a lot of freedom … since I used to work in small markets, I was able to do what I wanted in my place of work, and if the boss noticed, there was no big trouble. I used to drink a little bit, I never was falling [due to the alcohol use] and I drank more after my job, and I never fell, I could drink a lot and keep working. But when I started with meth, I had *tocado fondo* [touched bottom] with alcoholism, I was not able to work any more, it was very hard. On one occasion, I couldn't handle the hangover, I felt bad physically, but I was working, and someone told me that if I wanted to feel good, he had something for me to get better. I knew what he was talking about, but I had never tried meth; the guy left me some lines [of meth] on the table and I was

so desperate because I was not feeling good, so the first time that I used it, I just started and immediately I was feeling good, the physical discomfort disappeared. That experience was what attracted me and captured me more. The meth consumption made me a sociable person, what I couldn't do or say I did it under the effects of meth. I remember that I quit alcohol and I started to use meth regularly … I turned to my normal activities again and I was feeling better because, in the beginning, that's how it was.[6]

From the participants' perspective, using drugs for some years without experiencing negative consequences shaped their perceptions of not considering drug use to be a problem. Rather, drug use was a means to deal with their problems. The use of as a form of self-care to address their needs and discomforts reveals their perception and experience of drug use as a solution to problems, not an illness. Even though they experienced difficulties related to their drug consumption, those were lived and understood as extraordinary conditions that they have to struggle with constantly, in efforts to improve their lives. However, not perceiving their situation with drug use as a health problem is in some cases a result of the indifference of employers towards undocumented workers' conditions, in addition to the difficulty of accessing healthcare.

The notion of drug use as a problem

As mentioned earlier, the majority of participants identified different stages in their life trajectory where they managed drug use difficulties through self-care strategies, such as maintaining relative stability in their family relationships, job performance and economic position. However, in all the cases analysed, there are later stages where they experienced more difficulty in regulating the patterns of drug use, even if they were using the same self-care strategies, such as transitioning between different drugs or moving to a new context. These different conditions changed their perception and experiences related to drug use.

Once they were experiencing more difficulties in keeping a job or getting a new one if they were fired, they started to consider their drug use as a problem. In these cases, they were experiencing the situation of being at the margins of the system, which was expelling them once they were not economically functional for the employers. They often found themselves unable to provide for their families, which impacted their familial relationships and economic position. For participants in this study, the duty of being the worker and main provider is closely associated with gendered social expectations of them as the man of the house. Accordingly, when they were unable to perform their social role as provider, their family relationships broke down. Some of them found themselves in failing relationships, losing contact with their family members and eventually becoming homeless, as Alan recounts.

Alan was born in Guadalajara, Jalisco, and emigrated to the US at the age of 21. He tried to reunite with his wife in the US after having marital problems. His first employment in Texas was in agriculture, where he constantly experienced fear of deportation, leading him to live in precarious conditions in the field for some years. Later he reunited with his wife in Los Angeles, where he managed to get a job in upholstery. He was using alcohol in Mexico but began using meth in the US to do overtime and improve his performance at work. Eventually he started to lose control over his drug use.

> In the beginning, I was using meth, and everything was fine. I even wanted to work and to be more active and used to do overtime at work. But as time passed, everything changed … When I started using meth I was able to work, I was not using too much, around $20 per week. I was using just on Friday, Saturday and Sunday, when the party was over, and I was well rested and ready to work on Monday. For five years that's how it was, I didn't have economic or relationship problems. But when I started to spend the night with my friends drinking, I became more focused on drug use. That was when I began to have problems with my wife, and due to those problems with her, I increased my use. But what happened with that drug [meth] is that it is stronger than others. At the beginning I said, 'I control it', but later I lost control. I was using it to go to work and increased the quantity [of the drug]. Later, I started to miss work and had bad job performance. My social, labour and emotional responsibilities were affected. I said to my wife, 'I need help because I am not controlling it [the drug use]', and my wife said, 'That's your problem, don't count on me, because I didn't send you to use drugs', so I felt rebuffed. One time I heard her telling her sister, 'As long as he gives me what I need, he can do what he wants', but three years ago was when I was hitting bottom [having critical problems due to drug use]. My wife didn't want to be with me any more. I lost my job and became untrusty for other people and started falling down … I was still living with my wife, but our relationship was very hard, we were having economic problems, until the moment that she and her

family threw me out of my house. I lived 15 days in the street and a friend of mine who was also using drugs let me stay in his garage. I got a job in an upholstery where I was known, but I was lost already. I continued using every day ... to the point where in the morning if I got up, and I didn't drink a beer, I couldn't even walk. During the morning, I used to drink five beers and do meth at around noon, to reduce the beer effect so the boss couldn't notice. I was not using a lot of meth, the alcohol was what was disturbing me. The last 15 days were the heaviest because I started hallucinating and couldn't sleep at night. Those two weeks I was struggling with myself, due to the hallucinations.[7]

Alan's experience shows that failure as a provider (as a result of difficulties in keeping his job), and its consequences in the family context (being rejected by his family and becoming homeless), worsened his drug use problem, thereby exacerbating his conditions of precariousness. Most of the participants resorted to treatment once they were struggling with different problems or extraordinary conditions at the same time, such as the experiences of hearing voices, being homeless, lacking social support and suicidal ideation or attempting suicide.

The participants who had settled in Tijuana as returned migrants did not report seeking any treatment in the US. Compared with migrants arriving in the US for the first time, returned migrants with drug use problems experience conditions that are highly precarious once they are back in Mexico: a lack of social support networks, economic instability, limited employment and housing possibilities, as well as restrictions on receiving help in migrant shelters due to their drug use problems. This partially relates to their physical and mental health conditions stemming from their deportation (Rosales Martínez et al. 2017). Most of the participants interviewed on the Mexican side of the border reported that they become involved in treatment after their deportation. Their health conditions had worsened during their time in the US, due to their increased drug use. Once deported, they did not feel socially and economically able to integrate themselves in Mexico, leading them to voluntarily seek residential treatment as a temporary shelter.

From participants' perspectives, one critical consequence of drug use was the experience of auditory hallucinations, particularly when combined with suicidal ideation. For help with this they mainly turned to religious treatment, primarily because of social, economic and cultural difficulties in accessing any other sources of help. While some participants turned to psychiatric treatment, they did not feel comfortable being categorised as having a mental illness nor were they willing to begin psycho-pharmacological treatment. Therefore the preferred option was to seek religious support, where their hallucination experiences were interpreted as the presence of demons trying to bother them, rather than as a stigmatising mental problem. Alan recounted how he had turned to a charismatic Catholic group to take care of his problems related to drug use once he became homeless.

> When I couldn't keep my job, was when the voices [auditory hallu-cinations] were bothering me more. I talked with a person from the Catholic group … he told me that he knew what was going on with me. Then, the same day, I heard the voices again, telling me that I had broken the rules, that I wasn't supposed to have talked with them [the Catholics], it was something between them [the voices] and me. Later, I arrived here [at the religious rehabilitation cen-tre] and understood that what we face is a spiritual struggle. While reading the Bible, I found that seven demons attack us. I made sense of all that because I was listening to seven different voices by that time.[8]

All the participants sought institutionalised care based on the Twelve Steps or religious therapeutic models. This was in part because their economic condition prevented access to other kinds of treatments, since most of them only sought treatment once they became homeless. Fur-thermore, they identified with the community that constitutes those forms of care and the way they collectively addressed and understood their situation.

It is relevant to underline that Twelve Step treatments and religious models can be categorised as forms of care based on the self-help ethos, because service providers for those forms of care are often people who are also living through or have already undergone a rehabilitation pro-cess. In many cases, this caregiving community also provides social, cul-tural and sometimes economic support networks that migrants had been missing. This leads to two conclusions. First, turning to a form of low- or no-cost care sheds light on the conditions of social and economic pre-cariousness that undocumented migrants with drug use problems often experience. Second, it allows us to analyse the way in which the social group that constitutes the therapeutic community has taken a position on understanding, defining and caring for drug use problems contrast-ing with other hegemonic forms (medical, psychological, psychiatric) of treating their health condition.

According to Singer (1989), analysing the life course both inside and outside the health arena reveals disputes between individuals and groups whose social interests conflict; further, the fact that these different social groups (i.e. therapeutic communities and biomedical/psychological professionals) have unequal abilities legitimises certain forms of care and meanings attributed to illness. From this perspective, Singer suggests that we need to pay attention to the implicit and explicit social struggles that manifest in illness meanings and experiences, clinical interactions and the relationship between health systems and healthcare providers, as well as organised efforts by patients, workers and oppressed populations, such as self-help groups.

The wide dissemination of alternative forms of care (religious and Twelve Step) categorised as mutual-aid groups, as opposed to state-sponsored psychological services, makes visible the tension between the state as the provider of public healthcare services and its inability to meet the community's needs. Because of this, alternative forms of care have emerged within civil society (Galaviz and Odgers Ortiz 2014).

The difficulties experienced by undocumented and returnee migrants which ultimately lead to them accessing these forms of care reveal conditions of structural violence, social marginalisation and inequality. Being an undocumented or returnee migrant in the border region limits their labour possibilities to low-paid jobs with difficulties accessing healthcare, and with precarious housing conditions in segregated neighbourhoods, where drug use and violence are often community problems. These conditions worsen their problems with drug use, putting them in critical situations that make seeking treatment with mutual-aid groups a means to survive.

Conclusions

The problems that Mexican migrants face in their efforts to achieve social, economic, political and cultural inclusion in the border region significantly shape their mental and emotional health. The lived experience of the migration process increased the problems that these men were already experiencing in their places of origin, such as drug use. It is important to highlight that the participants in this study migrated to the border region under conditions of extreme precariousness. Most of them were children or young adults experiencing social and economic problems that motivated their migration; thus, they did not have a network that could act as an emotional, social and economic support in the border region.

As mentioned previously, this chapter used a life trajectories approach centred on the process of migration to analyse the subjective experience of drug use (changes, continuities, practices and meanings) and to address its relationship with the social, political, economic and cultural environment in the United States–Mexico border region. In the first stages of their trajectory, mainly in their places of origin, drug use (mainly marijuana and alcohol) was perceived as a recreational practice, but in some cases it was causing family problems because their parents perceived such practices as immoral. Once they migrated to the border region and faced different challenges related to the process of economic and social integration as an undocumented migrant in the US, it is possible to identify drug use (mainly methamphetamine, alcohol, psychotropic pills and crack) as a form of self-care to manage the (emotional and social) difficulties they faced at their destination. They also found social tolerance and easy access to drug use in low-paid informal jobs, since it helped them to improve their performance by working for long periods of time, to the employer's advantage.

From participants' perspective, drug use was part of their coping strategies, and it helped them to achieve economic, social and emotional stability. Changing patterns of consumption, like increasing drug use or substituting one drug for another, facilitated their adaptation to their new context for some years. From this perspective, drug use in daily life was among the resources and strategies they had to cope with the challenges of living as an undocumented migrant in the US, such as the fear of deportation, the high cost of living combined with low wages, lack of healthcare access and difficulties with social and cultural integration beyond the margins.

Undocumented migrants in the US were trying to be functional in the economic system and deal with emotional instability – in some cases as a result of not being able to visit their family in Mexico due to the militarisation of the border. Analysing the subjective experience of drug use from the participants' perspective, I argue, reveals that their understanding of their condition escapes the social framing of drug use as an illness. Focusing attention on their struggles allows us to identify the precarious conditions they faced when settling in the border region. Moreover, their experiences illuminate the lack of support in this region and the easy access to drugs, which reduced the discomfort they experienced in the process of settling into a new context. Yet their drug use experience transforms in later stages after the settlement process in the US, when they experience adverse social, cultural, economic and personal consequences of drug use.

When the experience of using drugs started to lead to other problems, such as not being socially and economically functional, not being productive at any job and unemployed, unable to be a provider and accomplish the role of the man of the house, and finally becoming homeless, the participants started to seek help and the meaning of using drugs changed. The marginalisation they experienced, not only at structural levels but also interpersonally, led them to seek residential mutual-aid treatment. This was the main source of help that the participants of this study had access to in the border region. The intersubjective experience of treatments that were based on the Twelve Steps and/or religiously oriented shaped their notion of drug use as an illness or suffering related to a spiritual problem; they then realised that they needed help from a therapeutic community to overcome this condition. The social network aiding these people was composed of those who were also marginalised and discriminated against by the health, political and economic system in the US.

Since having a sense of belonging (to a therapeutic community or, in this case, a self-help group) has a significant meaning in the process of recovery, joining this kind of community has improved their experience of social inclusion at the border region. The cases presented in this chapter shed light on the processes of marginalisation that drug users undergo in contemporary society. Furthermore, it reveals migrant men's capacity to assume active roles in the process of managing the problems associated with drug use through self-care strategies, and their ability to be part of a community that delineates alternative forms of understanding and caring for their health conditions.

Analysing this phenomenon from a CMA perspective contributes to scholarly understandings of the meanings that drug use practices can have in the daily lives of people living in conditions of precariousness, such as migrants in the US–Mexico border zone. This chapter has provided a window on the process of pathologising or criminalising drug use practices alongside an account of how drug use can be a strategy for self-care under stressful and emotional extraordinary conditions. The systematic, structural violence experienced in the border region sheds light on migrants' lack of resources for help in relation to their mental and emotional wellbeing, leading to the embodiment of illness experiences related to drug use.

Notes

1. The US Immigration and Customs Enforcement (ICE) implemented a Secure Communities Program from 2008 prioritising the removal of public safety and national security threats – people who have violated the nation's immigration laws, including those who have failed to comply with a final order removal. This deportation programme relies on partnership among federal, state, and local law enforcement agencies. Nonetheless, most of the people deported have committed minor offences and do not represent a threat to public safety and national security.

2. The original twelve-step programme was devised by Alcoholics Anonymous, founded in 1935 by Bill Wilson and Robert Holbrook Smith. The programme consisted of a set of guiding principles outlining a course of action for alcohol abuse problems. Later it was adapted to address a wide range of alcoholism, substance abuse and dependency problems and has been expanded worldwide.
3. Interview with Valentin in a religious rehabilitation centre in Los Angeles.
4. Interview with Ricardo in a religious rehabilitation centre in Los Angeles.
5. Interview with Dario in a Twelve Step rehabilitation centre in Tijuana.
6. Interview with Martín in an AA group in San Diego.
7. Interview with Alan in a religious rehabilitation centre in Los Angeles.
8. Interview with Alan in a religious rehabilitation centre in Los Angeles.

References

Alvarez, Josefina, Leonard A. Jason, Bradley D. Olson, Joseph R. Ferrari and Margaret I. Davis. 2007. 'Substance Abuse Prevalence and Treatment among Latinos and Latinas', *Journal of Ethnicity in Substance Abuse* 6 (2): 115–41.

APA (American Psychiatric Association). 2013. *Diagnostic and Statistical Manual of Mental Disorders: DSM-5*. 5th ed. Washington, DC: American Psychiatric Association.

Armenta, Amada. 2017. 'Racializing Crimmigration: Structural Racism, Colorblindness, and the Institutional Production of Immigrant Criminality', *Sociology of Race and Ethnicity* 3 (1): 82–95.

Brecht, Mary-Lynn. 2014. 'Drug Abuse Patterns and Trends in Los Angeles County – Update: January 2014'. National Institute on Drug Abuse. Accessed 14 September 2019. https://archives.drugabuse.gov/los-angeles-county-california.

Caetano, Raúl and María E. Medina Mora. 1988. 'Patrones de consumo de alcohol y problemas asociados en México y en población de origen mexicano que habita en Estados Unidos', *Nueva Antropología* 10 (34): 137–55.

Cajas Castro, Juan. 2013. 'Vigilar y sospechar: Violencia, estigmas y limpieza social en la guerra contra las drogas'. In *La marca de las drogas: Violencias y prácticas de consumo*, edited by María Dolores París Pombo and Lorena Raquel Pérez Floriano, 221–246. Tijuana: Colegio de la Frontera Norte.

Farmer, Paul. 2004. 'An Anthropology of Structural Violence', *Current Anthropology* 45 (3): 305–25.

Farmer, Paul E., Bruce Nizeye, Sara Stulac and Salmaan Keshavjee. 2006. 'Structural Violence and Clinical Medicine', *PLoS Medicine* 3 (10), Article e449: 1686–91.

Galaviz, Gloria and Olga Odgers Ortiz. 2014. 'Estado laico y alternativas terapéuticas religiosas: El caso de México en el tratamiento de adicciones', *Debates do NER* 15 (26): 253–76.

Galaviz Granados, Gloria. 2015. 'Mujeres, adicción y rehabilitación: Reflexiones desde la frontera noroeste de México', *Salud Colectiva* 11 (3): 367–79.

García Hernández, Ebermhi Federico. 2014. 'Renacer por la palabra: Identidad narrativa y experiencia espiritual de exadictos en centros de rehabilitación evangélicos en Tijuana, Baja California'. Master's thesis, Colegio de la Frontera Norte, Tijuana.

Gonzalez-Barrera, Ana and Jens Manuel Krogstad. 2019. 'What We Know about Illegal Immigration from Mexico'. Pew Research Center. Accessed 14 September 2019. http://www.pewresearch.org/fact-tank/2018/12/03/what-we-know-about-illegal-immigration-from-mexico/.

González Tamayo, Eduardo Yael. 2016. 'Hombres de esperanza: Transformación de la identidad masculina en la rehabilitación evangélica de la farmacodependencia'. In *Miradas multidisciplinarias a la diversidad religiosa mexicana*, edited by Luis Jesús Martínez Gómez and Genaro Zalpa Ramírez, 255–92. Tijuana: Colegio de la Frontera Norte.

Heyman, Josiah and Howard Campbell. 2012. 'The Militarization of the United States–Mexico Border Region', *Revista de Estudos Universitários* 38 (1): 75–94.

Holmes, Seth M. 2006. 'An Ethnographic Study of the Social Context of Migrant Health in the United States', *PLoS Medicine* 3 (10), Article e448: 1776–93.

Holmes, Seth M. 2013. *Fresh Fruit, Broken Bodies: Migrant Farmworkers in the United States*. Berkeley: University of California Press.

INPRFM (Instituto Nacional de Psiquiatría Ramón de la Fuente Muñiz; Instituto Nacional de Salud Pública; Secretaría de Salud). 2012. *Encuesta Nacional de Adicciones 2011: Drogas ilícitas*. Accessed 31 October 2019. http://www.conadic.salud.gob.mx/pdfs/ENA_2011_DROGAS_ILICITAS.pdf.

Jenkins, Janis Hunter. 1997. 'Subjective Experience of Persistent Schizophrenia and Depression among US Latinos and Euro-Americans', *British Journal of Psychiatry* 171 (1): 20–25.

Jenkins, Janis H. 2015. *Extraordinary Conditions: Culture and Experience in Mental Illness*. Oakland: University of California Press.

Jenkins, Janis Hunter and Norma Cofresi. 1998. 'The Sociosomatic Course of Depression and Trauma: A Cultural Analysis of Suffering and Resilience in the Life of a Puerto Rican Woman', *Psychosomatic Medicine* 60 (4): 439–47.

Jenkins, Janis H. and John G. Schumacher. 1999. 'Family Burden of Schizophrenia and Depressive Illness: Specifying the Effects of Ethnicity, Gender and Social Ecology', *British Journal of Psychiatry* 174 (1): 31–38.

Kleinman, Arthur and Erin Fitz-Henry. 2007. 'The Experiential Basis of Subjectivity: How Individuals Change in the Context of Societal Transformation'. In *Subjectivity: Ethnographic Investigations*, edited by João Biehl, Byron Good and Arthur Kleinman, 52–65. Berkeley: University of California Press.

Kozelka, Ellen Elizabeth. 2015. '(Not So) Fluid Borders, (Not So) Fluid Identities: Time, Space, and Social Categories in Tijuana Drug Rehabilitation Centers'. Master's thesis, University of California, San Diego.

Lerín Piñón, Sergio. 2004. 'Antropología y salud intercultural: Desafíos de una propuesta', *Desacatos* 15/16: 111–25.

Menéndez, Eduardo L. 1983. *Hacia una práctica médica alternativa: Hegemonía y autoatención (gestión) en salud*. Mexico City: Centro de Investigaciones y Estudios Superiores en Antropología Social.

Menéndez, Eduardo. 1994. 'La enfermedad y la curación: ¿Qué es medicina tradicional?', *Alteridades* 4 (7): 71–83.

Menéndez, Eduardo L. 2003. 'Modelos de atención de los padecimientos: De exclusiones teóricas y articulaciones prácticas', *Ciência e Saúde Coletiva* 8 (1): 185–207.

Menéndez, Eduardo L. 2009. 'De rituales y subjetividades: Reflexiones sobre algunas características de los grupos de Alcohólicos Anónimos', *Desacatos* 29: 107–20.

Meth Strike Force. 2018. 'MSF Report Card'. Accessed 14 September 2019. https://www.no2meth.org/local-statistics.

Módena, María Eugenia. 2009. 'Diferencias, desigualdades y conflicto en un grupo de Alcohólicos Anónimos', *Desacatos* 29: 31–46.

Odgers Ortiz, Olga and Gloria Galaviz Granados. 2016. 'Entre la espera y la esperanza: Construcción de la esperanza en internos de centros de rehabilitación para usuarios de drogas', *Nuevo Mundo Mundos Nuevos*, 25 January. Accessed 12 September 2019. https://journals.openedition.org/nuevomundo/68925.

Olivas Hernandez, Olga Lidia and Olga Odgers Ortiz. 2015. 'Renacer en Cristo: Cuerpo y subjetivación en la experiencia de rehabilitación de adicciones en los centros evangélico pentecostales', *Ciencias Sociales y Religión* 17 (22): 90–119.

Palacios Ramírez, José. 2009. 'La construcción del alcohólico en recuperación: Reflexiones a partir del estudio de una comunidad de Alcohólicos Anónimos en el norte de México', *Desacatos* 29: 47–68.

París Pombo, María Dolores. 2013. 'Criminalización del consumo de drogas y derechos humanos de los usuarios: El caso de Tijuana, Baja California'. In *La marca de las drogas: Violencias y prácticas de consumo*, edited by María Dolores París Pombo and Lorena Raquel Pérez Floriano, 109–36. Tijuana: Colegio de la Frontera Norte.

Pérez Floriano, Lorena Raquel. 2013. 'Marcas físicas y morales: Segregación y discriminación de las personas que consumen drogas y sus familiares'. In *La marca de las drogas: Violencias y prácticas de consumo*, edited by María Dolores París Pombo and Lorena Raquel Pérez Floriano, pp. 137–159. Tijuana: Colegio de la Frontera Norte.

Ramírez Navarro, Patricia. 2010. 'Análisis de la relación existente entre la cultura de género y la construcción de la depresión femenina'. In *La medicina social en México I: Experiencia, subjetividad y salud*, edited by Florencia Peña Saint Martin and Beatriz León Parra, pp. 55–76. Mexico City: Ediciones y Gráficos Eón.

Reséndiz García, Ramón R. 2013. 'Biografía: Proceso y nudos teórico-metodológicos'. In *Observar, escuchar y comprender: Sobre la tradición cualitativa en la investigación social*, edited by María Luisa Tarrés, 127–58. Mexico City: Colegio de México.

Rivera Sánchez, Liliana. 2012. 'Las trayectorias en los estudios de migración: Una herramienta para el análisis longitudinal cualitativo'. In *Métodos cualitativos y su aplicación empírica: Por los caminos de la investigación sobre migración internacional*, edited by Marina Ariza and Laura Velasco, 455–94. Mexico City: Universidad Nacional Autónoma de México.

Rosales Martínez, Yetzi, Ietza Bojorquez Chapela, René Leyva Flores and César Infante Xibille. 2017. 'Health Services Provision for Migrants Repatriated through Tijuana, Baja California: Inter-Agency Cooperation and Response Capacity', *Frontera Norte* 29 (57): 107–30.

Rosovsky, Haydée. 2009. 'Alcohólicos Anónimos en México: Fragmentación y fortalezas', *Desacatos* 29: 13–30.

Sánchez-Huesca, Ricardo and Jorge Luis Arellanez-Hernández. 2011. 'Uso de drogas en migrantes mexicanos captados en ciudades de la frontera noroccidental México–Estados Unidos', *Estudios Fronterizos* 12 (23): 9–26.

Sánchez-Huesca, Ricardo, Jorge Luis Arellanez-Hernández, Verónica Pérez-Islas and Solveig E. Rodríguez-Kuri. 2006. 'Estudio de la relación entre consumo de drogas y migración a la frontera norte de México y Estados Unidos', *Salud Mental* 29 (1): 35–43.

Scheper-Hughes, Nancy and Margaret M. Lock. 1986. 'Speaking "Truth" to Illness: Metaphors, Reification, and Pedagogy for Patients', *Medical Anthropology Quarterly* 17 (5): 137–40.

Secretaría de Gobernación. 2018. 'Boletín Estadístico V: Repatriación de mexicanos, 2018'. Accessed 31 October 2019. http://politicamigratoria.gob.mx/es/PoliticaMigratoria/Cuadro sBOLETIN?Anual=2018&Secc=5.

Singer, Merrill. 1989. 'The Coming of Age of Critical Medical Anthropology', *Social Science and Medicine* 28 (11): 1193–203.

Velázquez Fernández, Jareb Benelli. 2016. '"Si yo fuera yo, ya me habría fugado": El dispositivo de sanación pentecostal: Experiencia y proyectos de vida de mujeres internas en un centro de rehabiltación'. Master's thesis, Colegio de la Frontera Norte, Tijuana.

Wagner, Karla D. 2014. 'Drug Abuse Patterns and Trends in San Diego County – Update: January 2014'. National Institute on Drug Abuse. Accessed 14 September 2019. https://archives.drugabuse.gov/san-diego-county-california.

6

Border spaces: Stigma and social vulnerability to HIV/AIDS among Central American male migrants at the Mexico–Guatemala border

Rubén Muñoz Martínez, Carmen Fernández Casanueva, Sonia Morales Miranda and Kimberly C. Brouwer

I travelled to the north and I was deported, then I tried one more time and I came back to Mexico. In my country (Honduras), they want to kill me. There, they think I'm another person. Just by my haircut they think I belong to the Mara Chirizo, so Mara Salvatrucha and Mara 18 want to kill me by mistake. Sometimes you can be well dressed, beautiful, it doesn't matter, they kidnap you, and tomorrow you are in a plastic bag or floating in the river, dead.

(Honduran, 21 years old)

Listen, up to the north [of Mexico] there are the Zetas and mareros. *When you try to get close to the border the leaders will not let you go if you don't pay some money. We are travelling, begging to have something to eat. If they catch you and you don't have any money … you can imagine!*

(Honduran, 23 years old)

The main purpose of this chapter is to share and discuss the findings of an exploratory research study[1] conducted from a critical medical anthropology perspective. The study focuses on the processes of social vulnerability to HIV infection[2] that are faced by Central American male migrants en route to the United States, who are undocumented during their transit through Mexico, who were residing near the Mexico–Guatemala border when interviewed, and who perform sex work under the influence of non-injected drugs. Considering migration and/or displacement as non-linear processes, we explore the transit and temporary sojourn of these migrants in the following four border cities: Tecún Umán and Quetzaltenango (Guatemala), Ciudad Hidalgo and Tapachula (Mexico).

Drawing on Latin American critical medical anthropology, this research contributes to the development of a relational approach beyond the framework of the dialectical debate on subject versus structure (Menéndez 2009), enabling us to challenge a structural analysis that erases the actor's points of view and praxis, as well as to overcome individual 'rational choice' perspectives that ignore structural, symbolic and ideological processes determining actors' social praxis and representations. Additionally, this research elucidates different levels of the political economy of sex work and HIV risk, as Maternowska (2006) and Farmer (2006) explored in the case of Haiti. At the Mexico–Guatemala border, the reification of bodies and social spaces are mutual and transfigured conditions, encouraged by current public policies and practices on migration that, at the meso and micro levels, determine susceptibility to, for example, stigma, discrimination and the threat posed by organised crime. In this context, the bodily economy of sexual practices' exchange value, as Viveros (cited in Wade et al. 2008) and Stolcke (1974) have shown in Colombia and Cuba regarding racism and sexism in gender relationships, arises at the intersection of the subject's social class, country of origin, sex/gender identity and ethnicity. Our critical medical anthropology approach highlights the need to combine theoretical contributions with ethnographic field results in order to contribute to transforming a social reality marked by unequal social relations; in this we follow, among other authors, Singer (1995) and Scheper-Hughes (1995).

Our main interest in this research is the stigmatisation and discrimination experienced by low-income, undocumented, drug-using migrants, analysed in terms of their social vulnerability at three levels: macro-spaces (regions), intermediate spaces (urban/rural areas), and micro-spaces (drug use and sex exchange locations). We conducted social mapping in each of the four cities examined, based on an understanding of 'territory' as plural and using the subjects' knowledge about the 'places/spaces' as a fundamental element of the social research (Diez Tetamanti and Escudero 2012).

Social mapping was implemented for two types of spaces – locations of sexual exchange and locations of drug use – analysed in terms of both their social configurations and specific uses: *puntos* (points) and *pasos* (steps). Within this framework, spaces are understood as locations where social vulnerability to HIV is produced in accordance with their characteristics of social and urban placement in terms of unequal access to resources and capital (Harvey 2007). In the specific case of *pasos,* we also analyse places as generating strategies as the application of survival praxis and the recreation of labour networks.

Our understanding of social vulnerability opposes the stigmatising characterisation of at-risk groups, emphasising the social determinants of illness/sickness/disease and its ideological, structural and historic dimensions (Muñoz Martínez 2018). Viewed in this light, every person is vulnerable to misfortune, although the susceptibility to heightened factors of social vulnerability and their consequences on health/illness/attention/prevention varies based on one's position in the social structure (as a factor of ethnicity, social class, gender, age group or, as in the present case, migratory condition). We study the intersection of spaces, actors' viewpoints and strategies by documenting and analysing: 1) 'social representations' (Abric 2001) and practices surrounding the use of condoms, drug use during sexual exchange and HIV, and 2) the social use and configuration of the spaces where sex is exchanged under the influence of alcohol and other non-injected drugs. This is the first research study conducted at the Mexico–Guatemala border that documents and analyses these types of spaces from the perspective of health and migration-/displacement-related processes, as well as social vulnerability to HIV/AIDS of men engaging in commercial sexual intercourse with men and/or women.

The HIV epidemic in Mexico primarily affects vulnerable groups, and its main mode of transmission is sexual intercourse (CENSIDA 2015). It is most prevalent among population subgroups such as migrants, sex workers and men who have sex with men (CENSIDA 2013). In 2014, the state of Chiapas documented the fourth highest prevalence of new AIDS cases per 100,000 inhabitants in Mexico (CENSIDA 2015). This data is analogous for Guatemala (MSPA 2014a), in which the San Marcos department – where Tecún Umán is located – ranked third for HIV prevalence (MSPA 2014b).

There is little data regarding the prevalence of AIDS among the migrant population at the border; the cases documented on the Mexican side correspond to a foreign migrant population composed mainly of Guatemalans, followed by Hondurans and Salvadorans (Secretaría de Salud 2009), with a higher prevalence (following a concentrated pattern) than in their countries of origin (Leyva-Flores et al. 2016). One study conducted at the border with migrants who abuse alcohol or use non-injected drugs found an HIV prevalence of 1.3 per cent in men and 2.4 per cent in women (Conners et al. 2017). The Mexico–Guatemala border is crossed by 200,000 migrants[3] per year from the countries mentioned above, whose main destination is the United States (Rodríguez Chávez 2013); at the same time, mobile populations and circular and temporary migration are common.

The migrant route through Mexico toward the United States is considered one of the most dangerous in the world for undocumented migrants. Chiapas reports one of the highest rates of physical violence against migrants in Mexico (OIM/COLEF 2016), as well as rejection and discrimination against them (CIDH 2013), making migrants there particularly vulnerable to contracting HIV (Leyva-Flores et al. 2016) and/or experiencing difficulties accessing available services (Ledón Pereyra et al. 2015). While some studies of social vulnerability to HIV among the migrant population in this border region have been undertaken (Infante et al. 2009; Bronfman et al. 2002), as well as some specific studies of sex work by migrant women (Fernández-Casanueva 2009) and the violation of their sexual rights (Infante et al. 2013), little is known about HIV vulnerability for migrant men who have sex with men (Conners et al. 2017) and, in particular, the impact of their undocumented status on their susceptibility to contraction (Goldenberg et al. 2012).

When the so-called 'war on drugs' was launched in Mexico in 2006 (ACAPS 2014), the drug trade underwent a process of national and international diversification and reconfiguration; both sides of the Mexico–Guatemala border experienced an increase in drug trafficking, with a reported increase in the use of cocaine, ecstasy, methamphetamines and alcohol (OPS 2009). This phenomenon is a reflection of a national trend in Mexico,[4] where from 2008 to 2011 the number of those consuming methamphetamines, crack, cocaine and marijuana increased from 3.9 to 5.7 million people, and there was a rise in addiction rates from 450,000 to 550,000 people, according to the National Addiction Survey (Cacho Carranza 2015).

Multiple studies on various populations and contexts around the world have established a connection between drug use during sexual relations and unsafe sexual practices (Strathdee and Stockman 2010; Drumright and Colfax 2009). 'Crossing Borders'[5] is the first study undertaken at the Mexico–Guatemala border that specifically focuses on migration, drug use and HIV exposure. The study is coordinated by researchers from the University of California, San Diego (UCSD), Mexico's Center for Research and Advanced Studies in Social Anthropology (CIESAS-Sureste) and the Universidad del Valle de Guatemala. This chapter forms part of that research, specifically focusing on the analysis of some of the sociocultural data collected from 2010 to 2013 and during fieldwork conducted in 2016.

Geographic research context

There are three main routes for border crossing and migrant transit in southern Mexico: the route along the Pacific coast in Chiapas (Tecún Umán–Ciudad Hidalgo–Tapachula); one that borders the Gulf coast of Mexico (Tenosique, Tabasco); and one that crosses central Chiapas (La Mesilla, Comitán). The one most utilised by migrants is the Pacific coast route in Chiapas, since through it the train known as La Bestia (The Beast) is accessible. However, these routes have altered in recent years due to the pressure from immigration authorities and the violence of organised crime (Martínez et al. 2015).

Tecún Umán belongs to the municipality of Ayutla, Guatemala. Tecún Umán has 33,426 inhabitants and is located along the main Guatemala–Mexico border crossing (SEGEPLAN n.d.). According to official data, the municipality of Ayutla has a poverty rate of 37 per cent and an extreme poverty rate of 1.5 per cent (INE 2011).

With 300,000 inhabitants, Quetzaltenango is the second most populated city in Guatemala (CDUCIC 2016). It is located in the department of Quetzaltenango, and has an extreme poverty rate of 17.5 per cent (INE 2011). This city is a central crossing point along the migrant transit route to Tecún Umán/Ciudad Hidalgo or El Carmen (Guatemala)/Talismán (Mexico); it is also the place of origin of many migrants crossing for temporary work in Chiapas or on their way to the United States (Anguiano Téllez 2008).

Tapachula is the most populated city of the southern Mexican border region, with one of the largest migrant populations living there temporarily or permanently, as well as a large mobile population in transit (Alfonzo Melgar 2008). Tapachula has a population of 351,165 and presents an intermediate level of socio-economic marginalisation, according to the municipal and national Marginalization Index[6] (Gobierno del Estado de Chiapas 2017).

Ciudad Hidalgo neighbours Tecún Umán on the Mexican side of the border. It has 13,912 inhabitants and a high level of socio-economic marginalisation (Gobierno del Estado de Chiapas 2017).

Methodology

In-depth interviews were conducted with Salvadoran, Honduran and Guatemalan migrants (n = 28) and with professionals in the social, healthcare and migration sectors (n = 46)[7] in the four cities on the main migrant routes on the Mexico–Guatemala border named above. In Tapachula,

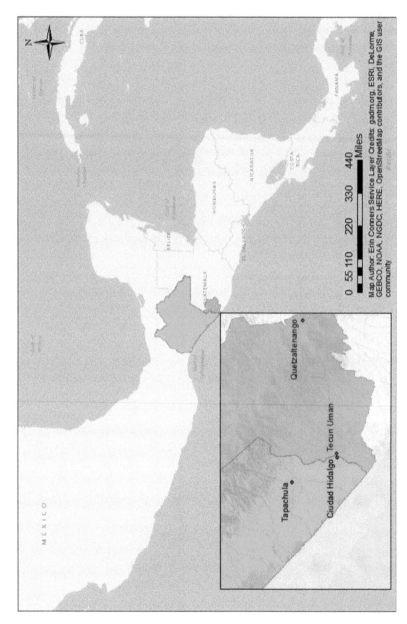

Figure 6.1   Map of Ciudad Hidalgo and surrounding region.

participant observation was conducted in addition to secondary data analysis, contrasting and triangulating empirical data obtained through testimonies and direct observations with other sources of information. The qualitative analysis sought a typological and/or analytical generalisation of the results, exploring the articulations between sociocultural and political processes affecting the production of social representations (Abric 2001), the migrant or displaced subjects' practices regarding the use of condoms and HIV, and the social use and configuration of spaces where sex is performed in exchange for drugs and/or money.

The present study represents an analysis of 13 in-depth interviews with migrants or displaced men obtained between 2010 and 2013 in 'Crossing Borders' and 15 in-depth interviews conducted with migrants in 2016 during ethnographic fieldwork. In 2016, we also spent 20 days (6 hours per day) in two public parks in Tapachula known to be locations for the solicitation of sex work, so that we could talk to those engaged in such work and observe the sociocultural and spatial dynamics of these locations. Participants were between 18 and 45 years of age; 44 per cent were between 18 and 25 years old; 28 per cent were Guatemalans, 35 per cent Hondurans and 37 per cent Salvadorans. Our interviews focused on the type and frequency of drugs consumed; sexual practices during sex work; the use of condoms; social representations of HIV; and migratory and displacement trajectory, among other health determinants. For security reasons, we did not ask about or record answers regarding details of organised crime, such as people's names or the specific addresses of places where drugs are sold.

Eligibility criteria included: participant age 18 or older; willingness and ability to provide informed consent; consumption of an illegal substance in the two previous months or alcohol abuse; being an international (or internal, in Guatemalan cases) migrant from Central America en route to the United States and having lived in one of the study's cities for at least one month; having engaged in commercial sexual exchange under the influence of non-injected drugs in the previous three months. We conducted the interviews in safe spaces that ensured privacy for the interviewee and safety for other people involved. The participants were recruited by colleagues from local non-profit organisations at locations where they are solicited by clients for sex work.

One of the study's main methodological limitations was the high level of social vulnerability of participants, which affected access to the interviewees, especially on the Mexican side, since some participants mistook us for immigration officers. This situation has parallels in other studies conducted in this region, emphasising the need for a responsible local approach to human rights (Goldenberg et al. 2016). Two potential participants were contacted in the process of fleeing the Mexican city of Tapachula, since, as they narrated and as we inferred from their visible wounds, they had been attacked and their lives threatened. At the same time, field observation was formally and temporally limited by the security measures that the researchers were compelled to adopt (for example, conducting interviews only during the day, in public spaces, and trying not to be excessively visible). We tried to include non-mestizo participants but were only able to include one Afro-Honduran migrant, as during our fieldwork period most migrants were mestizos and non-mestizos refused to participate. The data this migrant provided was very relevant and in line with findings from other regional research studies.[8]

All interviews were conducted after obtaining participants' informed consent, with approval from the institutional review boards of the University of California, San Diego, the Instituto de Salud del Estado de Chiapas and the Universidad del Valle de Guatemala. Participants were assured of confidentiality and anonymity. Identifying personal data was not recorded: for every interview only code numbers were used as identifiers. Participants were treated with respect, avoiding situations or topics that could cause psychological pressure or pose a security risk, and emphasising that participation was completely voluntary. Those who required drug treatment, or who were victims of violence (extortion, discrimination, etc.) were referred to local available support programmes. Free condoms and health information were also provided by interviewers.

Reasons for migrating

All participants began using illicit substances in their country of origin and, at the time of the interview, used them more than three times a week. The most commonly used drugs were cocaine (71 per cent) and marijuana (64 per cent). Other drugs included crack (36 per cent) and methamphetamines (17 per cent);[9] almost all participants combined the use of two or more substances. Alcohol was used more than three times a week by 82 per cent of the participants. Three participants had previously injected drugs, with two having injected only once. All injectors had had their first experience of intravenous use in the United States. Using and sharing crack pipes was also common in *puntos*, the spaces where drugs are purchased and consumed in a group.[10] The interviewees who had crossed or lived at the border several times over the previous five years or more, as well as the experts interviewed, perceived that drug availability (mainly cocaine, crack, methamphetamines and marijuana) had increased during that period.

Reasons that led participants to migrate to the United States were similar to those of non-drug-using migrants. These included a context of scant economic opportunity and, for most, violence associated with organised crime experienced in their cities of origin. The latter was especially the case with youths (18 to 25 years of age), some of whom had applied for asylum in Tapachula on the basis of forced displacement.

We found that certain specific reported motives, as recounted by participants, were linked to structural and family violence, and correlated to problems in their neighbourhoods that had led them to drug consumption; such systems of violence were replicated, at the individual and collective levels, through marginalisation and the mechanisms of recruitment by organised crime, among others.

> I came from El Salvador fleeing gangs, because death squads were about to start arriving [...] So what they [gangs] most need are people to be able to fight the police. When you get involved in that, they recruit you and they make you sell drugs, they make you keep guard to make sure the police don't come, or they send you somewhere else to kill the rival gang. And if you don't do it, they kill you. That's what I was running away from [...] no one has the right to take another person's life.
>
> (Salvadoran, 18 years old)

> I started [using drugs]; my dad used to beat me a lot and I was eight, seven years old. They would send me to do long errands and when I was about 12, 11 years old, I had many friends on the street and I started using drugs, marijuana and crack, in Honduras [...] Here in Tapachula it's beautiful because you don't see too many armed people and as much violence as in San Pedro Sula.
>
> (Honduran, 27 years old)

Under these circumstances, migration was perceived by many participants as an opportunity to stop using drugs and escape the problems stemming from the violence experienced in their countries of origin.

> [I arrived] destroyed by drugs, I came here looking for help because I had many problems, I was involved in many things there [...] I see that it's calmer here [Ciudad Hidalgo, Mexico] in terms of violence [...] It's hard moving ahead. I would like to change my life completely and I see more opportunities here.
>
> (Guatemalan, 32 years old)

Stigma and discrimination and the border as a temporary residence

There are four main transversal factors that cause participants to experience stigma and discrimination from the local border population, which associates them with criminal activity such as theft: a) having scarce economic resources and, in the case of Mexico, being undocumented; b) being an Honduran, Salvadoran or, in the case of Mexico, also Guatemalan migrant; c) using illicit drugs; d) being young and male.

According to our participants, the local population perceives that they are migrants from the Central American northern triangle because of their accents, appearance and attire – such as carrying a backpack – or practices such as begging. Skin colour, in the case of migrants of African descent, is a characteristic of 'otherness' in Mexico. Daily discrimination prevents their insertion in the formal job market because of their undocumented status or hinders their access to informal work or sources of income, such as begging.

> They pay you a pittance as a migrant [...] as soon as they look at you; in my case because of my colour, people who look at me know that I'm not Mexican. And others might be the same colour as they are, but [are identified as migrants] from the way they speak; we'll never get rid of our way of speaking.
>
> (Honduran, 24 years old)

> I was talking to them [government employees] about vulnerabilities and they said, 'Yes, we agree with these workshops, to be informed on how to orient migrants, but we're afraid because migrants are now sure of themselves, they think they have the authority to shout at us, to threaten us, everyone gives them priority, everyone believes that they are victims … but migrants murder, migrants steal.' I have heard this discourse everywhere.
>
> (Director of Doctors of the World, Tapachula)

Exclusion is exacerbated for those who are recognised as drug users by the local population. According to participants, substance users are recognisable through their dirty clothes and a haggard, unshaven appearance: 'Because of our looks, people don't support us to work, because we look haggard, some of us thin, others dirty, unshaved' (Guatemalan, 32 years old); '[...] like thieves. Because that type of drug [crack and cocaine] makes you too addicted; the more you have, the more you want, so some people start stealing' (Guatemalan, 30 years old).

Age, in turn, plays an important role in the case of young migrants, since, according to their own perception, they are mistaken for *maras* (gang members) and excluded from jobs because they are suspected to be thieves.

Interviewees stated that two of the main reasons for their temporary residence in the cities at the border were migrants' perception of a high risk of physical harm and/or being deported during their journey through Mexico. An additional reason was access to informal work related to the flow of merchandise, mainly across the river at the border, in addition to activities such as sex work, car washing, street sweeping or rubbish collection, in a context characterised by exclusion from the formal job market. Migrants conceive of the border as a temporary residence while they obtain the money necessary for continuing their journey to the United States, money necessary for minimising the risk of aggression by paying protection money to criminal groups during their travel.

> They're killing us up in the north […] In Reynosa, next to Laredo, things are uglier […] When I go north, I go through because I pay them [organised crime] $300 to let me through, because if I don't, they kill me.
>
> (Honduran, 27 years old)

At the same time, for those displaced by violence, the border is a place of anonymity that offers the perception of safety and greater security than their country or region of origin.[11]

The geography of sexual exchange: Drugs as access to sex, and sex to gain access to drugs

Empirical data showed two main types of sexual exchange for drugs: informal and formal sex work. Informal sex work consists of receiving goods such as food, lodging, money or drugs in exchange for sexual services of an occasional nature, in cases where another professional activity is the main source of income. Formal sex work consists of providing sexual services that are structured in location and time, within an economic framework of sex exchanged for money, with a frequency that results in a social 'professional profile', a designated location for the activity and, in the present case, the use of drugs during sex work as an end or a requirement for its performance.

While the analytical difference between formal and informal sex work is clear, the distinction is fuzzier in practice. The only empirical indicator observed that delimits one mode from the other is whether sex work is organised in groups and/or whether sex workers have to pay a pimp for working at a given location. From this standpoint, formal sex work is only performed by young participants, during their stopover on the way to the United States, in spaces such as the public park in the city of Tapachula.

There are two types of documented spaces where sex is exchanged for money or drugs. First, there are spaces for individual or collective consumption where drugs are not sold. Second, there are places where drugs are distributed and commercial sexual exchange takes place around that activity, mainly among consumers and, in some cases, with the seller.

In the first case, the spaces described are *pasos*, hostel rooms, repurposed rooms in abandoned buildings, public spaces away from roads (for example, temporary constructions among the shrubbery in dry rivers or ravines), public bathrooms and, in the cases of Tapachula and Ciudad Hidalgo, other public spaces where drugs are consumed and where the consumers are regularly or sporadically approached by people offering money in exchange for sex. Most of the time, the participants have not been previously contacted, since they do not have mobile phones or internet access.[12] In the case of Tapachula, since formal commercial sexual exchange takes place at a public park, drug consumption is held in check as a form of collective protection and to keep discrimination and police harassment from hindering sex work. Informal encounters are relegated to other parts of the city, since those that take place in the park are regulated by organised groups that control the territory.

The second case is the so-called *puntos* and some discotheques defined by the interviewees as 'sexual diversity' nightclubs. The types of drug consumed at these locations depend on the place and its characteristics.

> Consuming cocaine is good because you can do it anywhere, even in the restrooms, because it doesn't smell or require much [preparation] to be consumed [...] Crack, on the other hand, is definitely consumed at home or they go to some abandoned house to consume it, because it smells, like marijuana also smells.
>
> (Guatemalan, 28 years old)

Some spaces delimit a certain type of sexual practice for commercial exchange. Such is the case with Tapachula's public park, where the supply of sex is exclusively for local receptive men.[13] Thus, the structure of formal sex work and its territorial and economic organisation also define supply and demand.

Most of the participants in this study, who perform formal or informal sex work, identify as heterosexual. Most of those who occasionally offered informal sexual services in order to obtain drugs mentioned that they did so only with women, and some participants (20 per cent) also with men. Others suggested the latter possibility without overtly stating it. Another 15 per cent of the interviewees admitted to being men who have sex with men (MSM) and self-identified as bisexual or gay. In all spaces documented, except for the park in Tapachula, informal sexual exchange takes place with either men or women.

> Because of the need to get another dose […] I have to resort to those situations when a man offers you money for sex. I know […] that way I'll keep consuming, because there's no other option.
>
> (Guatemalan, 32 years old)

Spaces for sale, consumption and sexual exchange: *Puntos* and *pasos*

Puntos and *pasos* merit analysis because of their characteristics as public/private sectors of the city and their use by the study's subjects, as well as being the most representative spaces for sexual exchange and collective and clandestine drug consumption.

Puntos are spaces in the cities studied in Guatemala and in Ciudad Hidalgo (Mexico). In Tapachula, there are no such spaces. They are located on the outskirts or in under-developed locations (near rivers, for example) where drugs and alcohol are sold. They operate as informal bars with a guard at the entrance. Sugarcane alcohol and other drugs are usually sold in a separate section of the same space. Consumption on site is allowed and is, in fact, the main activity; the most common substances are crack, methamphetamines (in inhaled form) and marijuana. The interviewees mention that they consume alcohol to mitigate the effects of crack (called *paniqueo*, panicking).

> [*Puntos*] proliferate quickly or are welcomed by consumers because they no longer have to hide themselves; they arrive at the place and there they can buy alcohol, which serves as a tranquilliser for the drugs, and there they have it, so obviously they are very welcome to the drug-consuming clientele.
>
> (Guatemalan, 45 years old)

At some of these places, spaces for sexual exchange among men and women are improvised, for example, by hanging a bedsheet from the ceiling and walls. Sexual exchange (mainly among MSM) also takes place outside the *punto* where, according to all participants, condoms are not used. Women who engage in sexual exchange are generally drug users who go there with their male partners, who are also users and who often force them to do sex work in order to obtain drugs or money for drugs (inside or outside the *punto*). 'In one of those places there was a girl who had a partner, and when she would go in [to the *punto*] to get drugs and didn't get any for him, he would beat her badly' (Guatemalan, 30 years old).

Pasos are closed spaces similar to *puntos* but, in addition to being more improvised, these are places exclusively for drug consumption and not for sale. Another difference is that, in addition to consumption, people share other types of activities related to the space. *Pasos* are related to the spaces where *camareo* takes place (the transport of merchandise and informal trade across the border along the river). They are only present in Tecún Umán and Ciudad Hidalgo. Consumption takes place during the daytime; at night *pasos* are used as informal lodgings for those who have nowhere to sleep. One *paso* in Tecún Umán, located near a formal migrant shelter with a three-day maximum stay, is used as a refuge by the migrants who have reached this limit for staying at the shelter.

> There people cook, people live. We call it a *paso* [passage]. There we pass the time, there many helpers who work on the rubber inner tubes [used to carry people and goods across the border] get together. There they smoke and drink. Most of us do drugs. We always have to hide from other people, we can't do it publicly. There is the *paso* of the Coyote, of the Cruz Blanca, the Rojos …
>
> (Salvadoran, 44 years old)

The absence of police resistance to drug use in these spaces is one of the reasons for going there: 'In other words, it's because of the lack of pressure that we go there. You are free to smoke because there's no fear of the authorities' (Salvadoran, 44 years old).

At *pasos* drug use and commercial sexual exchange are not limited to the enclosed interior space: among regulars, these activities also take place outdoors, at the riverbanks; with people from outside the *pasos*, who go there in search of sexual services, drug use and commercial sexual exchange may occur at a private location. *Pasos* are also spaces to re-create labour networks: participants sometimes engage in remunerated informal activities, especially transporting merchandise across the river.

Desire, body technologies, risk perception and condom use

Evidence obtained from fieldwork allows us to identify five correlated variables that affect condom use during the sex work carried out by participants: formal or informal sex work; the client's gender and sexual orientation; the need for money and/or drugs; the type and amount of drugs used; and space as a condition for the availability of condoms.

When we asked participants about modes of HIV transmission, they were aware of the risks involved, according to a biomedical explanatory model, in engaging in unprotected sex as well as using shared syringes. Condom use during sex work was reported for two practices: insertive anal penetration with male clients and vaginal penetration with women. In informal sex work, few participants reported engaging in receptive anal sex, and in those cases they did not report using condoms; in formal sex work no interviewee reported engaging in receptive anal sex. None of the participants in the study carry condoms during sex work and they all report using them very sporadically. They acquire condoms in hotels, through a friend or client, or buy them in pharmacies.

Our data indicated more frequent condom use in formal as compared to informal sex work. In both cases, the client's gender and sexual orientation determined the perception of risk of contracting HIV. In this regard, the participants who use condoms reported a more frequent use with men than with women, since they relate 'promiscuity' and a greater risk of infection to MSM:

> It's more dangerous, dirtier, and you can get it [HIV], they do it with anyone. A prostitute does it maybe to feed her child, to earn a living, she knows who to do it with, she kind of chooses. With gays it's different. If they see a guy, they don't care, they don't ask what he has.
> (Salvadoran, 22 years old)

Drug use during sexual exchange functions as a means and/or end for obtaining both drugs and money in the practices documented. In both cases, commercial sexual exchange takes place under the influence of drugs and is performed to obtain more drugs, to obtain money to buy drugs or to obtain money for a different purpose. While for some of the participants obtaining drugs is an end in itself, others reported not wanting to begin or continue consuming certain substances such as cocaine or alcohol, and considered its use a compulsory job requirement. This was the case with formal sex work performed to obtain money for continuing the journey to the United States with reduced risk of violence from organised crime (by paying protection money). Thus, sex work as a source of money for buying drugs was less frequent in interviewees aged 18 to 25 years. For this group, the main reason mentioned was to save money for the journey, purchase food or pay for lodging. However, it is necessary to analyse this data with a larger population sample to determine whether access to drugs during sex work, the structure of sex work and/or migration plans, among others, are intervening variables.

Drug use during sex work is an instrument, as well as an end, that creates unequal negotiating conditions and becomes a source of tension between the client and the sex worker. All interviewees mentioned that once they are under the influence of drugs, they commonly forget to use a condom. Some of them recount that their clients, whether drug users or not, try to force them not to use a condom, urge them to use drugs or offer them more money for unprotected sex. The interviewees who reported using condoms frequently recounted that they were able to assert more control over the encounters by refraining from using drugs or controlling the amount and type of drug consumed during the sexual encounter:

> Some people tell you what you have to consume, and if you don't they get mad [...] but I prefer not to. You tell them, "that's enough or I'll leave" [...] Some invite you to snort cocaine [...] sometimes I agree; as long as it's not too much I feel that it relaxes me.
>
> (Honduran, 24 years old)

Although for some participants frequent or occasional consumption of some drugs acts as a sexual stimulant, several participants reported that one of the consequences of drug addiction, especially in the case of crack and cocaine,[14] is a negative impact on virility. On the one hand, drug use is associated with what some participants call 'loss of manliness', since 'men end up having sex with other men'; on the other, they relate it to reduced vigour, by diminishing erection and sexual drive. These testimonies reveal a connection between condom use – and concern about it – and sexual desire, regardless of whether the encounter is insertive or not, and a decreased use when the sexual encounter is unrelated to desire.

In cases of sex work where condoms are unavailable, and the participants prefer to protect themselves, they resort to strategies such as limiting the encounter to receiving oral sex as a prophylactic measure: 'When condoms are not available and you need to smoke badly, you come to an agreement when you enter the room, since they have to pay you, and you only let them do oral sex on you' (Salvadoran, 26 years old).

With the exception of hotels, in none of the spaces analysed do participants describe having access to condoms. No condoms are available at either *puntos* or *pasos*, and none of the people who go there carry condoms with them. Furthermore, these spaces are far from urban zones and pharmacies where condoms can be acquired. In this regard, they operate as self-contained, clandestine universes, separated from public spaces by stigma and discrimination against drug use and, in the case of *puntos*, the illegal nature of drug sales, in which the ease of practising sex work is among the main currencies in the dynamics of drug purchase and/or consumption.

The political production of inconsistent condom use and HIV exposure

The predominant approach by researchers and decision makers regarding drug use and HIV tends to focus on HIV prevention in the population that injects drugs, thus overshadowing attention from other modes of drug use. As a number of studies demonstrate, high-risk sexual behaviours associated with non-injected drug use can be an important contributing factor for HIV infection (Strathdee and Stockman 2010). The socio-economic, political and cultural conditions that affect HIV exposure at the Mexico–Guatemala border through high-risk sexual practices and under the influence of drugs, though specific to this context, exhibit characteristics that can be found in other settings that have not yet been studied. This is the first research study focusing on the Mexico–Guatemala border from this perspective, and one of the few that examines this problem in both countries as it is experienced by undocumented migrant men who perform sex work. It also contributes to the scant literature on HIV exposure and the effects of stigma towards drug users in Mexico (for example, in Tijuana, CONAPRED 2010) and Guatemala. Finally, it expands on studies that document the production of spaces of social vulnerability in places of drug consumption and/or sale and commercial sexual exchange in border regions of Central America and in the United States at large (Dickson-Gomez et al. 2012).

The territorial/political border is a place of residence for people who, due to forced displacement or migration, are en route to the United States. Conditions are determined at a macro level by the pressure exerted by both Mexican and United States immigration policies;[15] sex work becomes a strategy for making enough money to be able to continue the journey with fewer risks to physical safety by avoiding becoming victims of organised crime or deportation. In this regard, the number of deportations to Central America from the United States has exponentially decreased, while deportations from Mexico have increased (MIV 2015). The first immigration control point is located in Tapachula, constituting an initial fixed border that extends into a *mobile* border across the Mexican territory. The fixed border in Tapachula is a preview of the persecution to which migrants will be subjected due to their undocumented status.

At the same time, the border is also symbolic, consisting of the discriminatory prejudices held by a large sector of the local population about migrants from the Central American northern triangle, who, though historically considered an essential part of the region's economy and workforce, remain a vulnerable social group (Leyva and Quintino 2011). Local social prejudices are also present in Ciudad Hidalgo and Tecún Umán, linking migrants to crime (especially theft) and drug addiction (Canales et al. 2010).

The policies that led to current pressure by immigration authorities in Mexico and to the creation of the aforementioned stigmas promote the criminalisation and stigmatisation of migrants; they are related to the Mérida Initiative (2008) and Plan Frontera Sur (2014). Both these intergovernmental policies are indicative of the post-9/11 paradigm change and the development of a security strategy based on containing and thwarting migration (León Hernández 2011). A number of studies demonstrate the devastating effects of both policies in terms of immigration containment, leading to an increase in systematic violations of the human rights of migrants, especially in certain regions of southern, eastern and north-eastern Mexico. By fuelling the perception of insecurity, these policies undoubtedly seek to reduce the flow of migrants (Correa-Cabrera 2014).

The so-called 'war on drugs', based on military strategy, unleashed a proliferation of drug use in Mexico, as well as an increase of violence there and, as an extension of the conflict, in Guatemala and other Central American countries (ACAPS 2014). This scenario of violence and conflict is exacerbated by a lag in adopting policies decriminalising drug use, as is the case in Guatemala (Colussi 2013), and by failure to reduce social stigma and discriminatory treatment towards drug users by authorities and the local population[16] which leads migrant drug users to be subjected to various symbolic borders that make them resort to segregated spaces for drug purchase and consumption.

In addition, this policy lag removes otherness from common public spaces, thereby concealing this marginalised population from the local population in two ways: through *puntos*, as an intersection between purchase and consumption, and through *pasos*, which are linked to spaces for consumption near locations of informal work[17] to which migrant drug users are relegated, and often serve as an extension of informal shelters, condemning them to destitution. *Pasos* and *puntos* are socio-spatial phenomena characteristic of the Mexico–Guatemala border; yet *puntos* are also present in various Central American countries (Dickson-Gomez et al. 2012), but absent in other contexts of southern Mexico. Why? We believe that this is a compelling question for further research.

Stigma and discrimination against low-income, drug-using migrants function explicitly or implicitly by generating separate spaces on the basis of both factors of vulnerability; these spheres have uses and consequences in common with the non-drug-using migrant population as well as the local drug-using population. At the same time, these areas are also characterised by the juxtaposition of the symbolic and material marginalisation of both conditions – poverty and drug use.

The border is a place for transit that functions as a space for shelter, insofar as the current political logic imposes sojourns and territorial extensions by means of legal threats (deportation) or illegal ones (organised crime). In this context, stigma and discrimination against migrants and drug users operate through structural and symbolic mechanisms of exclusion from the formal job market and become determinants of health by increasing vulnerability to HIV contraction through risky sexual practices during sex work.

In this regard, an analysis of the triad 'border–*puntos/pasos*–body' explains the political dimension of a type of violence that can be defined as socio-spatial, and is characterised by its ability to transform those three elements. In other words, physical and symbolic spaces of inclusion and, as we have seen with *puntos* and *pasos*, exclusion – understood as social constructions produced by the local impacts of immigration policies and regulations on drug use and trade – are inscribed in the bodily economy of sexual practices' exchange value at the intersection of the subject's country of origin, social class, ethnicity and sex/gender identity.

The reifications of the body and the social space (in the terms of Bourdieu 1999) at the Mexico–Guatemala border, and along the mobile border with the United States in Mexico, are pre-existing conditions that transform and influence one another. The porous geographical border between Mexico and Guatemala also becomes a mobile border located within a network of non-static and non-linear geographical and symbolic points throughout Mexican territory, with its geography of immigration checkpoints, places of exposure to violence and physical or economic extortion by organised crime, and zones of shelter where migrants can obtain money to continue their journey. This geography finds its full expression in these mobile, symbolic and geographic micro-spaces of *borderisation*, determined and legitimised by an ideological landscape characterised by disdain for migrants' human rights and reinforced by stigma and discrimination; they represent a landscape produced by current migration policies and the threat posed by organised crime. In this context, conditions influencing social vulnerability to HIV infection in Tapachula, Tecún Umán, Ciudad Hidalgo and Quetzaltenango take the form of inconsistent condom use due to the power imbalance between clients and sex workers, and are mediated by informal/formal sex work, clients' gender and sexual orientation, the need for money or drugs, the type of drugs used and condom availability.

The type of sex work influences condom use by the space in which it occurs and its structure, among other factors. Theoretical contributions to the analysis of formal and informal sex work have been undertaken, for example, by Maternowska (2006) and Tabet (2005). Along the lines of these analyses, space determines access to places or to people who have condoms, while its structure, through the target clientele, alters perception of risks, due to homophobic prejudice based on gender and sexual orientation. The aforementioned conditions of discrimination and stigma impact the need for money or drugs and the willingness to engage in unprotected sexual practices, which are in turn influenced by the type of drugs used and amount consumed, making drugs an instrument of compulsion and resistance in unequal negotiations over condom use.[18] The evidence produced by this study contributes to elucidating, from an ethnographic perspective, the processes of social vulnerability to HIV for undocumented migrant and displaced male drug users, in a border context where no existing social research currently considers this problem, and where the recent epidemiological study by Conners et al. (2017) reveals a connection between drug use, unavailability of free condoms, occasional sexual encounters and inconsistent condom use.

Conclusions

Approaches to spaces of production of social vulnerability in processes related to health/illness/care and prevention are enhanced if they are connected to analyses of the macro-structural frameworks that configure them. They also benefit when they are interrelated to local character-istics and to the correspondences and linkages among bodies/subjects, spaces and borderisations in the access to an unequal distribution of sym-bolic and material resources. In the Mexico–Guatemala border context in general, and specifically regarding AIDS, a so-called epidemic of sig-nification (Treichler 1988), sociocultural and political analyses of spaces of migrant transit illuminate social determinants of health experienced by these migrants, and their strategies and perspectives for addressing them. This analysis challenges discriminatory views of migrants, and in this case migrant drug users, as a threatening blight upon the societies through which they pass or ultimately settle. For this purpose, a relational approach (Menéndez 2009) in critical medical anthropology questions the dialectic of micro-subject versus macro-structure as an opposition, and considers these analytical levels as linkages of the same processes.

Critical medical anthropology allows us to elucidate the effects of global forces and local ideologies on health by examining social practices and representations that occur in specific social relationships. In the pres-ent case, these social relationships are cemented through processes that increase the vulnerability to HIV infection, and occur in mobile spaces of territorial and symbolic borderisation that are conditioned by attitudes of stigma and discrimination and amplified through North American capitalist policies. The subjects' perspectives and survival strategies, resulting in exposure to HIV and practices to reduce exposure, do not automatically arise from Plan Frontera Sur or the Mérida Initiative, or the so-called 'war on drugs'. Nevertheless, these programmes, their local consequences and their link to socio-economic and political conditions in this region are co-factors in the updating of the dynamics of north/south dispossession, not only (re)producing but also justifying the misfortunes of other migrants.

This exploratory study highlights the need for ongoing critical medical anthropology studies of these issues at the Mexico–Guatemala border, exploring variables such as ethnicity, age, sex/gender identity and sexual orientation, forced displacement, local consumer networks of drug use/dependence, institutional and organisational programmes for sexual health and addictions, and their relationship, or lack thereof, to the various forms of sex work and exposure to HIV. We recommend fur-ther research on behaviours and social representations in spaces where processes producing social vulnerability to HIV occur throughout the mobile border between Central America and the United States, as well as other points of migrant transit through the geographical border between Mexico and Guatemala.

Notes

1. This study was supported by a grant from the US National Institute on Drug Abuse (NIDA, grant R01DA02989, Crossing Borders Project, PI Brouwer) and a post-doctoral grant awarded to Rubén Muñoz by NIDA, in collaboration with France's Agence Nationale de Recherches sur le Sida et les Hépatites Virales (ANRS). We would also like to thank Valerie Mercer, the Crossing Borders team and the Global Public Health Division and Family Medicine and Public Health personnel at the University of California, San Diego for their support.
2. The processes documented also expose the subjects to other sexually transmitted diseases, such as syphilis, as demonstrated by prevailing data in the study by Conners et al. (2017).
3. Extrapolated from the number of deportations from Mexico.
4. Guatemala has no records on the production, distribution and consumption of drugs, or systematic official reports or studies (PDH 2015).
5. Project number R01DA029899 at: https://projectreporter.nih.gov/reporter.cfm.
6. This index principally measures: education, housing infrastructure (sanitation services, running water, crowding, earthen floors) and income (less than minimum wage), and how these are affected by geographical location (for towns with fewer than 5,000 inhabitants). For more information see: https://www.gob.mx/cms/uploads/attachment/file/159052/01_Capitulo_1.pdf.
7. These were from governmental institutions and non-profit organisations that provide medical attention and advice on human rights to migrants and have experts on sexual health, HIV and addictions.
8. For example, Velázquez Gutiérrez and Iturralde 2012.
9. Other legal drugs used are Dormicum, Tranquilan, Sinterafin, Diazepam and phenobarbital.
10. It is currently under discussion whether they can be a mode of HIV transmission.
11. Other reasons, not examined in this paper, are the local communities of support and belonging created by drug users, and strategies for obtaining cheaper drugs on both sides of the border.
12. Some of the participants in the study with higher socio-economic status use online social networks to make contact with men or women whom they later meet at certain public spaces.
13. However, some of these people perform sporadic informal sex work with women in other spaces.
14. Future studies should focus on other variables, such as frequency of consumption, age and concomitant use of other substances, among others.
15. The United States provides resources for migration control, such as training for land and air patrols, among other initiatives for detecting and deporting undocumented Central American people (PCS 2015).
16. See the 'Escudo' police training programme in Tijuana: http://ucsdnews.ucsd.edu/pressrelease/binational_police_program_in_tijuana_targets_hiv_reduction.
17. Regarding *pasos* as informal trade across the border, see Ruiz Juárez and Martínez Velasco 2015.
18. The interaction between identity/sexual orientation, homophobia, drug use and sexual practices is not analysed here.

References

Abric, Jean-Claude. 2001. 'Metodología de recolección de las representaciones sociales'. In *Prácticas sociales y representaciones*, edited by Jean-Claude Abric, 27–37. Mexico City: Ediciones Coyoacán.

Alfonzo Melgar, Ana Silvia 2008. *La dinámica de los flujos migratorios mixtos en la Frontera Sur de México: Una breve interpretación*. Chiapas, México: ECOSUR. Accessed 17 September 2019. https://www.acnur.org/fileadmin/Documentos/nuevo_sitio/2010/conferencia/4.%20Mixed%20Migration%20Flows%20in%20the%20Americas/ECOSUR%20-%20REMISUR%20-%20La%20Dinamica%20de%20los%20Flujos%20Migratorios.pdf?view=1.

ACAPS (Assessment Capacities Project). 2014. *Otras situaciones de violencia en el Triángulo del Norte Centroamericano: Impacto humanitario*. Geneva: Assessment Capacities Project. Accessed 18 September 2019. http://www.iecah.org/images/stories/Otras_situaciones_de_violencia_ACAPS_Mayo_2014.pdf.

Anguiano Téllez, María Eugenia. 2008. 'Chiapas: Territorio de inmigración, emigración y tránsito migratorio', *Papeles de Población* 14 (56): 215–32.

Bourdieu, Pierre. 1999. *La miseria del mundo*. Buenos Aires: Fondo de Cultura Económica.

Bronfman, Mario N., Rene Leyva, Mirka J. Negroni and Celina M. Rueda. 2002. 'Mobile Populations and HIV/AIDS in Central America and Mexico: Research for Action', *AIDS* 16 (Supplement 3): S42–S49.

Cacho Carranza, Yureli. 2015. 'Epidemiología del consumo de drogas en México', Agencia Informativa Conacyt, 3 November. Accessed 17 September 2019. http://www.conacytprensa.mx/index.php/ciencia/salud/3725-drogadiccion-mexico.

Canales, Alejandro I., Patricia N. Vargas Becerra and Israel Montiel Armas. 2010. *Migración y salud en zonas fronterizas: Guatemala y México*. Santiago: Centro Latinoamericano y Caribeño de Demografía.

CDUCIC (Comisionado de Desarrollo Urbano, Competitividad local e Infraestructura Crítica), 2016. *Informe hábitat III*. Tercera Conferencia de la Naciones Unidas sobre Desarrollo Sostenible y Vivienda. Accessed 19 October 2019. http://habitat3.org/wp-content/uploads/Guatemala-Informe-Habitat-3_final-vf.pdf.

CENSIDA (Centro Nacional para la Prevención y el Control del VIH y el SIDA). 2013. *Vigilancia epidemiológica de casos de VIH/SIDA en México: Registro Nacional de Casos de SIDA: Actualización al cierre de 2013*. Mexico City: Secretaría de Salud. Accessed 17 September 2019. https://www.gob.mx/cms/uploads/attachment/file/215917/RN_CIERRE_2013A.pdf.

CENSIDA (Centro Nacional para la Prevención y el Control del VIH y el SIDA). 2015. *Vigilancia epidemiológica de casos de VIH/SIDA en México: Registro Nacional de Casos de SIDA: Actualización al cierre de 2015*. Mexico City: Secretaría de Salud. Accessed 17 September 2019. https://www.gob.mx/cms/uploads/attachment/file/215916/RN_Cierre_2015.pdf.

CIDH (Comisión Interamericana de Derechos Humanos). 2013. *Derechos humanos de los migrantes y otras personas en el contexto de la movilidad humana en México*. Washington, DC: Comisión Interamericana de Derechos Humanos. Accessed 18 September 2019. http://www.oas.org/es/cidh/migrantes/docs/pdf/Informe-Migrantes-Mexico-2013.pdf.

Colussi, Marcelo. 2013. *Despenalización de las drogas: Realidades y perspectivas en Guatemala*. Guatemala City: Instituto de Problemas Nacionales de la Universidad de San Carlos de Guatemala. Accessed 20 September 2019. https://www.tni.org/files/publication-downloads/gt-despenalizacion_de_las_drogas.pdf.

CONAPRED (Consejo Nacional para Prevenir la Discriminación). 2010. *Estigma y discriminación hacia las y los usuarios de drogas y sus familiares* (Dirección General Adjunta de Estudios, Legislación y Políticas Públicas Documento de Trabajo No. E052009). Mexico City: Consejo Nacional para Prevenir la Discriminación. Accessed 17 September 2019. https://www.conapred.org.mx/documentos_cedoc/E05-2009-1Co.pdf.

Conners, Erin E., Kate Swanson, Sonia Morales-Miranda, Carmen Fernández Casanueva, Valerie J. Mercer and Kimberly C. Brouwer. 2017. 'HIV Risk Behaviors and Correlates of Inconsistent Condom Use among Substance Using Migrants at the Mexico/Guatemala Border', *AIDS and Behavior* 21 (7): 2033–45.

Correa-Cabrera, Guadalupe. 2014. 'Seguridad y migración en las fronteras de México: Diagnóstico y recomendaciones de política y cooperación regional', *Migración y Desarrollo* 12 (22): 147–71.

Dickson-Gomez, Julia, Timothy McAuliffe, Lorena Rivas de Mendoza, Laura Glasman and Mauricio Gaborit. 2012. 'The Relationship between Community Structural Characteristics, the Context of Crack Use, and HIV Risk Behaviors in San Salvador, El Salvador', *Substance Use and Misuse* 47 (3): 265–77.

Diez Tetamanti, Juan Manuel and Beatríz Escudero, eds. 2012. *Cartografía social: Investigación e intervención desde las ciencias sociales, métodos y experiencias de aplicación*. Comodoro Rivadavia: Universitaria de la Patagonia.

Drumright, Lydia N. and Grant N. Colfax. 2009. 'HIV Risk and Prevention for Non-Injection Substance Users'. In *HIV Prevention: A Comprehensive Approach*, edited by Kenneth H. Mayer and H.F. Pizer, 340–75. London: Academic Press.

Farmer, Paul. 2006. *AIDS and Accusation: Haiti and the Geography of Blame*. Berkeley: University of California Press.

Fernández-Casanueva, Carmen. 2009. 'Experiencias de mujeres migrantes que trabajan en bares de la frontera Chiapas-Guatemala', *Papeles de Población* 15 (59): 173–92.

Gobierno del Estado de Chiapas. 2017. *Instrumentos normativos para la formulación del anteproyecto de presupuesto de egresos: Capítulo XXIII: Estadística de población*. Gobierno del Estado de

Chiapas. Accessed 17 September 2019. http://www.haciendachiapas.gob.mx/marco-juridico/Estatal/informacion/Lineamientos/Normativos/2017/XXIII-Estadistica-Poblacion.pdf.

Goldenberg, Shira M., Kimberly C. Brouwer, Teresita Rocha Jimenez, Sonia Morales Miranda and Monica Rivera Mindt. 2016. 'Enhancing the Ethical Conduct of HIV Research with Migrant Sex Workers: Human Rights, Policy, and Social Contextual Influences', PLoS ONE 11 (5), Article e0155048: 1–21. Accessed 12 September 2019. https://doi.org/10.1371/journal.pone.0155048.

Goldenberg, Shira M., Steffanie A. Strathdee, Maria D. Perez-Rosales and Omar Sued. 2012. 'Mobility and HIV in Central America and Mexico: A Critical Review', Journal of Immigrant and Minority Health 14 (1): 48–64.

Harvey, David. 2007. Espacios del capital: Hacia una geografía crítica, translated by Cristina Piña Aldao. Madrid: Akal.

INE. 2011. Mapas de pobreza rural en Guatemala 2011: Resumen ejecutivo. Guatemala: Instituto Nacional de Estadística. Accessed 21 October 2019. https://www.ine.gob.gt/sistema/uploads/2014/01/10/ifRRpEnfOcjUfRZGhyXD7RQjf7EQH2Er.pdf.

Infante, Cesar, Peter Aggleton and Pat Pridmore. 2009. 'Forms and Determinants of Migration and HIV/AIDS-Related Stigma on the Mexican–Guatemalan Border', Qualitative Health Research 19 (12): 1656–68.

Infante, César, Rubén Silván, Marta Caballero and Lourdes Campero. 2013. 'Sexualidad del migrante: Experiencias y derechos sexuales de centroamericanos en tránsito a los Estados Unidos', Salud Pública de México 55 (Supplement 1): S58–S64.

Ledón Pereyra, Aldo, Diego Lorente Pérez de Eulate, Santiago Martínez Junco, Gabriela Morales Gracia, Carolina Rivas Farfán, María de Lourdes Rosas Aguilar and Melissa Vertiz. 2015. 'México: Frontera sur'. In Niñez y migración en Centro y Norte América: Causas, políticas, prácticas y desafíos, edited by Karen Musalo, Lisa Frydman and Pablo Ceriani Cernadas, 251–325. San Francisco: Center for Gender and Refugee Studies. Accessed 17 September 2019. https://www.acnur.org/fileadmin/Documentos/Publicaciones/2015/9927.pdf.

León Hernández, Alba Izadó. 2011. 'When Cooperation and Intervention Meet: Sovereignty in the Mexico–United States Relationship', Amsterdam Law Forum 3 (4): 54–73.

Leyva, René and Frida Quintino. 2011. 'Introducción: La salud sexual y reproductiva en grupos móviles y migrantes'. In Migración y salud sexual y reproductiva en la frontera sur de México, edited by René Leyva Flores and Frida Quintino Pérez, 23–36. Cuernavaca: Instituto Nacional de Salud Pública.

Leyva-Flores, René, César Infante, Edson Servan-Mori, Frida Quintino-Pérez and Omar Silverman-Retana. 2016. 'HIV Prevalence among Central American Migrants in Transit through Mexico to the USA, 2009–2013', Journal of Immigrant and Minority Health 18 (6): 1482–88.

Martínez, Graciela, Salvador David Cobo and Juan Carlos Narváez. 2015. 'Trazando rutas de la migración de tránsito irregular o no documentada por México', Perfiles Latinoamericanos 23 (45): 127–55.

Maternowska, M. Catherine. 2006. Reproducing Inequities: Poverty and the Politics of Population in Haiti. New Brunswick, NJ: Rutgers University Press.

Menéndez, Eduardo L. 2009. De sujetos, saberes y estructuras: Introducción al enfoque relacional en el estudio de la salud colectiva. Buenos Aires: Lugar Editorial.

MIV (Misión Internacional de Verificación). 2015. 'Informe de la Misión Internacional de Verificación sobre la situación de los derechos humanos de la población migrante hondureña y su derecho a la protección internacional'. Accessed 18 September 2019. http://movilidadhumana.com/informe-de-la-mision-internacional-de-verificacion-sobre-la-situacion-de-los-derechos-humanos-de-la-poblacion-migrante-hondurena-y-su-derecho-a-la-proteccion-internacional/.

MSPA. 2014a. Estadísticas de VIH y VIH avanzado Guatemala, enero 1984–septiembre 2014. Accessed 18 September 2019. http://infecciosashr.org/wp-content/uploads/2014/12/VIH-GUATEMALA-Boletin-VIH-actualizadoSep2014.pdf.

MSPA. 2014b. 'Informe Nacional sobre los progresos realizados en la lucha contra el VIH y sida.' Ministerio de Salud Pública y Asistencia Social. Programa Nacional de Prevención y Control de ITS/VIH/SIDA.

Muñoz Martínez, Rubén. 2018. 'Estigma estructural, adherencia al tratamiento antirretroviral y cultura organizacional de cuidados en la atención hospitalaria en VIH y Sida en Guayaquil, Ecuador', Andamios 15 (36): 311–41.

OIM/COLEF. 2016. *Migrantes en México, vulnerabilidad y riesgos*. Geneva and Mexico City: Organización Internacional para las Migraciones y Colegio de la Frontera Norte. Accessed 1 November 2019. https://micicinitiative.iom.int/sites/default/files/document/micic_mexico_1. pdf.

OPS. 2009. 'Epidemiología del uso de drogas en América Latina y el Caribe: un enfoque de salud pública.' Organización Panamericana de la Salud. Washington, DC. Accessed 7 November 2019. https://www.paho.org/hq/dmdocuments/2009/epidemiologia_drogas_web.pdf?ua=1.

París Pombo, María Dolores, Melissa Ley Cervantes and Jesús Peña Muñoz. 2016. *Migrantes en México, vulnerabilidad y riesgos*. Geneva: Organización Internacional para las Migraciones. Accessed 18 September 2019. https://micicinitiative.iom.int/sites/default/files/document/ micic_mexico_1.pdf.

PCS. 2015. *Informe de la misión de internacional de verificación sobre la situación de los derechos humanos de la población migrante hondureña y su derecho a la protección internacional.* Project Counselling Service. Accessed 10 June 2016. http://pcslatin.org/portal/images/ InformeFinalMIV.pdf.

PDH (Procurador de los Derechos Humanos). 2015. *Recomendaciones sobre el respeto y la protección de los derechos humanos en el contexto del problema mundial de las drogas*. Procurador de los Derechos Humanos. Accessed 18 September 2019. https://www.ohchr.org/Documents/ HRBodies/HRCouncil/DrugProblem/NHRIGuatemala.pdf.

Rodríguez Chávez, Ernesto. 2013. 'Tendencias recientes de la migración centroamericana en tránsito irregular por México'. Paper presented at the 4th Coloquio de Migración Internacional: Políticas y gestión de la migración, San Cristóbal de las Casas, Chiapas, 13–15 November 2013.

Ruiz Juárez, Carlos Ernesto and Germán Martínez Velasco. 2015. 'Comercio informal transfronterizo México–Guatemala desde una perspectiva de frontera permisiva', *Estudios Fronterizos* 16 (31): 149–74.

Scheper-Hughes, Nancy. 1995. 'The Primacy of the Ethical: Propositions for a Militant Anthropology', *Current Anthropology* 36 (3): 409–40.

SEGEPLAN (n.d.). *Información demográfica del municipio de Ayutla, San Marcos*. Guatemala. Accessed 19 October 2019. http://sistemas.segeplan.gob.gt/sideplanw/SDPPGDM$PRINCIPAL. VISUALIZAR?pID=POBLACION_PDF_1217.

Singer, Merrill. 1995. 'Beyond the Ivory Tower: Critical Praxis in Medical Anthropology', *Medical Anthropology Quarterly* 9 (1): 80–106.

Stolcke, Verena. 1974. *Marriage, Class and Colour in Nineteenth-Century Cuba: A Study of Racial Attitudes and Sexual Values in a Slave Society*. London: Cambridge University Press.

Strathdee, Steffanie A. and Jamila K. Stockman. 2010. 'Epidemiology of HIV among Injecting and Non-Injecting Drug Users: Current Trends and Implications for Interventions', *Current HIV/ AIDS Reports* 7 (2): 99–106.

Tabet, Paola. 2005. *La grande arnaque: Sexualité des femmes et échange economico-sexuel*. Paris: L'Harmattan.

Treichler, Paula. 1988. 'AIDS, Homophobia and Biomedical Discourse: An Epidemic of Signification'. In *AIDS: Cultural Analysis, Cultural Activism*, edited by Douglas Crimp, 37–70. Cambridge, MA: MIT Press.

Velázquez Gutiérrez, María Elisa and Gabriela Iturralde. 2012. *Afrodescendientes en México: Una historia de silencio y discriminación*. Mexico City: Consejo Nacional para Prevenir la Discriminación.

Wade, Peter, Fernando Urrea Giraldo and Mara Viveros Vigoya, eds. 2008. *Raza, etnicidad y sexualidades: Ciudadanía y multiculturalismo en América Latina*. Bogotá: Universidad Nacional de Colombia.

7

The ethno-racial basis of chronic diseases: Rethinking race and ethnicity from a critical epidemiological perspective

Melania Calestani and Laura Montesi

An engaging five-day workshop on critical medical anthropology organ-ised by CIESAS and UCL was coming to an end. It was a sunny Friday in January and the Central Valleys of Oaxaca promised a spectacle of beauty and historical heritage to a group of anthropologists. We were about to visit Monte Albán, an archaeological site, testament to the Zapotec civ-ilisation and its power over the region. We were still riding the wave of the workshop debates when we met our tourist guide. We introduced ourselves to him and when Laura said that she worked with diabetes patients, the guide observed that diabetes is the largest epidemic in Mex-ico, caused by an unhealthy food system and by wrong eating behaviours triggering defective genes: 'We, Mexicans, are genetically predisposed to diabetes.'

We looked at each other and immediately understood that we were thinking along the same lines. We had been talking about racial-ised societies and health during the last few days, having found paral-lels between our respective works on social representations of diabetes in Mexico, and on chronic kidney disease and kidney transplant listing in the UK. We were wondering about the growing explanatory power of genetic aetiologies in health discourses and about how and why certain social groups, often detected on the basis of ethno-racial differences, end up being described by researchers, physicians and public health workers as genetically prone to many diseases and conditions, including type 2 diabetes (hereafter diabetes) and chronic kidney disease. We had also discussed the ways in which such representations and medical and sci-entific practices become part of the public imaginary, intersecting with popular notions of race, ethnicity, fitness and weakness.

In the 1990s, Lippman introduced the term 'geneticisation' to describe 'an ongoing process by which differences between individuals are reduced to their DNA codes, with most disorders, behaviours and physiological variations defined, at least in part, as genetic in origin. It refers as well to the process by which interventions employing genetic technologies are adopted to manage problems of health' (1991: 19).

The term geneticisation is resonant with 'medicalisation', which indicates processes 'by which nonmedical problems become defined and treated as medical problems, usually in terms of illnesses and disor-ders' (Conrad 1992: 209). Although medicalisation can have beneficial impacts, it has traditionally been seen with suspicion by medical anthro-pologists in light of the tendency by societies to label deviance and use medicine as a means of control, punishment or marginalisation. Finkler (2000) expressed concern about the mushrooming growth of beliefs in genetic inheritance because they are instrumental to the individualis-ation of health problems and the technification of solutions. Kinship and ethno-racial genetic explanations and solutions sit easily within the cur-rent global neoliberal climate and the growing 'economisation' of 'here-tofore noneconomic spheres and activities' (Brown 2015: 17). As Marks (2013) highlights, genetic and genomic research projects usually prom-ise solutions, mainly diagnostic tools, which are easily privatised (2013: 257). This raises more than one question about the interests behind sci-entific research, an issue that is becoming of paramount relevance as public funds diminish and corporations are increasingly being subsidised by state governments to promote research and provide health services (Clarke et al. 2003: 167).

To disentangle how political and economic forces shape scientific research and medical practice, we draw on Breilh's critical epidemiology (CE), which serves a double purpose: it supersedes the limits of con-ventional epidemiology with its multi-causal (yet still lineal) model of disease and rethinks 'health as a complex, multidimensional object, sub-mitted to a dialectical process of determination' (Breilh 2008: 747). By dissecting two case studies, social representations of diabetes in Mexico and ethnic minorities in transplant medicine in the UK, we analyse how science, considered in its broadest sense (as it is practised and communi-cated), reinvents race and ethnicity and can inadvertently contribute to deepening racialised inequalities in stratified societies. We examine how this over-emphasis on ethno-racial genetic aetiologies in chronic diseases diverts attention and resources from more important influences on populations' health, such as embedded health inequalities exacerbated by colonial pasts, neoliberal capitalism and institutionalised racism. In line with recent discussions in the anthropology of epigenetics (Lock 2013; Thayer and Non 2015), we draw on Kuzawa and Sweet's work to suggest how 'social influences can become embodied, having durable and even transgenerational influences' (2009: 2). Ethno-racial differences in disease patterns are then embedded in pathways of power, characterised by a somatisation of racial tensions (Guthman 2014) that profoundly affects local biologies (Lock and Nguyen 2010). We argue that CE permits us to move some of these discussions forward in specific ways: for instance, identifying how biologies are moulded within their larger ecological contexts, or webs of relationships, and how social systems, ways of life and health are inextricably linked.

Ethno-racial discourses and health

Concepts of race and ethnicity are among the most controversial and contentious classifications in our social and scientific landscapes. In health research, genotypes have often been associated with ethnic/cultural identity, showing poor consistency in terminology and reinforcing ethno-racial stereotypes (Sheldon and Parker 1992). Race and ethnicity have then become mere statistical categories, denying the complex interactions among political-economic processes, lived experiences, societal ways of living and human biologies (Goodman 2000; Krieger 2001).

In this chapter, rather than engaging with race as a physical or phenotypical category, we draw on Gilroy's and Ahmad's understandings of racialisation. The former talks about it as the existence and hegemony of 'raciological' thinking that affects the world and provides differential access to resources for members of different groups (Gilroy 2005: 39), while the latter conceptualises it as a process that 'assumes that "race" is the primary, natural, and neutral means of categorization, and that the groups are distinct also in behavioural characteristics, which result from their race' (Ahmad 1993: 18).

We argue that race and ethnicity are polysemic terms, acquiring a plurality of meanings according to the (inter)national and local circumstances in which they are employed. Moreover, their use responds to ideological and political propositions grounded in power unbalances. The rise of the race concept in the fifteenth century as part of the European conquest and as a means of legitimisation (Smedley 1998; Ahmad and Bradby 2007) reveals its political and colonial genesis. Historically, the involvement of health within racial representations has been instrumental, not incidental (Keval 2016). Arguments on health and hygiene were (and still are) racially coded and have been central to (post-)colonial practices of inclusion and exclusion (Mawani 2003; Shah 2001; Gilman 1988). Nineteenth-century health and hygiene movements were concerned with maintaining the boundaries between populations.[1]

In tandem with biological depictions of race, ethno-racial differences in health have also been explained in terms of cultural inadequacies, mobilising essentialised notions of 'culture' (Ahmad 1993). According to Menéndez (2001), since the 1950s, we have witnessed an expansion of biological understandings of everyday life and the rise of the concept of lifestyle as a signifier for (un)healthy behaviour, working as a mechanism of differentiation, stigmatisation and subalternisation. Likewise, in health research, racial and ethnic-group comparisons of health indices frequently are presented without stratifying or adjusting for socio-economic conditions that could affect the interpretation of the data (Lillie-Blanton and Laveist 1996).

CE provides a criticism of dominant biomedical and epidemiological explanations of health and illness, unveiling their reductive biological orientation and shedding light on how large-scale political economic processes 'get under the skin' (Leatherman and Goodman 2011): for instance, how racism and chronic stress affect local biologies through processes of somatisation (Kuzawa and Sweet 2009) or how the ever-growing reproduction of capital under market rules reduces the spaces 'for the fulfilment of life and health' (Breilh 2008: 747).

Amerindian genes and the Mexican susceptibility to diabetes

Diabetes in Mexico has become a top health, social and economic concern. Its prevalence rate ranges between 9.2 and 14 per cent, making it one of the highest worldwide (world prevalence in 2014 was 8.5 per cent of adults aged 18 and older (WHO 2016)) and the highest among Organisation for Economic Cooperation and Development (OECD) member countries (OECD 2015). In only 30 years (1980–2010) diabetes has gone from being the ninth to the second cause of death in the Mexican general population (Secretaría de Salud 2012: 38). People with diabetes often have to endure suffering and pain due to severe disability. According to a recent report (Secretaría de Salud 2015: 20), in 2013, 30 million disability-adjusted life years were lost, especially among two age groups, adults between 35 and 60 years of age and the over-80s. The statistics are indisputable. What is questionable is how this epidemiological panorama is portrayed and addressed by a number of institutional actors, from state representatives and public health workers to researchers and journalists.

State representatives say the diabetes epidemic is a national threat. The Mexican ex-Minister of Health, Mercedes Juan, described diabetes as a 'health emergency [...] capable of jeopardising [Mexico's] viability as a nation' (Secretaría de Salud 2013: 7). In 2013, President Peña Nieto launched the National Strategy for the Prevention and Control of Overweight, Obesity and Diabetes, designed to promote behavioural changes, increase epidemiological surveillance, make health services more accessible and regulate the sale of high-calorie food and beverage products. The strategy, contained in a 105-page document, showed a limited understanding of the role that social inequalities play in disease distribution. While launching his national strategy, President Peña expressed the need for citizens to be 'informed, active and healthy' and lamented the fact that the Mexican population 'suffers from overweight problems and lacks healthy habits'. He exhorted people to interrupt their sitting time with at least one hour of exercise per day (Presidencia de la República 2013). Discourses like these tend to frame diabetes not only as a Mexican problem but also as one that reflects *Mexicanness*, constructed around stereotypes of laziness, a propensity to over-eat and focus on the present, and the lack of a culture of prevention. In conjunction with behavioural/cultural explanations, the diabetes epidemic is also narrated in terms of ethno-racial predisposition, due to genetic variations that are 'exclusive of *mestizo* populations, whose *Amerindian* component is under study' (Secretaría de Salud 2013: 77; our emphasis). Although no national diabetes indicators by 'race' and/or ethnicity are available,[2] Mexico has taken a leading role in genomic research, searching for 'a genomic haplotype commonly found in Mexican and other Latin American *mestizo* populations and linked to *indigenous genetic ancestry*' (Saldaña-Tejeda and Wade 2018: 2733; our emphasis).

This scientific endeavour has spurred public interest and widespread media coverage, particularly after the foundation of the Instituto Nacional de Medicina Genómica (INMEGEN) in 2004 and the start of the Mexican Populations Genomic Diversity Project in 2005. In 2008, scientists at the National Autonomous University of Mexico (UNAM) inaugurated the Genoteca Indígena, a project that aims to form a DNA bank from Mexican native populations. The objective is to know more about frequent diseases in Mexico, particularly diabetes, 'from their origin' (El Informador 2012). The investigation aims to detect the genetic polymorphisms associated with diabetes, which are said to be more frequent among indigenous peoples and, consequently, in Mexicans, depicted as a mestizo population with a high percentage of indigenous genetic ancestry (El Informador 2012).

Interviews and reports on the Genoteca Indígena released in Mexican media indicate that researchers give credit to James Neel's thrifty gene hypothesis,[3] although it remains unexplained in what ways Mexican indigenous peoples might have had a more nomadic life in the past than other populations. The biochemist leading the Genoteca Indígena project argues: 'In the past, more than 6,000 years ago, when communities were nomadic, Mexican genetics allowed [Mexicans] to survive. This genetic make-up is today fattening them and making sugars harmful' (Menjívar Iraheta 2009).

Even though Neel's thrifty genotype is still an unproven hypothesis, its explanatory power has been astonishingly great (Fee 2006: 2990), as it provides an appealing answer to the high prevalence of diabetes and obesity among disparate ethnic groups, from the Pima of Arizona and the Oji-Cree of Ontario (Hegele et al. 1999) to Samoans (Minster et al. 2016) and Mexicans. Montoya (2011) underscores the fact that Neel's hypothesis remains elusive in at least two ways: the hypothesis rests upon disputable assertions about feast and famine cycles among populations, and the population groups deemed diabetes-prone are not biological but social groups (2011: 48). Thus, both minority groups and large national populations (but ones with strong links with indigeneity) end up lumped together because they share genetic 'ancestry'. In this regard, Ferreira and Lang ask: 'How can a genetic cause be applied across the borders of 300 million people divided into thousands of ethnic groups, living across the planet under strikingly different circumstances? What do these people have in common? Their genes?' (2006: 12).

Montoya (2011) suggests that the targeting of certain bodies as suitable DNA donors for research is made possible by the colonial practices that differentiated those bodies from the dominant ones in the first place, and confined them into poor neighbourhoods, plagued by poverty, neglect and therefore an excessive burden of disease. In the case of Mexico, it becomes clear that the reasoning by which (a) Mexicans are mestizos, (b) their indigenous genetic component is troublesome and (c) contemporary indigenous people should be targeted for DNA sampling is the direct result of Mexico's (post-)colonial history, which created the entire concept of the *indio* (Bonfil Batalla 1972), used it to place *indios* ('Indians') at the bottom of society, and pushed them into regions of refuge (Aguirre Beltrán 1967).

As several scholars have argued, *mestizaje* heralded 'the mixing of races rather than the separation of them, but without questioning the privilege of whiteness' (Saldívar 2014: 94). The proposition 'the whiter, the better' has structured Mexican racism, which works through 'distributed intensities' (Moreno Figueroa 2010) of white capital. The proposition 'the whiter, the less predisposed to diabetes', which seems implicit in the current scientific search for ancestral genetic backgrounds, sounds like the contemporary rendering of the Mexican *mestizaje* ideology. Indeed, the genomic enterprise – albeit not purposefully – articulates and is infused with racialised meanings that reflect cultural understandings of nationhood and alterity. As Wade et al. have pointed out:

> Racialized categories are implied in the use of concepts of genetic ancestry – usually talked of in terms of African, European, and Amerindian components. For the geneticists, genetic ancestry (understood as very specific sets of genetic markers) is distinct from race (which they understood as a set of coherent biological-bodily types). But the constant reference to African, European, and Amerindian ancestries evokes familiar racial meanings.
>
> (Wade et al. 2014: 497–8)

The Genoteca Indígena substantiates the idea of Mexicans as *mestizos* with a double genetic inheritance (the black component is largely overlooked) and of native peoples as the authentic, 'original' key to Mexican biology. Consistent with this perspective, Mexican media explain the Genoteca Indígena project in the following way: 'Indigenous genes: solution to diabetes' (Ocampo 2013). The article details how:

> Specialists agree that apart from promoting dietary and hygienic measures in the population, *the only way* to know *the origin*, complications and therapeutic management of diabetes, and to develop diagnostic, prognostic and control methodologies, *is to identify its hereditary components*.
>
> (Ocampo 2013; our emphasis)

In order to identify those hereditary components, researchers extract DNA from indigenous groups, the more 'isolated' the better. The logic is that isolated groups, being genetically more homogeneous, make for a good case study. One study on diabetes susceptibility, for example, found an association of genetic polymorphisms with the development of type 2 diabetes in Mayas (Lara-Riegos et al. 2015). Researchers selected participants who 'confirmed a Maya origin, with parents and grandparents born in the same communities, speak their native language and preserve traditional folks' (Lara-Riegos et al. 2015: 69).

It is interesting to note that cultural and ethnic qualities were used as indicators of genetic ancestry. The choice of taking DNA from this ethnic group was justified on the grounds that Mayas are said to have little contribution of continental ancestry (Silva-Zolezzi et al. 2009, cited in Lara-Riegos et al. 2015: 69) and that the region they live in presents a high prevalence of diabetes. The blood samples were later genotyped to confirm Amerindian ancestry. The search for 'isolated' groups recalls ideas of 'purity', which anthropological and ethno-historical scholarship has often demonstrated to be at best imprecise and, at worst, pernicious (Kuper 1988). Thus the isolation of the Mayas of south-east Mexico appears at odds with past and present history. The historical record, for example, demonstrates intense black–Maya relations in Yucatán (Lutz and Restall 2005: 189). Although mixing was much more common in urban than in rural areas, by the eighteenth century (often informal) miscegenation had become commonplace in Yucatán, especially 'between enslaved African men and native or mixed-race women and, to a lesser extent, between female slaves and Spaniards' (Lutz and Restall 2005: 193). Although the study mentions the importance of considering local environmental factors, lifestyles and modes of subsistence (Lara-Riegos et al. 2015: 73), virtually nothing is said about this region's social history and the processes of adaptation to changing political and environmental circumstances. Indigeneity appears, once more, as a biocultural unity (with specific genetic and linguistic/cultural markers) but socially and historically decontextualised.

Questions remain about how these ethno-racial representations of morbidity and alterity are appropriated by dominant and non-dominant sectors of society, and how indigenous peoples themselves make sense of diabetes as the institutions of science scrutinise their bodies.

In her ethnographic experience with Oaxacans from Santa Maria Atzompa, Everett (2011) found that the genetic aetiological accounts circulating in Mexico had not made inroads at the household level and genetic susceptibility was not part of the explanatory models of people with diabetes. A similar finding comes from Laura's ethnographic research among an ethnic minority in southern Oaxaca. During her year of fieldwork, nobody ever mentioned genetic susceptibility as depending on their ethnic belonging. When they were asked why they thought they got diabetes, they usually referred to strong emotions related to stressful life circumstances. Diabetes narratives revealed stories of poverty, unemployment, classism and physical and emotional abuse, phenomena that thrive in contexts where structural violence silently permeates social relations.

Cristina, a woman in her fifties, had been diagnosed with diabetes 18 years earlier. One year before Laura met her, she had started experiencing diabetes complications and had had a toe amputated. When asked why she got diabetes, she said: 'I got diabetes from a *susto* [fright], a *coraje* [anger] I had when I was young. My father was a prominent political figure and they killed him. I was only 25, the oldest among my siblings and I had to take care of them. That's how I got diabetes.' Cristina explained that her father's killing hit her hard and that from that moment her life had been punctuated by several illness episodes. Moreover, diabetes affected her financially as she resorted to private medical doctors and expensive medications.

Pancho, a teacher living with diabetes for more than 15 years, was emaciated, unable to stand and on dialysis when Laura met him. He explained that his diabetes was due to a terrible *susto* he had in Mexico City when he took part in a street protest with his fellow teachers: 'I was part of the struggle of the teachers' union and during the protest we were attacked by riot policemen. They trampled on my *compañeros* and when I saw them falling I got terribly scared.' He reacted so strongly to the violence he witnessed at the hands of the Mexican police, he said, that his blood turned sweet.

When research participants were asked about the great numbers of diabetics in their community, they talked about environmental and dietary change, culture loss and social disruption (Montesi 2017). Of the 38 people in Laura's sample, only four, all males (between 39 and 52 years of age), literate and with a relatively high socio-economic position (two had been in the past high-ranking officials in the municipality, one was a teacher and one co-owned a pharmacy) mentioned heredity as a possible causative factor. In these cases, genetics was related to family history, not to ethnic belonging. When she purposefully inquired about genetic susceptibility to diabetes, people denied such a predisposition, as the words of Anita, 55 years old and diagnosed with diabetes 18 years earlier, demonstrate: 'I don't think it's a matter of race because at the time of my grandmother and of my great-grandparents nobody had diabetes. Today everyone has diabetes, including the young.' Most of the people with diabetes Laura worked with were first-generation diabetics, with vivid memories of healthy parents.

Aetiological accounts may change in the future as people with diabetes begin to have memories of disease in their own families and genetic explanations become more commonplace. Research into how younger generations understand diabetes aetiology and ethno-racial health outcomes is critical and urgent. As our opening anecdote with the tourist guide shows, the Mexican susceptibility hypothesis is already being appropriated by urban people with greater access to media. Moreover, the genetic link of Mexicans (and 'Latinos' or 'Hispanos' more broadly) to diabetes has also found coverage in the US, strengthening racist attitudes towards Mexicans, as this comment in a racist website demonstrates:

> I have commented several times here re. the high cost of diabetes to a society. Diabetics' healthcare costs 2½ times the amount of non-diabetic healthcare. Diabetes is the cause of most blindness, amputations, kidney dialysis, & have 4x the chance of heart attack and stroke. A few years ago the *New York Times* had a week-long series of articles re. *Latinos' high rate of the disease. NYT claimed that 50% of them have it or will develop it!* And they brought up the issue of their diets, and lack of exercise. I also heard top US health officials express their concern over the coming diabetes epidemic *as we become a more Hispanic nation – and where the $$$$$$$$ is going to come from?*
> (SentryattheGate, comment on American Renaissance website, our emphasis)

In the current climate of white supremacism and rising numbers of hate crimes, it becomes imperative to look at the potentially stigmatising effects that racialising scientific narratives have on ethnic minorities.

Ethno-racial transplant medicine in the UK

Worldwide, increasing numbers of patients are affected by chronic kidney disease (CKD) and end-stage renal disease (ESRD), and are putting a substantial burden on global healthcare resources. This is due to the growing numbers of elderly people and the global pandemic of type 2 diabetes. In the UK, the annual incidence of ESRD has doubled over the past two decades to reach about 100 new patients per million of population (El Nahas and Bello 2005); this figure is expected to rise at an annual rate of 5–8 per cent (Lysaght 2002). 'Racial factors' have been described as playing a role in the susceptibility to CKD, as shown by the high prevalence of CKD related to hypertension, diabetes or both among BAME (black, Asian and minority ethnic) individuals in the UK (El Nahas and Bello 2005).

The National Institute for Health and Care Excellence (NICE) guidelines have identified higher-risk groups for diabetes, such as those aged 25–39 and of South Asian, Chinese, African-Caribbean or black

African descent (NICE 2017). In a research review from 2002, the UK's Department of Health and the Medical Research Council attempted to address the rise of diabetes cases in minority communities, suggesting the implementation of innovative lifestyle changes, such as, for instance, working with Indian restaurants to provide low-fat alternatives on their menus (Department of Health 2002). Embedded in this health strategy lay the assumption that there was something 'faulty' within the minorities' diets which required a fix, reinforcing simplistic notions of minority culture and/or identity. This has also been promoted through the work of national network organisations such as Diabetes UK (Keval 2016).

Minority communities have been represented over the years as being at higher risk of getting diabetes and hence of experiencing related complications, such as kidney failure. The NHS website on organ donations and ethnicity states that patients from BAME communities are more likely to need an organ transplant than the rest of the population as they are more susceptible to illnesses such as diabetes and hypertension, which may result in organ failure and the need for a transplant. ESRD or chronic renal failure is permanent kidney failure (Gordon 2001; Sehgal 1999) and is treated by one of three forms of renal replacement therapy: haemodialysis (mainly done in hospitals), peritoneal dialysis (done usually at home) and kidney transplantation (Gordon 2001). Dialysis is the clinical purification of blood and thus it is a substitute for the normal function of the kidney. Dialysis is generally considered more expensive than kidney transplantation (Laupacis et al. 1996; Yen et al. 2004). In the foreword to a report on the Transplant Summit of 2006, the All-Party Parliamentary Kidney Group in the UK states that: 'Transplantation is better for the patient. Furthermore, transplantation is cheaper than dialysis. Increasing transplantation rates would therefore be an all-round win' (All-Party Parliamentary Kidney Group 2006: 3).

This demonstrates how transplantation is depicted by modern biomedicine as the optimum treatment for end-of-stage kidney failure and as the cheapest option for healthcare systems. This solution to renal failure is represented as the best option not only for patients in terms of their quality of life but also for the rest of society in terms of expenditure on healthcare. However, despite this call for increasing the number of transplants, there is a shortage of organs, from living or cadaveric donors, across different countries. The 2006 Transplant Summit report also mentions that the UK currently has one of the lowest donation and transplantation rates amongst European countries. They continue by saying that this is considered to be partly because of differences in health service capacity and structure: for instance, the report cites Spain as an example, describing it as having almost three times as many intensive care unit beds (from where donor organs are often retrieved) compared to the UK. In addition, the report lists 'procedural and attitudinal short-comings' as possible reasons for the low rate of donations. The text continues by adding that:

> Innovative solutions must be found to maximise the opportunities for donation within the UK so that we can bridge the gap between accelerating demand and the declining supply of suitable organs available for transplantation. A national campaign should be launched to encourage potential donors to join the organ donor register. This should make clear to potential donors what the consequence of low donation rates are; not only for those individuals in need of an organ, but for the NHS as a whole.
>
> (All-Party Parliamentary Kidney Group 2006: 7)

As a consequence, a public campaign to increase donations in the UK has been developed in the last decade. In the case of kidney transplantation, the campaign aims particularly to raise the number of living donations. It is common to find news aimed at increasing donations in the media. For instance, on 20 December 2016, the London *Evening Standard* published an article titled 'Metropolitan police officer gives Christmas gift of life to sister by donating a kidney'. Interestingly, this is the story of two white siblings. The transplantation happened in a hospital in affluent Hampstead (north London). The article ends with a comment by one of the consultants, saying, 'If you know someone who needs an organ I would urge you to think about being a donor'. Readers then are redirected to the NHS website for further information.

Similarly, the charity Give a Kidney promotes non-directed (also known as altruistic) donation in the UK. More than 100 people donated in this way in the UK in both 2013/14 and 2014/15, and the numbers are expected to keep on track at more than 100 per year. Research on non-directed living kidney donations has shown that the anonymity of the donor and recipient appears to be seen as a benefit, freeing recipients from the obligations of the gift (Bailey et al. 2016).

However, medical anthropology research in Spain (Sánchez Hövel 2014) has shown that public campaigns describe living donations as 'altruistic' and 'supportive/caring', not taking into consideration the long-term holistic wellbeing of living donors and the regret of having donated a kidney on the part of living donors when their health deteriorates later in life. Further research is therefore needed to establish the long-term consequences of living donations for living donors.

Undoubtedly, linking donation with gift-giving, altruism and self-sacrifice creates a 'medical duty obligating both individuals and collectivities' (Kierans and Cooper 2013: 222) to act as donors. Research has shown that possible organ donors have different degrees of duty according to the racial and/or ethnic categories they are thought to belong to (Avera 2009; Gordon 2002; Kierans and Cooper 2011). This classificatory system is based on the assumption that some genetically inherited human leukocyte antigen (HLA) types as well as blood groups appear in certain 'ethnic' populations more commonly than others, meaning that patients may be more likely to find a transplant match with someone in the same 'ethnic' group (Avera 2009). Therefore, individuals and collectivities thought to belong to certain ethnic or racial categories receive greater attention in terms of health campaigns aimed at increasing organ donation. This is the case of ethnic minorities in the UK, which are often urged to discuss organ donation (Siddique and Morris 2016).

For instance, in September 2017 the NHS had a specific website on organ donations and ethnicity that described BAME groups as 'more likely to develop medical conditions that need blood, organs or tissue donations'. The website also mentioned that 'people needing bone marrow are more likely to find a match with someone with a similar ethnic background', crudely implying that genetics equates to 'ethnicity' and 'race'. This has slightly changed today, with 'More donors from black, Asian and minority ethnic groups are urgently needed to address an increase in patients from the same communities dying whilst waiting for an organ transplant'.

As highlighted by previous medical anthropological research (Gordon 2002; Kierans and Cooper 2011), biological differences have been combined with race and ethnicity in this context, emphasising the largely arbitrary character of racial categorisations based on shared characteristics, such as, for example, skin colour ('black', 'white') or geographic location ('Asian'). Moreover, 'white' HLA types are constructed as the standard against 'rare' 'black' HLA types, failing to account for racial mixing and mixed heritage (Kierans and Cooper 2011).

There is also the failure to acknowledge that developments in immunosuppressants make HLA (mis)matches increasingly irrelevant (Gordon 2002: 136). Cohen (2001) writes about how transplantation rapidly went global with the development, production and marketing of the immunosuppressant drug cyclosporine by the Swiss pharmaceutical corporation Sandoz. This made transplants possible from a far larger group of potential organ donors than before, profoundly affecting the harvesting of organs and transforming the productivity of transplant clinics and their organ-donation targets. Research on pharmaceuticals shows how the macro level of the pharmaceutical industry and health-care systems and the micro level of doctor–patient relations are inter-connected (Britten 2008), affecting the expansion of pharmaceutical markets (Busfield 2010) and providing a quick and easy solution to the complex issues emerging when facing inequalities in access to transplan-tation and transplant listing. Kierans and Cooper write that:

> In its attempts to accommodate 'rare' HLA types, transplant med-icine has fallen back on the same classificatory schemas that were implicated in the creation of the inequalities that recent policy shifts were intended to address – schemas that are based, primarily, on the assumption of a 'natural' basis for cultural differences.
>
> (Kierans and Cooper 2011: 13)

Therefore, 'ethnicity' and 'race' become biopolitical constructions in trans-plant medicine in the UK; these are often used to contrast the behaviour of ethnic minorities when it comes to donations in comparison to that of the 'white population', implying a higher moral stance for the latter. During an interview[4] in a renal unit in the UK, an Asian patient – we will call him Sadiq – in his forties told Melania:

> They [healthcare professionals] said to me that a lot of Asian peo-ple don't donate organs. My mum went through it and one of her kidneys was only 30 per cent efficient so they said no because she obviously was living on one; and my wife was not compatible and then after that I told the rest of the family not to go for it because I didn't want that responsibility. If it can happen to me it can happen to anybody in the family so I've just said I'd rather wait the time and wait for a donated dead one. […] Obviously, I got my brother and my sister, both of them went and had the tests done. I told them to go and have the tests done to make sure they don't have any possibility of kidney problems so that they are clear. I didn't want to take a kid-ney from any of those just in case. […] We spoke to a few people and again a few of my cousins came forward and said they would donate, but then again, the mental state I was in at the time. I refused to take it. […] I mean my cousin was only 20 at the time he offered as well; he was very fit, but I just said no. I'd rather wait it out and take it from someone that has already died rather than taking it form some-one that is living; and if they get any complication it's just mentally you wouldn't … you would feel responsible for that.

The words of Sadiq mirror the attitudes and feelings of other renal patients Melania interviewed. Despite the difficulties of living on dialysis and their daily suffering and pain – which Yannis, a Greek man in his fifties, described as a form of disability – patients find it extremely difficult to follow healthcare professionals' advice to ask family members if they can act as living donors. This was also common among those who identified themselves as 'white'; of the 53 people in the sample, many noted that they would feel 'guilty' and 'to blame' if the donor became sick later in life, following the donation. 'I wouldn't want anyone to carry that burden, you know', commented Scott, a 69-year-old white British man.

Another important point is the fact that patients like Sadiq internalise what healthcare professionals communicate to them regarding ethnic minorities and donations; this certainly has important repercussions in terms of self-identity as well as in terms of perceptions of their own communities. As Nazroo et al. (2007) have shown, treating categories – such as Caribbean, black and South Asian – as universal needs to be problematised. This challenges the ideology of transplant medicine in the UK, which identifies people from different continents as the same only because they are defined as ethnic minorities in the UK. Moreover, within the same ethnic groups there are many differences, and mixed heritage in an increasingly globalised world is not considered. For instance, in terms of vulnerability to cardiovascular disease, there are similarities between white British and South Asian British people when talking about their health experiences (Lambert and Sevak 1996). This leads to the conclusion that using 'race' or 'ethnicity' to explain disease in a specific group is not robust enough.

Minority groups are constructed as dangerous to themselves and in opposition to the white majority; the 'problematisation' of minority health generates binary states of normal/pathological trajectories, with the latter associated with minority groups in the NHS in Britain (Keval 2016). As the UK government has, decade after decade, attempted to 'manage race relations' (Craig et al. 2012), there has been a corresponding effect on concepts of health and health services, with the notion of taking responsibility for one's own health becoming a prime focus for governments (Keval 2016) – for instance, through encouraging lifestyle changes.[5]

Therefore, in this context, minority communities are not only represented as being at higher risk of becoming diabetic, showing an evident ethno-racialisation of the disease, but solutions to diabetes' further complications, such as kidney transplantation, are also constructed as ethno-racial issues, as minority individuals are represented as unwilling to act as donors.

Hence, it is difficult to consider transplant medicine as a neutral biomedical technology (Ohnuki-Tierney et al. 1994), as it deeply affects and is also affected by cultural definitions of personhood and the dynamics of social relations within families, communities and countries. It tests different boundaries (Kierans 2011: 1469) as bodies become artefacts for social and political control, through increasing fragmentation and commodification within the context of biomedicine and economics (Scheper-Hughes and Lock 1987). Through these medical and governmental ethno-racial discourses, we can engage with constructions of sameness and alterity as transplant medicine provides a space to discuss what it means to be human, shedding light on the cultural and social constructions of the self and the other (Sharp 1995; Douglas 2003, 2004).

Conclusions

The re-enchantment of scientists and lay people with genetic aetiologies and solutions to health problems is a social phenomenon that deserves full attention. It is important to recognise, though, that this is often an ambivalent re-enchantment (Bliss 2012). The cases of Mexico and the UK demonstrate the vitality of race and ethnicity as categories that shape biomedical and popular understandings of health and illness and, therefore, have an impact on how public health interventions are imagined. Transplant medicine and genetic modification (although not currently available) stand out as techno-fixes that operate at the individual level and simultaneously suit private interests. This has the inevitable consequence of shifting responsibilities for illnesses and conditions from the structural to the individual, yet they are marked by race and ethnicity. In Mexico, which is one of the largest consumers of sodas, the Coca-Cola Foundation has developed an interest in the genetic causes of diabetes: it is financially contributing to the Genoteca Indígena (Facultad de Química 2007). The suspicion is that the biggest producer of sugary drinks in the world has an interest in blaming faulty genes for the obesity and diabetes epidemic.

Epidemiology maps diseases along lines of race/ethnicity, gender or social class, providing a picture of a population's state of health. Its results can be used either to reinforce existing social hierarchies through racialised discourses of genetic predisposition compounded by unhealthy lifestyles or to explore social inequalities. CE offers theoretical tools to read ethnic and racial differences in this latter light, as the result of social histories marked by oppressive relationships that have an enduring, intergenerational impact on local biologies.

Breilh (2010) contends that the biological is always endowed with historicity; this means that physical, chemical and biological phenomena, as well as phenotypes and genotypes, are historically conditioned and cannot be isolated, fractioned or studied separately from their structuring social processes. Moreover, he adds, the connection between the biological and the social is not an extrinsic one but exists by virtue of subsumption (*subsunción*) (2010: 16). What are the implications of this theoretical standpoint?

A CE approach does not deny ethno-racial differences in disease patterns but sees them as incarnate results of pathways of power. This leads to novel conceptualisations of 'race'. For example, Guthman has explored non-genomic ways of thinking about 'race' and biology, suggesting that social constructions of race not only have material effects on social lives but can somatise 'race' (2014: 1156). Likewise, the concept of local biologies (Lock and Nguyen 2010) stresses the continuous, multi-level interactions among bodies within their life webs (Kuzawa and Sweet 2009).

Another relevant point of CE is the shift of gaze from 'health' to 'life'. Its object of inquiry is life itself, conceptualised as the sustaining web where everything happens or ceases to happen. This means that no aspect of our biology can be understood without taking into consideration its embeddedness in a complex ecology of mutually constitutive inter-relationships. Breilh criticises monocausal and multicausal explanations of disease because they favour proximate determinants of health over society-level ones. This critical posture has a practical, applied and political implication: if health has an intrinsic 'collective' nature, solutions to health crises have to be collective, too. Under this light, genes cannot be faulty, lifestyles cannot be bad and solutions can be technical only as a temporal relief. CE offers cues on how to overcome 'the epidemiological notion of the social as an inductive construction from the individual' (Breilh 2010: 17). A CE approach, therefore, does not analyse patterns of health and disease as the sum of individual risky behaviours or genetic make-ups but as the outcome of structures of power at work. It is social relations that empower or constrain people in and beyond their biologies. So what can a CE approach tell us about the appalling prevalence and incidence rates at which indigenous peoples and ethnic minorities worldwide experience diabetes or renal failure?

Ethnographic work on indigenous peoples with diabetes shows that diabetes sufferers link their illness to wider circumstances involving family and community disruption as well as social and environmental violence. The study of the narratives of people with diabetes reveals what a strong contribution ethnography can bring to health studies and why a mere account of lifestyles cannot be regarded as sufficient to stem diabetes. For instance, the seriousness with which anthropologists have approached and listened to life histories has led them to acknowledge the emotional dimension of experiences of vulnerability (see Jacobo and Orr, this volume), and the synergistic interactions between violence, suffering and diabetes (see Weaver and Mendenhall 2014, for instance). Biomedical studies have proved that 'chronic stressor exposure (such as living in poverty) has a health impact that goes beyond the supposedly bad behaviour of some people' (Kelly and Ismail 2015: 457).

Similarly, research on renal failure and transplantation can illuminate how ethno-racial difference and sameness are constructed, represented and internalised by different social actors. The communicative process is highly dependent on and structured by inequalities of power and resources; the organ shortage implies an assumption that organs go to waste if not donated, so every citizen should contribute to the transplant enterprise (Lock and Nguyen 2010). Normative theorists, clinicians and policy makers likely expect that patients make treatment decisions that enhance their health (Gordon 2001). Patients, however, make decisions according to non-normative factors, including their emotional and social notions about the repercussions of organ donation on a donor and on the patient's relationship with the donor. There is therefore a need for a renewed focus on patients' self-identity to explore how their treatment choices are embedded in the many relationships within which they are implicated.

The moral economy of transplantation has largely been boosted because of the global epidemic of chronic diseases such as renal failure, hypertension and diabetes. However, substantive research indicates that chronic diseases are themselves 'pathologies of power' (Farmer 2004) and symptoms of gender, class and ethno-racial inequalities that become embodied and are passed down from generation to generation. In order to break with this intergenerational cycle of violence, radical societal transformations are needed. CE recognises the practical and ultimately political nature of the scientific enterprise since 'there is an interdependence between how we *look* to reality, how we *think* it and how we *act* in it' (Breilh 2010: 8). CE offers 'collective health' as a theoretical, methodological and applied tool that focuses on group processes as they generate specific ways of living and dying. The 'social' is not an external variable useful to understand patterns of disease in individuals and groups, but the very condition that enables 'patterns' to occur (Breilh 2013: 20). Under this paradigm, biogenetic reductionism has no *raison d'être* and its exclusion from epidemiology clears the way for alternative explorations of race and ethnicity, which include the biological down to the genes but address them through a *longue durée* approach that links embodiment with social history.

Notes

1. See for instance the case of legal and spatial exclusion of Chinese immigrants suffering from leprosy in the province of British Columbia, Canada, where racialised governance came into practice through health strategies of segregation and isolation (Mawani 2003:3–21).
2. In 2012 the Mexican Ministry of Health started to include data on ethnicity in its administrative and epidemiological records, based on linguistic criteria (the patient speaks or does not speak an indigenous language). However, no data are available based on ethnic self-adscription.
3. In 1962, Neel proposed that the diabetic genotype was a 'thrifty' genotype, 'in the sense of being exceptionally efficient in the intake and/or utilization of food' (1962: 354). The spread and increase of diabetes worldwide was explained by Neel as an effect of 'civilisation'. Stripped down to its essentials, he suggested that 'genes and combinations of genes which were at one time an asset', especially in the feast-or-famine days of hunting and gathering cultures, had become a liability 'in the face of environmental change' (1962: 359).
4. This research was part of the ATTOM study, which was funded by a grant from the Programme Grants for Applied Research (PGfAR) funding stream, from the National Institute of Health Research (NIHR), United Kingdom (ref: RP-PG-0109-10116). This publication presents independent research. The views expressed in this publication are those of the authors and not necessarily those of the NHS, the NIHR or the Department of Health.
5. See Menéndez (1998) for further details on where the concept of lifestyle comes from and the disciplinary differences (between medical anthropology and biomedicine/public health) when analysing it.

References

Aguirre Beltrán, Gonzalo. 1967. *Regiones de refugio: El desarrollo de la comunidad y el proceso dominical en mestizo América*. Mexico City: Instituto Indigenista Interamericano.

Ahmad, Waqar I.U., ed. 1993. *'Race' and Health in Contemporary Britain*. Buckingham: Open University Press.

Ahmad, Waqar I.U. and Hannah Bradby. 2007. 'Locating Ethnicity and Health: Exploring Concepts and Contexts', *Sociology of Health and Illness* 29 (6): 795–810.

All-Party Parliamentary Kidney Group. 2006. *A Transplant Manifesto: More Transplants, Saving More Lives: A Report of the Findings of the 2006 Transplant Summit*. London: All-Party Parliamentary Kidney Group. Accessed 22 September 2019. https://www.kidney.org.uk/Handlers/Download.ashx?IDMF=b3254f80-4b1c-4507-a13a-12abd3175335.

Avera, Emily. 2009. 'Rationalisation and Racialisation in the Rainbow Nation: Inequalities and Identity in the South African Bone Marrow Transplant Network', *Anthropology and Medicine* 16 (2): 179–93.

Bailey, Phillippa K., Yoav Ben-Shlomo, Isabel de Salis, Charles Tomson and Amanda Owen-Smith. 2016. 'Better the Donor You Know? A Qualitative Study of Renal Patients' Views on "Altruistic" Live-Donor Kidney Transplantation', *Social Science and Medicine* 150: 104–11.

Bliss, Catherine. 2012. *Race Decoded: The Genomic Fight for Social Justice*. Stanford: Stanford University Press.

Bonfil Batalla, Guillermo. 1972. 'El concepto de indio en América: Una categoría de la situación colonial', *Anales de Antropología* 9: 105–24.

Breilh, Jaime. 2008. 'Latin American Critical ("Social") Epidemiology: New Settings for an Old Dream', *International Journal of Epidemiology* 37 (4): 745–50.

Breilh, Jaime. 2010. 'Las tres "S" de la determinación de la vida y el triángulo de la política', seminar presentation, 'Rediscutindo a questão da determinação social da saúde', CEBES Salvador, Brazil, 19–20 March.

Breilh, Jaime. 2013. 'La determinación social de la salud como herramienta de transformación hacia una nueva salud pública (salud colectiva)', *Revista Facultad Nacional de Salud Pública* 31 (Supplement 1): 13–27.

Britten, Nicky. 2008. *Medicines and Society: Patients, Professionals and the Dominance of Pharmaceuticals*. Basingstoke: Palgrave Macmillan.

Brown, Wendy. 2015. *Undoing the Demos: Neoliberalism's Stealth Revolution*. New York: Zone Books.

Busfield, Joan. 2010. '"A Pill for Every Ill": Explaining the Expansion in Medicine Use', *Social Science and Medicine* 70 (6): 934–41.

Clarke, Adele E., Janet K. Shim, Laura Mamo, Jennifer Ruth Fosket and Jennifer R. Fishman. 2003. 'Biomedicalization: Technoscientific Transformations of Health, Illness, and US Biomedicine', *American Sociological Review* 68 (2): 161–94.

Cohen, Lawrence. 2001. 'The Other Kidney: Biopolitics beyond Recognition', *Body and Society* 7 (2/3):9–29.

Conrad, Peter. 1992. 'Medicalization and Social Control', *Annual Review of Sociology* 18:209–32.

Craig, Gary, Karl Atkin, Sangeeta Chattoo and Ronny Flynn, eds. 2012. *Understanding "Race" and Ethnicity: Theory, History, Policy, Practice*. Bristol: Policy Press.

Department of Health. 2002. *National Service Framework for Diabetes: Delivery Strategy*. London: Department of Health. Accessed 25 June 2017. http://www.yearofcare.co.uk/sites/default/files/images/national%20service%20-%20delivery%20strategy.pdf.

Douglas, Mary. 2003. *Purity and Danger: An Analysis of Concepts of Pollution and Taboo*. London: Routledge.

Douglas, Mary. 2004. *Natural Symbols: Explorations in Cosmology*. London: Routledge.

El Informador. 2012. 'La UNAM progresa en consolidación de Genoteca Indígena', *El Informador*, 26 August. Accessed 27 June 2017. http://www.informador.com.mx/tecnologia/2012/400335/6/la-unam-progresa-en-consolidacion-de-genoteca-indigena.html.

El Nahas, A. Meguid and Aminu K. Bello. 2005. 'Chronic Kidney Disease: The Global Challenge', *The Lancet* 365 (9456):331–40.

Everett, Margaret. 2011. 'They Say It Runs in the Family: Diabetes and Inheritance in Oaxaca, Mexico', *Social Science and Medicine* 72 (11):1776–83.

Facultad de Química. 2007. 'Genoteca Indígena'. Accessed 2 September 2017. http://patronatofq.org.mx/proyectos/genoteca-indigena/.

Farmer, Paul. 2004. *Pathologies of Power: Health, Human Rights, and the New War on the Poor*. Berkeley: University of California Press.

Fee, Margery. 2006. 'Racializing Narratives: Obesity, Diabetes and the "Aboriginal" Thrifty Genotype', *Social Science and Medicine* 62 (12):2988–97.

Ferreira, Mariana Leal and Gretchen Chesley Lang. 2006. *Indigenous Peoples and Diabetes: Community Empowerment and Wellness*. Durham, NC: Carolina Academic Press.

Finkler, Kaja. 2000. *Experiencing the New Genetics: Family and Kinship on the Medical Frontier*. Philadelphia: University of Pennsylvania Press.

Gilman, Sander L. 1988. *Disease and Representation: Images of Illness from Madness to AIDS*. Ithaca, NY: Cornell University Press.

Gilroy, Paul. 2005. *Postcolonial Melancholia*. New York: Columbia University Press.

Goodman, Alan H. 2000. 'Why Genes Don't Count (for Racial Differences in Health)', *American Journal of Public Health* 90 (11):1699–702.

Gordon, Elisa J. 2001. '"They Don't Have to Suffer for Me": Why Dialysis Patients Refuse Offers of Living Donor Kidneys', *Medical Anthropology Quarterly* 15 (2):245–67.

Gordon, Elisa J. 2002. 'What "Race" Cannot Tell Us about Access to Kidney Transplantation', *Cambridge Quarterly of Healthcare Ethics* 11 (2):134–41.

Guthman, Julie. 2014. 'Doing Justice to Bodies? Reflections on Food Justice, Race, and Biology', *Antipode* 46 (5):1153–71.

Hegele, Robert A., Henian Cao, Stewart B. Harris, Anthony J.G. Hanley and Bernard Zinman. 1999. 'The Hepatic Nuclear Factor-1α G319S Variant is Associated with Early-Onset Type 2 Diabetes in Canadian Oji-Cree', *Journal of Clinical Endocrinology and Metabolism* 84 (3):1077–82.

Kelly, Shona J. and Mubarak Ismail. 2015. 'Stress and Type 2 Diabetes: A Review of How Stress Contributes to the Development of Type 2 Diabetes', *Annual Review of Public Health* 36: 441–62.

Keval, Harshad. 2016. *Health, Ethnicity and Diabetes: Racialised Constructions of "Risky" South Asian Bodies*. London: Palgrave Macmillan.

Kierans, Ciara. 2011. 'Anthropology, Organ Transplantation and the Immune System: Resituating Commodity and Gift Exchange', *Social Science and Medicine* 73 (10): 1469–76.

Kierans, Ciara and Jessie Cooper. 2011. 'Organ Donation, Genetics, Race and Culture: The Making of a Medical Problem', *Anthropology Today* 27 (6):11–14.

Kierans, Ciara and Jessie Cooper. 2013. 'The Emergence of the "Ethnic Donor": The Cultural Production and Relocation of Organ Donation in the UK', *Anthropology and Medicine* 20 (3):221–31.

Krieger, Nancy. 2001. 'Theories for Social Epidemiology in the 21st Century: An Ecosocial Perspective', *International Journal of Epidemiology* 30 (4):668–77.

Kuper, Adam. 1988. *The Invention of Primitive Society: Transformations of an Illusion*. London: Routledge.

Kuzawa, Christopher W. and Elizabeth Sweet. 2009. 'Epigenetics and the Embodiment of Race: Developmental Origins of US Racial Disparities in Cardiovascular Health', *American Journal of Human Biology* 21 (1):2–15.

Lambert, Helen and Leena Sevak. 1996. 'Is "Cultural Difference" a Useful Concept? Perceptions of Health and the Sources of Ill Health among Londoners of South Asian Origin'. In *Researching Cultural Differences in Health*, edited by David Kelleher and Sheila Hillier, 124–59. London: Routledge.

Lara-Riegos, J.C., M.G. Ortiz-López, B.I. Peña-Espinoza, I. Montúfar-Robles, M.A. Peña-Rico, K. Sánchez-Pozos, M.A. Granados-Silvestre and M. Menjivar. 2015. 'Diabetes Susceptibility in Mayas: Evidence for the Involvement of Polymorphisms in HHEX, HNF4α, KCNJ11, PPARγ, CDKN2A/2B, SLC30A8, CDC123/CAMK1D, TCF7L2, ABCA1 and SLC16A11 Genes', *Gene* 565 (1): 68–75.

Laupacis, Andreas, Paul Keown, Nancy Pus, Hans Krueger, Beryl Ferguson, Cindy Wong and Norman Muirhead. 1996. 'A Study of the Quality of Life and Cost-Utility of Renal Transplantation', *Kidney International* 50 (1):235–42.

Leatherman, Tom and Alan H. Goodman. 2011. 'Critical Biocultural Approaches in Medical Anthropology'. In *A Companion to Medical Anthropology*, edited by Merrill Singer and Pamela I. Erickson, 29–47. Chichester: Wiley-Blackwell.

Lillie-Blanton, Marsha and Thomas Laveist. 1996. 'Race/Ethnicity, the Social Environment, and Health', *Social Science and Medicine* 43(1): 83–91.

Lippman, Abby. 1991. 'Prenatal Genetic Testing and Screening: Constructing Needs and Reinforcing Inequities', *American Journal of Law & Medicine* 17 (1–2): 15–50.

Lock, Margaret. 2013. 'The Epigenome and Nature/Nurture Reunification: A Challenge for Anthropology', *Medical Anthropology* 32 (4): 291–308.

Lock, Margaret and Vinh-Kim Nguyen. 2010. *An Anthropology of Biomedicine*. Chichester: Wiley-Blackwell.

Lutz, Christopher and Matthew Restall. 2005. 'Wolves and Sheep? Black–Maya Relations in Colonial Guatemala and Yucatan'. In *Beyond Black and Red: African–Native Relations in Colonial Latin America*, edited by Matthew Restall, 185–221. Albuquerque: University of New Mexico Press.

Lydall, Ross. 2016. 'Metropolitan Police Officer Gives Christmas Gift of Life to Sister with Life Changing Kidney Donation', *Evening Standard*, 20 December 2016. Accessed 18 October 2019. https://www.standard.co.uk/news/health/metropolitan-police-officer-gives-christmas-gift-of-life-to-sister-with-lifechanging-kidney-donation-a3424781.html.

Lysaght, Michael J. 2002. 'Maintenance Dialysis Population Dynamics: Current Trends and Long-Term Implications', *Journal of the American Society of Nephrology* 13 (Supplement 1): S37–S40.

Marks, Jonathan. 2013. 'The Nature/Culture of Genetic Facts', *Annual Review of Anthropology* 42:247–67.

Mawani, Renisa. 2003. '"The Island of the Unclean": Race, Colonialism and "Chinese Leprosy" in British Columbia, 1891–1924', *Law, Social Justice and Global Development Journal* 5 (1): 3–21. Accessed 21 September 2019. https://warwick.ac.uk/fac/soc/law/elj/lgd/2003_1/mawani.

Menéndez, Eduardo L. 1998. 'Estilos de vida, riesgos y construcción social: Conceptos similares y significados diferentes', *Estudios Sociológicos* 16 (46): 37–67.

Menéndez, Eduardo. 2001. 'Biologización y racismo en la vida cotidiana', *Alteridades* 11 (21): 5–39.

Menjívar Iraheta, Marta Alicia. 2009. *Genética del mexicano propicia desarrollo de obesidad y diabetes* (Boletín UNAM-DGCS-351). Mexico City: Dirección General de Comunicación Social. Accessed 27 June 2017. http://www.dgcs.unam.mx/boletin/bdboletin/2009_351.html.

Minster, Ryan L., Nicola L. Hawley, Chi-Ting Su, Guangyun Sun, Erin E. Kershaw, Hong Cheng, Olive D. Buhule, Jerome Lin, Muagututi'a Sefuiva Reupena, Satupa'itea Viali, John Tuitele, Take Naseri, Zsolt Urban, Ranjan Deka, Daniel E. Weeks and Stephen T. McGarvey. 2016. 'A Thrifty Variant in CREBRF Strongly Influences Body Mass Index in Samoans', *Nature Genetics* 48: 1049–54.

Montesi, Laura. 2017. 'La diabetes como metáfora de vulnerabilidad: El caso de los ikojts de Oaxaca', *Revista Pueblos y Fronteras Digital* 12 (23):46–76.

Montoya, Michael J. 2011. *Making the Mexican Diabetic: Race, Science, and the Genetics of Inequality.* Berkeley: University of California Press.

Moreno Figueroa, Mónica G. 2010. 'Distributed Intensities: Whiteness, Mestizaje and the Logics of Mexican Racism', *Ethnicities* 10 (3):387–401.

Nazroo, James, James Jackson, Saffron Karlsen and Myriam Torres. 2007. 'The Black Diaspora and Health Inequalities in the US and England: Does Where You Go and How You Get There Make a Difference?', *Sociology of Health and Illness* 29 (6):811–30.

Neel, James V. 1962. 'Diabetes Mellitus: A "Thrifty" Genotype Rendered Detrimental by "Progress"?', *American Journal of Human Genetics* 14 (4):353–62.

NHS Organ Donation. 'Organ Donation and Ethnicity'. Accessed 2 September 2017. https://www.organdonation.nhs.uk/about-donation/organ-donation-and-ethnicity/

NHS Organ Donation. 'Organ Donation and Ethnicity'. Accessed 21 September 2019. https://www.organdonation.nhs.uk/about-donation/organ-donation-and-ethnicity/.

NICE (National Institute for Health and Care Excellence). 2017. 'Type 2 Diabetes: Prevention in People at High Risk'. Accessed 21 September 2019. https://www.nice.org.uk/guidance/ph38.

Ocampo, Mónica. 2013. 'Genes indígenas, solución a la diabetes', *SinEmbargo*, 16 April. Accessed 21 September 2019. http://www.sinembargo.mx/16-04-2013/588062.

OECD (Organisation for Economic Co-operation and Development). 2014. *OECD Economic Surveys: Mexico: January 2015: Overview.* Paris: Organisation for Economic Co-operation and Development.

OECD (Organisation for Economic Co-operation and Development). 2015. *Health at a Glance.* Washington, DC: Brookings Institution Press.

Ohnuki-Tierney, Emiko, Michael V. Angrosino, Carl Becker, A.S. Daar, Takeo Funabiki and Marc I. Lorber. 1994. 'Brain Death and Organ Transplantation: Cultural Bases of Medical Technology [and Comments and Reply]', *Current Anthropology* 35 (3):233–54.

Presidencia de la República. 2013. 'Encabeza el Presidente Peña Nieto la Estrategia Nacional para prevenir y controlar sobrepeso, obesidad y diabetes'. Accessed 21 September 2019. https://corporacioncomunicativaojeda.wordpress.com/2013/10/31/encabeza-el-presidente-pena-nieto-la-estrategia-nacional-para-prevenir-y-controlar-sobrepeso-obesidad-y-diabetes/.

Saldaña-Tejeda, Abril and Peter Wade. 2018. 'Obesity, Race and the Indigenous Origins of Health Risks among Mexican Mestizos', *Ethnic and Racial Studies* 41 (15):2731–49.

Saldívar, Emiko. 2014. '"It's Not Race, It's Culture": Untangling Racial Politics in Mexico', *Latin American and Caribbean Ethnic Studies* 9 (1):89–108.

Sánchez Hövel, Natascha. 2014. 'La donación de vivo en el trasplante renal: Entre el regalo de vida y la tiranía del regalo', *Anales de la Fundación Joaquín Costa* 28:165–90.

Scheper-Hughes, Nancy and Margaret M. Lock. 1987. 'The Mindful Body: A Prolegomenon to Future Work in Medical Anthropology', *Medical Anthropology Quarterly* 1 (1):6–41.

Secretaría de Salud. 2012. *Panorama epidemiológico y estadístico de la mortalidad en México 2010.* Mexico City: Secretaría de Salud. Accessed 22 September 2019. https://www.gob.mx/cms/uploads/attachment/file/267597/Mortalidad_2010.pdf.

Secretaría de Salud. 2013. *Estrategia nacional para la prevención y el control del sobrepeso, la obesidad y la diabetes.* Mexico City: Secretaría de Salud. Accessed 22 September 2019. https://www.gob.mx/cms/uploads/attachment/file/276108/estrategia_sobrepeso_diabetes_obesidad.pdf.

Secretaría de Salud. 2015. *Informe sobre la salud de los mexicanos 2015: Diagnóstico general de la salud poblacional.* Mexico City: Secretaría de Salud. Accessed 22 September 2019. https://www.gob.mx/cms/uploads/attachment/file/64176/INFORME_LA_SALUD_DE_LOS_MEXICANOS_2015_S.pdf.

Sehgal, A.R. 1999. 'End Stage Renal Disease Epidemiology and Outcomes'. In *Nephrology Secrets*, edited by Donald E. Hricik, John R. Sedor and Michael B. Ganz, 131–32. Philadelphia : Hanley and Belfus.

SentryattheGate. 2015. Comment on the article 'Maya Ancestry May Help Explain the High Risk of Diabetes in Mexico', *American Renaissance*, 9 June. Accessed 21 September 2019. https://www.amren.com/news/2015/06/maya-ancestry-may-help-explain-the-high-risk-of-diabetes-in-mexico/.

Shah, Nayan. 2001. *Contagious Divides: Epidemics and Race in San Francisco's Chinatown*. Berkeley: University of California Press.

Sharp, Lesley A. 1995. 'Organ Transplantation as a Transformative Experience: Anthropological Insights into the Restructuring of the Self', *Medical Anthropology Quarterly* 9 (3):357–89.

Sheldon, Trevor A. and Hilda Parker. 1992. 'Race and Ethnicity in Health Research', *Journal of Public Health Medicine* 14 (2): 104–10.

Siddique, Haroon and Steven Morris. 2016. 'Organ Donation Rates for Transplants Still Too Low in UK, Says NHS'. *The Guardian*, 1 September. Accessed 22 September 2019. https://www.theguardian.com/society/2016/sep/01/organ-donation-rates-for-transplants-still-too-low-in-uk-says-nhs.

Silva-Zolezzi, I., A. Hidalgo-Miranda, J. Estrada-Gil, J.C. Fernandez-Lopez, L. Uribe-Figueroa, A. Contreras, E. Balam-Ortiz, L. del Bosque-Plata, D. Velazquez-Fernandez, C. Lara et al. 2009. 'Analysis of Genomic Diversity in Mexican Mestizo Populations to Develop Genomic Medicine in Mexico', *Proceedings of the National Academy of Sciences of the USA* 106 (21): 8611–16.

Smedley, Audrey. 1998. '"Race" and the Construction of Human Identity', *American Anthropologist* 100 (3): 690–702.

Thayer, Zaneta M. and Amy L. Non. 2015. 'Anthropology Meets Epigenetics: Current and Future Directions', *American Anthropologist* 117 (4): 722–35.

Wade, Peter, Vivette García Deister, Michael Kent, María Fernanda Olarte Sierra and Adriana Díaz del Castillo Hernández. 2014. 'Nation and the Absent Presence of Race in Latin American Genomics', *Current Anthropology* 55 (5): 497–522.

Weaver, Lesley Jo and Emily Mendenhall. 2014. 'Applying Syndemics and Chronicity: Interpretations from Studies of Poverty, Depression, and Diabetes', *Medical Anthropology* 33 (2): 92–108.

WHO (World Health Organization). 2016. *Global Report on Diabetes*. Geneva: World Health Organization.

Yen, Eugene F., Karen Hardinger, Daniel C. Brennan, Robert S. Woodward, Niraj M. Desai, Jeffrey S. Crippin, Brian F. Gage and Mark A. Schnitzler. 2004. 'Cost-Effectiveness of Extending Medicare Coverage of Immunosuppressive Medications to the Life of a Kidney Transplant', *American Journal of Transplantation* 4 (10):1703–8.

Part III
Political economy and judicialisation

8
Consultation rooms annexed to pharmacies: The Mexican private, low-cost healthcare system

Rosa María Osorio Carranza

Recent years have witnessed the expansion in Mexico of a private healthcare system promoted by the pharmaceutical industry, whose healthcare infrastructure consists of consultation rooms adjacent to pharmacies. These have been spreading throughout the country in connection with various pharmaceutical chains, chain stores, self-service stores or independent pharmacies. This healthcare system has become known as 'consultation rooms annexed to pharmacies'. It is defined as 'consultation rooms that are adjacent to a pharmacy with a direct or indirect connection such as belonging to the same business group, being on the same property, sharing a commercial brand and where the pharmaceutical company can determine the operating procedures of a consultation room' (FUNSALUD 2014: 15).

This chapter considers some of the characteristics of the growing number of consultation rooms annexed to pharmacies (CRPs) where a general practitioner (GP) provides primary healthcare services. Since 2010, these healthcare services have grown substantially, giving rise to a private system that is parallel with and complementary to the public primary healthcare system.

Using available information about this private general practice system, I will show how its emergence can be framed within the context of public policies aimed towards the privatisation of healthcare services and the simultaneous retreat of the Mexican public health sector. Finally, I describe how some users evaluate this kind of service and their motivations for using it.

GP consultation rooms compete to provide medical care for certain primary-level health problems, with qualified physicians providing very low-cost (between 35 and 70 pesos[1]) or even free consultations. They have a wide and growing geographical distribution throughout the country, mainly in urban areas, so that users have the option of consulting a physician very close to their homes, with a relatively short waiting time, and without admission requirements; all these factors establish it as the private medical system for primary care level with the greatest economic, geographic and institutional accessibility for certain socio-economic groups and populations.

Pharmaceutical chains account for nearly 80 per cent of all consultation rooms. The most relevant are: Farmacias Similares, Farmacias del Ahorro, Farmacias Unión, Farmacias Guadalajara, Farmacias Benavides, Farmacias de Genéricos Intercambiables, Farmacias Dr Descuento, Farmacias Multigenéricos and Red Médica Yza. Some are associated with certain commercial brands such as FEMSA (Oxxo-Coca Cola); others are linked to self-service stores such as Walmart, Soriana and Waldos, as well as a number of independent pharmacies that have installed their own consultation rooms.

From the pharmaceutical industry's point of view, and judging by its rapid expansion,[2] this system represents an excellent new business niche, attracting and generating real or potential clientele for the medications sold in the adjacent pharmacy. Not only does this model expand the market, but it also creates consumers (users/patients/clients); thereby the processes of medicalisation induces and increases the consumption of pharmaceuticals, a process known as pharmaceuticalisation:

> Pharmaceuticalisation denotes the translation or transformation of human conditions, capabilities and capacities into opportunities for pharmaceutical intervention. These processes potentially extend far beyond the realms of the strictly medical or the medicalised (Conrad 2007) to encompass other non-medical uses for lifestyle, augmentation or enhancement purposes (amongst 'healthy' people).
>
> (Williams, Martin and Gabe 2011: 711)

These two processes – medicalisation and pharmaceuticalisation – inherently draw attention and resources to pharmaceutical interests. Medicalisation does so by allowing a growing variety and quantity of biological conditions and sociocultural behaviours to be incorporated into, recognised or even generated within the sphere of biomedicine (Conrad 2007). The pharmaceuticalisation process is focused on making prescription drugs – biomedicine's principal and hallmark therapeutic standard for treating medical conditions under professional medical authority – whether that is justified or not.

The entire range of positive and negative consequences, affecting the population's health at micro and macro levels, has not been completely identified and analysed; neither has the quality of care given in the CRP system been evaluated. It would be simplistic to attempt to reduce an analysis of this system to the pharmaceutical industry's business marketing (Torres Guerra and Gutiérrez 2009). There are other actors and interests to be considered within the CRP system, for example those of the users themselves, who undoubtedly have greater access to professional medical care when CRPs are available.

From the point of view of the medical profession, this system provides a significant number of jobs for doctors, and forms a source of employment even though their contracts expose them to precarious labour conditions. Most of them are practitioners who are at the beginning or end of their careers as health professionals. They are not part of the complex training circuit of medical specialisation and sub-specialisation, nor are they part of the public or private healthcare system at secondary or tertiary levels of care.

For the Ministry of Health and other government agencies, the CRP system is challenging because it is a continually expanding private system that grows without any clearly defined role within the three levels of the public health system, nor is it regulated as a private medical practice. This lack of clarity exists despite the important role it currently plays in out-patient medical care; particularly in urban areas, and sometimes even in rural communities, it is one of few available services.

From the point of view of critical medical anthropology, the pharmaceutical industry's expansion of market pre-eminence and the conditions favouring the monopolistic consolidation of large pharmacy chains are issues that merit scrutiny. Policy decisions taken by the public health sector have been crucial to the exponential growth of this system. In light of these issues, I consider that it is critical to focus the analysis on the importance of the CRP system's medical, cultural and political-economic dimensions. Hence this study will attempt to consider different perspectives on this complex issue, as well as the view of the social actors involved (Singer and Baer 1995).

Several questions arise: for example, how have the dynamics of treatment processes for common ailments been transformed? How do these clinics fit in alongside public healthcare services at all three levels? How has increased access to health services and the over-prescription of medicines impacted new processes of medicalisation or pharmaceuticalisation?

Based on these questions, I set out to explore the experiences of CRP users and to understand their opinions about their quality of care and the perceived advantages and disadvantages when they compare service at these sites to care to a primary health centre or private practice.

In other papers, I have analysed the systems of knowledge and practice that are adopted in relation to the health-seeking process (Osorio Carranza 2001, 2013, 2016). Different social groups can, in relation to their own socio-economic conditions, adequately, empirically and theoretically assess the social performance and practices that involve technical and ideological symbolic knowledge. This ability enables them to make their own decisions about which healthcare resources they should seek in their therapeutic process, as well as determine their choice among available services to which they have realistic access.

Those seeking medical care initially treat themselves at home or with basic care, at least for some non-serious conditions or follow-up of certain chronic conditions; but this treatment process may be rechannelled into the CRP network of private out-patient coverage, which provides patients with faster and more timely medical care. Such micro-social processes parallel macro-social structural trends, such as medicalisation and medication of health-disease-treatment processes: the expansion of the pharmaceutical industry, its economic gains in the drug market and its control of the medical labour market, as well as the consolidation of national or international monopolies (Conrad and Schneider 1980, 1992).

Based on these factors, I propose an overview of the conditions in which the CRP system arises and operates, enabling us to contextualise its impact. I will offer several lines of analysis that allow us to compare it with the public system at the primary level; in order to do so I shall present the opinions of a set of CRP users that explain the rationale for their choice and convey their experiences as clients.

Given the fertile terrain for research, in this paper I gathered information from different available sources. Insofar as this system of medical care is an 'alternative' or 'parallel' system, available data is scattered among and does not necessarily coincide between different sources. This data, consisting of fragmented information from different sources, reveals not only ignorance about how the CRP system is working, but also the lack of systematic information and, above all, the absence of regulation by corresponding governmental agencies. To date, few detailed studies consider this field of medical care in detail. These include FUNSALUD 2014; Díaz Portillo 2012; Pérez Cuevas et al. 2012; Leyva Piña and Pichardo Palacios 2012; Leyva-Flores et al. 1998; Wirtz et al. 2011; Hayden, 2007, 2008, 2013; Gutiérrez et al. 2012, Oláiz Fernández

2013. Additionally, a great deal of information is available through printed news, digital media and the companies' own websites. In general, it can be said that only scant information is available about the operation of the system of GP consultation rooms annexed to pharmacies.

An approach to primary healthcare: Public and private health services

In this section I will present an overview of the public health system[3] at the primary level, which provides care for basic health issues that can also be addressed through out-patient services; these issues are also the most sought-for services by users of the pharmacy-dependent consultation rooms. The goal is to have a reference for identifying and comparing the growing importance of the private CRP system versus the public primary healthcare system throughout the country.

Despite a prior trend (since the 1970s) towards universal healthcare coverage (through various social security institutions or programmes implemented by the Ministry of Health directed towards rural or impoverished populations), because certain conditions are requisites for eligibility, the goal of universal coverage has not been met.

Data from the National Health and Nutrition Survey (Gutiérrez et al. 2012: 35) reports that over 24 million (21.4 per cent of the national population, estimated at 115 million) Mexicans do not have healthcare coverage or insurance. The official data for 2015 report coverage of 98 per cent of the national population, estimated at 120 million Mexicans (DENUE-INEGI 2017). However, it is worth mentioning that coverage statistics refer here to the condition of having a right to some kind of social security scheme and do not necessarily reflect the real access of the population to public health services.

According to the national data provided by the National Survey (Gutiérrez et al. 2012), on out-patient care services (over the 15 days prior to the survey), 61.1 per cent of the total number of consultations took place in public sector healthcare services, compared to 38.9 per cent in the private sector. Of those occurring in the private sector, the survey reveals that independent medical offices account for 58.5 per cent of private out-patient consultations, while pharmacy-dependent consultation rooms provide 41.5 per cent of the total.

On their own, pharmacy-dependent consultation rooms treat 16.1 per cent of total out-patient visits, reinforcing the importance of taking this sub-group into account. This breakdown of the private sector was not investigated in the 2006 survey, hence it is not possible to assess the changes over this period of time (Gutiérrez et al. 2012: 44).

In terms of infrastructure, according to the 2012 data provided by the Ministry of Health there are 71,767 public clinics, of which 29,208 medical units (40.7 per cent) corresponded to state or federal social security institutions, while 42,559 out-patient clinics (59.3 per cent) were accessible to the non-beneficiary population. The Ministry of Health oversaw 51 per cent of clinics, followed by the Mexican Institute of Social Security (IMSS) with 26 per cent of clinics, the Social Security Institute for Federal Workers (ISSSTE) with 8.8 per cent of the primary-level medical units, and finally, Petroleos Mexicanos workers (PEMEX), the Defence Ministry (SEDENA) and Marine Ministry (SEMAR) together constituted 4 per cent (Secretaría de Salud 2013). Notably, the Federal Commission for the Protection of Health Risks (COFEPRIS) identified approximately 10,000 consultation rooms attached to pharmacies for the same year, 2012, signifying that about 12 per cent of the national total number of sites providing care would correspond to the CRP system. The most recent figures would approximate a total of 16,000 CRPs in 2016 (COFEPRIS 2016).

These figures allow us to comprehend not only the scale of private care, but also its relationship with the public health sector. According to data from the National Health Survey, one-third of people affiliated to some type of public insurance reported using CRP, while two-thirds of the population without any coverage resorted to the private sector for out-patient consultation (Gutiérrez et al. 2012: 44).

The growth of CRP has skyrocketed since 2010: in only four years the number of establishments tripled; it is to be expected that the utilisation rates have correspondingly increased, similarly modifying the recourse to public out-patient health services. However, it is worth noticing that ENSANUT 2012 does not record the impact of the increase in medical consultations at CRPs, since its general conclusions about the use of out-patient services indicate that:

> The use of health and out-patient services shows similar performance to that observed in 2000 and 2006 […] In terms of provision, public services as a whole represent more than 60% of total consultations, a percentage similar to the one observed in 2006. This means the pattern of utilization of out-patient services has not changed. It shows that about 3 out of 10 healthcare system users with public healthcare coverage opted for private care, a significant part of which occurred at pharmacies with out-patient care.
> (Gutiérrez et al. 2012: 54)

In order to compare the total number of out-patient consultations provided by the public healthcare system to those of the CRP system, I used the number of general medical consultations offered in all the public health services as an index, close to 223.5 million out-patient consultations per year. According to COFEPRIS (2014), about 9.7 million consultations per month take place within the entire CRP system, or 117 million consultations per year. However, it should be emphasised that, given that no precise survey of the system's operation or enumeration of CRP facilities exists, the above figures are only estimates. These data reveal the growing importance of the private out-patient care system that would be equivalent to half of all medical consultations of the public primary care system.

The director of COFEPRIS recognised that 'the CRP system should be used to implement prevention programs and health policies; and the 32,000 doctors who attend these clinics can apply the same prevention and control measures used in public facilities' (Rodríguez 2014).

Critiques of this model are principally oriented at emphasising the inadequacies of the public healthcare system and its inability to respond to the growing demands of a population prone to acute and chronic diseases, requiring long-term care and continued use of pharmaceuticals.

Although the expansion of the CRP system means greater access to medical care, the encroachment of the private healthcare sector and the pharmaceutical industry, and concurrent influence on increased drug consumption and out-of-pocket patient expenditure, cannot be ignored.

Public health policies: The driving force behind the CRP system

I start by considering that one of the principal functions of the state is to guarantee the right to health, and to increase effective and timely access to public health services in terms of equity, quality and accessibility, especially for the most disadvantaged sectors of the population. However, this function is affected when the supply of public services stagnates or is reduced relative to growing demand, while its services are replaced by contracting to private companies. In this sense, one can say that the expansion of the private system of primary care has been promoted and permitted by the state through certain public health policies. For practical purposes, this implies recognising the weakening or diminishing of the state supply of basic care services, opening the way for the pharmaceutical industry to provide this function.

One of the public policies that favoured such exponential growth of CRP had its origin in the August 2010 agreement issued by the Ministry of Health prohibiting the sale of antibiotics without a medical prescription, which had been a common practice in Mexico until the time. The official argument was that the inappropriate or excessive use of antibiotics generates a problem of bacterial resistance; it emphasised the risks of self-medication, attributing a large proportion of the deaths recorded during the AH1N1 influenza epidemic in Mexico in 2009 to poor self-administration of antibiotics (COFEPRIS 2013):

> The inappropriate use of antibiotics poses a risk to the health of individuals and increases the costs incurred by families and healthcare services. Additionally, it contributes to the growing epidemic of bacterial resistance, consequently creating the need for more expensive treatments and higher mortality from infectious diseases, for which reasons it is considered a serious global public health problem. In this context, antibiotics are considered a global public good [… t]he growing negative consequences of the indiscriminate use of antibiotics in our country [Mexico] reveals the need to take stricter regulatory action in the short term, such that patient safety is ensured and public health protected. These regulatory actions include restricting the sale of those antibiotics that are of critical importance as soon as possible, requiring that they be dispensed only by medical prescription.
>
> (COFEPRIS 2010c)

According to data provided by COFEPRIS (2010a), this government decision led to a reduction in the sale of antibiotics (the second most sold drug in the country) of almost 14 per cent in the period from 2010 to 2012 – from approximately 61 million units sold in 2010 to 49 million in 2011 and almost 45 million in 2012.

As per this agreement, with the justification of not leaving the population unprotected and guaranteeing regulated antibiotics prescription, the public health sector modified its policy towards the pharmaceutical industry; beginning in 2010 it authorised the general establishment of this type of medical practice annexed to pharmacies.

In the same year, a wide variety of drugs that until then were classified as 'similar' were certified as 'generic': that is, they could be considered as pharmacological equivalents or chemically biocompatible with the respective patented drugs. This pharmacological equivalence was certified after five years of clinical trials. Thus, in 2010 drug classification decreased from three categories (patent, interchangeable generics and similar) to only two (patent and generic) (COFEPRIS 2010a). This reclassification boosted the mass production of generic drugs prescribed and distributed in CRPs that are associated with pharmaceutical laboratories, each producing generic medications under its own brand.

The detailed analysis by Hayden of the relationship between drug patents, trademarks and the increased production of generic drugs in different countries states that:

> In Latin America, where my research is concentrated, generic drugs have become new and important features of national pharmaceutical landscapes [...] and the category 'unbranded generics' is the fastest growing pharmaceutical niche in both Mexico and Brazil. [...] We might make the simultaneously obvious and strange argument that the pharmaceutical market is becoming commodified; that is, it is being genericized and the commercial landscapes [are] saturated by sameness.
>
> (Hayden 2013: 604)

Since the late 1990s, a part of the international pharmaceutical sector has reoriented its research and production towards interchangeable medicines. A sector of the industry is directed to the elaboration and commercialisation of drugs that are copies of the original, when the patent of the laboratory that designed them has passed into the public domain; these copies are called similar, generic, interchangeable generic or biosimilar, and are sold at a lower price than the patented originals.

However, there are different levels or kinds of sameness or similarity, depending on national public policies and specific norms and regulations that change across time and place. For example, the dominant criteria may be bioequivalence (similarity in the chemical substance) or bioavailability (similarity in the blood absorption rate of the active substance) when evaluating the active substance, its effectiveness, safety and time of action – notions that influence determinations of 'pharmaceutical equivalence' and 'interchangeability' (Hayden 2013: 606).

The generic market in Mexico has grown to 40 per cent of the total drug market. The proliferation of generics, aided by their low price, has helped to establish a new category of drugs and a growing consumer market. The most notable example is the market-leading Mexican pharmaceutical chain Farmacias Similares, whose advertising emphasises: 'The same but cheaper', 'We call ourselves Similar, we are generic'; or the case of Farmacias GI (Generic Interchangeable), whose advertising motto is '[We are] Your generic expert'. The same applies to other pharmaceutical chains who have launched their generic 'own brand', announcing only the generic chemical formula and distribution company on packaging: for example, generic GI; generic FarmAhorro (Farmacias del Ahorro); generic Medimart (Walmart); generic FABE (Farmacias Benavides). The circuit of production, distribution and marketing of generic drugs is therefore perfectly complemented by a physician's prescription from a CRP, and by their sale through partner pharmacies (Hayden 2007, 2008).

The two aforementioned Ministry of Health public policy decisions that coincided in 2010 would, together, spark the proliferation of this type of clinic and drugs throughout the country. The pharmaceutical industry's response was quick and definitive: consultation rooms were installed next to pharmacies and the production of cheap generic medicines marketed under the particular pharmaceutical brand increased.

Based on the COFEPRIS data, at the beginning of 2015, over half (53 per cent) of the 28,000 pharmacies in the country had a clinic. The regulatory organisation itself noted that as of 2010, the date of the aforementioned agreement, the number of CRPs quadrupled, from 4,370 to 16, 000. Over only five years (2010–16) they increased by 366 per cent (Table 8.1).

The accelerated growth is highlighted by the comparative sluggishness or absence of regulation by the public healthcare sector. Only in 2013 did the governing entity, COFEPRIS, propose the need to regulate and supervise these establishments, implementing guidelines for best

Table 8.1 Growth of consultation rooms annexed to pharmacies in Mexico, 2010–16[4]

Year	Number
2010	4,370
2011	6,611
2012	10,000
2013	13,000
2014	15,000
2016*	16,000

Source: COFEPRIS data at: http://interactivo.eluniversal.com.mx/2018/mapa-consultorios-farmacias/mapa-consultorios.html (accessed 1 November 2019).

practice and penalties for breach of regulations, fines, and in extreme cases, temporary or permanent closure of the CRP (COFEPRIS 2013). Among the main regulations are the prohibition of direct communication between CRP and pharmacy, and the requirement that physicians have professional qualifications, with appropriate facilities for diagnosis, examination and maintaining clinical files.

This private healthcare system was gradually made operational by several pharmaceutical brands. By the end of June 2014, CRP distribution in pharmacy chains represented 62 per cent of the market. They were present in 16 per cent of self-service stores and 16 per cent of private pharmacies (Table 8.2).

It is useful to analyse the CRP healthcare system within the framework of public health policies: that is, by examining authorisations, regulations and government negotiations with the pharmaceutical industry, and through the work of regulatory agencies. By 2013, the director of COFEPRIS, Mikel Arriola Peñalosa – later appointed (in 2016) as director of the Mexican Institute of Social Security – gave the following perspective on this kind of connection between pharmacies and clinics:

> This is good news for healthcare coverage because pharmacies have even more [market] penetration than banks; we are talking about almost 2.5 pharmacies per 10,000 inhabitants [...] and for pharmacies and self-service chains, the outlook is even more favourable. An anticipated 90% of dispensed drugs will come from these two channels in 2014, of which 60% correspond to the [pharmaceutical] chains [...] as a regulatory authority and in accordance with occurring economic and health phenomena, adapting to new areas of business is always a challenge for us, but we cannot lag behind anymore.
>
> (Arteaga 2013)

Table 8.2 Number of CRPs in principal pharmaceutical chains, June 2015.

Pharmaceutical Brand	Number	Percentage
Similares	5,120	52%
Genéricos Intercambiables	1,623	16%
Del Ahorro	1,300	13%
Benavides	1,029	10%
FEMSA	800	8%
Total	9,872	100%

Source: El Universal newspaper, 4 September 2015, page B3.

Almost 15 years after the emergence of the first CRP, although the regulatory agency was already well aware of the importance of this phenomenon and its impact both on health coverage and on prescription drugs, only in 2013 was the necessity of adapting to these growing economic and health processes taken seriously, when regulatory best practices to control and supervise such establishments were put into effect. The public policy determined by the Health Ministry thus allowed and promoted the expansion of these offices throughout the country. However, it has since shirked its role through its failure to regulate and monitor their proper functioning.

Another aspect of this relapse of state governance regards the provision of health coverage to the population. For health issues considered 'non-serious', taking a balance of time, needs and results into account, people will usually go to a CRP or directly to the pharmacy near their home, instead of their affiliated public health centre or clinic. For this reason, the growing number of CRPs represents a diversification and expansion of access to primary healthcare for the entire population, and particularly for those sectors that do not have effective and timely access to public health services. In this sense, there is a general, indirect decrease in the demand for public health centres and clinics, not only for medical consultation but also for the free medication supplied through social security institutions and those dependent on the Ministry of Health.

The production, distribution and sale of generic medicines at low cost through the CRP system transfers public-sector expenses to users/ clients/patients, who buy them at the pharmacy next to the CRP, absorbing their cost, and increasing their out-of-pocket expenses.[5] This decrease in the demand for public-sector consultations and drugs reduces public health spending and functions as a safety valve to relieve pressure from the need to expand public health coverage.

In this sense, it is important to understand and analyse healthcare policies and services systemically and relationally, being aware of their contradictions and complementarities, and identifying the connections and decision-making between the public and the private health sectors, in which there are different social actors with potentially different goals and challenges. For example: the government has determined public policies through the Ministry of Health and other public institutions; the pharmaceutical industry seeks to meet its economic interests and business objectives; medical professionals are aware of their labour needs. Above all, the population that requests and uses accessible health services makes specific choices from the available options based on a set of conditions and factors: they are users of specific services, patients who expect medical care from a practitioner who fits a certain profile; they are also clients: potential consumers of prescription drugs.

User feedback: Why do they prefer consultation rooms attached to the pharmacies?

It is clear that an extensive and low-cost private healthcare system has been developed at the primary care level. This system complements the public out-patient system and, in a certain sense, displaces or at least competes with the traditional scheme of the private physician whose office is independent, but whose consultations are comparatively more expensive.

I interviewed users of three CRPs located in very close proximity to each other. They were asked about their opinions regarding the care received at these consultation rooms and how these compared with the public ambulatory care services and with other private GPs which they had attended. My research conducted short interviews in a middle-class neighbourhood in the south of Mexico City,[6] where three consultation rooms annexed to the pharmaceutical chains Similares, Unión and Ahorro are located within 50 metres of one another, with a high number of users: neighbourhood residents, passers-by or local workers.

According to the observations of this study, at the Similares and Unión pharmacies medical care is available from 9 a.m. to 10 p.m. from Monday to Saturday, and from 10 a.m. to 5 p.m. on Sundays, with doctors attending in two shifts. Free medical advice was offered in Farmacias del Ahorro only from Monday to Saturday, from 9 a.m. to 7 p.m., with a pause for lunch. The influx of customers varies according to the day of the week, time of day and the attending professional. On weekends and some evenings there are more users in Farmacias Similares CRP, while during the week, the doctor who attends at the Unión pharmacy has gained the confidence of users and some report that this doctor is 'very experienced' and 'very effective'.

During this preliminary inquiry, I interviewed 10 women who had used the services of these CRPs at least once, asking questions about the condition for which they sought treatment, their experience in the type of care received and how this compared to other primary healthcare services, like that of the health centre and Mexican Institute of Social Security (IMSS) clinics.

Generally, the reasons for seeking treatment are mostly episodes of acute respiratory or gastrointestinal infections, although the patients also mentioned accidents, treatment and monitoring of chronic diseases such as diabetes and hypertension, and issuance of medical certificates:

> So far this year [over a four-month period] I have been to Similares four times: to take a blood test [glucose], for the flu, for a medical certificate for my daughter, and I [went] with my eldest son [28 years old] to get vitamins because he was very thin; he asked me to accompany him. For the whole family [five members] I think we go about eight times a year; my husband almost never goes. I always go for minor issues. Now there are also some pharmacies with consultation rooms where you can also go for fractures, to have stitches removed or get [saline] solution. [You] can't [go] for more serious problems since they do not have enough medical equipment.[7]

> I have gone to the Similares when there are minor issues and I have no one to accompany me. It is more practical, because I don't have to cross the city, [or] stand in line; it is an accessible service when it is nothing serious; it solves my problem. When more attention is required, then I go to the private doctor, which of course is much more expensive. I don't go to ISSSTE.[8]

This frequency of use can be compared to those who have social insurance but who end up only using the CRPs:

> I usually go to the health centre, or social security. On Saturday, both are closed and so I went to the Farmacias Similares because there they treat flu and coughing, and as I felt as though I were choking. They gave me medicine that does not have the same name as the patent, but thank God, I recovered. About Farmacias Similares, my sons and my daughters-in-law go there a lot. They get blood work done there. My daughter-in-law fell and fractured her foot; they took X-rays and treated her foot right there. She also takes her three small children there. They go for a headache, or upset stomach.[9]

> I once went to the ISSSTE for emergency [care] because it was a Sunday night. I was vomiting and had a stomach ache, but when I got to the emergency room, they told me that the doctor had gone to dinner. The only open service nearby was a Farmacia Similar that attended patients at night. I went there, but there were about 10 people ahead of me, children, adults; they looked bad. It took a while, but at least I was given something to ease the momentary discomfort.[10]

In general, the difference in frequency of use is determined principally by the socio-economic status of the user, as reflected in occupation and schooling, as well as their neighbourhood and access to social security or private medical insurance. It was expected that people in the most unfavourable conditions would report a greater use of the CRP system. Less obvious was that that even people from comparatively better socio-economic conditions have also used them on occasions, or at least once. It is important to mention that in all cases users frequently used the CRP to buy generic drugs on account of their lower cost compared to patented medicines.

The interviewees recognise differential care among the major pharmaceutical chains, even when they have only used CRPs once or twice. There is a clear preference for Farmacias Similares,[11] whose advertising campaign used the popular image of 'Dr Simi' (a caricature of an elderly, congenial cartoon doctor).

> I think the [system of] pharmacies is beginning to grow. Around the year 2000, the first one was Similares. I go [to] the Similar more. I've been to the Farmacia del Ahorro only once in my life and that was last year. I had a very bad stomach ache but they didn't attend me, actually the doctor didn't see me. He was there [in the office] and came out and said, 'I will be back in a minute', but he left me there waiting for half an hour. I asked [for] him directly; but he didn't come out any more and I stayed there alone. After that I said, even though they do not charge for the consultation, what is the use if the doctor is not there; that is why I prefer to pay for the consultation in the Similares and they see me. It is the one I rely on the most and the one that has the most [branches]. I like it because the consultation and the medicine end up being a little cheaper when I do not have money; it is the most practical and most economical.
>
> (AC)

> Dr Simi is closer and always open. The medicines are cheaper, almost half the cost of patent [drugs]. I do not find any deficiencies with the Farmacias Similares. I've been to Farmacias del Ahorro to buy the medicine about three times.
>
> (AB)

> In the Similares there are [good] doctors and there are [less able] doctors; but in the one I go to, medical care is good because [the practitioner] examines you, and prescribes medicine according to the diagnosis. Before they did not do that, previously they would

just prescribe the medication. Now they prescribe the medicine for three days, for example, and say 'In three days please return for a check-up, to see how things are going.' If the medication they gave you was the right one, and you are already feeling better, you don't go back. If you [do] return on for your scheduled follow-up appointment, then you do not have to pay for the consultation. But if you return on another day, then you have to pay again. I think that the treatments are [just] ok, because sometimes they work and sometimes they don't.

(FT)

I come here (Unión) because the afternoon [attending] doctor is very good. I once came for a throat infection and he cured it very fast. You can see that he has a lot of experience and there are always people waiting for him. Now I came because of a backache.[12]

The interviewees also compared the care received at different primary care public and private facilities in relation to GPs at CRPs. The basic differences in types of service are: waiting time for consultation, out-of-pocket expenses, quality of care and available infrastructure.

I think Similar is better than the primary health centre because at Similar, it's your turn and that's all; there's one doctor who examines you calmly. At my health centre, the doctors have barely had [time for] their coffee, when they see so many people [already there] that they become disheartened and they [only] see patients as long as they want to.

(AC)

At the Similar, to exaggerate, it takes about two to three hours at most to get medical care when there are a lot of people; but at the health centre it is almost a full day. If I want to be among the first [in line], I have to arrive by 5 a.m. in order to the 24th or 30th turn. They begin to distribute the numbers at 8 a.m. and only distribute between 40 and 60. It is like in the IMSS; it is exactly the same, it takes all day.

(TI)

The way the doctor attends at Similar is more practical; at the health centre, the nurses are mean, very rude; it goes back to the same thing, there are so many people that the attention is not good. For example, with the sugar-glucose test, they don't do the test [at its scheduled time]; [they] only say that it was [supposed to be] at 8 a.m., and at 9 a.m. they say [the test] can't be done any more. If we are fasting, what is the problem with doing it, even at noon? If you go there fasting, I say that they can do it.

(AB)

On the other hand, the main comparative disadvantages of the CRP are the professional qualifications of the doctors, the clinic's equipment and the quality of the medicines. With regard to the attending physicians, the main comparison is made with private doctors who have traditionally practised in their neighbourhoods:

I feel that there are differences between doctors. In the Similar, I feel that they, as they themselves say [...] are rotating doctors. They are [still students] writing their theses, while [the doctors] at the health centre have already graduated; they already have their diplomas, their title.

(LU)

The doctors at Similar are young people who have just finished studying; they have no experience, but they do attend well. The medicines are the same, but cheaper. I think the private doctors are best; but there, since you are paying, the consultation is better. It is very expensive, that is why I prefer the health centre, because with popular insurance, they do not charge me.

(AB)

I think that to improve the Similares, they should have a better stock at the pharmacy, the most necessary that cannot be found else-where. The clinic could also have better more up to date equipment; Farmacias Similares gave us a glimpse of a private practice, where there are more things, more [medical] devices. It should be better equipped in order to be like a private physician's practice.

(TI)

The statements about the types of prescribed medications indicate that the population recognises a qualitative difference between patent drugs, generic drugs and those of the 'Similar' brand. Thus, the slogan 'The same, but cheaper' is not assumed to be entirely true, since these drugs are con-sidered to be lower quality or to have less therapeutic efficacy. This evalu-ation is similar to the one made regarding private physicians, in which it seems that quality is directly proportional to the price paid for care:

You can buy the prescription in any Farmacia Similar; almost always the medicines are Similar brand. It cannot be patent [medication], because in the Similar there is no patent [medication] and vice versa, in the patent pharmacies there are no Similar brand drugs. The patent medicine is more concentrated. For example, when Amoxilina [sic] was prescribed to my daughter for an infection, the Similar brand came in a light pink colour, pale, more discoloured; the patent [medication] comes in strong pink, like strawberry. The Similar brand comes discoloured and the patent has more colour. In the health centre the generic medication is also a little weaker, but not as much as the Similar.

(AC)

Finally, I requested an overall assessment of the public health services used by interviewees in order to verify the positive and negative representations made about them. Complaints refer to the waiting time for consultations, the lack of organisation, the lack of warm and friendly staff and waiting lists, even when they recognise the out-of-pocket savings, both in consultation fees and medicine:

I have not been back to the health centre for years; because, though there is no charge for the consultation, it is always chaos there and better that I do not go. [Some] people use the health centre a lot because they have to go there to submit documentation to receive their government assistance in the Opportunities Programme. But since I don't have to do any of that, I do not go. They will see me [there] but give priority to those who are enrolled in the programme. I have *Seguro Popular* insurance, but that is only valid in hospitals; at least there, it does work. Or, for example, when my daughter had surgery for her appendicitis, I was seen under the *Seguro Popular* insurance.

(AC)

The testimonies note the factors that influence the choice of services, such as long waiting times, the consultation hours, mistreatment and inadequate facilities; all of these issues can dissuade users from seeking treatment in public health centres, although all recognise that care is free for those who have public insurance benefits.

Overall, choosing CRPs – mostly the Similares – is explained by the shorter waiting times, lower comparative costs and adequate relative efficacy for conditions considered not serious. Their disadvantages include less training for physicians; infrastructure limitations that prohibit attending for other major health problems; lower quality of generic drugs compared to patent medicines; and out-of-pocket expense.

In all cases, users acknowledge that better care would be offered by private doctors, private clinics or even private hospitals, because the doctors would be better prepared and better patent medicines would be prescribed. Of course, the obstacle to accessing them is the high cost of the consultation and of the medicines.

Final considerations

Throughout this chapter, I have tried to describe and analyse how over 20 years a parallel system of out-patient medical care delivered through pharmaceutical companies has been built. This system complements or even replaces the public health system at a primary care level, thanks to ease of access to facilities, its low cost and broad geographical distribution. I have also emphasised how policies implemented by the public health sector have promoted and consolidated this private system; finally, I have explored the main reasons why these pharmacies have become so popular.

By means of conclusion, I will take a political economy perspective to understand the macro, meso and micro dimensions of this phenomenon and to identify stakeholders and interests in both the public and private arenas of the Mexican health system (Singer and Baer 1995). At the macro-social level, it is essential to consider the economic dimensions of the pharmaceutical sector and its impact on the national economy in terms of its contribution to gross domestic product. The industry of health and disease not only involves the production and manufacture of drugs, but also depends on a complex circuit involving the certification, marketing, distribution and sale of drugs, where the prescription constitutes a strategic link in the chain, and the CRP system becomes a privileged space for this purpose, especially if an over-prescription of the drug is supplied.

In the past decade some progress has been made in terms of extending healthcare coverage to populations that did not have any form of social security. Although it can be said that at present there is institutional coverage for a basic suite of diseases and medicines, serious deficiencies persist in terms of real and timely access to services, particularly for people living in conditions of poverty and extreme poverty. The emergence of a private health system accessed through economic and political power directly or indirectly corrects these shortcomings, even at the expense of transferring costs to the user and devaluing the professional knowledge of doctors.

The shortage of medicines, lack of material, financial and human resources, long waiting lists and disarticulation between the three levels of care should be questioned as part of a social health policy. Research must respond to this by identifying resources that provide analytical and collaborative instruments to generate a counter-hegemonic social response based on a greater awareness of the rights of the population to demand and secure their right to health. As for the state, a greater regulation of the CRP system would be desirable to take advantage of and promote, from this same private-sector platform, prevention and health promotion policies. From a critical anthropological approach, it is expected that the CRP system will continue to generate greater privatisation of services, the commodification of health and disease and a greater biomedical hegemony through the medicalisation and pharmaceutisalisation of social representations and medical practices.

The hegemony of biomedical knowledge manifests itself not only through the clinical encounter, the patient–physician relationship and biomedical prescription, but also in self-medication processes or the search for 'magic pills' that solve everyday problems, as widely discussed in the media (Menéndez 1983, 1990). Examining the articulations between the processes of medicalisation and pharmaceuticalisation exceeds the objectives of this paper, but nevertheless it can be said that these processes feed into and strengthen each other. With biomedical hegemony and the processes of medicalisation in our societies preponderantly focusing on the consumption of drugs, the prescription process itself has become a pillar of this hierarchy. However, the social responses of the population depend on multiple transactions between social actors. We have seen that their choices regarding the use of services are mediated by multiple conditions such as the type of medical condition, their socio-economic profile and the specific context within which the need for care is generated. Decisions involve a set of representations, practices and experiences associated with public and private health services (Osorio Carranza 2001).

The main advantages of CRPs are their relative therapeutic efficacy when treating certain health problems, geographical accessibility, the lack of enrolment requirements, minimum waiting times and reduced consultation costs. The disadvantages are the almost non-existent regulation and supervision by the relevant institutions, limited infrastructure, unstable working conditions and low medical qualifications, drug over-prescription and the paucity of information regarding the doctor–patient relationship and quality of care within these clinics.

This state of affairs is complemented by the negative popular evaluation of public healthcare services due to prolonged waiting times and poor quality of service, despite recognition of the benefit of free consultations and medications. Private practitioners – in the traditional sense – are identified as being better care providers and simultaneously the most expensive.

The large number of consultations taking place within the CRPs' clinical network seems to indicate that broad sectors of the vulnerable population, especially those without social security or the middle class, which need or would prefer a fully qualified physician, are reorienting their search for medical care towards these clinics. This system offers the possibility of medical care to disadvantaged sectors of Mexican society and is often the only possibility of professional medical care available to them. The new type of service offered by CRPs has become the second most important system of out-patient care at the national level, and is increasingly relevant to the health-seeking and treatment paths for different medical problems.

In this sense, it is worth pointing out that having a medical practice associated with a pharmacy is not a new phenomenon. Throughout the twentieth century, private medicine was expanded by GPs, who would install their practices in rural and urban areas and subsequently open their own pharmacy where their patients could purchase the medicines they prescribed. The private doctor's practice would append a pharmacy adjacent to it; here the medical professional was pre-eminent and the commercial function of medication sales passed into the background.

In the current context, this relationship has become reversed: the pharmacy will add a medical practice. Nowadays the large pharmaceutical chains that install and control CRPs are also the ones who hire the doctor to work for them.

Pharmaceutical industry operation displaces and imposes itself over the medical professional; the interweaving cogs between the pharmaceutical industry and the medical profession are highly sophisticated. By prescribing medicine in their practices, private doctors became principal distribution agents of retail drugs; realising this, pharmaceutical representatives would strive to influence private physicians to prescribe a particular drug. Now, through the installation of CRPs – along with the mass production of generic drugs – the pharmaceutical industry has managed to incorporate autonomous medical professionals among its employees; within its operational functions the pharmaceutical industry has managed to, literally and in a very specific way, put the medical profession entirely at its service, including ceding its autonomy. The role of the pharmaceutical industry as a healthcare services provider – beyond just providing medicine – is becoming fundamental, to the extent that the Mexican government and its public policies have focused on prioritising the economic dimensions of the CRP system above those of healthcare itself.

In this sense, it is significant that much of the information about the CRP system found in various printed or digital media gives commercial and business perspectives, as if this issue were purely entrepreneurial or transactional. This stands in contrast to the paucity of information available from the perspectives of healthcare systems or the consideration of medical and health outcomes.

Along the same line of analysis, it has been noted that in the results of the 2012 National Health Survey, the impact of this system was poorly recognised and the Ministry of Health is not generating systematic information about it. It is striking that it is easier to find statistical information under the category 'general practice doctors' offices in the private sector' in the Statistical Directory of Economic Units (DENUE-INEGI) than available Ministry of Health data about private out-patient health services.

However, the problem appears to lie not only in the expansion of this network of clinics and in its minimal regulation, but in the fact that, rather than being a supplementary alternative to health centres and public clinics, it has gradually become the most accessible option for certain sectors of the population. It could be a positive addition to existing public or private services that users could access without obstacles, one alternative among many that allow the public to access the healthcare service and medical professionals of their choice; such a situation now appears utopian.

As we have seen, public policies explain how and why this privatisation process is in line with the state's contraction and growing deficiencies in the public healthcare system. From this perspective, the main critique must be directed at the public healthcare sector and governmental institutions that should guarantee the right to health for the population and offer a real universal coverage scheme that, minimally, provides effective and timely access to primary care.

In Mexico's current political context, the federal government is promoting change to the national health system, which would include reforms to the Health Law, the gradual unification of social security services, the creation of a National Institute of Welfare (INSABI) that will replace the Popular Health Insurance and absorb the IMSS Welfare Programme (formerly IMSS-Prospera) and the health services of each state, in the logic of financial, physical and human resources efficiency.

Health Law reforms and the combining of services may lead to greater restrictions on medical treatment: for example, chronic conditions that lead to catastrophic health costs are not necessarily covered by out-patient care systems. The population's right to choose is affected when public services deteriorate, important budgets are reduced, medicines are unavailable and demand for treatment overwhelms available care; when there are few medical and paramedical personnel, long waiting lists and welfare programmes are inadequate – and so on.

The reorganisation of the public health system proposes goals – or promises – of a different order, such as increasing the coverage of medical assistance to the uninsured population, hiring a greater number of doctors, particularly in rural areas, and the free provision of all medicines instead of only a guaranteed basic pool. It also refers to the need to make transparent the acquisition of prescribed medications and the possibility of carrying out massive imports of medicines to reduce costs.

These goals would be commendable as long as they move beyond official discourse and achieve a real positive impact on public policies and specific programmes to ensure that people have effective and timely access to services, and thereby guarantee the population's right to health. However, judging by recent decisions made in public policy, budget reductions and inefficient management, I believe that serious consequences are being generated which are currently affecting the functioning of an already deficient and insufficient public health system.

There is no clear route forward and there are too many uncertainties regarding the scope and limitations of these transformations of the public health system. It is expected that serious operational, institutional and financial difficulties will arise, involving different social actors and interests, sometimes opposed to each other. It may be unrealistic or even utopian to expect that, with so many other goals still to be achieved, the Mexican government should focus serious attention on the CRP system and the need to regulate its operation.

In the light of this, it can be seen that the government has delegated part of its responsibility. It has transferred the social function of medical care to private pharmaceutical companies, which, though effective at providing services, are intrinsically commercial ventures, and therefore do so with an eye to business and profit making. In short, it is a further aspect of the global trend towards the privatisation of health and disease as a generator of market profit.

It seems difficult to reverse this privatisation process, so a comprehensive analysis of these issues is necessary. The economic cost–benefit ratio, the commercialisation of health, the expansion of the pharmaceutical industry and the retreat of the public healthcare sector are all important. Additionally, it is important not to ignore the perspective of the user population who – through the CRP system – can at least treat some of their medical issues in an effective and accessible way.

The current challenge for the Ministry of Health is the implementation of public policies that guarantee the quality of the treatment offered within this model of private care, regulating its growth and operation, reducing the problem of over-prescription and ensuring that the doctors have accredited training. The goal is to optimise this service and merge it adequately with the other public and private services in the three levels of medical care.

The state should not cede its leading role in the provision of health services and simply leave the population's needs in the hands of private enterprise, in the free market of supply and demand, where health issues are the source of major earnings for the highly profitable business of the pharmaceutical industry.

It is imperative to demand from the state better regulation and standardisation of the services offered by these clinics in order to guarantee patients high-quality and humane care. This network of private clinics could be used as a platform to implement and improve epidemiological surveillance systems, prevention programmes and health promotion campaigns that already operate in the public health system. Given the importance of their day-to-day work, the role of physicians in the CRP system needs to be restored, not only in terms of social prestige within and outside their profession, but also in improving their labour conditions.

Finally, I believe that it is fundamental to regain the perspectives of all the actors involved, the interests and needs that are at stake, and to recognise the advantages and disadvantages, possibilities and risks that this new private healthcare system can offer in the present and in the immediate future. It is a system that, for better or for worse, is doubtless here to stay.

Notes

1. Prices fluctuate depending on the commercial company, the service hours and urban location. This amount is equivalent to between US$2 and $3, exchange rate September 2017.
2. In the period 2010–16, the number of consultation rooms in Mexico increased from 4,000 to over 16,000.
3. The health system in Mexico is of a mixed type: public and private. The public health system is institutionally divided by which sector of the population it covers. First, people with social security benefits are attended at specific institutions such as the Mexican Institute of Social Security (IMSS), the Institute for Security and Social Services for Federal Government Workers (ISSSTE), Petróleos Mexicanos (PEMEX), the National Defense Ministry (SEDENA) and the

Marine Ministry (SEMAR); among those treated are also workers (and their familial beneficiaries) who are part of the formal economy. This system is financed by the government, the workers and, where applicable, entrepreneur-employers. Second, the public sector groups and the institutions that protect or provide services to the population outside the social security system; they are attended by the Ministry of Health (SSA), the State Health Services (SESA) and certain social assistance and protection programmes such as Seguro Popular or the IMSS-Prospera programme, which provide medical care for a basic set of health problems in order to expand healthcare coverage for the low-income population in urban and rural areas. It is financed by the federal government, and the beneficiaries may contribute minimal charges. In order to qualify, beneficiaries must comply with specific requirements. The private health sector provides services to the population with payment capacity in the three levels of care. The system of pharmacies and annexed consultation rooms is one facet of private primary healthcare.

4. Despite an extensive search for more current information, no official data was found for the years 2017–18. Presumably, the trend of accelerated growth rate continued.
5. According to the World Health Organization, out-of-pocket expenses 'encompass all types of sanitary expenses done at the moment in which a home is benefited by the health services, e.g. doctors' fees, medication purchase and hospitalization receipts [...] without taking in[to] consideration transport expenses incurred or special nutrition' (quoted in Murayama and Ruesga 2016: 25).
6. The research was conducted on a central and heavily transited avenue of the Benito Juárez Delegation of Mexico City, in a middle- and upper middle-class neighbourhood.
7. Mrs AC, 44 years old with three children, working in domestic service, educated to second grade of primary school; she does not use the public health centre.
8. Mrs FT, 45 years old, is divorced, childless and a professional with a college degree; she is a foreigner who has lived in Mexico for 15 years. She has social security in ISSSTE and private medical insurance.
9. Mrs AB, 58 years old, is divorced, with three children and three grandchildren; she is of Nahua indigenous origin, completed her third year of primary school, and migrated to the greater metropolitan area of Mexico City 32 years ago. She has social insurance, although she mainly goes to the primary health centre.
10. Mrs RJ, 58 years old, has a son; she is a professional, educated to PhD level, with social security and private insurance.
11. The company Farmacias Similares, founded in 1997, covers the chain of production, marketing, distribution and sale of drugs in Mexico and other countries in Latin America. It is the national market leader with 30 per cent of the total CRPs, and is diversifying and expanding its services towards clinical analysis, radiological studies, dental services and psychological care. A central axis of its expansion has been the distribution and sale of cheap medicines, with prices up to 60–75 per cent less than the commercial value. These drugs were initially recognised as 'similar drugs' because they were not yet granted the registration of interchangeable generics, and in 2010 they were granted pharmacological equivalence. Their advertising is based on the slogans 'The same, but cheaper' and 'We call ourselves Similar, we are generic'. According to their own data, as of February 2016, they had 6,368 offices, employing 12,857 doctors. During 2016, they report having granted more than 80 million consultations throughout the country (Fundación Best 2019). Their dominance in the market is such that it is common for the population to identify the CRP and/or their doctors with the generic denomination of 'Similar'.
12. TI, 30 years old, no children, secretary, technical career, no social security.

References

Arteaga, José Roberto. 2013. 'Oxxo-farmacias, ¿la nueva estrategia de Femsa?', *Forbes México*, 27 December. Accessed 12 September 2019. http://www.forbes.com.mx/nuevos-formatos-de-farmacia-cuales-son-sus-retos/.

COFEPRIS (Comisión Federal para la Protección contra Riesgos Sanitarios). 2010a. 'El Mercado de los antibióticos en México'. Accessed 15 September 2019. https://www.gob.mx/cms/uploads/attachment/file/310791/Gu_a_Dispensaci_n_de_Antibioticos.pdf.

COFEPRIS (Comisión Federal para la Protección contra Riesgos Sanitarios). 2010b. 'Acuerdo sobre venta de antibióticos'. Accessed 29 September 2015. http://dof.gob.mx/nota_detalle.php?codigo=5144336&fecha=27/05/2010.

COFEPRIS (Comisión Federal para la Protección contra Riesgos Sanitarios). 2010c. 'Regulación y promoción para el uso adecuado de antibióticos en México: Propuesta de lineamientos para la acción'. Accessed 1 November 2019. http://www.insp.mx/images/stories/Lineas/medicamentos/doc/acciones_antibioticos.pdf.

COFEPRIS (Comisión Federal para la Protección contra Riesgos Sanitarios). 2013. 'Guía para las buenas prácticas sanitarias en farmacias y consultorios'. Accessed 1 November 2019. https://www.anafarmex.com.mx/wp-content/uploads/2013/08/Guia-Consultorios1.pdf.

COFEPRIS (Comisión Federal para la Protección contra Riesgos Sanitarios). 2014. Documento 12022015, Comisión Federal para la Protección del Riesgo sanitario. Regulación de establecimientos, April 2014. https://www.gob.mx/cofepris/prensa/avanza-la-estrategia-para-regular-consultorios-en-farmacias–62847.

Conrad, Peter. 2007. *The Medicalization of Society: On the Transformation of Human Conditions into Treatable Disorders*. Baltimore: Johns Hopkins University Press.

Conrad, Peter and Joseph W. Schneider. 1980. 'Looking at Levels of Medicalization: A Comment on Strong's Critique of the Thesis of Medical Imperialism', *Social Science and Medicine – Part A: Medical Psychology and Medical Sociology* 14 (1): 75–79.

Conrad, Peter and Joseph W. Schneider. 1992. *Deviance and Medicalization: From Badness to Sickness*. Expanded ed. Philadelphia: Temple University Press.

DENUE–INEGI. 2017. 'Derechohabiencia'. Directorio Estadístico de Unidades Económicas. Instituto Nacional de Estadística, Geografía e Informática. Accessed 15 September 2019. https://www.inegi.org.mx/temas/derechohabiencia/.

Díaz Portillo, Sandra P. 2012. 'Percepción del entorno laboral y de los servicios ofrecidos del personal de salud en los consultorios médicos privados en México'. Master's thesis, Instituto Nacional de Salud Pública, Cuernavaca.

Fundación Best. 2019. 'Salud'. Accessed 15 September 2019. http://www.fundacionbest.org.mx/div-salud.html.

FUNSALUD (Fundación Mexicana para la Salud). 2014. *Estudio sobre la práctica de la atención médica en consultorios médicos adyacentes a farmacias privadas*. Mexico City: Fundación Mexicana para la Salud.

Gutiérrez, Juan Pablo, Juan Rivera, Teresa Shamah, Carlos Oropeza and Mauricio Hernández Ávila (eds). 2012. *Encuesta Nacional de Salud y Nutrición 2012: Resultados nacionales*. Cuernavaca: Instituto Nacional de Salud Pública. Accessed 15 September 2019. http://ensanut.insp.mx/informes/ENSANUT2012ResultadosNacionales.pdf.

Hayden, Cori. 2007. 'A Generic Solution? Pharmaceuticals and the Politics of the Similar in Mexico', *Current Anthropology* 48 (4): 475–95.

Hayden, Cori. 2008. 'Sem patente não há genérico: Acesso farmacêutico e políticas de cópia', *Sociologias* 10 (19): 62–91.

Hayden, Cori. 2013. 'Distinctively Similar: A Generic Problem', *UC Davis Law Review* 47 (2): 601–32.

INEGI (Instituto Nacional de Estadística y Geografía e Informática). 2015. 'Encuesta Intercensal 2015'. Accessed 15 September 2019. https://www.inegi.org.mx/programas/intercensal/2015/.

Leyva-Flores, René, Joaquina Erviti-Erice, María de la Luz Kageyama-Escobar and Armando Arredondo. 1998. 'Prescripción, acceso y gasto en medicamentos entre usuarios de servicios de salud en México', *Salud Pública de México* 40 (1): 1–8.

Leyva Piña, Marco Antonio and Santiago Pichardo Palacios. 2012. 'Los médicos de las Farmacias Similares: ¿Degradación de la profesión médica?', *Polis: Investigación y Análisis Sociopolítico y Psicosocial* 8 (1): 143–75.

Martínez Soria, Jesuswaldo and Ciro Murayama Rendón. 2016. 'El sistema de atención a la salud en México'. In *Hacia un sistema nacional público de salud en México: Una propuesta integral a partir de experiencias internacionales*, edited by Ciro Murayama and Santos M. Ruesga, 19–124. Mexico City: Universidad Nacional Autónoma de México.

Menéndez, Eduardo L. 1983. *Hacia una práctica médica alternativa: Hegemonía y autoatención (gestión) en salud*. Mexico City: Centro de Investigaciones y Estudios Superiores en Antropología Social.

Menéndez, Eduardo L. 1990. *Antropología médica: Orientaciones, desigualdades y transacciones*. Mexico City: Centro de Investigaciones y Estudios Superiores en Antropología Social.

Murayama, Ciro and Santos M. Ruesga, eds. 2016. *Hacia un sistema nacional público de salud en México: Una propuesta integral a partir de experiencias internacionales*. Mexico City: Universidad Nacional Autónoma de México.

Olaiz Fernández, Gustavo. 2013. 'Resultados en Salud Pública ENSANUT 2012'. Accessed 1 November 2019. https://ensanut.insp.mx/encuestas/ensanut2012/doctos/seminario/SAPSC04.pdf.

Osorio Carranza, Rosa María. 2001. *Entender y atender la enfermedad: Los saberes maternos frente a los padecimientos infantiles*. Mexico City: Centro de Investigaciones y Estudios Superiores en Antropología Social.

Osorio Carranza, Rosa María. 2013. 'La cultura médica materna y la salud infantil: Un análisis de las enfermedades respiratorias desde la epidemiología popular en México'. In *Sexo y género en medicina: Una introducción a los estudios de las mujeres y de género en ciencias de la salud*, edited by Montserrat Cabré i Pairet and Fernando Salmón Muñiz, 229–51. Santander: Editorial de la Universidad de Cantabria.

Osorio Carranza, Rosa María. 2016. 'La cultura de atención médica materna en las enfermedades infantiles'. In *Antropología médica e interculturalidad*, edited by Roberto Campos Navarro, 201–13. Mexico City: McGraw-Hill.

Pérez Cuevas, Ricardo, Svetlana V. Doubova, Veronika J. Wirtz, Anahí Dreser, Edson E. Serván Mori and Mauricio Hernández Ávila. 2012. *Consultorios médicos en farmacias privadas: Efectos inesperados en el uso de servicios de salud y el acceso a medicamentos*. Cuernavaca: Instituto Nacional de Salud Pública. Accessed 15 September 2019. https://ensanut.insp.mx/doctos/analiticos/UsoConsultorio.pdf.

Rodríguez, Ruth. 2014. 'Farmacias arrebatan consultas al sector salud', *El Universal*, 10 February. Accessed 15 September 2019. http://archivo.eluniversal.com.mx/nacion-mexico/2014/farmacias-arrebatan-consultas-al-sector-salud-986292.html.

Secretaría de Salud. 2013. 'Servicios otorgados y programas sustantivos', *Boletín de Información Estadística* 32 (3). Accessed 1 November 2019. http://www.dgis.salud.gob.mx/contenidos/publicaciones/p_bie_gobmx.html.

Singer, Merrill and Hans Baer. 1995. *Critical Medical Anthropology*. Amityville, NY: Baywood Publishing Company.

Torres Guerra, Sandra and Juan Pablo Gutiérrez. 2009. 'Mercado farmacéutico en México: Tamaño, valor y concentración', *Revista Panamericana de Salud Pública* 26 (1): 46–50.

Williams, Simon J., Paul Martin and Jonathan Gabe. 2011. 'The Pharmaceuticalisation of Society? A Framework for Analysis', *Sociology of Health and Illness* 33 (5): 710–25.

Wirtz, Verónika, René Leyva Flores, Anahí Dreser, et al. 2011. 'Organización y funcionamiento de las farmacias en México'. In *Las farmacias, los farmacéuticos y el uso adecuado de medicamentos en América Latina*, edited by Núria Homedes and Antonio Ugalde, 59–81. Buenos Aires: Lugar Editorial.

9

Naming, framing and shaming through obstetric violence: A critical approach to the judicialisation of maternal health rights violations in Mexico

Paola M. Sesia

Between October 2013 and September 2014, eight cases of human rights violations against Mexican women during childbirth were denounced to human rights oversight bodies by civil society organisations. Cases were petitioned at Mexico's National Commission on Human Rights (NCHR) as well as at the Inter-American Commission on Human Rights (IACHR), requesting intervention regarding the Mexican government's acts or omissions on this issue.

The violations occurred during expectant mothers' failed attempts to obtain care in the public health system, over the course of obstetric care or as a fatal consequence of the care provided, resulting in the woman's death. The majority of these cases refer to low-income, indigenous and rural women from the poorest and most marginalised states of the country, such as Oaxaca. These cases were litigated pro bono as 'public interest' or 'strategic litigation' cases (Coral-Díaz et al. 2010), that, while benefitting the victims, simultaneously sought a transformation of the Mexican healthcare system through legal mechanisms and from a rights-based perspective.

The practice of litigating human rights violations against pregnant women is a recent phenomenon in Latin America; even more so, in Mexico. In order for this phenomenon to take place, it was first necessary to argue in the political and legal arenas that access to high-quality and respectful maternal healthcare is a right for all pregnant women. This has become even more urgent for women who have been historically and socially excluded and discriminated against. Simultaneously, in Mexico a novel type of argument was being framed, using the concept of 'obstetric violence' to name and judicialise these violations.

In this chapter, I will examine how this concept was constructed and how it has begun to be used as a tool for demanding justice in human rights oversight bodies. I will explain what we mean by judicialisation in maternal health and how this process is being broached in Mexico by analysing some characteristics and problems of the public maternal healthcare system, in order to understand the context in which judicialisation occurs.

I will analyse one specific case of a violation committed against an indigenous woman from Oaxaca, review the characteristics of the case, the timeline of its progression, the responses from health authorities and the discursive and material strategies adopted by the litigating organisation in constructing and handling the legal case. Through this example, I will share some thoughts about the achievements and limitations of judicialising violations of maternal healthcare, keeping in mind that in Mexico these are incipient, incomplete and evolving processes. In particular, I will analyse the use of obstetric violence arguments and the capacity of judicialisation as a means for compensating victims, as well as its potential for transforming health policy and healthcare delivery to make them less discriminatory and more responsive to poor indigenous women's needs and rights.

The judicialisation of human rights violations in maternal healthcare and their framing as obstetric violence provide a fruitful ground for anthropological inquiries from a critical medical anthropology (CMA) perspective. CMA can be defined as a theoretical and methodological orientation that is vigilant of structural determinants and power relations around health, illness and health-seeking and whose field of inquiry includes individual and collective responses embedded in those social determinants and relations (Seppilli and Otegui 2005).

The litigation of human rights in maternal health is a social practice that can benefit from becoming the subject of anthropological critique – even more so, when this critique is sensitive to power relations, multiple inequalities and the quest for social justice (Farmer 1999). Unlike the language and practice of law that tends to stress a formalistic, unspecific and universalist reading of human rights including the right to health, CMA provides an analytical lens that highlights their context-specific, relational, disputed, power-related and transforming (as well as transformative) nature in practice.

Moreover, and as Farmer reminds us in relation to human rights abuses, such a critique allows us to understand how violations are related to dominance and the production and reproduction of social inequalities. A CMA perspective also helps to discern the almost inevitable interplay of social class, racism and/or gender discrimination in their occurrence, including in healthcare. In Farmer's own words:

> [Anthropology] permit[s] us to ground our understanding of human rights violations in broader analyses of power and social inequality. Whereas a purely legal view of human rights tends to obscure the dynamics of human rights violations, the contextualizing disciplines [anthropology, history and sociology] reveal them to be 'pathologies of power'. Social inequalities based on race or ethnicity, gender, religious creed, and – above all – social class are the motive force behind most human rights violations.
>
> (Farmer 1999: 1488)

In particular, we can read the litigation of human rights violations in maternal healthcare through the framing of obstetric violence as a conflictive relational social field (Bourdieu and Wacquant 1995) whose discursive and material stakes are greatly disputed among multiple contenders. Here, a CMA perspective is able to unravel the power dynamics implicit in those contentions; to dissect the differing motives, reasoning and strategies of actors involved in arguing for or against the occurrence of obstetric violence in human rights violations; to understand the underlying meanings attributed to such a conceptual framing in building the legal arguments; to unpack the hegemonic social representations that coalesce around constructions of otherness attributed to subaltern social subjects such as indigenous pregnant women in the clinical encounter; to identify counter-hegemonic representations that arise in subaltern responses during the unfolding of the judicial dispute; and to highlight the socio-political consequences of those contentions and resolutions in victims' redress as well as in the transformation of the healthcare system from a rights-based perspective.

Judicialisation, human rights and obstetric violence

Judicialisation is defined here as the phenomenon of bringing problems, controversies, requirements and violations of human rights to judicial authorities or to human rights oversight agencies at the national or international levels, so that they can be defined, discussed and legally resolved; these resolutions and recommendations may include enforceable consequences for the state and its institutions, ones that will frequently require states and their agencies to act in the sphere of public policy. This is possible as part of democratic governance (Domingo 2011) in which the state is accountable for its policies and has an obligation to defend, promote and respect the human rights of all its citizens. Rights, in turn and by definition, are enforceable and justiciable in the framework of international human rights treaties ratified by these countries.

Resorting to legal strategies is a phenomenon that has increasingly characterised Latin America since the early 1990s (Sieder et al. 2011; Couso et al. 2010),[1] in order to resolve social and political conflicts, to make the state comply with existing economic, social and cultural rights, to broaden the scope of rights through jurisprudence, and to intervene in social public policy through the courts and human rights oversight bodies. This process has been referred to as the 'judicialisation of politics' in the region (Sieder et al. 2011).

Since the end of the 1990s, the judicialisation of public policy in some Latin American countries has included the right to health (Alzate Mora 2014; Biehl 2013; Biehl et al. 2012; Gutiérrez-Rivas and Rivera-Maldonado 2009; Lamprea 2017; additionally, various case studies in Yamin and Gloppen 2011; and Aureliano and Gibbon, in this volume). Rulings by courts and human rights bodies have recognised violations of this right in vulnerable population groups and have legally forced these countries to implement measures that guarantee access to services, clinical treatment and pharmaceuticals, such as the case of antiretroviral therapies for HIV/AIDS patients in Brazil (Biehl et al. 2009), or lawsuits seeking healthcare coverage and access to drugs litigated through the Colombian *tutela* system (Yamin and Parra-Vera 2009).

This increasing judicialisation of the right to health in Latin America has been controversial. Crucial debates have been opened about the limits or even the counter-productive effects of judicial intervention in public health systems. Questions have been raised about whether the judicialisation of this right, especially through individual claims, is able to improve or limit collective access to services, treatment and pharmaceuticals, and to promote or hamper equity and social justice within the healthcare system (Alzate Mora 2014; Lamprea 2017; Yamin 2011).

Moreover, the judicialisation of the right to health reaches its structural limitations in a context of public healthcare systems that are deeply unequal and unevenly distributed, and whose medical services are deficient, lacking, overstretched and insufficiently financed – situations that have worsened after over 30 years of neoliberal policies in Latin America (de Currea-Lugo 2006; Lamprea 2014). This may be so even when judicial decisions attempt to promote a restructuring of the public health system for the common good and in order to guarantee the collective right to health (Alzate Mora 2014).

Beyond these debates, the judicialisation of the right to health certainly implies a formal recognition that health, medical care and access to pharmaceuticals are human rights that should be enforceable, precisely because they can be tried in the courts or legally resolved by oversight bodies. In particular, General Comment No. 14 by the United Nations' Committee on Economic Social and Cultural Rights (CESCR) has contributed to the enforceability of the right to care, specifying that the right to health include access to medical care, and that health services must be available, physically accessible, economically feasible, culturally acceptable and of high quality for everyone without discrimination, above all when those affected are part of disadvantaged and excluded social groups; this is the case with poor, rural and indigenous women who should have access to adequate and effective maternal health services.[2]

In Mexico, the judicialisation of the right to health is taking place in a more limited manner and more recently than elsewhere in Latin America. Partly this is related to a justice system that until 2011 was not auspicious for protecting human rights, and even less so for litigation that seeks jurisprudence that is rights-enforcing and socio-politically transformative (Pou Giménez 2014). That year, the Mexican Supreme Court of Justice (SCJ) ruled that international human rights treaties signed by Mexico enjoy the same status as the Constitution; and all public authorities have a legal obligation to respect and guarantee human rights in their areas of competence, opening up a window of opportunity for pro-rights litigation.

The concept of obstetric violence deserves a separate mention for at least two reasons. First, it is central to the construction and appeals process, as well as to the enduring political, legislative and juridical effects in the case that we will consider below. Moreover, it constitutes a powerful epistemic construct to name a multifaceted and widely diffuse problem in many Latin American public hospitals, thus contributing to CMA readings of bio-obstetrics as a sociocultural system that reflects and reproduces inequalities and discrimination on the basis of gender, ethnicity and social class.

Following Medina (2009), obstetric violence is conceptualised as follows:

Any act or omission by healthcare staff that damages, harms or denigrates a woman during delivery, as well as negligence in her medical care, expressed by treatment that is dehumanizing and/or discriminatory, in which there is abuse of medication, or natural processes are pathologised, in detriment to her rights to autonomy and reproductive freedom, or informed consent, including as such, the omission of timely and effective emergency obstetric care.

(Parto Libre and GIRE 2014: 1–2)

This broad definition merges the violence perpetrated against women by virtue of their gender (gender violence) with institutional violence; that is, violence that is perpetuated, often in an organised manner and through the exercise of legitimate power, within hierarchical institutions (hospitals, schools, jails, police headquarters, asylums, military barracks etc.) where individuals tend to lose their personal autonomy.

Medina distinguishes between physical and psychological obstetric violence. The first occurs when a woman in childbirth is subjected to invasive procedures, unnecessary drugs are administered or the course of a physiological delivery is not respected – in other words, when a woman's body is unnecessarily medicalised or pathologised, transforming her into the passive recipient of external clinical decisions. Psychological violence, on the other hand, includes 'dehumanising, rude, discriminatory, humiliating treatment when the woman comes seeking advice or medical care, or during the course of provided obstetric care' (Medina 2009: 4).

Although I would argue that obstetric violence lacks some semantic precision, as an umbrella term it is a powerful tool for legal and political action while, at the same time, helping to explain a complex sociocultural phenomenon that commonly happens during institutional childbirth. As I strive to show in the following pages, it makes an epistemic contribution to CMA studies of biomedicine and bio-obstetrics as sociocultural systems, both embedded in and reproducing societal power asymmetries, while they normalise and naturalise ideologically laden medical practices on the grounds of, supposedly, ideological neutrality, moral superiority, pragmatic efficacy and scientific rationality (Martínez Hernáez 2008; Menéndez 1983), and, I would add, an altruistic value-free science at the exclusive service and benefit of mankind.

The context of the Mexican maternal healthcare system

Mexico has reached a very high level of coverage of qualified care during delivery, going from 77 per cent of all births in 1990 to 98 per cent in

2016.[3] The expansion of coverage is the result of deliberate policies after the turn of the millennium, designed so that Mexican women could give birth in institutional hospitals as part of a strategy for reducing maternal mortality.

However, the expanded coverage is not synonymous with quality of care. This is so much the case that no correlation has been found between the reduction of maternal mortality and more widespread institutional delivery care (Lazcano-Ponce et al. 2013). This data reveals, on the contrary, that institutional obstetric care in Mexico is facing a complex and multidimensional problem.

At the structural level, services are inadequately distributed over the country; they are under-used in primary healthcare due to lack of equipment, personnel or financial means to operate, while hospitals are overburdened by excessive demand; they face frequent supplies and drugs shortages; financial resources are inadequate or unequally distributed among states, between levels of care or between institutions; and human resources are also insufficient and poorly distributed between units, levels of care, by shifts, specialisation and type or level of training (Lazcano-Ponce et al. 2013). These problems are particularly pronounced in primary healthcare, in the most impoverished states in the country and in rural and indigenous regions (CNEGySR 2009; Freyermuth 2011; Lazcano-Ponce et al. 2013; Sachse et al. 2012).

At the organisational level, the Mexican healthcare system suffers from segmentation and fragmentation in service provision, financing, clinical auditing processes and performance evaluation. System administration governance is weak, as are the mechanisms for supervision, oversight and regulation (Lazcano-Ponce et al. 2013). Moreover, serious problems have been detected regarding technical skills and medical staff knowledge in the provision of maternal healthcare (Walker et al. 2012), as well as the failure to comply with technical norms and guidelines (Freyermuth 2011; Lazcano-Ponce et al. 2013; Sachse et al. 2012).

This issue is reflected, for example, in the medicalisation of physiological birth through the routine use of invasive, unnecessary, painful, dehumanising and even harmful practices on women (DeMaria et al. 2012; Sachse et al. 2012; Valdez-Santiago et al. 2013, Walker et al. 2012). These routine procedures and practices are contrary to national norms[4] and international guidelines that are grounded in evidence-based medicine (EMB) (Chalmers et al. 2001; FIGO 2012).

These problems are deeper than mere ignorance about EMB or norms, or deficiencies in management of the system. They reflect systematic and structural issues of over-medicalisation and the pathologisation of natural physiological processes, as well as the abuse and 'dehumanis-ing' treatment of patients: in other words, of the problem of institutional obstetric violence (GIRE 2013; Medina 2009). One national survey revealed that 40 per cent of Mexican women were subjected to mistreat-ment, abuse and lack of respect during their last deliveries in the public healthcare system.[5] Available qualitative information points to a systemic phenomenon, especially in public hospitals that attend to women who are disenfranchised, poor and/or indigenous (Castro and Erviti 2003; Valdez-Santiago et al. 2013).

The emblematic case of Irma López Aurelio

A photograph began to circulate on social media on 2 October 2013 and immediately generated strong reactions; it went viral within a few hours.[6] The picture was published by the leading national newspapers and the for-eign press, and became the subject of various television, radio and internet news reports both within and outside Mexico in following days and weeks.[7]

The photo depicts a young, light brown-skinned woman kneeling in the grass; her face is framed by straight black hair; she wears rubber flip-flops; and her light dress is raised up in the front by her right hand while she props herself up in the grass with her left. In front of her, where her right hand lifts the hem, a naked newborn is lying in the grass; the umbil-ical cord stretches from the middle of its navel, rising vertically to what can easily be imagined as the mother's vulva, which is barely covered by the hem of the dress. Her face displays suffering and desperation; her other mixed feelings can only be guessed at – perhaps incredulity, fear and rage. In her face, a cry for help can be imagined, possibly audible in the moment, or maybe drowned in her throat.

This is Irma López Aurelio, a woman from Jalapa de Díaz, an indig-enous Mazatec area with approximately 20,000 residents in the southern Mexican state of Oaxaca. Irma was 28 years old when she gave birth to her third child in the grass and without any assistance, because when she arrived, already in labour, at the community healthcare centre at 6 a.m., the nurse on duty told her to go for a walk and return to the clinic at 8 a.m., when the attending physician's shift would start. An hour and a half later, unable to restrain the urge to push, Irma gave birth alone on the clinic's patio, since her husband had run to get help. Someone captured the photo on a mobile phone and posted it on social media. Becoming aware of what had transpired, the clinic staff admitted her; nevertheless, before releasing her and the baby that same night, they charged Irma for drugs and other materials provided during the care. In Mexico, maternal healthcare should be free of charge in the public health system; charging Irma for medical supplies and drugs represented another violation of her right to health.

The local primary care clinic only attends patients from Monday to Friday during daytime operating hours. This situation makes it impossible to provide obstetric care during the night, the early morning and weekends.

Immediately following these events, the clinic staff and state health authorities tried to deflect attention and responsibility for the situation onto others. First, they argued that this was a spontaneous birth: accidental births that occur suddenly are beyond anyone's responsibility, such as those occurring in taxis, on the street or when a woman is caught unprepared before she is able to reach a hospital. On the second day, facing devastating evidence that Irma had been denied care, the clinic staff began to argue that Irma was indigenous, that she did not speak Spanish and was unable to explain the situation to the nurse when she first approached the clinic. This version was openly supported and disseminated by the regional health authorities, who stated that 'the child's mother distorted the information because she spoke only the Mazatec language and was unable to explain what was happening in Spanish'.[8]

In slightly more neutral language, the Secretary of the State Ministry of Health stated that the publication of the photo was unfortunate in that this contributed to 'fuelling morbidness' on social media, and was damaging to the public image of the clinic staff. He again argued that Irma had not received care because she could not make herself understood to the attending nurse. The expectation of the Secretary was that Irma would not contend his official explanation and would keep silent. Instead, Irma decided to speak out and refuted his thesis. Interviewed by various state and national media the following day, she related in correct and perfectly comprehensible Spanish not only that she had not been attended when she arrived at the healthcare centre and explained that she was already in labour, but that even after what had occurred, they admitted her for examination and charged her 400 pesos[9] for the medications and hygienic materials used. Moreover, she stated that she had been subjected to threats and pressure after expressing dissatisfaction and her intention to formally file a complaint.

The broad media coverage revealed the poor state of healthcare services in Jalapa de Díaz and the serious crisis in maternal healthcare, especially in rural and indigenous areas. It also highlighted Irma López' indignation not only about the treatment she received, but also about the public statements of the Health Secretary, and additionally revealed her intention not to remain silent and her desire to denounce the issue. Finally, it emphasised the paltry and clumsy response of the Ministry of Health, which, instead of recognising the seriousness of the issue and the systemic crisis that the situation displayed, tried to deflect responsibility onto the victim, in a process of naturalising substandard care and the re-victimisation of Irma, while expecting simultaneously that media attention would cease and the usual amnesia prevail.

Nevertheless, this did not occur. Seeing the turmoil on social networks and in the press, the National Commission on Human Rights (NCHR) – the highest human rights oversight agency in Mexico – decided almost immediately to open an investigation of the case. Founded by presidential decree in 1990, with a mandate to supervise the Mexican public administration's handling of rights and to promote a culture of respect towards human rights, the NCHR is an autonomous, decentralised and well-financed body. Its different inspectorates have pursued and documented systematic violations of human rights, including cases of abuses in healthcare provision or in the denial of care. The recommendations issued by the NCHR remain the country's main avenue for achieving restorative justice (Pérez Sauceda et al. 2011) in cases of human rights violations perpetrated by public authorities.[10]

Media coverage continued to increase, feeding off of new statements, interviews and reports about the case, while over the following weeks, four similar cases of women denied care came to light, three of them in Oaxaca. The following days brought Irma together with GIRE AC, which formally assumed her legal representation and began to construe the argument that Irma had been a victim of institutional and obstetric violence.[11]

Facing growing pressure from public opinion, a week later the state authorities felt forced to change their strategy. They recognised that the staff of the health clinic had not attended to Irma in a timely manner, putting her and her baby at risk. The removal of the local clinic's director and the head of the regional health authority were announced, and two new doctors hired. The dismissals took place despite the fact that previously the medical staff of the healthcare unit had acknowledged the lack of material and human resources with which to attend to the women who went there for care during delivery. In the case of rural clinics, these do not have enough birth rooms and frequently lack medicines.[12]

Although the NCHR investigation was already underway, Irma – as advised by GIRE – filed a complaint to the Commission expressly requesting measures that she considered appropriate for repairing the harm caused, including measures for non-recurrence. Four months later, the

Commission issued a recommendation to the Government of the State of Oaxaca,[13] citing the exercise of institutional and obstetric violence and claiming violations to the right to a life free from violence, the right to equality, the right to non-discrimination and the right to protection; these violations were due to the lack of adequate medical care and the absence of necessary infrastructure for the provision of healthcare services. In this recommendation, the NCHR requested reparation of the damage, and that measures be taken against non-recurrence; but the recommendation failed to state explicitly what these measures should be, except for mentioning generic courses for staff training in human rights and the need of better staff training on filling medical charts and records. This last point left the corresponding decisions about specific measures of reparations and non-recurrence (how to improve the maternal healthcare system) up to the same authorities that had perpetrated the violations in the first place.

Responding to this situation, GIRE publicly stated that the NCHR was not complying satisfactorily with its role as defender and guarantor of the human rights of Irma and her child; at the same time and among other actions, the organisation entered into direct negotiations with the Oaxaca government, with whom it ensured reparations: economic compensation, permanent medical care for Irma and for her child, a grant for the child's education and a public apology, offered by the Secretary of the State Ministry of Health in a press release in March 2014. Finally, they agreed to transformational measures in healthcare services: opening new positions for medical staff; a state-level staff training plan in human rights, intercultural health and gender equity; a sensitisation programme for healthcare staff about their civic responsibilities as public servants; the establishment of 50 new birthing rooms in the state; and the completion and opening of the basic community hospital in Jalapa de Díaz.

As an additional action, GIRE, together with two other Mexican NGOs,[14] petitioned in a hearing at the Inter-American Commission of Human Rights (IACHR)[15] in Washington DC, exposing the issue of violations of the reproductive rights of four Mexican indigenous women during a presentation on public maternal healthcare provision that highlighted Irma's case. The organisation argued that these human rights violations present common traits, that these flaws are structural and systemic and that Mexican government policies and programmes on maternal healthcare and the reduction of maternal mortality are not sufficient nor necessarily the most suitable for resolving problems that discriminate against women and jeopardise their security and integrity. GIRE noted that in the face of these violations, opening criminal cases and the penalisation of the responsible healthcare staff through individual trials is not the best solution; rather, it is essential to find solutions that transform the healthcare system instead.

GIRE emphasised the poor treatment of the victims by the NCHR and their precarious access to justice in denouncing the increasing violations that indigenous Mexican women experience in public healthcare facilities. It argued that the NCHR did not listen to the victims, did not incorporate their demands for compensation in the scant recommendations that it issued, did not include concrete measures to avoid recurrence of these issues, and above all did not provide any information about whether recommendations accepted by the corresponding authorities were being complied with.

The Mexican government was present at the IACHR hearing, with a committee composed of high-level representatives, including the Deputy Secretary of the federal Ministry of Health and the Secretary of Health from Oaxaca. In his statement, the Deputy Secretary acknowledged that Irma's case was highly regrettable and violated her rights. He explained that this case had provoked reaction and many responses including the adoption of a nationwide 'zero rejection' policy on pregnant women by public institutions in the healthcare sector. He added that the country's 32 federal entities had committed to effecting it immediately. Nevertheless, he denied that what happened to Irma was symptomatic of a systemic and structural problem. Rather than the concept of obstetric violence, he used the terminology of malpractice and spontaneous birth to explain that, by his estimation, the cases similar to that of Irma in Oaxaca represent a very small number of total births (CIDH 2014).

As months and then years passed, following the issuing of the NCHR recommendation and the signing of the compensation agreement with the Oaxacan government, GIRE waited for the Oaxacan Ministry of Health to comply with the agreements. One year after the recommendation and 10 months after the agreement was signed, the organisation issued a press release expressing concern about the total lack of compliance with measures designed to prevent a recurrence, including the incompletion of the basic community hospital in San Felipe Jalapa de Díaz. In the statement, it called on the NCHR to follow up on the recommendation issued the previous year, in order to ensure that the Government of Oaxaca complied with the agreed-upon commitments of 'guaranteeing that healthcare services be safe, and have necessary infrastructure, and respect the human rights of women'.[16] Four years later, the Oaxacan Ministry of Health still has to comply with most of the non-recurrence measures recommended by the NCHR and agreed upon with GIRE.

Discussion

The case of Irma allows us to reconsider broader questions about actions, strategies, goals and effects of judicialisation on the violations of the rights of indigenous women in the area of maternal healthcare and to analyse them in light of what this concrete example reveals. The discussion is informed by a CMA perspective and includes the following points: the interactions among intervening and disputing actors and some of the underlying meanings and representations behind their actions; arguments used in the judicialisation process; the strategies deployed; and the impact of judicialisation on victims' redress as well as on the transformation of the healthcare system.

The social interactions among contenders: Hegemonic biomedical representations of the indigenous other

Reading the case from a CMA perspective allows us to dissect how discrimination and racism against indigenous women are construed in the healthcare system through stereotyping and how they come to foster and then justify human rights abuses. It also reveals how power relations work within the health system so that the weakest chain-links are those who receive the blame and pay the costs *vis-à-vis* an outcry by victims and the media.

Irma was repeatedly stereotyped by the clinic's medical personnel, the regional health authorities and, finally, the Secretary of the Oaxacan Health Ministry as an indigenous woman who did not speak Spanish and could not make herself understood to the attending nurse. This argument placed the blame on the victim and constituted the initial justification behind the denial of care. In all cases, the expectation was that Irma would remain silent, not replying to these arguments. This is the case because indigenous women are commonly perceived by healthcare personnel and authorities as docile, uncomplaining and submissive.

This expectation should not be surprising since – as I highlighted in a previous ethnographic study of hospital births (Sesia et al. 2014) – at least three interrelated dominant social representations commonly converge in the medical encounter with indigenous women, in which differences of class, ethnicity/race and gender permeate established and essentialist conceptions about the supposedly passive, acquiescent and compliant nature of the indigenous expectant mother. On one hand, these women are conceived as part of the *other*, considered not only different, but hierarchically inferior (backward, ignorant, uneducated and unable to speak Spanish well) with respect to *us* (the medical cadre) that consider themselves educated, scientific, modern and urban. Simultaneously, the indigenous women are conceived of as obedient, docile and permissive patients who, by nature, do not question the work of doctors or nurses – even less so the official word of a health authority. Finally, it is common to consider them as noble in mind and heart and, in general, grateful for the free maternal healthcare they receive, independently of how they are treated and the outcomes of the care they were given.

If the patients are perceived as inferior, submissive, grateful and ignorant, then they can be the objects of condescending, disrespectful and despotic treatment within institutional healthcare, without these behaviours being considered blameworthy or punishable by those who perform them, but rather as normal, routine and natural. In this context, even refusing care can be conceived as an act without repercussions, since indigenous women are seen as subject-objects that do not complain or make demands on the system. We can see here how otherness is created and differential discriminatory treatment or even denial of care can be justified in the medical encounter through the essentialisation of cultural characteristics. This should come to no wonder since, as Menéndez (2017), a leading voice in Latin American CMA, reminds us, in Mexico everyday racism (and, I would add, institutional violence in health settings) is constituted, normalised and virulently reproduced mostly through singling out specific cultural traits (such as 'not speaking Spanish') through which the other is made different and inferior.

Irma's response was unexpected and caught the clinic's personnel and health authorities off guard because it effectively broke with this hegemonic stereotyping. In the midst of the media uproar, it took days for the Secretary of Health to take in this unexpected turn of events and change discourse and strategies.

In general, the public healthcare system in Mexico considers its users as recipients of care and not as rights-bearing subjects. When violations such as this occur, it is common that clinical auditing and internal administrative sanction mechanisms at the healthcare facilities are weak, or are simply not activated when the doctor in charge is a member of a union or otherwise protected. On the other hand, and particularly for members of staff who are unable to defend themselves, institutional sanctions are harsh, without taking attenuating circumstances into account such as the systemic structural deficiencies that often inhibit staff from properly doing their jobs. When there is political or media pressure to act and sanction violations – as was the case here – the authorities do not assume institutional responsibility, but rather find accountable persons among the weakest staff and place the blame on targeted individuals.

It is our understanding that the doctors who were fired had temporary contracts and were not protected by the health workers' union.

Naming and framing through obstetric violence: The arguments used in judicialisation and a cultural critique of bio-obstetrics

In Irma's case, the concept of obstetric violence was used in order to argue the violation of the right to care during childbirth. The case could have been argued differently and possibly even more solidly, as a violation of the right to health, integrity and security, in addition to Irma's having suffered discrimination.

Appealing to obstetric violence, nevertheless, was a deliberate strategy for strengthening arguments that these violations occurred not only because Irma is an indigenous woman who was denied care at a public health institution, but also because she is a member of a group of women who all tend to endure similar violations. At the CNHR and the IACHR hearings, denial of the right to obstetric care, a preventable maternal death and a case of substandard quality of care were all argued as obstetric violence, using Irma's case as a paradigmatic example of the systemic violations that poor, indigenous, pregnant women endure in the public healthcare system.

Framing these diverse violations as obstetric violence permits a shift from the status of an individual victim who accidentally suffered denial of care, mistreatment, poor-quality care or medical malpractice, to being part of a collective of victims. Simultaneously, it allows a conceptual and ideological shift from conceiving of these occurrences as accidental and random situations to seeing them as a structural condition that the public maternal healthcare system tolerates at best, or, at worst, reproduces and even promotes. Framing the issue this way offers the advantage of construing a single legal argument out of multiple, intertwined and combined violations of human rights at the intersection of gender, race/ethnicity and class discrimination – conceptualising them as acts that infringe not against random individuals, but against a collective of women, at the most vulnerable moment in their lives when they are giving birth.

The use of the obstetric violence frame became possible because the cases filed by GIRE all share specific characteristics that permit the construction of this argument as a structural and shared phenomenon: indigenous pregnant women with scarce economic resources and few possibilities, if any, for accessing the justice system, who have been victims of systematic acts or omissions perpetrated in the Mexican public healthcare system.

In practice, recourse to the conceptual frame of obstetric violence has entailed that GIRE gambled, initially with a considerable degree of uncertainty, on using a novel epistemological category in legal terminology and litigation in defence of women's human rights and in an attempt to improve the performance of the healthcare system rather than targeting the specific conduct of the obstetric care staff. Irma's case reveals that this strategy was successful, at least in its purpose of defending the rights of women giving birth. For the first time, the NCHR used this same conceptual framework in its recommendation to the Oaxaca state government. Moreover, the IACHR hearing was the very first occasion that the Commission heard a petition on HR violations because of obstetric violence. After hearing GIRE's arguments, the president of the Inter-American Commission recognised and legitimised those arguments. She affirmed that the issue of obstetric violence is relevant, disturbing and pertinent throughout the Americas, not only in the case of Mexico.

At the same time, Irma's case reveals that obstetric violence is not only a semantic category used in the construction of a new legal framework for defending pregnant women's human rights. It is also an epistemic category that defines a social field of medical performance, providing a radical critique of hegemonic bio-obstetrics whose ramifications are both discursive and material.

Obstetric violence reads institutional childbirth by exposing its rationale, doings and possible effects and by subverting the value of its underlying ideological premises. In bio-obstetrics, various forms of hegemonic knowledge and practices, and different biopowers (Foucault 1977) converge; this constructs – and explains – what obstetric violence names as a systemic and structural phenomenon. On one hand, we find the hegemony of biomedicine as a model of scientific knowledge, organisation of work and practices of care: biomedicine tends to medicalise and pathologise all physiological processes and, in the hospitalisation context, it has a dominant voice in decision making and in the course of medical treatment (Menéndez 2003). On the other hand, and more specifically in obstetric care, biopower or disciplinary control over the body are not exercised over any individual, but rather specifically over the female person/body, with the effect that women's subjectivity and agency are objectified, made passive and silenced within hierarchical and authoritarian structures of a medical specialty – Ob-Gyn – that is deeply patriarchal in its historical origin, medical practice and socio-clinical interactions (Oakley 1984).

Finally, when women who arrive in public hospitals within the Mexican healthcare system are indigenous, rural and poor, the intersecting characteristics of otherness that differentiate them on the basis of social class, race/ethnicity and gender begin to multiply, intensify and solidify in stereotypes, relations, attitudes and behaviours that easily become authoritarian, discriminatory and disrespectful on the part of healthcare staff. Such behaviours and attitudes have been naturalised and normalised across the board: from hospital lobbies to delivery rooms (Castro 2014; Sesia et al. 2014). The epistemic category 'obstetric violence' can easily account for all these deployments of institutional power.

As Foucault reminds us, naming something is more than isomorphic description: it constitutes a privileged technology of knowledge (Foucault 1968) and a sophisticated technology of power (Foucault 1966). Foucault was primarily interested in studying the evolution of language, the social construction of knowledge and technologies of state power towards its dominated subjects. Unlike Foucauldian discursive power technologies, with the promotion of the obstetric violence category as a way of reading the clinical encounter, to expose its doings and to litigate its consequences, we have a 'subversive' or 'counter-hegemonic' process of naming, framing and acting. The endeavour is to designate, explain and deconstruct predominant naturalised forms of caring and treating obstetric patients of the healthcare system – forms that, in turn, are technologies of power exerted by the hegemonic biomedical system on its most deeply subaltern social subjects: impoverished, indigenous, expectant mothers. By naming such behaviours and attitudes during maternal healthcare as obstetric violence, by arguing that this problem is systemic within public healthcare and by shaming attending physicians for their obstetric practices and treatment of patients, GIRE and accompanying NGOs engage in an interesting and consistent counter-hegemonic act (Santos and Rodríguez Garavito 2007) against the state, its healthcare system and bio-obstetrics in Mexico.

Because it is rather subversive in what it names, the category of obstetric violence has faced outright semantic, ideological and political opposition from the medical field. Mexican government healthcare officials and professional medical associations have denied the existence of obstetric violence as a problem afflicting the Mexican public healthcare system, and have rejected, sometimes vehemently, its use as a conceptual frame for describing a social problem affecting public obstetric services. It is no coincidence that, during the IACHR hearing, the federal Deputy Secretary of Health did not accept, either in his statement or rebuttal, the argument that the violation to Irma's human rights constituted obstetric violence. By refuting the argument, he was denying that obstetric care in the country is facing a structural and systemic problem of violence against female patients. It allowed him to affirm that Irma's experience was instead an isolated event, indisputably revealing medical malpractice and even discrimination by the healthcare providers, and that, in Irma's case, this had already been dutifully punished by the authorities.

The dispute is not only about an epistemological category that allows us to perceive and understand the significance of a given social problem from innovative interpretive angles. Here we are also facing that which, by acknowledging its existence, has concrete legal and tangible consequences that seem threatening to healthcare professionals and healthcare officials alike, though not for the same reasons. Recognising that obstetric violence exists and plagues the public healthcare system implies admitting the existence of systemic institutional responsibility of authorities, and the identification, attribution and/or limitation of individual responsibility of healthcare professionals towards women victims. In both cases, this entails adopting sanctions or responses that correspond to the seriousness of the situation. Finally, it entails seriously questioning the hegemonic obstetric practices that are deeply engrained and naturalised in the healthcare system; moreover, it challenges the medical community that controls this care and is not very inclined to listen, let alone to accept the fact that this is a real, tangible and serious problem that requires transformation.

This debate plays out not only in courts and the legislature, with laws and bills opposing obstetric violence, but also in mass media and in street-level public protests.[17] In this struggle GIRE has wagered, both from conviction and strategy, on openly opposing the criminalisation of individual medical conduct,[18] emphasising instead the structural failures of the healthcare system that do not allow its staff to undertake their work in an adequate and timely manner. GIRE has also publicly questioned the idiosyncratic, partial and sometimes plainly unjust responses of healthcare officials – such as applying draconian measures to the supposedly identified culprits, without taking the inadequacies and deficiencies of the context into account.[19]

In this debate, the positioning, interests and concerns of healthcare officials do not always coincide with those of the service providers; the latter resist what they perceive as a disturbing and offensive term that entails blaming them for being *violent* persons, beside the fear that they will bear the blame, even when health facilities present conditions that do not allow them to perform their work satisfactorily.

Beyond convergences or divergences, it nevertheless remains clear that naming and framing the problems of maternal healthcare as obstetric violence has become an anathema to many physicians, above all those who work in public healthcare institutions in obstetric care. Unsurprisingly, and despite the fact that GIRE's position of non-criminalisation has been open, repeatedly pronounced and public, the reception of this posture and proposals 'has been costly, because, being lawyers, it is assumed that we want to put doctors behind bars', according to the organisation's director.[20] In this context, GIRE may be over-optimistic in wagering that it would not incur opposition from the physicians' professional associations in the current proposed federal bill that includes the term *obstetric violence*, since the proposal avoids criminalisation of medical practice.[21]

The impact of judicialisation on victim redress and on the transformation of the healthcare system

Besides the legal petitions, GIRE resorted to multiple extra-legal strategies, among them media visibility, public shaming, political pressure and direct negotiation with the Oaxacan Ministry of Health. Applying political pressure and openly shaming the public health system through mass media coverage was particularly effective. The combination of these strategies opened a door for reaching successful compensation agreements from a perspective of human rights and restorative justice: first, negotiating redress from a comprehensive approach that included, but also went beyond, simple economic compensation; second, the fact that the public healthcare system accepted responsibility for the damage caused to Irma and her child and publicly apologised for it; and third, by jointly defining the claims and transformative measures for the Oaxacan public healthcare system, in order to avoid repetition of these occurrences.

The publicity that Irma's case received in the media also had the ripple effect of encouraging other victims to come forward and denounce similar violations. In the following weeks, several other cases began to crop up in the press in Oaxaca and elsewhere, and several women or their families petitioned the state human rights oversight agencies or the NCHR in relation to maternal healthcare violations. Some of these cases were picked up by GIRE, which began to defend other women who had suffered similar abuses. Here we can see how judicialisation can be successful insofar as other women see it as a legitimate and effective avenue for seeking redress in their own cases.

Judicialisation seems to prove successful in Irma's case by considering that all the claims for compensation were accepted and were carried out by the government of Oaxaca. Nevertheless, it remains to be seen whether future administrations in the state government will continue honouring the long-term agreements of providing complete medical care throughout Irma and the child's life, and an education grant to support the child's schooling, since there are no established mechanisms that assure long-term compliance with these agreements.

Conversely, we can identify serious shortcomings in what judicialisation can achieve in the intent to transform the healthcare system, beginning with the content of the agreements themselves. The definition of the measures that the healthcare system needs to take in order to guarantee access and improve the quality of maternal healthcare obviously surpasses GIRE's level of expertise. GIRE is dedicated to advocacy and the legal defence of women's reproductive rights, not in the field of the maternal healthcare system, and even less in the specific context of its working and performance in the state of Oaxaca. The agreed-upon measures did not include, for instance, a commitment to advancing the restructuring of maternal health services in the state,[22] starting with the regional network that encompasses Jalapa de Díaz, Irma's community.

Judicialisation finds its major limitation precisely in effecting the transformation of the healthcare system. Four years after having signed the agreement, the Health Ministry of Oaxaca has not complied with the majority of the points included. The local clinic continues to face the same shortages as in 2013. The community hospital under construction has not opened its doors yet. The Ministry of Health in Oaxaca has implemented some workshops on human rights sensitisation and obstetric violence eradication among health personnel in some jurisdictions, but this amounts to a drop in the ocean. And the problems besetting the Oaxacan maternal healthcare system do not show any signs of improvement (Sesia 2017). Questions arise here in assessing the impact of judicialisation: how, through which mechanisms, in how much time and who can verify satisfactory compliance with the agreements? And what does 'satisfactory compliance' mean for the different parties involved? In this case, it seems clear that the expectations of Irma (the injured party), her family and her representatives were noticeably different and encompassed more than those of the healthcare officials, for whom compliance signified formal closure of the legal proceeding, without implying any structural transformation of the system. In this context, reforming healthcare through judicialisation seems to amount to beating the air.

These concerns are not new, since the literature on health, human rights and litigation warns about the intrinsic limits of using the courts as a tool for potential transformation of the healthcare system (Cook 2013; Yamin 2011). Above all, it underscores the major contradiction that the legal approach in human rights violations 'consists of appeals to the perpetrators' (Farmer 1999: 1493), who can be expected to be recalcitrant.

Nevertheless, some interesting developments have taken place, within and beyond the judicialisation process initiated by GIRE. The visibility of Irma's case, the discrediting of the public healthcare institutions, the pressure and political costs that this broad coverage of the episode entailed, the coming forward of other women denouncing similar occurrences and the Commission's decision to investigate the human rights violations caused the federal healthcare system to make important agreements with the states, such as the 'zero rejection' policy for pregnant women. This agreement remains in force at the time of writing.

In hindsight, though, it seems that, more than attaining its intended goals, the judicialisation of this case was successful in exposing the multifaceted problems plaguing obstetric care in the public healthcare system, including the discrimination, rejection and mistreatment experienced by many indigenous women. The expression 'obstetric violence' is incisive and unsparing towards attending health personnel: naming and framing the issue in such a way allows full and unforgiving disclosure of what often happens in institutional care; and it places blame and shame on nurses, doctors and health authorities alike.

In 2015, the Mexican Federation of Ob-Gyn Organisations issued a public statement against the inclusion of obstetric violence in states' legislation on gender violence; and they condemned its use as a valid conceptual category, especially when used to refer to the (ab)use of established obstetric practices. Such staunch opposition, though, did not stem the tide: obstetric violence has become a powerful construct in framing human rights violations in obstetric care and it has acquired much greater political recognition, social legitimacy and public popularity in naming and making visible an increasingly recognisable problem in Mexican healthcare delivery.

Since 2014, the NCHR has fully adopted the term, and issued 37 recommendations against obstetric violence cases between 2015 and 2017. This number represents over 50 per cent of all recommendations in cases of health-related human rights violations and 20 per cent of the total number of recommendations in reviewed human rights abuses in those three years. In 2017, the NCHR issued a general recommendation against the occurrence of obstetric violence within the public healthcare system; this is one of only three general recommendations that the Commission has issued towards the healthcare system in the almost 30 years of its existence. Meanwhile, 20 Mexican states have incorporated legislation against obstetric violence, the great majority after 2014; others are discussing similar proposals, including now in the federal legislature.[23]

In conclusion, reflecting on these issues can contribute to an understanding of the complexities, advantages and limitations of rights-based litigation as an instrument to pursue social justice in health. This production of knowledge does not need to be an end in itself. It can also be useful for designing strategies and when engaging in emancipatory politics (Biehl 2013; Santos and Rodríguez Garavito 2007) for the many critical medical anthropologists who are also involved in social activism with the goal of ensuring that the public healthcare system in Mexico becomes more equitable, better performing, less discriminatory and more just and respectful of all women patients.

Notes

1. For experiences elsewhere in the Global South, see Gauri and Brinks 2008; Lamprea 2017; and Mæstad et al. 2011.
2. General Comment No. 14: The Right to the Highest Attainable Standard of Health (Art. 12), adopted at the 22nd Session of the CESCR, 11 August 2000 (https://www.refworld.org/pdfid/4538838d0.pdf).
3. For coverage data see: Indicator 31 in: https://public.tableau.com/views/Indicadoresde Resultado/IR2?:embed=y&:display_count=yes&:showTabs=y&:toolbar=no&:showViz Home=no (accessed 31 October 2019). 'Qualified staff' refers to physicians: medical students who finished their training and take the mandatory one-year social service programme in primary health clinics, general practitioners, resident physicians and specialists.
4. Diario Oficial de la Federación. 'Official Mexican Norm 007-SSA-2-2016', published in 2016 (http://www.dof.gob.mx/nota_detalle.php?codigo=5432289&fecha=07/04/2016).
5. INEGI, 'National Survey on Household Relationships' Dynamics' (ENDIREH), 2016 (https://www.inegi.org.mx/programas/endireh/2016/).
6. The case is emblematic in being the first (of the 32 registered and eight cases) to be catapulted into the public light by mass media, the first case to be legally represented by GIRE, the first to be litigated nationally and internationally as a case of obstetric violence, and additionally the most advanced in terms of resolutions achieved. The facts presented here were reconstructed in countless news stories between October 2013 and January 2015, in *Proceso* magazine; national newspapers *El Universal*, *La Jornada*, *El Excelsior*, *Milenio* and *Reforma*; in foreign media such as *El País*, *Univisión*, *Telemundo*; and various internet news agencies and in radio reports. I also reviewed the recommendation issued by the NCHR (available online), the petition made by GIRE to the CIHR, Irma's complaints to the NCHR, and a series of press releases by GIRE during litigation of the case. Finally, I reviewed a video recording of the hearing at the CIHR available online, and I conducted an extensive interview with 'RT', the director of GIRE in September 2014, in order to clarify the legal and extra-legal channels taken by Irma and GIRE since October of 2013. I use the woman's real name because it is public knowledge.
7. Pedro Matías, 'Irma, la indígena mazateca que parió en el patio de un hospital', *Revista Proceso* (2013), http://www.proceso.com.mx/?p=354510.
8. José de Jesús Cortés, 'Cobran servicio a mujer que dio a luz en jardín de Oaxaca', *Periódico Excelsior* (2013), http://www.excelsior.com.mx/nacional/2013/10/07/922216.
9. Equivalent to approximately US $30 at the time.
10. The Commission has been criticised for not fully complying with its mandate: not always ensuring effective compensation for victims of rights violations, not providing enough follow-up to ensure compliance with its own recommendations, not adequately informing or involving victims in the development of recommendations and reconciliation agreements, not sufficiently utilising international human rights treaties in its recommendations and reports, not promoting the structural reforms the country needs with regard to respecting and

guaranteeing human rights. Finally, there has been ongoing scrutiny about the fact that the recommendation, the NCHR's strongest instrument for enforcing HR, is used insufficiently; its reception and acceptance is not mandatory and, when formally accepted, authorities frequently do not comply with it. See Magaloni and Mayer-Serra 2014.

11. The Information Group on Reproductive Choice (GIRE) is a non-profit organisation that promotes women's reproductive rights in Mexico. Founded in 1991 by a group of Mexican feminist intellectuals, it is dedicated to systematising and disseminating scientific, secular, rational and unprejudiced information about reproductive rights and promoting public policy and legal reforms that guarantee such rights, beginning with freedom of choice in motherhood, the right to abortion and the right to quality reproductive health services. Since 2010, it has begun strategic public-interest litigation against violations of reproductive rights in the national and international arenas, including in cases of maternal mortality and obstetric violence (information from the web page https://gire.org.mx, and interview with 'RT').

12. Pedro Matías, 'Irma, la indígena mazateca que parió en el patio de un hospital', *Revista Proceso* (2013) https://www.proceso.com.mx/354510/irma-la-indigena-mazateca-que-pario-en-el-patio-de-un-hospital.

13. Recommendation 001/2014 (https://www.cndh.org.mx/sites/default/files/doc/Recomendaciones/2014/REC_2014_001.pdf).

14. Parto Libre and Sakil Nichim Anzetik. The hearing was held on 27 March 2014 (http://www.oas.org/es/cidh/audiencias/Hearings.aspx?Lang=En&Session=134&page=2 and (https://www.youtube.com/watch?v=UCy0mR6Gp5c).

15. The IACHR is the human rights oversight body of the American States Organisation. When the national appeals channels are exhausted, and human rights organisations can show that the state has failed to comply with its obligations, they can undertake the appeal at the IACHR (Macaulay 2011), not only to denounce and publicly document the failures and violations committed by the authorities of the country but also to generate ethical, political and media pressure on their government. Even though IACHR resolutions are not binding, resolutions may well affect the actions of the Mexican government because of the Commission's moral stature and Mexico's sensitivity to international pressure (Domingo 2011).

16. GIRE Bulletin, 5 January 2015.

17. See, for example, the movement among health care staff #Yosoy17 that arose in 2014, from the criminalisation of medical malpractice without authorities taking a share of the structural responsibility (https://www.proceso.com.mx/374625/crean-movimiento-yosoy17-en-respaldo-a-criminalizacion-de-medicos and https://es.wikipedia.org/wiki/Movimiento_YoSoy17). As an example of the antagonism of the association to the concept of obstetric violence, see this news article: http://www.milenio.com/region/Medicos-movimiento-YoSoy17-alistan-marcha_0_386961543.html. For an example of the intersection of antagonism and the legal category of obstetric violence in criminal law, with the opposition to changing the forms of care during delivery, see: https://www.milenio.com/estados/medicos-oponen-tipificar-violencia-obstetrica-delito.

18. With the exception of serious acts that are criminally punished and punishable, such as forced sterilisation (GIRE 2013).

19. Interview with the director of GIRE, 'RT', in person, 2014.

20. Interview with the director of GIRE, 'RT', in person, 2014.

21. Interview with the director of GIRE, 'RT', in person, 2014.

22. Public maternal health services should be organised into networks where primary health clinics cluster around a secondary-level hospital to which women requiring emergency obstetric care are referred. Primary health clinics and the referral hospital need to fulfil certain requirements in terms of equipment and infrastructure, availability of human resources and drug supplies, as well as in obstetric emergencies training, geographical location and distance, and transport.

23. After a failed attempt to include obstetric violence in the legislation against gender violence in 2015, a new legislative proposal to eradicate obstetric violence was submitted in the Senate by the new party in power in December 2018 (http://comunicacion.senado.gob.mx/index.php/informacion/boletines/43015-presentan-reformas-para-erradicar-violencia-obstetrica-y-asegurar-atencion-materno-infantil.html).

References

Alzate Mora, Daniel. 2014. 'Health Litigation in Colombia: Have We Reached the Limit for the Judicialization of Health?', *Health and Human Rights Journal*, 23 September. Accessed 12 September 2019. https://www.hhrjournal.org/2014/09/health-litigation-in-colombia-have-we-reached-the-limit-for-the-judicialization-of-health/.

Biehl, João. 2013. 'The Judicialization of Biopolitics: Claiming the Right to Pharmaceuticals in Brazilian Courts', *American Ethnologist* 40 (3): 419–36.

Biehl, João, Joseph J. Amon, Mariana P. Socal and Adriana Petryna. 2012. 'Between the Court and the Clinic: Lawsuits for Medicines and the Right to Health in Brazil', *Health and Human Rights* 14 (1): 1–17.

Biehl, João, Adriana Petryna, Alex Gertner, Joseph J. Amon and Paulo D. Picon. 2009. 'Judicialisation of the Right to Health in Brazil', *The Lancet* 373 (9682): 2182–84.

Bourdieu, Pierre and Loïc J.D. Wacquant. 1995. *Respuestas: Por una antropología reflexiva*. Mexico City: Grijalbo.

Breilh, Jaime. 2010. *Ciencia emancipadora, pensamiento crítico e interculturalidad*. Quito: UASB-Digital. Accessed 13 September 2019. http://repositorio.uasb.edu.ec/bitstream/10644/3353/1/Breilh%2C%20J-CON-078-Ciencia.pdf.

Castro, Roberto. 2014. 'Génesis y práctica del habitus médico autoritario en México', *Revista Mexicana de Sociología* 76 (2): 167–97.

Castro, Roberto and Joaquina Erviti. 2003. 'Violations of Reproductive Rights during Hospital Births in Mexico', *Health and Human Rights* 7 (1): 90–110.

Chalmers, Beverley, Viviana Mangiaterra and Richard Porter. 2001. 'WHO Principles of Perinatal Care: The Essential Antenatal, Perinatal, and Postpartum Care Course', *Birth* 28 (3): 202–7.

CIDH (Comisión Interamericana de Derechos Humanos). 2014. 'Salud materna y denuncias de violencia obstétrica en México'. 150 Período de Sesiones, Thursday 27 March. Accessed 13 September 2019. http://www.oas.org/es/cidh/multimedia/sesiones/150/default.asp.

CNEGySR (Centro Nacional de Equidad de Género y Salud Reproductiva). 2009. *Estrategia integral para acelerar la reducción de la mortalidad materna en México*. Mexico City: Secretaría de Salud.

Cook, Rebecca J. 2013. 'Human Rights and Maternal Health: Exploring the Effectiveness of the Alyne Decision', *Journal of Law, Medicine and Ethics* 41 (1): 103–23.

Coral-Díaz, Ana Milena, Beatriz Londoño-Toro and Lina Marcela Muñoz-Ávila. 2010. 'El concepto de litigio estratégico en América Latina: 1990–2010', *Vniversitas* 121: 49–76.

Couso, Javier A., Alexandra Huneeus and Rachel Sieder, eds. 2010. *Cultures of Legality: Judicialization and Political Activism in Latin America*. Cambridge: Cambridge University Press.

De Currea-Lugo, Víctor. 2006. 'La encrucijada del derecho a la salud en América Latina'. In *Derechos económicos, sociales y culturales en América Latina: Del invento a la herramienta*, edited by Alicia Ely Yamin, 215–34. Mexico City: Plaza y Valdés.

DeMaria, Lisa M., Lourdes Campero, Marianne Vidler and Dilys Walker. 2012. 'Non-Physician Providers of Obstetric Care in Mexico: Perspectives of Physicians, Obstetric Nurses and Professional Midwives', *Human Resources for Health* 10, Article 6: 1–9. Accessed 12 September 2019. https://doi.org/10.1186/1478-4491-10-6.

Domingo, Pilar. 2011. 'Judicialización de la política: El cambio de papel político del Poder Judicial en México'. In *La judicialización de la política en América Latina*, edited by Rachel Sieder, Line Schjolden and Alan Angell, 21–46. Mexico City: Centro de Investigaciones y Estudios Superiores en Antropología Social.

Farmer, Paul. 1999. 'Pathologies of Power: Rethinking Health and Human Rights', *American Journal of Public Health* 89 (10): 1486–96.

FIGO Safe Motherhood and Newborn Health (SMNH) Committee. 2012. 'Management of the Second Stage of Labor', *International Journal of Gynecology and Obstetrics* 119 (2): 111–16.

Foucault, Michel. 1966. *El nacimiento de la clínica: Una arqueología de la mirada médica*, translated by Francisca Perujo. Mexico City: Siglo XXI Editores.

Foucault, Michel. 1968. *Las palabras y las cosas: Una arqueología de las ciencias humanas*, translated by Elsa Cecilia Frost. Mexico City: Siglo XXI Editores.

Foucault, Michel. 1977. *Historia de la sexualidad, I: La voluntad de saber*. Mexico City: Siglo XXI Editores.

Freyermuth, Graciela. 2011. 'Programa de atención materna y perinatal'. In *Monitoreo de la atención a las mujeres en servicios públicos del sector salud*, 54–123. Mexico City: Instituto Nacional de las Mujeres.

Gauri, Varun and Daniel M. Brinks, eds. 2008. *Courting Social Justice: Judicial Enforcement of Social and Economic Rights in the Developing World*. Cambridge: Cambridge University Press.

GIRE (Grupo de Información en Reproducción Elegida). 2013. 'Violencia obstétrica'. In *Omisión e indiferencia: Derechos reproductivos en México*, 119–47. Mexico City: Grupo de Información en Reproducción Elegida.

Gutiérrez Rivas, Rodrigo and Aline Rivera Maldonado. 2009. 'El caso "Mininuma": Un litigio estratégico para la justiciabilidad de los derechos sociales y la no discriminación en México', *Revista de la Facultad de Derecho de México* 59 (251): 89–122.

Lamprea, Everaldo. 2014. 'Colombia's Right-to-Health Litigation in a Context of Health Care Reform'. In *The Right to Health at the Public/Private Divide: A Global Comparative Study*, edited by Colleen M. Flood and Aeyal Gross, 131–58. New York: Cambridge University Press.

Lamprea, Everaldo. 2017. 'The Judicialization of Health Care: A Global South Perspective', *Annual Review of Law and Social Science* 13: 431–49.

Lazcano-Ponce, Eduardo, Raffaela Schiavon, Patricia Uribe-Zúñiga, Dilys Walker, Leticia Suárez-López, Rufino Luna-Gordillo and Alfredo Ulloa-Aguirre. 2013. 'Cobertura de atención del parto en México: Su interpretación en el contexto de la mortalidad materna', *Salud Pública de México* 55 (Supplement 2): S214–S224.

Macaulay, Fiona. 2011. 'Conflictos privados, poderes públicos: Violencia doméstica en los tribunales de América Latina'. In *La judicialización de la política en América Latina*, edited by Rachel Sieder, Line Schjolden and Alan Angell, 227–47. Mexico City: Centro de Investigaciones y Estudios Superiores en Antropología Social.

Mæstad, Ottar, Lise Rakner and Octavio L. Motta Ferraz. 2011. 'Assessing the Impact of Health Rights Litigation: A Comparative Analysis of Argentina, Brazil, Colombia, Costa Rica, India, and South Africa'. In *Litigating Health Rights: Can Courts Bring More Justice to Health?*, edited by Alicia Ely Yamin and Siri Gloppen, 273–303. Cambridge, MA: Harvard University Press.

Magaloni, Ana Laura and Carlos Elizondo Mayer-Serra. 2014. '¿Qué hacer con la CNDH?', *Nexos*, 1 November. Accessed 12 September 2019. https://www.nexos.com.mx/?p=23111.

Martínez Hernáez, Ángel. 2008. *Antropología médica: Teorías sobre la cultura, el poder y la enfermedad*. Barcelona: Anthropos.

Medina, Graciela. 2009. 'Violencia obstétrica'. *Revista de Derecho y Familia de las Personas*, 4.

Menéndez, Eduardo L. 1983. *Hacia una práctica médica alternativa: Hegemonía y autoatención (gestión) en salud*. Mexico City: Centro de Investigaciones y Estudios Superiores en Antropología Social.

Menéndez, Eduardo L. 2003. 'Modelos de atención de los padecimientos: De exclusiones teóricas y articulaciones prácticas', *Ciência e Saúde Coletiva* 8 (1): 185–207.

Menéndez, Eduardo L. 2017. *Los racismos son eternos, pero los racistas no*. Mexico City: Universidad Nacional Autónoma de México.

Oakley, Ann. 1984. *The Captured Womb: A History of the Medical Care of Pregnant Women*. Oxford: Blackwell.

Parto Libre and GIRE. 2014. 'Audiencia sobre salud materna y denuncias de violencia obstétrica en México'. 150 Período de Sesiones, Thursday 27 March: 1–8. Accessed 13 September 2019. http://www.oas.org/es/cidh/multimedia/sesiones/150/default.asp.

Pérez Sauceda, José Benito and José Zaragoza Huerta. 2011. 'Justicia restaurativa: Del castigo a la reparación'. In *Entre libertad y castigo: Dilemas del estado contemporáneo*, edited by Fernando Gerardo Campos Domínguez, David Cienfuegos Salgado, Luis Gerardo Rodríguez Lozano and José Zaragoza Huerta, 639–54. Mexico City: Universidad Nacional Autónoma de México.

Pou Giménez, Francisca. 2014. 'El nuevo amparo mexicano y la protección de los derechos: ¿Ni tan nuevo ni tan protector?', *Anuario de Derechos Humanos* 10: 91–103.

Sachse, Matthias, Paola Sesia, Azalia Pintado and Zaira Lastra. 2012. 'Calidad de la atención obstétrica, desde la perspectiva de derechos, equidad e interculturalidad en centros de salud en Oaxaca', *Revista CONAMED* 17 (Supplement 1): S4–S15.

Santos, Boaventura de Sousa and César A. Rodríguez Garavito, eds 2007. *El derecho y la globalización desde abajo: Hacia una legalidad cosmopolita*, translated by Carlos F. Morales de Setién Ravina. Barcelona: Anthropos.

Seppilli, Tullio and Rosario Otegui. 2005. 'Antropología médica crítica: Presentación', *Revista de Antropología Social* 14: 7–13.

Sesia, Paola. 2017. 'Quince años de investigaciones en la prevención y la reducción de la muerte materna en Oaxaca'. In *La muerte materna en México: Contribuciones a la investigación desde la academia*, edited by Graciela Freyermuth, 202–51. Mexico City: CIESAS.

Sesia, Paola, Marieke van Dijk and Matthias Sachse Aguilera. 2014. 'Características del manejo obstétrico en la atención pública de segundo nivel en la era del seguro popular: Un estudio de caso en un hospital público de Oaxaca'. In *Enfermedades del rezago y emergentes desde las ciencias sociales y la salud pública*, edited by Jaime Tomás Page Pliego, 241–65. Mexico City: Universidad Nacional Autónoma de México.

Sieder, Rachel, Line Schjolden and Alan Angell, eds. 2011. *La judicialización de la política en América Latina*. Mexico City: Centro de Investigaciones y Estudios Superiores en Antropología Social.

Valdez-Santiago, Rosario, Elisa Hidalgo-Solórzano, Mariana Mojarro-Iñiguez and Luz María Arenas-Monreal. 2013. 'Nueva evidencia a un viejo problema: El abuso de las mujeres en las salas de parto', *Revista CONAMED* 18 (1): 14–20.

Walker, Dilys, Lisa M. DeMaria, Leticia Suarez and Leslie Cragin. 2012. 'Skilled Birth Attendants in Mexico: How Does Care during Normal Birth by General Physicians, Obstetric Nurses, and Professional Midwives Compare with World Health Organization Evidence-Based Practice Guidelines?', *Journal of Midwifery and Women's Health* 57 (1): 18–27.

Yamin, Alicia Ely. 2011. 'Power, Suffering, and Courts: Reflections on Promoting Health Rights through Judicialization'. In *Litigating Health Rights: Can Courts Bring More Justice to Health?*, edited by Alicia Ely Yamin and Siri Gloppen, 333–72. Cambridge, MA: Harvard University Press.

Yamin, Alicia Ely and Siri Gloppen, eds. 2011. *Litigating Health Rights: Can Courts Bring More Justice to Health?* Cambridge, MA: Harvard University Press.

Yamin, Alicia Ely and Oscar Parra-Vera. 2009. 'How Do Courts Set Health Policy? The Case of the Colombian Constitutional Court', *PLoS Medicine* 6 (2), Article e1000032: 147–50.

10

Judicialisation and the politics of rare disease in Brazil: Rethinking activism and inequalities

Waleska Aureliano and Sahra Gibbon

According to the World Health Organization, diseases classified as 'rare' are those that affect 65 people in every 100,000, or 1.3 people in every 2,000, and it is estimated that about 8 per cent of the world's population is affected by some form of rare disease (Huyard 2009). They are generally chronic and/or degenerative conditions, with a high degree of morbidity and mortality and often without cure or effective treatment. It is estimated that there are between 6,000 and 8,000 rare diseases, of which 80 per cent are of genetic origin, and in many cases they are hereditary. In Brazil there are thought to be between 13 and 15 million people with some form of rare disease.[1] Due to the fact that they are not common conditions and the fractured and inequitable nature of the Brazilian healthcare system, obtaining a diagnosis is frequently a lengthy and time-consuming process (Aureliano 2015, 2018; Barbosa 2015). Moreover, there is no effective treatment for the majority of rare diseases currently identified, with only an estimated 10 per cent having a specific drug treatment. In a considerable number of cases this is a high-cost medication (Barbosa and Monsores 2016; Monsores 2013) that is often unavailable for those in the public health system and for those with private health insurance. As a result, for many Brazilian rare-disease patients and their families the only way of accessing medications is through judicialisation: a legal process of seeking the right to healthcare resources.[2]

While the judicialisation of health is a phenomenon that has unfolded across a range of international arenas (Comaroff and Comaroff 2006; Gauri and Brinks 2008; Yamin and Gloppen 2011), the number of individual legal cases in Brazil has risen particularly sharply in the last decade (Biehl 2013; Biehl and Petryna 2011; Biehl et al. 2009; Ministério da Saude 2005; Diniz, Medeiros and Schwartz 2012). This emerged initially in Brazil in the context of broadening access to and provision of antiretroviral drugs for those with HIV/AIDS.[3] It has now expanded to include provision of medication and access to health services for other conditions, particularly cancer and rare diseases. Nevertheless, recourse to the judiciary as a health-seeking strategy is debated both inside and outside Brazil, where the tension between individual rights or collective benefits and social justice is frequently contested (Biehl 2013; Ministério da Saude 2005; Diniz, Medeiros and Schwartz 2012). In this chapter we draw on research that highlights how complex entanglements between the court and the clinic (Harper, Kelly and Khanna 2015) in the context of judicialisation and rare disease in Brazil generate particular kinds of 'ambiguous political subjectivities' (Biehl 2015: 169) that require reflective critical engagement. We argue that this raises important questions for critical medical anthropology in addressing, examining and accounting for activism and inequalities.

Drawing from ethnographic research undertaken with patient organisations, and by examining policy documents and popular media discussion, we analyse the cultural and political context in which judicial processes involving the demands of patients with rare diseases are unfolding in Brazil and how this has become an important avenue for accessing health rights. Addressing the intersections in Brazil between rare disease and judicialisation, we explore how government, civil society and the pharmaceutical industry are complexly situated around disputes that involve on the one hand the constitutional right to health and the budgetary limits of the state, and, on the other, the commercial interests of the market. In this way we contribute to wider discussions in anthropology and beyond concerning how rights are legitimated with reference to a humanitarian or a universalist ethos (Ticktin 2011). This has been described by Fassin (2009) as a form of 'biolegitimacy', where rights are increasingly legitimised in terms of the 'suffering body'. Building on work highlighting how 'affective economies' have become key strategies for political action in diverse healthcare spheres and specifically the treatment of rare diseases (Buchbinder and Timmermans 2014), we examine how multiple and variable claims about the value or price of life are mobilised as part of the 'governing work' (Feldman and Ticktin 2010) that constitutes the terrain of judicialisation and high-cost drugs for rare diseases in Brazil. We illuminate the complex economic and power relations that have placed patients and their families in situations of profound uncertainty and instability, whilst also revealing the dangers of commodifying health that ultimately weaken the public health assistance offered by the Brazilian state to its citizens. In conclusion, we reflect on how from a critical medical anthropology perspective, expanding rates of judicialisation related to rare diseases in Brazil and a growing economic and political crisis, including the rise to power of the extreme right-wing and authoritarian government led by Jair Bolsonaro, raises further questions about the evolving dynamics between inequities, social justice and activism.

The chapter is informed by qualitative ethnographic research that has been undertaken since 2013. This research has aimed to understand how the question of judicialisation is being constituted among health professionals, in the media, in legal domains and principally among people living with rare genetic diseases in Brazil. It has included an examination of the discourse and practice of judicialisation on the internet and within high-profile Brazilian media outlets (*Folha* and *O Globo*), as well as fieldwork with patients' associations, at scientific congresses and public policy meetings and in public hospitals. The community encompassed by this analysis is therefore heterogeneous with respect not only to rare diseases themselves but also to different interests and investments and the material conditions of working lives and lived social contexts. Patients in doctors' offices or involved in support networks do not always participate in scientific or political events concerning rare diseases, nor are they necessarily included, acknowledged or directly involved with either the pharmaceutical industry or the state. We argue that an understanding of and perspective on how people are variably positioned in relation to the phenomenon of judicialisation, including those with variable access to the health system and with particular needs for treatment and care, have implications for how the politics of rare diseases in Brazil are perceived and experienced. The first part of this chapter demonstrates how the history of Brazilian sanitary reform, social medicine and the establishment of the constitutional right to health is central to understanding how judicial strategies have emerged in dialogue and how they have, in some cases, come to substitute the logic of public health.

The Brazilian healthcare system: Sanitary reform, the 1988 Constitution and Sistema Único de Saude (SUS)

During the last four decades of the twentieth century the Brazilian health system underwent several transformations, with the current model consolidated in the latter part of that period, following the move towards

CRITICAL MEDICAL ANTHROPOLOGY: PERSPECTIVES IN AND FROM LATIN AMERICA political democracy (Paim et al. 2011). In this sense the history of the reform of the Brazilian health system provides an important context that has both informed and propelled judicialisation.

In the first decades of the twentieth century, access to social and civil rights, including the right to health, was established through labour agreements for specific categories of work, including civil servants, bank officers and others. Other workers, or people with more informal work arrangements, continued to depend on precarious public assistance, through voluntary contributions to social security[4] or philanthropic institutions and paid services. This model, which linked access to health with a job position, offered a fragmented and unequal public service. As a result it facilitated, both directly and indirectly, the expansion of private health services, which continued to grow both during and beyond the period of military government in Brazil, from 1964 to 1985. While the state widened healthcare assistance, extending social security to rural workers, it also financed private health organisations, reformed private hospitals and provided subsidies or discounts for companies able to provide health assistance to their employees. This system also led to the concentration of health services in urban centres that housed the majority of the formally employed population and healthcare companies, thereby creating a centralised system that was focused on hospital medical assistance.

However, from the 1970s onwards, the struggle for democratic openness became linked to the health reform movement in Brazil. This movement included broad sectors of civil society, from grassroots movements to unions, from the middle classes to health managers. These groups demanded a care model that considered health a social and political concern, and were connected to a progressive agenda that emphasised access to health as a basic human right. Several actions were taken by civil society groups to consolidate health reform, including the Eighth National Health Conference (1986) which eventually provided a framework for the current public health system known as the Sistema Único de Saúde or SUS. In 1988 a new Brazilian constitution was established, and despite the expansion of the private health system, new healthcare reform was approved. Health came to be defined as the right of the citizen and an obligation of the state. However, the constitution was reformed at a time of deep economic recession as well as hyper-inflation and when there was an expanding neoliberal political agenda increasingly attuned to the market; this has made implementation of the healthcare reform uneven and difficult.

Since the beginning of the twenty-first century, with greater economic stability and the reorganisation and activism of different social movements, the Brazilian public health system has expanded its scope and reach. One example of this was the National Neo-natal Screening Programme (PNTN), popularly known as the national *teste do pezinho* or 'blood spot test', which tests all newborns in the country for certain diseases (including some considered rare, such as phenylketonuria). Another illustration was the approval in 2000 of a new mental health policy that aimed to consolidate the psychiatric reform movement in Brazil. Finally, also under the leadership of the governing Workers' Party, which began in 2003, so-called 'popular pharmacies' were created, and the free production and distribution of medicines for prevalent diseases such as hypertension and diabetes was expanded.[5]

In parallel with these developments there has also been, somewhat paradoxically, a growth and expansion of legal actions against the state for the right to access medicines and treatments not offered by the SUS. This is because of a stated scarcity, poor management of resources or because these have simply not been incorporated into the public health system. The judicialisation of health began in the 1990s with the HIV/AIDS movement, but in the following decade it assumed greater proportions involving, mainly, cancer patients and those with rare diseases. It has also emerged in close connection with new forms of capitalisation of the health market by private-sector interests, represented especially by the pharmaceutical industry.

Judicialisation: Between global innovations and local boundaries

The judicialisation of health has grown exponentially in Brazil in the last 10 years (Biehl 2013; Biehl and Petryna 2011; Biehl et al. 2009; Diniz 2009). The constitutional premise that the state must provide healthcare to every Brazilian citizen has led many to seek and in some cases successfully secure this legal right through the Brazilian courts. This recourse to the judiciary and the legal system in Brazil is focused on access to medicines, but it also frequently includes non-medicated treatments, hospital services and sometimes routine health technologies.

In practice the phenomenon of health judicialisation began with the implementation of SUS in the 1990s, and was initially informed by the Brazilian HIV/AIDS movement. With the development of drugs for treatment and control of the disease, HIV virus carriers in Brazil were among the first to lodge judicial claims for the right to access to medicines and healthcare. This demand was built, mainly, from the collective mobilisation of organised groups of civil society. The first successful action was in 1996, the same year the Brazilian National Congress passed law 9313, which obliged the state to provide antiretroviral (ARV) drugs. In this sense, the initial movement towards the use of judicialisation for access to drugs such as ARVs leveraged the construction of a specific public policy for this population, supported by financial agreements with the World Bank (Ministério da Saude 2005).

From 1999, with the value of the dollar rising, the Brazilian state began to claim that there was a lack of resources to maintain the HIV/ AIDS programme. The demand from NGOs linked to the 'global' HIV/ AIDS movement was then directed to challenging patent monopolies as a means of guaranteeing access to drugs in Brazil and in other developing countries. These challenges were ultimately successful, precipitating the internal production of medication and helping to sustain a policy of free distribution of these drugs in Brazil. The pharmaceutical industry, however, developed and in fact continues to develop new, more effective drugs, ensuring that, despite a commitment by the government to provide free access to certain medication, there continue to be new lawsuits brought to the courts by Brazilian HIV-positive patients seeking to access the most up-to-date medication. Thus, even within the context of a well-established national treatment programme, such as HIV/AIDS initiatives, the Brazilian state continues to be subject to legal demands for drugs.

Currently, however, processes of judicialisation in Brazil are dominated by cases concerning new drugs for treatment for cancer and rare diseases. In the case of rare diseases, lawsuits can involve the right to have a genetic test as well as access to basic health services such as physiotherapy and the use of drugs not yet approved in Brazil, or those approved but not yet included on the SUS lists (Diniz, Medeiros and Schwartz 2012; Boy et al. 2011; Boy and Schramm 2009). These lawsuits involve individual patients, families and collective claims, including from patient associations. Despite structural and financial constraints, such associations have played an important role in the Brazilian political arena, informing the construction of public policies for people with rare diseases (Grudzinski 2013; Barbosa 2015). However, it is important to note that unlike many Euro-American patient associations (Rabeharisoa et al. 2014), Brazilian patient associations are not mobilised around finding a cure for rare diseases. Rather, as the work of Grudzinski (2013) shows, they are engaged in efforts to legally oblige the state to care for those affected by rare diseases and their families; most frequently this translates into having access to high-cost drugs.

Since the 1990s, with the implementation of SUS, legislation has responded to the activism and engagement of Brazilian patients' associations, to focus state resources and attention on rare diseases, even before this term became common. For example, in the 1990s medicines for treating a particular rare condition, Gaucher disease, were included in the federal government's Exceptional Medicines Programme, following legal action against the state by a patient association (Boy et al. 2011). Similarly, efforts by other patient associations have led to the regulated inclusion of rare diseases such as cystic fibrosis and phenylketonuria in national programmes of neo-natal screening along with a specified treatment protocol. However, this has not prevented new legal demands for conditions which are at least nominally now included in public health programmes – a situation generated by both a lack of available medicines and a demand for newer and potentially more effective medications.

Thus there are two processes that fuel the growth of health judicialisation in Brazil, whether for antiretrovirals, cancer medications or rare disease medications: the expanding development of new high-cost drugs at a global level (not always with guarantees of long-term effectiveness), and the management of state resources at the local level.

Global innovation, costly drugs and the promise of health

By investing in the development of new drugs, the pharmaceutical industry seeks not only to improve technologies and to develop medicines, but also to renew its patents, guarantee competitiveness in the global market and increase profits (Gagnon 2015). The history of HIV/AIDS in Brazil is a useful example of this. As treatments initially caused profound side effects, there were continued efforts to develop newer medications, but at a speed which was not always accompanied by the ability of either government or individuals to purchase or acquire the drug. The breaking of patent monopolies, which was so crucial for enabling the effectiveness of the Brazilian treatment programme in the case of ARVs, is therefore constantly confronted by the emergence of new drugs, which promise fewer side effects, but at a cost that is usually unfeasible to meet the demand of all patients.

For cancer, new drugs arise continuously. The case of anti-cancer drugs in the UK is emblematic of this difficult equation between the high cost of new technologies, the urgency for patients of acquiring them, their not always proven efficacy and state budgetary limits. In 2010, the

UK government set up the Cancer Drug Fund (CDF). The fund's expected value was £50 million but it reached £340 million by 2016. The CDF was a parallel investment to the government's unique cancer treatment programme, created exclusively for new drugs, with the promise of faster treatment pathways. Critical reviews of the programme have challenged this investment – noting, among other indicators, that the effectiveness of the drugs selected is not always known (Aggarwal et al. 2017). Of 47 drugs recommended by the CDF, only 18 (38 per cent) were statistically significant in promoting patient survival. The review also showed that many drugs were approved without studies that presented statistical data for survival rates. According to Aggarwal et al. (2017), doctors are prescribing drugs to avoid 'moral blame' or the accusation that they have not done enough to test or know whether a particular drug can bring some benefit, even if studies provide little evidence that this is the case.

The dynamics between the struggle for access to 'life-saving' medication by cancer patients and the acceleration and timing of drug production is mirrored but also made more complex in the context of rare diseases, given that for the vast majority there are no medications. In 1983, the US government launched the Orphan Drug Act to stimulate research and production of rare-disease drugs by offering subsidies to pharmaceutical companies and market exclusivity. The initiative was followed by other countries such as Japan (1993), Singapore (1997), Australia (1998) and the European Union (2000). The term 'rare disease' emerged from a raft of new international legislation that allowed state governments to offer economic incentives for pharmaceutical companies to develop medicines. As the work of Huyard (2009) demonstrates, 'rare disease' was a concept that emerged from and was directly linked to the market for orphan drugs and was thus based in economic rather than clinical logic.

Brazil is no exception. Here, as elsewhere, the process of having a drug approved and included in the public health system involves conflicting and contrasting dynamics between the interest of government, the pharmaceutical industry and patients' urgent desires and needs for treatment. These are shaped by and further inform legal and economic disputes involving patients, government and the pharmaceutical industry concerning access to these drugs.

Laboratories must request to register new drugs with the Agência de Vigilância Sanitária (ANVISA), a sector of government that regulates the commercialisation of any drug in Brazil. The petition to register a drug needs to be based in clinical trials, after which the price for new medicines is further defined, and where industry will suggest a price to commercialise the drug in the country. At this point, government will try to lower the price, in an effort to include the drug in the programmes of the national health system too. In different events that we have followed in Brasilia and in interviews with government representatives, it was suggested that pharmaceutical companies do not routinely apply for registration of new drugs for rare diseases. It is claimed by government officials that this is a situation that stimulates judicialisation internally, as soon as the drug is approved by international organisations. The government's argument is that for industry, judicialisation is more profitable, as once a court order is issued it must be fulfilled in a short time, preventing the negotiation of the price.

The pharmaceutical industry, for its part, says that it seeks to register drugs, but that this is compromised by bureaucratic processes and the current criteria for registration. Materials published by Interfarma, an international company that brings together several Brazilian laboratories, state that the pharmaceutical industry does not support judicialisation but that in the face of delays by the Brazilian federal state in approving new drugs, families have no alternative but to resort to judicialisation, which they consider a 'democratic instrument' for accessing rights to medication (Interfarma 2016). Another complaint by the pharmaceutical industry, also endorsed by patient associations, is that current norms in Brazil to validate research and clinical trials make it difficult to analyse and approve medications for rare diseases. They ask for alternative standards for registering these drugs and other criteria, such as not requiring a high number of participants to validate a study, since most rare diseases affect only up to a few hundred people. Brazilian rare-disease patient associations have also raised questions about the legal obligation for pharmaceutical companies to offer the drug to study participants indefinitely if they are proved effective since, the associations argue, this discourages laboratories from conducting clinical trials in Brazil (Castro 2015; see also Aureliano 2018).

The Brazilian government's argument is that there are no resources to cover the costs of incorporating all the medications developed as soon as they are approved in their countries of origin, so they have to individually analyse cost-effectiveness as well as demonstrate the efficacy of medication. In their defence, they evoke the notion of 'possible reserve' (*a reserva do possível*; see Chiavassa et al. 2014)[6] to secure the constitutional right to health, and to emphasise that while individual demands are infinite, state resources are finite. The argument that judicialisation is contributing to the dismantling of the SUS provokes in turn both malaise and indignation from patients or their families with rare diseases, who find themselves situated quite literally in the middle of this contested terrain.

This is therefore a domain where, because of the role of the Brazilian Defensoria Pública (which provides free juridical assistance to patients and publics), the judiciary has effectively, as Flores (2016) points out, become an agent within the state to litigate against the state. That is where state agents both argue against *and* defend the state in the case of access to health and medicines. As a result it is not perhaps surprising to find that an affective discourse concerning 'life' and 'value' is appropriated by the different social actors encompassed by and constituted within these processes. While in general there is a sense of opposition to judicialisation – whether from within patient associations, government or industry – each of these spheres nevertheless defends itself in this process, putting to work legitimating social and moral categories in particular ways. Social theorists have become increasingly interested in how human life is not simply constituted (or denied) through the workings of biopolitics (Foucault 1976; Agamben 1998) but how it has become part of a governing apparatus in terms of sustaining but also sometimes contesting power and inequalities (Fassin 2009). Building on work in Brazil that has considered how the power 'of life' and not simply the power 'over life' has made 'biolegitimacy' a powerful tool in particular fields of social policy and practice (Maluf 2015), we examine how patients and patient associations mobilise affective articulations of 'life' and 'value' in their efforts to pressure the public and the judiciary in seeking to oblige the state to pay for high-cost drugs.

'My life has no price': Rare diseases in the Supreme Court and the value of life

In 2016 two lawsuits concerning access to medication reached the Brazilian Federal Supreme Court (STF). In one, the state of Rio Grande do Norte questioned the obligation to provide a high-cost drug to a patient with cardiomyopathy and pulmonary arterial hypertension who had obtained, through a separate judicial process, the right to the drug, which was not currently available in the SUS. The other action was a patient from the state of Minas Gerais, who had been seeking through local state judicial processes to have access to a drug that was not yet approved in Brazil for the treatment of chronic kidney disease. The patient had turned to the STF in a further effort to gain access to this medication.

The public unfolding of these different lawsuits in the Supreme Court in 2016 mobilised rare-disease patients from all over Brazil, leading to a social media campaign focused around the slogan 'my life has no price – *Minha Vida Não Tem Preço*'. An online petition gathered more than 500,000 signatures. On Change.org, which hosted the petition, the text of the campaign is as follows:

> Imagine you – or someone you love – with a serious, chronic and rare illness. Now imagine that the remedy is too expensive, much more expensive than you can afford. And, finally, imagine that even the courts cannot force the state to supply this medicine. This is precisely the risk we are facing today in Brazil. The Federal Supreme Court will decide whether governments are obligated or not to provide expensive medicines to people who need them and who do not have the financial means to get them. These are high-cost drugs that are not yet included in SUS and those that do not yet have Anvisa's approval.[7]

In 2016 patients held a vigil in front of the STF and achieved wide coverage of the case in the media, which focused on the high costs of health judicialisation in Brazil. However, only three votes were handed down by judges in relation to the two lawsuits, and one minister called for more time to better analyse the process. While the legal action on both cases has been suspended, with no date as yet for when it will be resumed, the public campaign and its messages about the value of life in the context of rare diseases have continued, spilling out far beyond the domain of popular and social media. It has been a prominent feature at several rare-disease events held in 2017 and 2018, and a key campaigning message for a diverse range of individual and umbrella rare-disease patient organisations.

The motto of the campaign mobilises the concept of 'life' as a 'value' that cannot be measured in monetary terms. The argument of patients and public defenders is that the Brazilian government cannot consider the concept of the 'possible reserve' to deal with the demands of patients with rare diseases, since the state budget is not more important than the life of patients. Public advocates who work with patients rebut the thesis of the 'possible reserve' with another legal concept, also drawn from German jurisprudence, the 'existential minimum' (*minimo existencial*). This asserts that 'the state has a duty to allow its jurisdictions to enjoy their fundamental social rights at a minimally acceptable level so that they have a dignified life' (Chiavassa et al. 2014). Access to medicines that, in theory, allow, prolong or improve the quality of life of people would therefore be a fundamental right, situated within the existential minimum that the state must provide.

The notion of a life/death scenario along with the idea of 'dignified' life is most visibly evoked in the discourse of patients and their legal representatives and in public debate. But it is also present, albeit in more collective terms, in the rhetoric of the public lawyers who defend the government and who seek to avoid prosecution by patient litigants, as this statement by one Brazilian state lawyer illustrates:

> The state defends the right for the planning and organisation of the [health] system to be maintained, so that it is possible to serve *the community*. One is not here, in any way, disregarding the serious situations that affect the Brazilian citizen, but the fact is that the resources of the state are limited. It is necessary to have a regulated [health] system to serve the *community* [emphasis added].[8]

We see therefore here a dispute between the Brazilian state and rare-disease patient associations that is framed through narratives about the value of life and the financial means of maintaining it, with emotional appeals that move between despair and hope and which, at the same time, speak of individual and collective forms of social justice.

Ambivalence and the 'moral criminalisation' of rare-disease activism

In the materials we analysed, it was evident that patients and their families are aware that the value of their lives oscillates when assessed by the market and public health. In certain circumstances, instead of being perceived as victims they are seen as destabilising the public health system, accused of causing damage to the community in their efforts to ensure their treatment through judicialisation. This awareness was reflected in the comments of one patient association leader at a rare-disease event in Rio de Janeiro in March 2017:

> I do not like the word judicialisation, because I think that judicialisation is used precisely to criminalise whoever turns to justice for the constitutional right to health [...] it is as if it were something that would break the SUS, that would end the financing of the Unified Health System. There are treatments that are more expensive, but it is not by choice [...] if I could I would treat myself with aspirin, but I did not choose the treatment [...] who would want to have a rare disease and need medicine for life? That will often partially

solve your problem, it will give you better quality of life, but it will not solve your problem fully. So it seems like we're going there to ask a privilege for a few people. The people you see talking, even the Supreme Minister saying 'a few people want to take the right to have a hospital bed', that's not it, that's not it at all.

In striking contrast to the situation of HIV/AIDS activism in Brazil in the 1990s, there is a sense among rare-disease patients of being stigmatised for pursuing their right to health through the judiciary. The self-defensive tone evident in these comments reflects how the discussion in the media is often presented in terms of rare-disease patients draining resources from the SUS and undermining the health system as a whole, or limiting others' rights by personally advocating for expensive medicines. Yet at the same time these comments also suggest such patients and those involved with patient associations are profoundly reflective in confronting contested debates concerning judicialisation.

While there are clearly alignments between the pharmaceutical industry and some rare-disease patients' interests in seeking to obtain medications, there is a diversity of response, with many of these individuals and organisations determined not to ignore the economic interests of the industry. On the contrary, some clearly recognise that these are profit-seeking companies, and may try to disassociate themselves from any idea that are being financed by the pharmaceutical industry to pursue a process of judicialisation. This is evident in the criticism of the sociologist Barbosa (2015), who is also the father of a girl with a rare disease and founder of a major Brazilian patient association. He is particularly critical of what he calls the 'utility model of care' for the rare disease, centred on drugs. For him, the perception of care as access to medicines is far removed from what he proposes as a holistic approach to care: an approach that he suggests might be especially important given that in most cases concerning rare diseases there are no available remedies.

Nevertheless, for those conditions where there is a possibility of using a drug, patients and their families enthusiastically receive the results regarding research and the development of new drugs. In a scenario of desperation, often where nothing or very little exists, the possibility of participating in a clinical study is also perceived with interest and the approval of a new drug abroad shapes an unending hope of healing or improving the quality of life of a patient or family member with a rare disease.

In interviews with leaders of patient associations and by following the public debate on newspapers, it is possible to understand that judicialisation for many patients is not something sought or always desired. Rather it is for many the only possible way of accessing some form of treatment. Many, particularly parents and especially mothers of patients with rare diseases, who make up a significant portion of the Brazilian rare-disease activist community, are aware of the moral criminalisation of patients who seek access to medications and services in this way. In the context of our interviews a number commented further on this.

> I'm really afraid to hear someone talk about judicialisation, because as a patient if we go somewhere where we talk about this topic, we are really thought as the biggest thug, the biggest enemy, *persona non grata* in society.
>
> (patient in an event about rare diseases in Rio de Janeiro, March 2017)

> The cost [of judicialisation] is much higher, nothing is solved, the patient is not making money, the patient is gaining health. So if we are to blame for our interest in saving the lives of our children then I am guilty, mainly because I was one that judicialised to get my son's treatment and he did for six years [...] I do not think it's right that I have to judicialise to get my son's treatment, I do not think so, but I have no other way, what should I do? I will wait, [but] if there is already a law, constitutionally a right to health and life, which in fact does not work, I expect the sky to fall before they take pity! No, if I have the option to prosecute, I will go to court, it is not right what they say about the judicialisation.
>
> (leader of a patient association who has a son with rare disease)

As these comments suggest, a notion of responsibility (frequently translated as 'maternal' responsibility, given the gendered profile of many involved in patient associations) is often evoked in efforts to pursue the right to life in these reflections by patients involved in associations. Similarly for adults with rare diseases, the expectation of a decent or 'dignified' life is central to an argument that is used to justify the judicial pursuit of care and medication. With the motto 'my life has no price', families with rare diseases aim to encourage the Brazilian state to attend to a basic right that the lack of a medicine can limit, namely the right to life and health.

The 'exceptional' market value of rare-disease lives in Brazil

For those who produce drugs capable of saving patients' lives or providing them with better conditions, life and health have significant monetary value. For the pharmaceutical industry, rare diseases have become a highly attractive and lucrative market. In 2016, an American executive from the pharmaceutical industry at a speech in Brasilia explained to the audience that the market for rare diseases in Latin America was estimated at about 37 to 50 million patients. While quantifying the data, the speaker evoked human rights and compliance with international treaties on economic, social and cultural rights to argue that national governments should bear the costs of such demand. He called attention to the construction of a public agenda to finance the purchase of medicines. Thus, a representative of the market advocated for public financing to provide resources for private initiative. At one point, he explicitly stated that developing 'diagnosis and treatment for very few patients is very expensive', before rhetorically asking, 'Who will pay the bill?'

His speech was not lost on the patient activists who were present, especially those who are directly affected by rare diseases or who are relatives of people with rare diseases for which there is no drug treatment. In his blog, one such activist later responded to the talk he had witnessed, highlighting how this reflected and informed differences amongst rare-disease associations in the way they perceive the role of pharmaceutical companies:

> This 'business in search of profit' was explicit in one of the lectures, the one made by Dr Fernando Ferrer of Multinational Partnerships, who ended his speech inviting multinational businessmen from the pharmaceutical industry to invest in Latin America, as it would be an excellent business opportunity here in the field of rare diseases. I believe that these differences are reflected inside the rare diseases field where they fit into the political struggle between the public health model (universal, for all, and therefore state) and the private health model (only for those who can afford it). (https://amanf. org.br/2016/10/, accessed 31 October 2019).

Industry representatives do not deny that their companies are looking for profit. In material published in 2017 by EvaluatePharma, a company dedicated to providing guidance to pharmaceutical investors, orphan drugs are presented as a major potential market niche. The 26-page report shows in detail the potential and actual profits from this market, which by 2022 will, according to its estimates, generate $209 billion, accounting for 21 per cent of all medical prescriptions worldwide. While it mentions all the benefits and subsidies offered by governments of various nations with legislation like the Orphan Drug Act, more affordable pricing for these drugs is not at issue in this document. Instead, fiscal and financial incentives and market exclusivity are listed as yet another way to boost profits.[9]

Gagnon (2015) argues that the pharmaceutical market today is marked by 'nichebusters', which have become more profitable than the earlier model of 'blockbusters', produced for prevalent diseases and sold to thousands of people. Over the years, patent infringement and loss of sales exclusivity have made so called blockbuster drugs unprofitable. The alternative profit-seeking pathway is to develop new patents, but this is not always feasible when previous cheaper drugs remain in the market. Blockbusters have thus lost competitiveness on the global stage, and specific niche markets, such as rare diseases, have become the focus of industry.

Thus, if for the state and patient associations the life of patients with rare diseases should not have a price, for the pharmaceutical industry it has, by contrast – and somewhat ironically, given the campaigning slogan of rare-disease associations in Brazil – exceptional value. In all rare-disease events in Brazil the industry is present or represented. Its largest representative in the region is Interfarma, a pharmaceutical research association that brings together 51 national and international laboratories, among them giants such as Bayer, Novartis and Sanofi. Among the materials published by Interfarma is a special issue on the judicialisation of medicines (Interfarma 2016). In this document, the company says it is against judicialisation, but it affirms that it exists because of 'failures' of the Brazilian public health system. It presents official data on the costs of judicialisation for the government's budget and understands that the best way to stop this process, which is considered harmful to every society, is to create more effective and quicker ways of incorporating medicines into SUS. It is unclear how prices would change as a result, although it is mentioned that this would 'enable' price negotiation.

The state in turn, in its defence, always claims that industry is not interested in registering medicines. In 2017, some changes were made to speed up the registration processes for orphan drugs. Even with these changes, the government says that few companies seek to register these drugs, and when they do, requests are not always properly substantiated or documented and are as a result eventually turned down.

The whole process is slow, and patients find themselves in the midst of an economic and bureaucratic dispute between government and business. The former seeks to ensure adequate allocation of finite resources and constantly argues that paying dearly for drugs for rare diseases limits other health actions that would reach a larger number of people, such as vaccination programmes and basic care. The industry also appeals to the small number of patients to justify abusive prices. In this equation, where a few people are seen as too expensive and quantified in monetary terms, life ceases to be a value in itself but becomes a commodity, qualified according to perspectives of economic management and profit.

Concluding comments and future developments

We have seen in this chapter how the value of life and the forms of 'biolegitimacy' (Fassin 2009; Maluf 2015) this entails are multiple and contested across the diverse terrain in which judicialisation is unfolding in relation to rare diseases in Brazil. Patients caught in the midst of this dispute see their lives quantified and valued in different ways: on the one hand as expense and cost, and on the other as an inestimable individual value, masking possibilities of profit and financial interests. The Brazilian state alleges that judicialisation impacts the budget of the public health system, causing damage to the community, since the money spent to meet judicial demands entails a cut in other services. As one government representative put it in one of the hearings observed in Brasilia, managing the health bill is like carrying out a 'Sophie's choice' (*uma escolha de Sofia*) given the budgetary limits of the state. The 'life' that is valued here is that of the greatest possible number of people who can be served with these limited resources. Industry, in turn, bets on the unique character of an individual life and the possibility of its extension at any cost. Publicity produced by industry is routinely aimed at the general public, usually focusing on particular cases of improvement in the quality of life, with the use of individual life histories highlighting elements related to family and work. Nothing is said in these contexts about the soaring costs of drugs and their possible limited benefits.

While illuminating how the ethical value and category of 'life' gains traction across different spheres of social action in the context of contestation and debates concerning judicialisation and rare disease, this chapter has also aimed to further contextualise how we might understand the way that particular forms of activism and inequalities inform these developments. Whilst an affective discourse of life and value in pursuing access and rights to medication is prominent, these do not, as Buchbinder and Timmermans (2014) suggest, serve to 'obscure' fiscal costs and opportunities of public health programmes; rather, in Brazil, they are brought into sharp relief. We see very clearly in the Brazilian context the complex 'paradoxes and prospects of citizenship' (Petryna and Follis 2015) or what Biehl describes as the 'ambiguous political subjectivities' (2015) at stake in the judicialisation of health in relation to rare disease. Shaped at the nexus between the state, patient associations and the judiciary, such activism can facilitate access to urgent healthcare in the context of a fractured healthcare system, even as it does little to redress underlying structural inequalities. The sense of being left with little choice but to judicialise was conveyed by one rare-disease patient in an interview with a major newspaper: 'I do not want to be demanding an unapproved drug, except that the company has no interest in approving it in Brazil. My life cannot wait until the company has an interest. *We are hostage to industries and government*' (our emphasis).

The activism of rare-disease patients in Brazil confronts serious challenges. Some are similar to those which the HIV-positive community in Brazil faced in the mid-1990s in their efforts to arouse the interest of the pharmaceutical industry and to get the state to build a solid policy of assistance. Nevertheless, this is quite a different context. People with rare diseases, because of an increased and highly diverse variability and specificity in terms of the condition (often undiagnosed) and treatment (often non-existent and of uncertain efficacy), confront different problems and challenges. Without the large media appeal that HIV/AIDS had or which certain forms of cancer now have, nor the possibility of more effective cure or control, it is very difficult to raise public awareness. Equally problematic are the market protections provided by legislation in the countries where the drugs are produced, and patent monopoly, which make it more difficult to put pressure on the industry to demand the reduction of drug prices or challenge patents, as happened in the case of HIV/AIDS in Brazil.

The wave of austerity policies in Brazil during the last few years has not diminished cases of judicialisation – in fact, quite the opposite. However, with the worsening of the political and financial crisis in Brazil it is not surprising that the Supreme Court has not, to date, been very swift to judge lawsuits such as those outlined earlier. The enactment of Constitutional Amendment 95 (EC 95) in 2017, which freezes social investments for 20 years, has already had consequences for healthcare in Brazil, with drastic reductions in budgetary resources. Brazilian states and municipalities cannot shore up this situation, given the fall in revenues as a result of recent austerity policies, which in turn affects health budgets. Judicial proceedings continue to be filed, but they no longer have the same effects, and even the drugs already approved or intended to be purchased are not being bought in the necessary quantities. In October 2017, one of the authors attended an event organised by a large association of patients, which brought together associations from Latin America in Rio de Janeiro. At the close, a manifesto was read that would be delivered to the Senate the following week. This highlighted that for the year 2017 substantial cuts were made in the acquisition of nine medicines for rare diseases, meaning that dozens of patients would have their treatments stopped if new purchases were not authorised.

In 2017, Directive 199, which legally instituted the national policy of guaranteeing care for people with rare diseases, was reviewed. This legislation had envisaged the accreditation of centres in Brazil aimed at providing integrated public health services for patients with rare diseases, as well as providing funds for staff costs, routine examinations and treatment. Seven such centres were planned across the country, but only one of them has thus far secured some of the resources budgeted for these developments. The others continue to function as before, without new financial and resource contributions and facing the same challenges in efforts to care for patients with rare diseases. In May 2018, at an event organised by the authors to return research data to participants from a number of patient associations, we were informed that Directive 199 was revoked and incorporated into other legislation in a new document published by the federal government a few days before the meeting. The leaders of the associations lamented that as soon as the directive had begun to be implemented, it was appropriated by new management that has shown little interest in strengthening SUS. On the other hand, in July 2018 the federal Senate approved a complementary bill that intends to institute the National Policy for Rare Diseases in the SUS. It is envisaged that actions aimed at the care of people with rare diseases will be implemented within three years. However, the text of the bill does not clarify how resources will be allocated for this process: a significant challenge, given the promised freezing of public spending on health for the next 20 years.

The current political and economic scenario in Brazil, including the presidential victory in 2018 of the extreme right-wing politician Jair Bolsonaro who has declared a commitment to 'eliminate activism',[10] points to the ongoing process of dismantling SUS, the commercialisation of health and the promotion of healthcare companies to the detriment of users. This reflects not only the growing entrenchment of a neoliberal agenda but also the active erosion of many public healthcare benefits and rights. In this process, the place of people with rare diseases in Brazil remains uncertain, raising further questions about how justice can continue to be sought in a context of increasing and ongoing limits to health rights and resources.

Notes

1. See Ministério da Saúde 2014.
2. As the work of Sesia (this volume) shows, judicialisation is also a much wider phenomenon and can be a mechanism for seeking redress for victims of human rights violations in healthcare contexts.
3. But this has not been the case everywhere: see for instance Sesia (this volume) for an account of how judicialisation in Mexico was initially articulated in the context of ensuring access to healthcare resources for indigenous communities.
4. In Brazil, all people with a formal job (in a company or factory, for example) contribute to social security, a tax collected to provide retirement income to employees in the future. This social security is controlled by federal government. Self-employed workers may choose whether they want to contribute to social security.
5. Ministerio de Saúde, 'Sobre o Programa' http://portalms.saude.gov.br/acoes-e-programas/farmacia-popular/sobre-o-programa (accessed in 2018).
6. This is a legal term that arose from a case in West Germany in 1972 involving young adults who, having failed the admission process at the public university, legally appealed the decision, evoking the precept of a fundamental law which guaranteed German citizens the choice of profession, workplace and training. The German justice system denied the request, instituting the theory of the 'possible reserve' that limits the state's action to address the constitutional right of private interest above the right of the majority. In Brazil, the theory is associated with the scarcity of public resources and consequent inability to fulfil all the demands related to social rights.
7. See www.change.org/minhavidanaotempreco (accessed in September 2016).
8. 'Ministro muda voto sobre remédios fora do SUS ou sem aval da Anvisa', *O Globo*, 28 September 2016, http://oglobo.globo.com/sociedade/saude/ministro-muda-voto-sobre-remedios-fora-do-sus-ou-sem-aval-da-anvisa-20194447#ixzz4MJt2OBgC (accessed 28 September 2016).
9. See this document at www.evaluategroup.com/orphandrug2017 (accessed in December 2017).
10. See for example https://www1.folha.uol.com.br/poder/2018/10/organizacoes-repudiam-fala-de-bolsonaro-contra-ativismos.shtml.

References

Agamben, Giorgio. 1998. *Homo Sacer: Sovereign Power and Bare Life*, translated by Daniel Heller-Roazen. Stanford: Stanford University Press.
Aggarwal, A., T. Fojo, C. Chamberlain, C. Davis and R. Sullivan. 2017. 'Do Patient Access Schemes for High-Cost Cancer Drugs Deliver Value to Society? Lessons from the NHS Cancer Drugs Fund', *Annals of Oncology* 28 (8): 1738–50.
Aureliano, Waleska. 2015. 'Health and the Value of Inheritance: The Meanings Surrounding a Rare Genetic Disease', *Vibrant: Virtual Brazilian Anthropology* 12 (1): 109–40.
Aureliano, Waleska. 2018. 'Trajetórias terapêuticas familiares: Doenças raras hereditárias como sofrimento de longa duração', *Ciência e Saúde Coletiva* 23 (2): 369–79.

Barbosa, Larissa and Natan Monsores. 2016. 'Linhas de cuidado e itinerários terapêuticos para doenças raras no distrito federal', *Tempus: Actas de Saúde Coletiva* 10 (3): 69–80.

Barbosa, Rogério L. 2015. *Pele de Cordeiro: Associativismo e mercado na produção de cuidado para as doenças raras*. Lisbon: Chiado Editora.

Biehl, João. 2013. 'The Judicialization of Biopolitics: Claiming the Right to Pharmaceuticals in Brazilian Courts', *American Ethnologist* 40 (3): 419–36.

Biehl, João. 2015. 'The Juridical Hospital: Claiming the Right to Pharmaceuticals in Brazilian Courts'. In *The Clinic and the Court: Law, Medicine and Anthropology*, edited by Ian Harper, Tobias Kelly and Akshay Khanna, 163–96. Cambridge: Cambridge University Press.

Biehl, João and Adriana Petryna. 2011. 'Bodies of Rights and Therapeutic Markets', *Social Research* 78 (2): 359–86.

Biehl, João, Adriana Petryna, Alex Gertner, Joseph J. Amon and Paulo D. Picon. 2009. 'Judicialisation of the Right to Health in Brazil', *The Lancet* 373 (9682): 2182–84.

Boy, Raquel and Fermin Roland Schramm. 2009. 'Bioética da proteção e tratamento de doenças genéticas raras no Brasil: O caso das doenças de depósito lisossomal', *Cadernos de Saúde Pública* 25 (6): 1276–84.

Boy, Raquel, Ida V.D. Schwartz, Bárbara C. Krug, Luiz C. Santana-da-Silva, Carlos E. Steiner, Angelina X. Acosta, Erlane M. Ribeiro, Marcial F. Galera, Paulo G.C. Leivas and Marlene Braz. 2011. 'Ethical Issues Related to the Access to Orphan Drugs in Brazil: The Case of Mucopolysaccharidosis Type I', *Journal of Medical Ethics* 37 (4): 233–39.

Buchbinder, Mara and Stefan Timmermans. 2014. 'Affective Economies and the Politics of Saving Babies' Lives', *Public Culture* 26 (1): 101–26.

Castro, Rosana. 2015. 'Reivindicações por participação em pesquisas clínicas e desafios à regulamentação ética da investigação científica no Brasil'. Paper presented at the XI Reunião de Antropologia do MERCOSUL, Montevideo, Uruguay, 30 November–4 December 2015.

Chiavassa, Rosana, Guilherme Guimarães Coam, Marcelo Chiavassa de Mello Paula Lima and Thiago de Miranda Queiroz Moreira. 2014. 'Direito à saúde: Dever do Estado – considerações sobre a judicialização do acesso à saúde nas hipóteses de doenças raras', *Jornal Brasileiro de Economia da Saúde* Supplement 1: 30–40.

Comaroff, John L. and Jean Comaroff. 2006. 'Law and Disorder in the Postcolony: An Introduction'. In *Law and Disorder in the Postcolony*, edited by Jean Comaroff and John L. Comaroff, 1–56. Chicago: Chicago University Press.

Diniz, Debora. 2009. 'Judicialização de medicamentos no SUS: Memorial ao STF', *Série ANIS* 66: 1–5.

Diniz, Debora, Marcelo Medeiros and Ida Vanessa D. Schwartz. 2012. 'Consequências da judicialização das políticas de saúde: Custos de medicamentos para as mucopolissacaridoses', *Cadernos de Saúde Pública* 28 (3): 479–89.

Fassin, Didier. 2009. 'Another Politics of Life is Possible', *Theory, Culture and Society* 26 (5): 44–60.

Feldman, Ilana and Miriam Ticktin, eds. 2010. *In the Name of Humanity: The Government of Threat and Care*. Durham, NC: Duke University Press.

Flores, Lise Vogt. 2016. '"Na minha mão não morre": Uma etnografia das ações judiciais de medicamentos'. Master's thesis, Universidade Federal do Paraná.

Foucault, Michel. 1976. *The History of Sexuality Volume 1*, translated by Robert Hurley. London: Allen Lane.

Gagnon, Marc-André. 2015. 'New Drug Pricing: Does It Make Any Sense?', *Prescrire International* 24 (162): 192–95.

Gauri, Varun and Daniel M. Brinks, eds. 2008. *Courting Social Justice: Judicial Enforcement of Social and Economic Rights in the Developing World*. Cambridge: Cambridge University Press.

Grudzinski, Roberta Reis. 2013. 'A nossa batalha é fazer o governo trabalhar: Estudo etnográfico acerca das práticas de governo de uma associação de pacientes'. Master's thesis, Universidade Federal do Rio Grande do Sul.

Harper, Ian, Tobias Kelly and Akshay Khanna, eds. 2015. *The Clinic and the Court: Law, Medicine and Anthropology*. Cambridge: Cambridge University Press.

Huyard, Caroline. 2009. 'How Did Uncommon Disorders Become "Rare Diseases"? History of a Boundary Object', *Sociology of Health and Illness* 31 (4): 463–77.

Interfarma. 2016. *Por que o brasileiro recorre à Justiça para adquirir medicamentos? Entenda o que é a judicialização da saúde*. São Paulo: Interfarma – Associação da Indústria Farmacêutica de Pesquisa.

Maluf, Sônia. 2015. 'Biolegitimacy, Rights and Social Policies: New Biopolitical Regimes in Mental Healthcare in Brazil', *Vibrant: Virtual Brazilian Anthropology* 12 (1): 321–50.

Ministério da Saúde [Secretária de Vigilância em Saúde]. 2005. *Programa Nacional de DST e Aids. O Remédio via Justiça: Um estudo sobre o acesso a novos medicamentos e exames em HIV/aids no Brasil por meio de ações judiciais.* Brasília: Ministério da Saúde.

Ministério da Saúde. 2014. 'Portaria N° 199, de 30 de Janeiro de 2014'. Accessed 2 March 2015. http://bvsms.saude.gov.br/bvs/saudelegis/gm/2014/prt0199_30_01_2014.html.

Monsores, Natan. 2013. 'Questões bioéticas sobre doenças genéticas raras: Câmara dos Deputados: 54a Legislatura – 3a Sessão Legislativa'. In *Série Separatas de Discursos, Pareceres e Projetos*, n° 21/2013.

Paim, Jairnilson, Claudia Travassos, Celia Almeida, Ligia Bahia and James Macinko. 2011. 'O sistema de saúde brasileiro: História, avanços e desafios', *The Lancet (Série Saúde no Brasil)* 1: 11–31.

Petryna, Adriana and Karolina Follis. 2015. 'Risks of Citizenship and Fault Lines of Survival', *Annual Review of Anthropology* 44: 401–17.

Rabeharisoa, Vololona, Michel Callon, Angela Marques Filipe, João Arriscado Nunes, Florence Paterson and Frédéric Vergnaud. 2014. 'From "Politics of Numbers" to "Politics of Singularisation": Patients' Activism and Engagement in Research on Rare Diseases in France and Portugal', *BioSocieties* 9 (2): 194–217.

Scheffer, Mário, Andrea Lazzarini Salazar and Karina Bozola Grou. 2005. *O Remédio via Justiça: Um estudo sobre o acesso a novos medicamentos e exames em HIV/Aids no Brasil por meio de ações judiciais.* Brasília: Ministério da Saúde.

Ticktin, Miriam. 2011. *Casualties of Care: Immigration and Politics of Humanitarianism in France.* Berkeley: University of California Press.

Yamin, Alicia Ely and Siri Gloppen, eds. 2011. *Litigating Health Rights: Can Courts Bring More Justice to Health?* Cambridge, MA: Harvard University Press.

Afterword

Claudia Fonseca

Fruit of the singular encounter of scholars working on health-connected issues in countries as diverse as Mexico, Guatemala, Peru and Brazil, this book registers as much as it helps forge a burgeoning field of critical medical anthropology in Latin America. The subjects are varied – from rare genetic disease to drug addiction, from diabetes to abortion, from obstetric violence in maternity wards to low-cost health services provided by pharmacies. However, the authors of this volume are connected by certain common concerns. On the one hand, they consistently place problems of health, illness and care within the framework of enduring structural inequalities, exacerbated in recent years by the dynamics of globalisation. On the other hand, by framing biomedical knowledge as one among many cultural systems for understanding mental and bodily wellbeing, the authors explore the dynamics (and efficacy) of varied practices of care, including those based on 'local' conceptions of health. But perhaps most important is the way in which, counteracting the generalising, model-building tendency of much contemporary scholarship, they share an evident commitment to ethnography, valued not only for detailing the description of local processes but also for establishing dialogues that lead to more symmetrical relations between researchers and their interlocutors. The net outcome of this process (in common with a number of other 'critical' forms of social science) is the necessary coupling of 'a sense of moral purpose and practical solidarity that might animate both critical thought and social action' (Biehl 2016).

The structural violence responsible for much of the world's poverty and illness (Menéndez 1998; Farmer 2011), tacitly evoked in the majority of chapters, acquires sharp contours in Muñoz et al.'s work on Central American migrants on Mexico's southern border. Fleeing from situations of war and famine in their own countries and suffering persistent discrimination – both because of skin colour and because of their undocumented status – the young men depicted here are left with few options aside from sex work in exchange for drugs or a pittance of money. Through an analysis anchored in the viewpoint of the migrants, who are left by local police and health services to fend for themselves, the reader comes to recognise a situation of extreme social and economic vulnerability that the usual analytical paradigms of 'rational choice' and 'risk groups' simply do not account for. Addressing another facet of structural violence, Paola Sesia's research on obstetric violence in Mexican maternity hospitals examines the stumbling blocks of racial prejudice and stigmatised cultural difference as they appear in the very fabric of public health systems. Working through a well-publicised episode, her analysis revolves around the story of an indigenous woman in Oaxaca who, told to 'come back later' by hospital personnel, was forced to give birth in a public park. Thanks to the author's deft analysis, the event emerges not as an isolated incident, but as part of a repeated pattern of discrimination against indigenous mothers – seen by hospital authorities as under-educated, incomprehensible and passive – who bring birth-related disasters upon themselves.

Yet another, more subtle, form of ethno-racial prejudice comes to the fore in Calestani and Montesi's chapter, inspired to a great extent by Breilh's 'critical epidemiology' (2008), on alleged connections between race and chronic disease. Whether dealing with the Amerindian 'thrifty gene' that would explain a propensity towards diabetes, Mexicans' purportedly inadequate dietary habits or the supposed reluctance of minority groups in the UK to donate organs, the authors make a convincing argument that culturalist and genetic explanations for chronic disease have been 're-enchanted'. As a result, scientists as well as lay observers tend to cast minority groups as intrinsically vulnerable, if not 'dangerous to themselves', diverting attention from social and economic inequalities embedded in the very structures of society.

Aside from the dire living conditions and institutionalised forms of prejudice that undermine the health of people from poor and minority groups, the critical medical anthropology of this volume also examines the monetarisation of biomedical care – and the corollary problem of access to increasingly high-cost technologies. The anguish of Brazilian patients and their families trying to deal with a rare genetic disease, described by Aureliano and Gibbon, is a case in point. Confronting situations of life and death, these people grasp for even the most uncertain of pharmaceutical innovations, summoning judicial authorities to oblige the state to foot the bill for experimental treatments of enormous cost. Encouraged by the prospect of high profits, the pharmaceutical companies invest ever more energies in this market 'niche', producing medicines that, although beyond the reach of most family budgets, can be purchased by public health administrations (Petryna 2009). The dilemma here is between a citizen's supposedly state-guaranteed 'right to health' and health as a high-cost commodity that, in extreme cases, might ultimately deplete public resources and so undermine the quality of routine care.

Carranza's discussion of small-scale health clinics adjacent to commercial pharmacies in Mexico broaches precisely the problem of democratic access to routine primary healthcare. The clinics, recently authorised by the government, allow patients convenient low-cost consultations in close-to-home facilities by competent physicians without the long waiting lines they experience at often distant public health posts. The pharmacy chains are, for their part, more than happy to thus shore up inadequacies in the national health services, foreseeing a profitable niche for the promotion of their prescription drugs. Questions, however, remain. Does this particular form of 'facilitating access' to health services not induce people to conceive good health as defined and promoted primarily by the consumption of prescription drugs? In what ways does this public–private partnership involving stakeholders of unequal political clout shape basic notions about public service and citizens' rights?

If, on the one hand, these scholars of critical medical anthropology bring steady proof of the structural inequalities that undermine good health, their contextualised descriptions of real-life practices also reveal the creativity of patients who, through individual and collective strategies, find alternative ways of imagining practices for health and wellbeing. In this 'pluralist' arena of conceptions (Menéndez 1998), there are many ways to contest the biomedical diagnosis of an illness, just as there are to doubt treatments and so-called cures. The traditional Mesoamerican and Andean category *susto*, referring to disturbances caused by a person's loss of soul, aptly illustrates this point. As Orr and Herrera show us, healers specialising in this ailment go beyond patient symptoms, resorting to a variety of diagnostic techniques – from dream travels to the reading of coca leaves – in their quest to alleviate bodily and mental suffering. The analysis of different cases in contemporary Peru and Mexico not only fuels reflection on the central role of emotions in local conceptions and practices of health, it also underlines how the various circumstances of poverty, gender oppression and other forms of vulnerability give rise to disruptive fears that call for varied forms of treatment.

Although analysts in this volume shed light on the practices of local healers and their specialised forms of knowledge, their ethnographic 'empirical lanterns' (Biehl 2016) call attention above all to what the pioneering scholar Eduardo Menéndez (1983) has named techniques of 'self-care' (*autoatención*), devised through individual or group strate-gies to influence, alleviate or cure health problems. Hernandéz' study of Mexicans migrating back and forth across the US–Mexican border fur-nishes insight into the use of illegal drugs as a form of self-care for deal-ing with the stress and exhaustion of exploitative work conditions. As subjects navigate between routine and extreme situations in their daily struggles, the very distinction between the 'healthy' and the 'pathologi-cal' blurs. It is through negotiating varied therapeutic strategies – ranging from personal networks to religious associations and rehab centres – that people determine when they are actually ill, and select appropriate paths to a cure according to the lifestyles they value. In yet another context, Irons brings the question of self-care to the dilemma of Peruvian women faced with the possibility of an unwanted pregnancy. For most women, surgical intervention – illegal and generally costly – is not an option, but many will resort to pills, legally procured at local pharmacies. Here, dif-ferent local perceptions of time and foetal development afford a certain flexibility about the start of personhood, permitting women to think of their condition as 'delayed menses' rather than pregnancy. Such ambi-guities, inherent in the decision-making process, mean that what some women see as an abortive pill, others may see as a contraceptive meas-ure, or even as a way of simply disintegrating a clot of menstrual blood. In this setting, not only biomedical perspectives but also religious doctrines are creatively integrated into the pluralist dynamics of self-care.

Once the legitimacy of diverse health conceptions and practices is recognised, a major challenge facing Latin American specialists is how to integrate this diversity into national health systems. Langdon and Diehl address precisely this issue in their discussion about the joint efforts of anthropologists, collective health agents and the various indigenous communities to forge a 'differentiated' health service in Brazil. During the first phase of this process – in the 1980s and 1990s – committed scholars invested their energies in identifying indigenous perceptions and practices linked to systems of health/illness/care in an attempt to attenuate the biomedical hegemony inherent in national health services. With the consolidation of a National Policy of Healthcare for Indigenous Peoples, a new and highly relevant phase of inquiry began, questioning to what extent indigenous groups are able to exercise agency and citi-zenship in the 'border spaces' of intercultural (and 'intermedical') inter-actions created by the state. The preliminary response to this question, formulated through ethnographic fieldwork rooted in the perspective of the communities, underlines how, in addition to racial prejudice and cultural miscomprehensions, the confusions and disagreements among state administrators, together with chronically unstable funding, present serious obstacles to democratic inclusion in a comprehensive health programme.

Sesia's chapter, already mentioned above, looks at a form of extra-governmental collective action (by a feminist NGO) channelled through judicial action to combat the gender and racial violence observed in Mexican maternities. The interesting point here is how a novel epistemological category, 'obstetric violence', is consciously wielded as a tool not only to call attention to a recurrent form of medical abuse, but also to form a counter-hegemonic discourse and rally public support for a collective cause. Using this rhetoric, activists achieved considerable gains in the national courts and the Mexican Commission for Human Rights – in terms of both individual reparation and the enactment of accords for the non-recurrence of institutional infractions. Nonetheless, as the author points out, results were still far from ideal. Despite the judicial accords packed with alluring promises, the lack of effective political activity to guarantee follow-up supervision meant that, four years later, few changes had actually been made in hospital practices for maternal health.

Berrio and Gamlin tell of yet another form of collaboration between indigenous groups and feminists that involves an active role for the anthropologist-researcher. Embracing what they call a 'post-critical' stance that takes into account the ongoing processes of coloniality, the authors propose negotiated practices of intervention that would highlight indigenous knowledge forms and therapeutic practices, and, at the same time, question well-entrenched structures of gender inequality. Bringing an innovative twist to the idea of structural violence, their analysis underlines the 'participant agency' of midwives and other members of local networks in the promotion of maternal health. Introduced, through ethnographic narratives, into the lives of pregnant women in two different Mexican states, the reader comes to recognise the fundamental role played by such intermediaries in promoting a pluralist approach to healthcare that might succeed in attenuating, if not completely overcoming, extremely asymmetrical hierarchies of gender and medical authority. Throughout their discussion, Berrio and Gamlin drive home the importance of collaborative efforts – between anthropologists, activists and indigenous peoples – in collective action aimed at ensuring not only improved health outcomes, but also enhanced academic theory and analysis.

Altogether, the chapters in this book nourish reflection on the way health problems such as malnutrition, drug addiction and exposure to violence follow on the heels of 'local' policies of economic austerity imposed by a neoliberal economy of global dimensions. The irony of a globalised apparatus of high-technology medicine existing side by side with vast numbers of people who have no access even to the basic necessities for decent health threads its way through the different case studies in this volume. The reader is thus invited to step back from traditional biomedical conceptions of cause and effect to consider wider historicised networks of causality. One way or another, the different chapters converge towards a powerful conclusion that places biomedicine between brackets, revealing it to be but one among the possible systems of efficient care. In this scenario, ethnography becomes more crucial than ever, as it furnishes glimpses of possible 'alternative routes' – nurtured by plural concepts and differentiated practices – that might lead towards a more egalitarian distribution of health and wellbeing.

As in any other collective work, there still exist a few matters left out that make the reader anticipate with pleasure a second volume. Firstly, it would be interesting to think more about how to identify and enlist, among the agents of biomedicine, critical allies – professionals who, having experienced a certain ambivalence about their practice, might be open to dialogue and creative alterations in their own knowledge and practices. In this case, it would be useful to reflect on communicative strategies that could effectively mediate the different perspectives without creating warring blocs (see Hansen, Holmes and Lindemann 2013; Briggs 2005). Secondly, when looking at the wider context of health issues, we might include in our critical perspective the seemingly progressive influence of the various international agencies – from the OAS (Organization of American States) to the WHO (World Health Organization). As analysts have repeatedly demonstrated, the humanitarian efforts of international organisations often come suspiciously coupled with military interventions and economic blockades – raising questions not only about motivations, but also about the ultimate effects of certain campaigns (Fassin 2012; Roodsaz and Van Raemdonck 2018). Finally – and above all – we might reiterate a feeling that emerges already from the pages of this volume: that the issues are not simple, and there are no magic-bullet solutions. Thus, the engagement of researchers, although understandably spurred by outrage and indignation, should come backed with a patient involvement in sorting our way through the labyrinth of complex reality to help formulate new, more effective alternatives to combat the embodied inequalities that plague our contemporary world.

References

Biehl, João. 2016. 'Theorizing Global Health', *Medicine Anthropology Theory* 3 (2): 127–42.

Breilh, Jaime. 2008. 'Latin American Critical ("Social") Epidemiology: New Settings for an Old Dream', *International Journal of Epidemiology* 37 (4): 745–50.

Briggs, Charles L. 2005. 'Perspectivas críticas de salud y hegemonía comunicativa: Aperturas progresistas, enlaces letales', *Revista de Antropología Social* 14: 101–24.

Farmer, Paul. 2004. 'An Anthropology of Structural Violence', *Current Anthropology* 45 (3): 305–25.

Farmer, Paul. 2011. *Haiti after the Earthquake*. New York: PublicAffairs.

Fassin, Didier. 2012. *Humanitarian Reason: A Moral History of the Present*, translated by Rachel Gomme. Berkeley: University of California Press.

Hansen, Helena, Seth Holmes and Danielle Lindemann. 2013. 'Ethnography of Health for Social Change: Impact on Public Perception and Policy', *Social Science and Medicine* 99: 116–18.

Menéndez, Eduardo L. 1983. *Hacia una práctica médica alternativa: Hegemonía y autoatención (gestión) en salud*. Mexico City: Centro de Investigaciones y Estudios Superiores en Antropología Social.

Menéndez, Eduardo L. 1998. 'Estilos de vida, riesgos y construcción social: Conceptos similares y significados diferentes', *Estudios Sociológicos* 16 (46): 37–67.

Menéndez, Eduardo. 2001. 'Biologización y racismo en la vida cotidiana', *Alteridades* 11 (21): 5–39.

Menéndez, Eduardo L. 2003. 'Modelos de atención de los padecimientos: De exclusiones teóricas y articulaciones prácticas', *Ciência e Saúde Coletiva* 8 (1): 185–207.

Petryna, Adriana. 2009. *When Experiments Travel: Clinical Trials and the Global Search for Human Subjects*. Princeton: Princeton University Press.

Roodsaz, Rahil and An Van Raemdonck. 2018. 'The Traps of International Scripts: Making a Case for a Critical Anthropology of Gender and Sexuality in Development', *Social Inclusion* 6 (4): 16–24.

Index

Illustrations and tables are denoted by the use of *italics*. Notes are indicated by 'n' after a page number, i.e. '37n7'.

Bolsonaro, Jair, 250, 266
bone marrow donation, 182
Bonfil Batalla, Guillermo, 21, 44–5
borderisation, 164, 165
border populations, stigma/discrimination from, 154–5
border spaces, 8–9, 28, 30, 32, 145–65
Brazil
    anthropologists, 36, 37n2
    healthcare system, 250–2, 267
    indigenous health in, 19–37, 22–5
    judicialisation, and the politics of rare disease in, 248–67
    pharmaceutical industry, 203
    social security, 267n4
Brazil Plural (IBP), 26, 37n7
Breilh, Jaime, 61, 64, 171, 186
Brower, Kimberly C., 128, 145–65
brujos (witches), 79
Buchbinder, Mara, 265

caboclo (traditional peoples of mixed ethnic heritage), 29
Cajas Castro, Juan, 127
Calestani, Melania, 170–88
California (CA), US, 119–20
CAMI (*Casa de la Mujer Indigena* – Indigenous Women's House), 49, 53–5, 59, 77, 78
Campos-Navarro, Roberto, 111
cancer, 249, 252, 254–5
Cancer Drug Fund (CDF), 255
cardiovascular disease, 184
Casa de la Mujer Indigena – Indigenous Women's House (CAMI), 49, 53–5, 59, 77, 78
case studies
    childbirth, 229–42
    diabetes, 178
    drug use, 131–7
    Juana's pregnancy, 49, 53–5, 56, 57, 59
    Sukulima's pregnancy, 50–2, 56, 57, 58–9
    susto, 82–3
Catholicism
    Catholic church, 84, 91, 93, 100
    Peru, 97–8
    popular, 29
    Yachaq practices and, 79
CDF (Cancer Drug Fund), 255
CE (critical epidemiology), 9, 171–3, 185–6, 187, 271
Central America, 145–65, 162, 166n15
centralisation, state, 36
CESCR (Committee on Economic Social and Cultural Rights), UN, 226
chains, pharmaceutical
    and CRPs, 196, 204–5, *204–5*
    hiring doctors, 215
    preference for, 207, 209
childbirth
    dangers of, 76
    human rights violations, 222
    Irma López Aurelio case, 229–42
    medicalisation of, 59, 228–9
    qualified care during, 227–9
child malnutrition, 79, 81–2

Chinese immigrants, 188n1
chronic diseases
    ethno-racial basis of, 170–88
    Mexico and, 201, 208, 217
    world's population and, 248
chronic kidney disease (CKD), 170, 179
chronic stressor exposure, 187
Church of Health, Brazil, 29
CISI (Intersectoral Commission of Indigenous Health), 23, 25
Ciudad Hidalgo, Mexico, 146, 149, *150*, 158, 162
cleansing (*limpia*), 78
clinics, private, 109, 213, 218
CMA (critical medical anthropology)
    definition, 223
    framework, 91
Cobo, Father Bernabé, *Historia del Nuevo Mundo*, 80
Coca-Cola Foundation, 185
cocaine use
    Mexico–Guatemala border, 148, 152, 156, 160
    Mexico–United States border, 131, 132
COFEPRIS (Federal Commission for the Protection of Health Risks), 200–1, 202–5, *204*
Cohen, Lawrence, 182
collective health (*saúde coletiva*), 19, 60, 186, 187
collective health movement, 35
Colombia, 146, 225
coloniality, of care, 56–8, 60–2, 274
coloniality/colonialism and inequality, 44–5, 48, 52–3
Committee on Economic Social and Cultural Rights (CESCR), UN, 226
communicative hegemony, 29
conception, and concepts of time, 94–5, 96–100
condom use
    and HIV/AIDS, 147, 151, 159, 160–1, 164
    Peru, 97
Conners, Erin E., 164
conos (poor northern neighbourhoods, Lima)
    abortions, 95, 105
    contraception and, 102, 107
    definition, 113n2
    migrants, undocumented, 96
Constitutional Amendment 95 (EC 95), 265
Constitution of Brazil (1988), 250–2
consultation rooms annexed to pharmacies (CRPs), 195–218, 218n2, 272
contraception
    conos and, 102, 107
    emergency, 90–112
    See also condoms
controle social (social oversight), 23, 32
Conway, Janet M., 48
Cooper, Jessie, 183
Coordination of Indian Health (Coordenação da Saúde do Índio/COSAI), 23, 24
councillors, indigenous, 32–3
crack use, 131, 148, 152, 156–7, 160
Crandon, Libbet, 72
crime, organised, 149, 153, 155, 159–60, 163–4

human leukocyte antigen (HLA) types, 182
human rights, 127
  violations, 222–43
hunger, 79, 81–2
Huyard, Caroline, 255
hypertension (high blood pressure), 29, 179, 180

IACHR (Inter-American Commission of Human
    Rights)
  background, 244n15
  hearings, 222, 232–3, 236, 237, 238
Ifaluk communities, 74
illnesses, emotional, 69–86
immigrants
  Chinese, 188n1
  illegal, 124
  US Mexican, 119–20
Immigration and Customs Enforcement (ICE),
    US, 123, 141n1
immunosuppressant drugs, 182–3
IMSS (Mexican Institute of Social Security),
    200, 218–19n3
indigeneity
  definition, 44
indigenous communities
  Brazil, 19–37
  health policies, 22–5, 56, 59
  Ifaluk, 74
  Irma López Aurelio case, 229–42
  justice, 236
  Kaingáng, 28–30, 31–2, 33–4, 36–7
  Maya, 176–7
  Mazatec, 229
  Mexico, 42–64, 234–6
  Nahua, 75–7, 80
  Oaxacan, 177
  Quechua, 103
  Shipibo-Conibo, 28
  type 2 diabetes, 186–7
  Wixárika, 46, 49–52
  women and healthcare, 223, 233, 234–5,
    236–8, 271
  Zapotec, 72, 170
Indigenous Health Subsystem, Brazil, 19–20,
    23–4, 26, 28, 30
Indigenous Health Workgroup of the
    Brazilian Association of Collective Health
    (Associação Brasileira de Saúde Coletiva/
    ABRASCO), 20, 24–5, 26
indigenous models of health, 46–8
indigenous therapeutic systems and medical
    pluralism, 45–6, 272
individual vs. collective, 46–8
inequality, 72
  and activism, 224, 248–67
  and coloniality/colonialism, 44–5, 48, 52–3
  gender, 49, 53, 58–62, 71, 274
  health, 43, 44
  racial, 62, 123, 124, 128, 130
infant/maternal health, 42–64
  arrebato, 70
  malnutrition, 79, 81–2
  mortality, 79
  responsibility, 261
infectious diseases, 202

influenza epidemic, Mexico, 202
informal sex work, 155, 156–7, 159, 164
Information Group on Reproductive Choice
    (GIRE), 231–3, 236–7, 239–42, 244n11
Institute for Security and Social Services for
    Federal Government Workers (ISSSTE),
    200, 208, 218–19n3
Inter-American Commission of Human Rights
    (IACHR)
  background, 244n15
  hearings, 222, 232–3, 236, 237, 238
intercultural health: critical approaches and
    current challenges, 7–8, 55–6, 111
Interfarma, Brazil, 256, 263
intergovernmental policies, 162
intermedicality, 28, 29
Intersectoral Commission of Indigenous
    Health (CISI), 23, 25
isolation, social, 131, 132, 141
ISSSTE (Institute for Security and Social
    Services for Federal Government
    Workers), 200, 208, 218–19n3

Jacobo Herrera, Frida, 69–86, 80, 272
Jalapa de Díaz, Mexico, 230, 232, 233
Jenkins, Janis Hunter, 124
Juan, Mercedes, 174
judicialisation
  definition, 224–5
  between global innovations and local
    boundaries, 252–4
  of maternal health rights violations, 222–43
  and the politics of rare disease in Brazil,
    248–67

Kaingáng communities, 28–30, 31–2, 33–4,
    36–7
kidney disease, chronic, 170
kidney failure, 179, 180, 187
kidney transplant, UK, 170
Kierans, Ciara, 183
Kleinman, Arthur, 122
knowledge co-production, 62–4
Kozelka, Ellen Elizabeth, 127
Kuczynksi, Pedro Pablo, 110, 113n6
Kuzawa, Christopher W., 172

Lamas, Marta, 94, 104
Lang, Gretchen Chesley, 175
Langdon, Esther Jean, 19–37, 56–7, 64, 273
language, 28, 44, 79, 129, 188n2
language barriers, 77, 119, 230
Latin America, 25, 26, 203, 225–6
Latin American critical medical anthropology
    (LA-CMA), 1–3, 21–2, 35–6, 47, 121
  definition, 3–6
lawsuits, health, 225, 253, 257–9
lightning, 77–8
Lima, Peru, 90–112
limpia (cleansing), 78, 86n3
Lippman, Abby, 171
llamadas espirituales (soul callings), 78, 86n6
local biologies, 92, 111, 186
local boundaries, and global innovations,
    252–4